KINDRED AND
RELATED SPIRITS

KINDRED AND
RELATED SPIRITS

The Letters of John Muir and
Jeanne C. Carr

EDITED BY

Bonnie Johanna Gisel

FOREWORD BY

Ronald H. Limbaugh

THE UNIVERSITY OF UTAH PRESS
Salt Lake City

Printed on acid-free paper

ACKNOWLEDGMENT IS MADE FOR PERMISSION TO REPRODUCE THE FOLLOWING:

John Muir's drawing of the geology of Yosemite (with the letter dated "Autumn 1872"). The John Muir Papers, Holt-Atherton Department of Special Collections, University of the Pacific Libraries. Copyright 1984 Muir-Hanna Trust.

"The Grasshopper Letter" written by John Muir to Jeanne C. Carr from Yosemite Valley, September 27, 1874. The Huntington Library.

Jeanne C. Carr's botanical drawings, courtesy of the Archives at the Pasadena Historical Museum: Part One, Fern and Leaves; Part Two, Mushrooms; Part Three, "Untitled"; Part Four, *Sarcoscypha occidentalis*; Part Five, *Salix discolor*; Part Six, "*Geoglossum glutinosum,* Slimy earthtongue"; Part Seven, Pine Cone (Sketch attributed to Jeanne C. Carr); Part Eight, *Anemone occidentalis.*

All letters in this volume not in public domain appear courtesy of the John Muir Papers, Holt-Atherton Department of Special Collections, University of the Pacific Libraries. Copyright 1984 Muir-Hanna Trust.

ISBN 0-87480-682-8

LIBRARY OF CONGRESS CATALOGING-IN-PUBLICATION DATA

Muir, John 1838–1914
    Kindred and related spirits : the letters of John Muir
and Jeanne C. Carr / edited by Bonnie Johanna Gisel ;
foreword by Ronald H. Limbaugh.
    p.   cm.
Includes bibliographical references.
ISBN 0-87480-682-8 (hardcover : alk. paper)
    1. Muir, John, 1838–1914—Correspondence.   2. Carr, Jeanne C.
Smith—Correspondence.
    I. Carr, Jeanne C. Smith.   II. Gisel, Bonnie Johanna, 1948–
QH31.M9A4   2001
333.7/2/092—dc21 [B]

                    2001001176

FOR Able

CONTENTS

Samoset.

(Mariposa, California)

"Samoset," a Sequoia named by Ralph Waldo Emerson when he was in Yosemite Valley in 1871 and drawn by John Muir, who sent the sketch to Emerson probably with his letter of July 6, 1871. Courtesy of the Houghton Library, Harvard University.

SONG OF NATURE

Mine are the night and morning,
The pits of air, the gulf of space,
The sportive sun, the gibbous moon,
The innumerable days.

I hide in the solar glory,
I am dumb in the pealing song,
I rest on the pitch of the torrent,
In slumber I am strong.

No numbers have counted my tallies,
No tribes my house can fill,
I sit by the shining Fount of Life,
And pour the deluge still;

And ever by delicate powers
Gathering along the centuries
From race on race the rarest flowers,
My wreath shall nothing miss.

And many a thousand summers
My apples ripened well,
And light from meliorating stars
With firmer glory fell.

I wrote the past in characters
Of rock and fire the scroll,
The building in the coral sea,
The planting of the coal.

And thefts from satellites and rings
And broken stars I drew,
And out of spent and aged things
I formed the world anew;

What time the gods kept carnival,
Tricked out in star and flower,
And in cramp elf and saurian forms
They swathed their too much power.

Time and Thought were my surveyors,
They laid their courses well,
They boiled the sea, and baked the layers
Of granite, marl, and shell.

But he, the man-child glorious,—
Where tarries he the while?
The rainbow shines his harbinger,
The sunset gleams his smile.

My boreal lights leap upward,
Forthright my planets roll,
And still the man-child is not born,
The summit of the whole.

Must time and tide forever run?
Will never my winds go sleep in the west?
Will never my wheels which whirl the sun
And satellites have rest?

Too much of donning and doffing,
Too slow the rainbow fades,
I weary of my robe of snow,
My leaves and my cascades;
I tire of globes and races,
Too long the game is played;
What without him is summer's pomp,
Or winter's frozen shade?

I travail in pain for him,
My creatures travail and wait;
His couriers come by squadrons,
He comes not to the gate.

Twice I have moulded an image,
And thrice outstretched my hand,
Made one of day, and one of night,
And one of the salt sea-sand.

One in a Judaean manger,
And one by Avon stream,
One over against the mouths of Nile,
And one in the Academe.

I moulded kings and saviours,
And bards o'er kings to rule;—
But fell the starry influence short,
The cup was never full.

Yet whirl the glowing wheels once more,
And mix the bowl again;
Seethe, Fate! the ancient elements,
Heat, cold, wet, dry, and peace, and pain.

Let war and trade and creeds and song
Blend, ripen race on race,
The sunburnt world a man shall breed
Of all the zones, and countless days.

No ray is dimmed, no atom worn,
My oldest force is good as new,
And the fresh rose on yonder thorn
Gives back the bending heavens in dew.

Ralph Waldo Emerson

FOREWORD

THIS INTEGRATED PUBLICATION OF CORRESPONDENCE BETWEEN JOHN Muir and Jeanne C. Carr has been inevitable ever since a heavily emended edition of Muir's letters to Carr was published as *Letters to a Friend* in 1915, the year after Muir's death. Ironically, the daughters of John Muir, in trying to prevent others from capitalizing on their father's intimate letters, provided the means and the motive for further publication of Muir's personal correspondence. Knowing only one side of a complex personal relationship, who could resist wanting to know more?

Muir's written words to Carr, however fragmented and diversely interpreted, have been available to general audiences for eighty-five years. What has remained unavailable to all but selected scholars since Muir's death are the letters of Jeanne C. Carr, Muir's most intimate lifelong friend. Her role as fellow botanist, spiritual soulmate, literary critic, publishing agent, financial advisor, surrogate mother, matchmaker, and personal friend can now be fully explored for the first time in a chronological sequence of letters that begin in the early 1860s when Muir was a student at the University of Wisconsin, where Carr's husband was employed as Professor of Natural History, and end only with Carr's death in 1903.

The full story of the Muir-Carr relationship remains to be written, but this combined edition takes a giant step toward that end. Muir and Carr were more than just friends, but Muir biographers still argue over the nature of their relationship. The speculation began even before the publication of *Letters to a Friend,* but remained largely beyond public purview until modern times. A renewed search for the "real" John Muir coincided with the emergence of the modern environmental movement in the 1960s and the opening of the Muir papers in 1970. It reached its most salacious form after Stephen Fox's Muir biography, *John Muir and His Legacy: The American Conservation Movement,* was published in 1981. Fox addressed in some detail Muir's relationships with Carr,

Emily Pelton, Elvira Hutchings, Theresa Yelverton, and other women with whom Muir came into contact over his long career. One reviewer took Fox's book as evidence that Muir was a "womanizer." Later biographers have revised and refined these early impressions, and most have discounted notions of sexual intimacy between Muir and any of his early female acquaintances. Yet the definitive word on the Muir-Carr nexus remained unspoken until 1998, when Bonnie Johanna Gisel completed her Ph.D. dissertation, "Into the Sun: Jeanne C. Carr, A Woman's Experience in Nature and Wilderness in Nineteenth-Century America." Bringing together all the extant correspondence between Muir and Carr for the first time, and exploring the lives of two individuals bonded by common love of the natural world, Gisel draws a deeper and richer picture of the Muir-Carr friendship than has heretofore been presented. It is a portrait drawn from the larger perspective of social and personal relationships in Victorian America. Gisel sees intimacy in a spiritual context, where human relationships are viewed as part of a larger bond between all the forms of creation.

Bonnie Johanna Gisel has meticulously researched the original correspondence, and has reconstructed letters from originals wherever possible. She has supplemented the two-way correspondence with a few third-party letters to provide a better contextual framework when necessary for clarity and fuller explanation. She has enriched the narrative with Carr drawings and with photo images of the principal characters. Her introductions provide a scholar's perspective on the relationship, and explore what others have said about it. They also clarify the record of previous publications, and explain why Muir's daughters felt compelled to rush into print with *Letters to a Friend*. A glossary of botanical terms and a chronology round out this valuable collection.

John Muir's place in American letters remains uncertain, but few doubt his role as publicist and popularizer of wilderness. This book provides a new benchmark for exploring the meaning of Muir's life, and opens a broader vista into his mystic correspondence with Jeanne C. Carr. But it also shows how important Carr was to the development of Muir's career, and invites us to speculate on the life of a woman caught between maternal responsibilities and limited professional options. As her correspondence reveals, Carr had unbounded energy and ambition, yet managed to subordinate her own personal predilections and remain true to the nurturing role carved out for nineteenth-century women in Victorian America. Carol Gilligan called this "goodness as self-sacrifice."[1] Carr did not stray from the "cult of true womanhood," in Barbara Welter's terms.[2] But we see in this series of letters a woman at times frustrated by the limits of her culture, yet finding power and perhaps self-satisfaction, if not contentment, in helping her younger friend along the road to fame and fortune.

By any standard in any age, nature's impact on the human heart has never been more profoundly revealed than in this remarkable series of letters. Muir and Carr together invite us to join their passionate quest for nature's "glad tidings."

Ronald Limbaugh
University of the Pacific

ACKNOWLEDGMENTS

THE RESEARCH AND preparation of this book would not have been possible without the contributions of many individuals and institutions. I owe a debt of gratitude to them all.

My deepest debt is to Ronald H. Limbaugh, Professor Emeritus, University of the Pacific, and Director Emeritus of the John Muir Center for Regional Studies, who provides the Foreword in this book, to whom and for which I am sincerely grateful; and who generously devoted time and his vast knowledge of Muir and the Muir Papers to my research. His support and encouragement were the impetus for this edited edition of the John Muir and Jeanne C. Carr letters. Thanks are also due to Marilyn Norton, a staff associate in the History Department, University of the Pacific, who provided assistance that expedited research.

I am grateful to Daryl Morrison, Head, Holt-Atherton Department of Special Collections, University of the Pacific Libraries, and her staff, particularly Janene Ford, Photo Archivist, for every kind consideration directed toward the research and preparation of this book. I am much obliged to Tania Rizzo, Archivist, Pasadena Historical Museum, for the attention devoted to the retrieval of photographs and the sketches of Jeanne C. Carr. I owe special thanks to Jennifer L. Martinez, Curator, Western Historical Manuscripts, and Erin Chase, Library Assistant, Rare Book Department, Huntington Library, for their time and effort contributed to the research of letters and photographs.

I am also appreciative of the assistance given by staff of other institutions that are repositories of Muir materials and items of related interest. These include the Bancroft Library, University of California, Berkeley, and Anthony Bliss, Curator, Rare Books and Literary Manuscripts, and Lisa de Larios, Project Archivist; the L. H. Bailey Hortorium Library, Cornell University, and Peter R. Fraissinet and Melanie Schori; the Yosemite Museum, National Park Service, and Barbara Beroza, Curator; and the State Historical Society of Wisconsin.

To James G. Ball, who freely gave of his time to collect letters and articles at the Library of Congress and read through the introduction and endnotes, thank you. I am forever grateful for his friendship. I would also like to thank Daniel E. Flisser, with whom I explored botanical nomenclature, for his assistance and review of the Botanical Glossary. A special thank you goes to Robert E. Lee, a descendant of Jeanne C. Carr, who encouraged the publication of Carr's letters.

Last and most important, I want to thank Nikolaus Paris Gisel, to whom my research and teaching in environmental studies is dedicated. Through his Music he has always understood my devotion to the study of Nature and Wilderness.

Ithaca, New York

January 2000

INTRODUCTION

JOHN MUIR LEFT HIS HOME NEAR PORTAGE, WISCONSIN, IN THE
autumn of 1860, boarded a train to Madison, and headed for the Wisconsin State Agricultural Society Fair to exhibit his wooden inventions.
He was twenty-two, charming, gentle, and humorous, and had twinkling
blue eyes, a tangle of wild unshorn auburn hair, and a beard. His appearance was rustic and his clothes were hand-made; and he was wholly
unsophisticated. He entered the fairgrounds, found his way to the fine-
arts hall, and set his clocks and thermometer on a shelf where they
drew an inordinate amount of attention from visitors and reporters.
Fair officials sent Jeanne C. Carr, a thirty-five-year-old woman who had
a sweet expression and a charming voice, and who was five feet two
inches tall, with tawny hair parted evenly in the center, as an emissary
to report on Muir's "meritorious inventions." She recommended that
Muir be given a special commendation. For his clocks and thermometer
presented in the Fine Arts and Miscellaneous Department, Muir received
a diploma and a monetary award of five dollars.

In addition to his entries at the fair, Muir prepared a "side-show"
with his early rising bed, a contraption that raised its occupants to an
upright position with feet upon the footboard. As Carr proceeded across
the fairgrounds with the official to whom she reported the special pre-
mium awarded in Muir's behalf, they encountered Muir. With the assistance of one of Carr's sons (probably Allie) and Henry Butler, the son
of James D. Butler, Professor of Greek at the University of Wisconsin,
Muir demonstrated the unique features of the bed. His enthusiasm drew
a receptive crowd of onlookers who cheered each time the boys, feign-
ing sleep, were abruptly brought to their feet. Carr recalled that her introduction to Muir would probably have been forgotten if her husband,
Ezra S. Carr, Professor of Chemistry and Natural History at the University of Wisconsin, had not reported Muir's attendance in his lectures.
Nonetheless, the clocks, thermometer, and early rising bed contributed

to Muir's being remembered by her. The inventions, both original and promising, would open doors for Muir. Perhaps the most important of these doors literally belonged to the home of Jeanne and Ezra Carr at 114 Gilman Street, in Madison, Wisconsin.

Early in 1861 Muir matriculated in the second term at the University of Wisconsin. When Carr's son and Henry Butler heard he was at the university they badgered Carr until she agreed to pay him a visit in his dormitory room in North Hall. Along with clocks and the early rising bed, Muir's room was furnished with a desk that moved the textbooks required in each study to the front and opened them at the proper place, and also with an apparatus for registering the growth of an ascending plant stem during each hour. Carr was captivated by this latter device.

While he was at the University of Wisconsin, three elements converged in Muir's life that profoundly affected his future. First, James Butler, Professor of Classics, and an Emerson enthusiast, encouraged Muir to keep a commonplace book of daily events, which Muir adapted to a botanical journal. Second, Milton Griswold, a fellow student, introduced Muir to the formal study of botany. And third, by the time he left the university in 1863, Muir and the Carrs were close friends.

Having initially invited Muir into their home to tutor their sons, the Carrs quickly befriended him, recognizing his pure mind, unsophisticated nature, inherent curiosity, scholarly acumen, and independent thought. Jeanne Carr liked him for his individualized acceptance of religious truths with which she sympathized. Her own religious experience—grounded in Puritan tradition, steeped in Calvinism, synchronized with evangelicalism, and experienced in nature—melded well with Muir's Calvinist upbringing, which was washed in evangelicalism and infused with Scottish Common Sense philosophy that encouraged empirical evidence of God in the natural world. For both Carr and Muir, worship was not limited to the Sabbath or to church. Their faith, predicated on the Book of Nature, called them to engage in the multiplicity of images God provided in nature. Religious iconography was not limited to the Cross, and worship could be celebrated anywhere, at any time, and in different ways in God's sacred world.

Muir enjoyed study and borrowing privileges in the library at the Carrs' home. With Carr he discussed the plants she grew in the indoor garden, an enclosed porch that wrapped around the front and side of their yellow sandstone house. Carr's garden was her classroom, and into it she welcomed students who applied themselves to the study of practical knowledge. Botany was important to both Carr and Muir, and the depth of their mutual love of plants both strengthened their friendship and was a vehicle for the expression of their faith.

At some point the Carrs offered Muir a room in their home, an invitation he declined. Carr later recalled of Muir that no quail "ever hid her nest more effectually—or more truly enjoyed its privacy." In early 1864, having spent five semesters at the university and three summers botanizing, Muir left Madison, taking with him a commitment to the study of botany, a genuine aptitude for recording his experiences and discoveries in a journal, and his friendship with the Carrs. He left "the Wisconsin University for the University of the Wilderness." In March, after plans to attend medical school at the University of Michigan failed to materialize, Muir went to Canada to botanize in glorious freedom. There he encountered the shy orchid, *Calypso borealis,* that he had hoped so long to find. A letter from the Carrs reached him in Trouts Mills near Meaford, Canada, where Muir was manufacturing and improving wooden rakes, calling it earnest labor. Encouraged by Carr's proposal to exchange thoughts, Muir's missive to her in September 1865 began a correspondence that continued for thirty years.

Muir returned to the United States, and while he was employed in a factory in Indianapolis, an industrial accident resulted in the temporary loss of sight in his right eye. At the time of the accident Carr's influence on him was already taking hold. She had suggested, perhaps insisted, that Muir read Lamartine's *The Stonemason of Saint Point,* whose protagonist, a poor man with a pure heart, found in nature divine lessons and saw all of God's creatures as interconnected—belonging to one family with no species of greater value than any other. His life grounded in nature was for Carr emblematic of the values she hoped would metabolize in Muir and was a projection of the life she envisioned for him. Muir read the book prior to his accident, but his response would have to wait until his health improved. While he convalesced Carr encouraged him to have a friend read him a description of Yosemite Valley. Muir responded to Carr that he had read an illustrated folder about the Valley the previous year and had not forgotten it since.

With rest Muir's sight returned. His promise to be true to himself and to spend the remainder of his life studying the works of God began to materialize when he walked one thousand miles from Kentucky to Florida. Like the stonemason, Muir found his joy in wilderness and the study of nature, where God resounded free from the influence of society. And in accord with those of the stonemason, Muir's feelings of tenderness for God's creation resulted from the fact that the common dust of the earth was the source from which *Homo sapiens* and all other creatures were made. Elements of the stonemason's understanding of the relation between humanity and nature coalesced with Muir's and appeared in his journal and in later correspondence to Carr.

As Muir traveled Carr tried to follow him with a trail of letters. In May 1868 she wrote to Merrill Moores, hoping he knew of Muir's whereabouts. Incapacitated with malaria, Muir aborted his plan to continue on to South America. Remembering Yosemite Valley, he headed west, arriving in California in March 1868. By 1869 he was headquartered in Yosemite Valley and spent the next four years exploring the Sierra for evidence of glacial action.

When Ezra Carr came under academic scrutiny during the winter of 1867, resulting from his concerns over issues related to governance of the university, curriculum development, faculty vacancies, reduced salaries, and economic constraints, he resigned his professorship at the University of Wisconsin. By June, with Jeanne and their sons in Castleton, Vermont, with her parents, Dr. and Mrs. Albert Smith, Ezra had sold their Madison home ("everything but books and pictures") and had gone east to spend the summer in Vermont. Jeanne favored a move to California, and when the Carrs' plans were finalized, Muir rejoiced. Carr would read for herself "the glorious lessons of sky and plains and mountains," and Muir without "a single friend in California" would be rich with their company.[1]

The Carrs arrived in San Francisco in early 1869. Ezra accepted a professorship in agriculture, chemistry, and horticulture at the burgeoning University of California in Oakland. By summer Jeanne was in Yosemite looking for Muir, whom she never found. On July 13, he was three miles north of the Valley on the banks of the Yosemite Creek; on July 17, one mile from the Yosemite wall; by July 30, Carr had looked for him daily and hourly. Not fewer than eight of her letters traveled in search of him. Certain the mountains knew of her arrival, Muir thanked God for turning her face to them and hoped Carr would worship among them.

For Carr as well as Muir, Yosemite Valley was a gateway to the spiritual world. Her miscellaneous notes and manuscripts express her belief that in drinking the natural beauty there she would be turned to Yosemite's lessons of purity, constancy, and endurance. Overpowered by the view at Inspiration Point, she crouched under a boulder, shut her eyes to the view, and sailed through the depths of space touched by the inexplicable power of the divine.

During the next four years Carr introduced Muir to her friends and sent many of them to meet him in Yosemite to share the *sanctum sanctorum* of the Sierras and to hear him preach the gospel of the mountains. The most notable was Ralph Waldo Emerson. She also introduced him to the letters of Walter R. Brooks, a minister and lecturer on natural history, whom she had met in Madison, Wisconsin, in 1856, and who shared her interest in the study of the relation between nature and religion. Brooks's views centered on the unity and sacredness of the world and the revelation of spiritual truth through nature. The influence Brooks had upon Muir is difficult to measure. Muir was certainly inspired enough to mention his ideas to Emerson when he was in the Valley in 1871.

Muir's letters to Carr revealed thoughts and feelings he had never shared with anyone. He drew close to her and she often traveled in his thoughts with him—his letters are filled with examples of her spiritual presence. Her letters reassured him and inspired him, and through his letters to her he developed a voice and purpose. Carr, for her part, soon recognized Muir's unique gift for writing. In early 1872 she began submitting Muir's letters to the *Overland Monthly* for publication. Later that year, sensing the need for him to save his writing for the public, she encouraged him to allow acres of silence between letters regardless of personal loss. It was, she said, not those who cling, but those who walk apart yet ever with you who are true companions.

Carr's role cannot be overestimated as Muir's writing career advanced while he remained in the Valley and she resided in Oakland. However, Muir applied himself to the publication of his letters and essays and purposefully undertook the processing and presentation of his writing. He may have been inexperienced, but he was no fool. Trusting Carr as his spiritual mother, with their friendship "like a planet burning along its own path," he recognized her value to him and accepted and learned from the gracious gifts of effort and influence she bestowed upon him. For Carr it was not difficult to support Muir's empirical wilderness studies, which closely aligned with her belief that those who rooted themselves firmly to the earth had a fairer chance to rise and endure than those in the overcrowded callings and professions.

In 1873 Carr accompanied Muir, Albert Kellogg, and William Keith on a trip to Tuolumne Canyon and the sources of the Merced and San Joaquin Rivers. Carr, who venerated David Douglas, the Scottish botanist-explorer, as a "poet naturalist," surely saw a resemblance between Douglas and Muir. Literally hoping to follow in Douglas's footsteps, albeit forty years later, she botanized and sketched in the region above Hetch Hetchy with yet another Scotsman, John Muir. The death on October 23, 1873, of Carr's oldest son, Ezra Smith Carr, a railroad brakeman who was crushed between two railroad cars, prevented her from traveling north in search of Muir later that year; and the Carrs' bereavement made it impossible for them to board Muir when he spent the winter in Oakland working on his Sierra studies for the *Overland Monthly*. He stayed with J. B. McChesney, superintendent of schools in Oakland and a "true nature-lover."[2]

For Muir, writing for publication without Carr as a facilitator was agonizing, and life in Oakland was confining. The first of his Sierra studies appeared in the *Overland Monthly* in May 1874. By September he was back in Yosemite Valley. A long letter to Carr addressed the transition from town life to wilderness. Though he was weary and footsore, his reentry into Yosemite returned him to simple earnest work. For Muir, life was in the Valley; death in town. In Yosemite *Hemizonia virgata*, steadfast *Eriogonums,* larks, lizards, mice, butterflies, and briar roses surrounded him and he bathed in life and in the sacred stream, though he felt as though a stranger in the Valley. Gathering a handful of leaves for Carr and for Mrs. McChesney, he headed north and climbed Shasta in November, wishing Carr were there. On the advent of another period of "town dark" he was nervous and fearful. When he returned to Oakland he boarded at the home of John Swett, a San Francisco teacher, principal, state superintendent of schools, and a friend, who urged Muir to adopt a narrative writing style less imbued with revisions. His second extended sojourn in Oakland was decisive. Forever bound to mountains, ice, rivers, and trees as well as to writing, he would divide the remainder of his life between wilderness, which was timeless, and civilization, which he resisted, though friends and friendships were irresistible.

Carr's proximity to Muir, living in Oakland and then in Berkeley, enabled her to introduce him to friends who visited the Carrs, sometimes en route to Yosemite. This was made possible by Ezra Carr's professorship at the University of California. His position also provided a climate in which the Carrs could advance their educational and agricultural objectives. No calling was as useful or pleasurable as agriculture, and their efforts to improve agricultural literacy led to their participation in the organization of the California grange, known for advocating women's educational equality and leadership. Through meetings of the California State Agricultural Society and the grange, the Carrs met Dr. and Mrs. John T. Strentzel and their daughter, Louie Wanda. In 1872 Carr was already suggesting that Muir and Louie were a match.

Ezra Carr opposed the proposal to establish a liberal arts curriculum at the University of California in 1874. He supported and encouraged the development of a practical curriculum that emphasized the study of agriculture and mechanical arts. Locked in a bitter dispute over the future of the university that involved the grangers, the Mechanics' Deliberation Assembly, the Mechanics' Council, and the newspapers, he was asked to resign his professorship. He refused and was dismissed. Assuming in December 1875 the position of Superintendent of Public Instruction for the State of California located in Sacramento, Ezra appointed Jeanne Deputy Superintendent. Jeanne was among the first women to hold public office in California. As Deputy Superintendent she attended the United States "Centennial," taking with her a book of ferns representative of California flora and two bound volumes of papers, maps, and drawings from a school in Del Norte County. When Ezra's rheumatism compromised his tenure as superintendent, Carr took over his responsibilities. Muir described Carr as lost in conventions, elections, and women's rights. He suggested she not grind too hard in the "Sacramento mills."[3]

The Carrs purchased forty-two acres of land in Pasadena on the northeast corner of Orange Grove Avenue and Colorado Street, upon which they would build their retirement home, Carmelita. Muir visited their "sunny patch" in August 1877. His enthusiasm for the land tempted him to consider investing himself. Following the death of their third son, John Henry Carr, who committed suicide on April 9, 1877, with a Smith & Wesson revolver, the Carrs found some refuge at their homestead. Ezra, however, had been worn thin by academic battles. Overcome with rheumatism, his body had become brittle and he was largely immobilized. Carr planted an orange grove and an arboretum and hoped to open a school of horticulture for women. Muir envisioned Carmelita as an exhaustive miniature of all the leafy organisms of the earth.[4]

Though Carr attempted to arrange a meeting with the Strentzels and Muir, her effort was of no avail. In 1877 Muir stopped in Martinez of his own volition on his way back to San Francisco to visit the Strentzels. Over the next year his visits to the Strentzel ranch obviously became more intended for Louie. Their engagement in June 1879 was a private affair; not even Carr knew. Muir's letter to Carr written shortly after his betrothal to Louie and before he left for Alaska mentioned that he was going home and nothing more. When Muir and Louie married in April 1880, Carr maintained that the marriage had been foreordained in heaven. The Strentzel family was now complete. Muir spent the next ten years in Martinez.

Four hundred people were residing in Pasadena when the Carrs formally arrived in early 1880. In May Carr wrote to Louie's mother, Louisiana E. Strentzel, describing life there. Deer came down from the mountains every few days and her sons, Edward (Ned) and Albert (Allie), had been hunting a grizzly bear. At night coyotes howled on her doorstep and tarantulas crawled across the hard adobe soil. Citrus culture was a gamble. The hesperian fruit was not indigenous to southern California and could not exist in a wild, untended state. Unprecedented frosts during the winter of 1879–1880 destroyed nursery stock as well as five- and six-year-old trees, and the season of 1882–1883 provided further setbacks. Late frosts nipped the fruit and trees were unusually full, dwarfing the oranges and detracting from their quality. The Strentzels received a letter from Carr that hinted at the inevitable. They were shivering with cold and their orange trees were frozen. With little strength remaining, Carr abandoned agricultural pursuits and established Carmelita as a boarding house.[5]

While Carr's crops failed, Muir took over the Strentzel ranch in Martinez and made it prosper. Farming was a business for Muir, and he was up before the earliest bird stirred in the morning. He transformed the ranch into a commercial enterprise. Louie for her part had taken an active role in her father's fruit ranching operations and carried on during the growing season, enabling Muir to leave Martinez between June and October. Louie was a charming hostess to the distinguished guests who visited their home, and her own interests included world affairs, new inventions, and astronomy. She read the *Review of Reviews* and the *World's Work*. The Muirs had two daughters, Wanda and Helen, to whom Muir was a devoted father.[6]

Muir resumed writing in 1888. As editor of *Picturesque California,* Carr was asked to write the essay on "Southern California." From his letter to her it was clear she was having difficulty formulating a manuscript. Write freely, he suggested, and listen for no further instruction. Muir's own writing in defense of wilderness preservation challenged many Americans who believed the nation was a repository of limitless land and natural resources. In collaboration with Robert Underwood Johnson in 1890, Muir's articles made a significant and lasting contribution to the protection of Yosemite Valley National Park. As one of the founding members and the first president of the Sierra Club, Muir became a powerful advocate for the preservation of wilderness. *The Mountains of California,* published in 1894, was the first of ten books Muir wrote focused on his wilderness experiences. The fact that they remain popular is an affirmation of Carr's faith in Muir's writing and a witness to the timelessness with which Carr believed Muir's words were imbued.

As Muir prospered, Carr experienced hardship and loss. The sale of Carmelita in 1892 was followed by the death of Ezra Carr in 1894. Carr wrote to a friend that nothing new filled her life, which she described as characterized by advanced age carrying advanced opinions. Dementia consumed Carr's mind and drew her into a world of her own. Although she was isolated from the present, her recollections of past events remained clear and accessible. Muir visited her sometime between 1896 and 1898. He described her as cheerfully holding on to life with wonderful tenacity, like a storm-beaten Sequoia. Carr resided with Elijah Melanthon Carr, Ezra's brother, on a ranch in Santa Paula. Muir wrote to Theodore Parker Lukens, a friend, forester, and naturalist, who had been the president of the Pasadena National Bank, on several occasions regarding Carr's health and care. In December 1903, Muir received a final letter from Elijah Melanthon Carr, notifying him of Carr's death, which brought closure to a noble life.

When President Theodore Roosevelt and Muir camped in Yosemite in 1903, Muir was encouraged that national policy would be established rightfully preserving wilderness in perpetuity. During his greatest public battle over the damming of Hetch Hetchy Valley, Yosemite Valley's twin and scenic counterpart, Muir discovered that even a national park was for sale. Just as Louie's death in 1905 was a reminder of the fragility of life, the unprecedented loss of Hetch Hetchy in 1913 was a reminder to Muir of the fragility of wilderness. With his home and heart always in the mountains, Muir saw the loss of Hetch Hetchy as the loss of another refuge of peace. Muir died in December 1914, believing the battle for preservation would go on forever, a universal battle between right and wrong.

Early in their friendship Carr recognized Muir as one of God's beloved. She believed in his right to the journey he freely chose—a leap of faith for them both. To him she gave that which is immeasurable—time, support, and understanding. If and when he suffered on his pathless journey, she hoped he always remembered her love. Carr listened to Muir; his letters to her are proof of that. Upon the death of Carr's husband she wrote to Muir, her beloved friend, that her heart continued to build precious hope in his life. She rejoiced in all that honored him and all that brought him happiness.

For all that bound Muir and Carr together, what distinguished them clearly set Muir apart. Whereas Carr worked from within the framework of society to reform it, utilizing individuals and institutions to create order and content, Muir was a visionary, acting along the boundaries of society and culture to create new paradigms and new structure. For Muir to accomplish this, instead of existing on the cutting edge of human invention, he turned to that which God first created "and finally concluded to stay out till sundown, for going out, [*he*] found, was really going in."[7]

The Letters to a Friend

While the letters Jeanne C. Carr wrote to John Muir remained unknown, the letters Muir wrote to Carr have had an illustrious history. Following the appointment in 1897 of an executor for Carr, who was infirm with advanced dementia, several boxes of her letters, books, papers, and manuscripts were directed to George Wharton James, though Muir claimed he was the intended recipient of his letters to her. As associate editor of the *Craftsman,* James selected the longest letter and published it in March 1905. In receipt of copies of the article "John Muir: Geologist, Explorer, Naturalist," sent to him by James, Muir responded on May 17, 1905, admonishing James for publishing his letters without permission.[8]

Muir had nothing kind to say about James on December 15, 1906, when he wrote to Robert Underwood Johnson. James, who had not responded to his letter, was in Muir's estimation "an unscrupulous ex-minister" whose only purpose with Muir's letters was to make money. Muir described the letters, some written forty years before and most from Yosemite, as important to his studies and useful for their "first impressions." If unable to retrieve them from James, Muir stated he would rather have them published "notwithstanding the fringe of sentimental rubbish" James would draw around them.[9]

In July 1908 James wrote to Muir regarding "incorrect ideas" as to how he came by the letters and his intended purpose. He had not surreptitiously and underhandedly acquired Muir's letters to Carr from one of her "degenerate sons," nor was he hawking Muir's private affairs to magazine publishers. James claimed he went to Bliss Perry, editor of the *Atlantic Monthly,* and suggested that the nearly two hundred letters he possessed be edited and "given to the world." His letter to Muir appeared benign. "I have not yet looked through a fifth part of the letters, but as far as I have seen and know there is not a letter that contains a line that could not be given to the world. . . . As far as I personally am concerned I have too long loved you and revered you and reveled with joy in your work to do or say one single thing that would not glorify you and your work." In James's words Carr believed the letters contained wonderful lessons. She requested he pledge to edit and publish the letters after Muir's death. There is no record of Muir calling upon Carr to return his letters. In a letter to Theodore Parker Lukens written in November 1901, Muir inquired about the letters and implied that Carr had repeatedly promised to collect and send them to him.[10]

By the end of January 1909 A. C. Vroman borrowed the letters from James and had them transcribed. When they were returned to James in April, Muir had included a list of letters he wished expurgated in part or whole. There were sixteen letters on Muir's list, eight to be destroyed and eight to be cut. Upon Muir's death James publicly announced he would publish the letters. He wrote to Wanda Muir Hanna, Muir's older daughter, regarding his proposal, offering her the option to publish the letters. Hanna, as special administrator of the estate of her father, responded with an injunction based on the contention that though the letters were James's property, the rights to publish their contents rested solely with Muir's heirs. A restraining order was issued in February 1915 preventing James from publishing the letters. Hanna arranged with Houghton Mifflin to copyright and publish Muir's letters to Carr, eliminating the edition James intended to publish.[11]

Muir's anger had been, perhaps, fueled by past experience. Early in his career James D. Butler literally took a letter Muir had written to Carr off the table in her home and published it in the *Boston Recorder* in December 1866. Carr was indignant. There was no law against so indelicate an abuse of the privilege of friendship except "the law of one's own mind." Samuel Kneeland, secretary of the Massachusetts Institute of Technology, incorporated several of Muir's letters and his *Tribune* article and delivered the resulting paper before the Boston Historical Society. According to Muir, he received credit "for all of the small sayings and doings" while Kneeland stole the broadest truths for himself. Joseph Le Conte borrowed and "hashed" Muir's research, presenting a lecture on "Sierra glaciers and new theories" for which Muir felt certain Le Conte would not claim discovery—though apparently he did. Following the actions of Kneeland and Le Conte, Muir wrote to Carr offering her the first chance to steal his experiments on living "Glaciers of the Sierras." Thereafter he would independently give his thoughts to the public. Muir's hostility toward what he viewed as James's theft of his personal documents opened old wounds.[12]

As a national figure involved in controversial preservation and conservation issues, Muir was sensitive to the circulation of his letters to Carr, but he had suggested to Johnson that James could publish them, and accordingly he selected and edited them for publication. They have remained vulnerable to misinterpretation due in part to the excisions that have subsequently led to speculation about Muir's character, his friendship with Carr, and other relations.

Muir requested that eight letters be destroyed. Of these letters four are partially intact because he also requested that these four letters be destroyed only in part. These included his letters to Carr dated August 7, 1870, Spring 1872, August 5, 1872, and September 13, 1872. His request to have them expurgated in whole was complied with in that the original letters were destroyed. His request to have them excised in part was also complied with in that transcriptions of these letters were cut. As a result four of the eight letters were not expurgated in whole.[13]

Of the four letters that were destroyed, three were written by Muir. They included the letters dated June 2, 1871, May 22, 1872, and December 18, 1872. The fourth letter, dated June 1, 1873, was written by Jeanne Carr prior to her visit to Yosemite Valley with Albert Kellogg and William Keith. This letter may have been a response (following Carr's letter of May 27, 1873, in a private collection) to Muir regarding his relationship with Elvira Hutchings, which Elvira had brought to light at the time she was planning to leave her husband, James Hutchings, proprietor of the Hutchings Hotel in the Valley. The highly vulnerable and deeply misconstrued relation between Muir and Elvira appears to have been little more than a noble friendship grounded in Christian fellowship. In her letter of May 27 Carr nonetheless took the opportunity to chastise Muir for his relationship with Elvira, and she put in doubt her hopes for his future if his behavior toward Elvira was less than proper. Muir was not above the laws of Christian propriety and certainly not above the standards Carr set for him. Even if God forgave him, she would not forgive his indiscretion, if it were true. Carr's June 1 letter may have brought closure to her letter of May 27, and paved the way for her visit to the Valley that summer.[14]

Muir also requested that eight letters have sections excised. These included his letters to Carr dated Midnight, April 3, 1871, April 15, 1871, September–October 1871, April 1872, May 31, 1872, October 8, 1872, May 15, 1873, and November 3, 1873. Three of these letters are complete, April 15, 1871, April 1872, and October 8, 1872. Sections of Muir's letters of September-October 1871 and November 3, 1873, are extant. Although one sentence of the original letter of September–October 17, 1871, was erased, the three sentences that precede it are complete (all four sentences were excised from Vroman's transcribed copy). These sentences disclosed a problem Muir was having with James Hutchings. Perhaps Muir thought this a personal matter that need not be exposed to public scrutiny. "Did I tell you in my last that I had set-tled up with Hutchings. He used me very shabbily trying to keep back part of my wages. If I am about the Valley hotels at all next summer I shall stop at Blacks." For an unknown reason these sentences were not erased from the original letter.[15]

Muir requested that the lower third of his letter of November 3 be excised. Though the lower third of the letter was cut from Vroman's transcribed copy (the final paragraph), the two paragraphs preceding it are intact. When the lower third of the original letter was excised all three paragraphs were expurgated, since the letter was written on both sides. These two paragraphs expressed Muir's diminished hopes of seeing Carr at Lake Tahoe. "Somehow I had no hopes of meeting you here [*Lake Tahoe*], I could not hear you or see you." (Carr, who explored Tuolumne Canyon and the sources of the Merced and San Joaquin Rivers with Muir, Kellogg, and Keith that summer, had returned to Oakland to make arrangements for the move to her new home in Berke-ley near the University of California. She anticipated meeting Muir and Kellogg in Tahoe City in November. The death of her son Ezra Smith Carr made it impossible for her to join them.) There has been much speculation that sections like this one might have revealed an affair be-tween Muir and Jeanne Carr, but this section was certainly no overture to intimacy.[16]

Muir also requested that several sentences of his Midnight, April 3, 1871, letter be expurgated. These sentences were erased from the orig-inal letter, but nine words of what appear to be the first sentence and the entire second sentence are extant in Vroman's transcribed copy of this letter: "...you might read the glory that I cannot write. The notes of this nights song echo in every fibre and all the grandeur of form is engraved not in sheet perspective but in life proportions and surely you would find it." The letters of May 31, 1872, and May 15, 1873, were cut as requested.[17]

That in some cases Muir's request was not complied with may simply be a matter of working with the original letters and with Vroman's transcribed copies, which may have led to confusion. Who actually cut the transcribed copies and who cut, scratched out, or erased the original letters is unknown. It may have been Muir, Vroman, or James, or someone else.

Whereas Muir viewed the letters as first impressions and a source of personal reflection and study, Carr thought of them as a source of lessons from which others would gain knowledge. Motivated by a desire to have them published, Carr, who first mentioned James to Muir in 1894, may have believed that James was a reliable conduit for following through with their publication. James was present in 1894, and Carr's decision may have stemmed from his attention. When Muir married Louie Strentzel in 1880 his letters to Carr became less frequent and in content were domestic and professional. Carr remained faithful to Muir, her beloved friend for whom she always had a special hope. Distance may have graced their friendship. At the very least Carr may have aspired to preserve the letters in their natural unedited state—she knew Muir well. Whatever her reasons, the letters were hers, a gift from Muir, and while in her possession their destiny rested with her.[18]

Muir was angry at James for not requesting permission to publish the letters. Concerned for the effect the circulation of material of a personal nature would have upon his career and credibility, he sought to control public access to them. In 1890 he had weathered an attack that strengthened his resolve. The charge came from John P. Irish, secretary and treasurer of the Yosemite Commission, who accused him of despoiling the Valley, logging and sawing trees with as willing a hand as any lumberman. Muir, who responded that he had never cut a single Yosemite tree, may have viewed James's self-promotion as fuel for the frustration and anger that already burned. Still, the letters contained accusations, words Muir wished to forever silence. In addition, the affection Muir and Carr shared was also vulnerable to attack. In James's and Carr's estimation the letters were invaluable because they presented Muir as a work in progress. They demonstrated that his development was in large part dependent on the friendship, guidance, and love bestowed upon him by Carr and the many friends and acquaintances she directed to him. Galen Clark, the official guardian of Yosemite Valley, believed Carr to be the one person who gave to Muir the greatest encouragement and assistance.[19]

Muir's correspondence revealed lessons, obstacles, and insights, and rendered visible his commitment to places and ideas in which he believed. Capturing his development, Carr's devotion to him and to others, and the rich cultural and social milieu in which they resided, their letters to each other serve as a window through which we may learn something about their humanity and the qualities of relation that connects them to us. This may have been more than Muir wanted revealed. By dismissing the sentimentality of James's interpretation, he may have been dismissing his own emotional and spiritual attachments, with which he felt the letters abounded, seeing himself as somehow disconnected from his past as he headed more sternly into the greatest fight of his life, Hetch Hetchy.

The Letters of John Muir and Jeanne C. Carr

Though several passages from the letters Carr wrote Muir appeared in *Son of the Wilderness: The Life of John Muir* and in *The Life and Letters of John Muir,* here for the first time Carr's collected letters present a voice silent all too long. Together with the letters Muir wrote to her, they provide a unique opportunity to explore their friendship and the meaning of nature, wilderness, and faith in their lives. Both were seasoned travelers and explorers. Both observed principles and progress, and each in his and her own way invested in individuals and institutions.[20]

The letters are a witness to Muir's dedication to unraveling the lessons to be learned from wilderness, and to Carr's role as mentor and friend as he walked his pathless journey. Carr helped to guide and shape Muir and his career with the support of her husband, Ezra S. Carr, her sons, and her friends and associates—a remarkable undertaking offering little personal gain and a testimony to her Christian faith and her love of nature, botany, and humankind. Blanketing Muir with encouragement, Carr helped to shape his destiny and his resolve. Their correspondence created a fabric that affirmed their beliefs, revealed truth as Muir and Carr saw it, and dispelled misinterpretations resulting from having access to Muir's letters alone.

The letters, which began in 1865 and concluded in 1895, are divided into eight sections by year or years, depending on the number of letters within any given year. Each chapter begins with an introduction that weaves together the letters and events.

While there are many letters to and from family members and friends that contribute to a better understanding of the relationship and letters shared by Muir and Carr, sixteen were selected and integrated here for their contribution to the portrayal of people, events, and places. These include letters written by Muir to Ralph Waldo Emerson, Charles Warren Stoddard, and Theodore Parker Lukens; by Carr to Ada Brooks, Merrill Moores, Mrs. C. L. Waterston, the *Overland Monthly,* Ezra S. Carr, Louie Wanda Strentzel, and Louisiana E. Strentzel; and received from friends: Mrs. C. L. Waterston to Carr, Mrs. M. R. Moore to Muir, Emelie T. Y. Parkhurst to Carr, and Theodore Parker Lukens to Muir. Last is the letter from Elijah Melanthon Carr to Muir written in 1903 to inform him of Jeanne Carr's death.

Kindred and Related Spirits: The Letters of John Muir and Jeanne C. Carr is enhanced by the inclusion of a photo album of individuals and places referred to in the letters, and by a collection of Jeanne Carr's sketches. A sketch created by her son Allie Carr has also been included. Many of Carr's sketches were completed while exploring Tuolumne Canyon and the sources of the Merced and San Joaquin Rivers with Muir, Kellogg, and Keith in 1873. A brief epilogue is followed by notes that include citations for authors and resources, and by a botanical glossary that identifies trees, plants, and wildflowers discussed by Muir and Carr. The research undertaken in the preparation of this glossary provides considerable insight into the depth of the study of botany in which Muir and Carr engaged. As this glossary has expanded my appreciation of their knowledge of botany and the level of their observation and encouraged my own study, it is my hope that it will be of assistance to readers as well. Following the glossary are a bibliography of botanical sources, a list of articles and manuscripts by Jeanne C. Carr, and a list of selected readings for further study. A chronology of events and lists of the letters in this volume and the letters that are missing precede the index. In making every attempt to provide clarity, full names have been included or on occasion a word has been added to complete a sentence. These additions appear within brackets and are italicized.

My purpose in compiling this book has been to preserve, for Muir scholars and for those who believe that Muir's pathless way is also theirs, a record that will cast new light on the lives of John Muir and Jeanne Carr and further our understanding of the relation between humanity and nature.

PART ONE

1865–1868

*You propose, Mrs. Carr, an
exchange of thoughts, for which
I thank you very sincerely.*

John Muir

One Baptized of
Nature and the Spirit

IN MARCH 1864 JOHN MUIR DEPARTED FOR THE UNIVERSITY OF THE WILDERNESS, urged on in search of beauty and knowledge, refuge and nurture. He headed north into Canada. In April he waded into swamps. In May he traveled as far as Simcoe and Grey counties. In July he botanized north of Toronto in the Holland River swamps. In August he found his way to the shores of Lake Ontario, near Niagara Falls. In October Muir and his brother, Daniel, secured employment at "Trout's Hollow," Meaford, Canada West, and worked for William Trout and Charles Jay at the Trout sawmill. They engaged in building an addition to a rake factory. Muir stayed on under contract to make twelve thousand rakes and thirty thousand broom handles and to improve machinery. He remained at Meaford for nearly a year and a half.

When Muir did not return to the University of Wisconsin in the autumn of 1864, the faculty invited him to matriculate as a free student. Professor John W. Sterling's letter of invitation that asked Muir to return never reached him in Meaford. Jeanne C. Carr, who had befriended Muir during his years at the University of Wisconsin from 1861 until 1863 while he studied a course in geology with her husband, Ezra S. Carr, and James D. Butler, also hoped he would return to the university. Carr and Muir met during the autumn of 1860 at the Wisconsin State Agricultural Society Fair. Carr, thirty-five, quickly recognized Muir, twenty-two, as well principled in nature and virtuous in character. What he lacked in knowledge and experience of "social life and forms" he more than made up for with his pure mind, unsophisticated manners, inventiveness, and interest in science. Carr invited Muir to her home at 114 Gilman Street to benefit her sons, Ezra Smith, Edward Carver, John Henry, and Albert Lee. They would learn by Muir's example.[1]

The Carrs' yellow sandstone cubicle villa with a mansard roof and a cupola with a wide overhang had a large enclosed glass porch that wrapped around the west front corner of the house. The vestibule opened to a hall that led directly forward into the library, to the left of which stood, one behind the other, a formal parlor for entertaining, a sitting room, and a dining room. In the library were two large windows that looked east. Bookshelves were fitted into the wall around the door and there was a large desk. In September 1865 Carr wished Muir in the kernel of her home. Muir confided how frequently when lonely and weary he wished that like a hungry worm he might creep into the Carrs' library and into the blossoms and verdure of Jeanne's little plant kingdom complete with garden and fruit trees, plants and gooseberry bushes, and mosses and ferns.

Carr began to study botany at the age of seven and collected over four hundred species of plants that she pressed into an herbarium. She began her formal education when she was nine, in 1834, at the Castleton Seminary in Castleton, Vermont, studying under the tutelage of Dr. William Tully, a professor at Castleton Medical College with whom Carr explored the cedar swamp behind Carvers Corners looking for a *Cypripedium arietinum,* a lady's-slipper orchid. The study of plants was for Carr fertile ground for friendships that harkened back to her experience with Tully in Vermont. Carr felt a kinship with young men who loved plants. From the porch of her home on Gilman Street she taught botanical science and cultivated plants for study as well as for beauty. Carr and Muir grounded their friendship in the study of botany and in their Christian faith located in the Book of Nature. In the complex of inquiry and spirituality they sought truth and peace and hoped to live useful lives. Their kindred friendship provided a source of nurture and clarity for them both. If not in the kernel of her home then from a distance through letters that bound each to the other Carr would help to unfurl in Muir the budding botanist and naturalist he was to become. Carr's first letter to Muir, written in 1865 and now lost, marked the beginning of the correspondence between two like-minded botanists that continued for thirty years. Muir's response to Carr's letter is the first letter in this edition.[2]

In early March 1866 the thirty thousand broom handles Muir made for the Trouts at the rake factory were destroyed in a factory fire that began as the result of a blizzard. The factory was a total loss and required complete rebuilding. Muir decided not to remain in Canada. Disagreements with the Trouts over religion and a growing sense that he could accomplish more in the United States drew him to Indianapolis, which had many manufactories. He found employment at Osgood & Smith, a carriage-material factory. He wrote to his sister Sarah that he felt utterly homeless. Success at inventing labor-saving improvements at Osgood & Smith interrupted Muir's botanical studies. Carr wrote to him in October, tried to assuage his loneliness, inquired as to whether he had found *Calypso borealis,* and invited him to return to Madison. Throughout 1866 Muir found himself drawn to the power and goodness of God manifest in the natural world. The Book of Nature and the Bible harmonized and each contained enough divine truth for the study of all eternity; however, it was easier for Muir to employ his faculties on beautiful tangible forms than to wrestle with a faith that called for a literal reading of the Scriptures—the discipleship that his father, Daniel Muir, practiced and preached.[3]

In response to Carr's inquiry about the *Calypso borealis,* Muir wrote after October 12 but sometime before December 16, 1866, describing his encounter with the orchid. James Butler took Muir's letter from a table at Carr's home and without her consent submitted it to the *Boston Recorder* with a letter of his own. Muir's letter, published on December 22, 1866, did not mention him by name. The article was brought to Muir's attention perhaps as early as December 28 or 29. Butler, who spent Christmas with his family in Madison, traveled to Indianapolis after the holiday. In Indianapolis he most likely stayed with Colonel Samuel Merrill. Muir wrote to his brother, Daniel, on December 31 and described his visit with Butler and an evening at the Merrills' home. Butler probably had a copy of the *Boston Recorder* article with him that he intended to show Muir. In autobiographical notes written later in life, Muir altered his account of the publication of the *Calypso* article. He stated that he wrote to Butler about his encounter with the *Calypso* and that Butler then sent the letter to the *Boston Recorder* for publication.[4]

Carr knew Muir would not willingly leave Indianapolis and return to Wisconsin. In October, in place of a home in which to hibernate she offered him a literary refuge in Alphonse de Lamartine's *Stonemason of Saint Point.* Carr recommended that Muir read the classic tale of the life of a humble Christian peasant stonemason who understood the unity of creation. She suggested he read the book in 1865. Her copy arrived in December 1866. Lamartine's stonemason's life style and work ethic were emblematic of Carr's expectations for Muir's life. Borrowing his principles of Christian service in relation to the natural world, she hoped to provide a foundation for Muir. The virtue of the stonemason resided not in his humble and timid character but in his understanding of the harmony of creation expressed as a catechism of nature and in his love for nature and his relation to God's creation. This was the path Carr believed divinely fitted Muir's life and destiny. She rejoiced in handing him a perfect vision of his future.[5]

Muir wrote to Carr that he had read the *Stonemason* with great pleasure. His remarks would have to wait as would his botanical studies, suspended due to a serious eye injury that resulted from his having installed a countershaft for a new circular saw at the Osgood & Smith factory. The belt that connected to the mainshaft was new, stretched during use, and required shortening. A file that Muir used to unlace the belt slipped and pierced his right eye on the edge near the cornea. Muir feared his eye was gone, closed forever on all God's beauty. The Carrs and Butler introduced Muir to the Merrill family when he arrived in Indianapolis, and by the end of summer they had engaged Muir in informal nature walks beyond the city. It was the Merrills who sent for an oculist to see Muir following his eye injury.

While Muir convalesced Carr wrote several letters of encouragement. In March she mentioned Butler, the *Calypso* letter, and the article in the *Boston Recorder*. There are no extant letters between December 16 and March 15, 1866, that might provide clues as to whether Muir told Carr about his meeting with Butler in late December. Carr's letter to Muir in March suggested she was unaware that he knew about the publication of the letter. The tone of her objection to Butler's indiscreet snatching of the letter suggests concern that seems immediate rather than reminiscent. In Carr's estimation there was no law against the "abuse of the privileges of friendship." Butler's punishment, however, was to never again lay a finger on a letter belonging to her.

In April Carr once again wrote to Muir about his meeting with *Calypso*, this time writing as if she personally accompanied him on his journey in the Canadian swamp in which he found the orchid. She fused her thoughts on Muir's encounter with an introduction to her "best beloved friend" the Reverend Walter R. Brooks and Brooks's understanding of nature's spiritual existence. Though Carr would formally introduce Muir to Brooks's writings in July 1870, she explained in April 1867 that Muir's *Calypso* epiphany evoked within her a strong emotional association with nature, best explained in Brooks's writings that centered on the unity and sacredness of the creation, on the revelation of spiritual truth through nature and scripture, and on the dialogue between natural history and religion. For Brooks books were a second-hand source of truth. He believed they were samples upon a shelf, a faint weak murmur, providing a limited connection to the real world. Nature, the great ocean, was the true revealer of knowledge. And nature was the revealer of the thoughts of God, who created nature, filled it with His own presence, power, and wisdom, set it in motion and perpetual change, and brought our spirits into it to think and study nature. According to Brooks God did all this in order to awaken human feelings, to touch our sentiments, and to instruct our souls by the influence of the world upon us. Brooks saw the entire world as one and as sacred as a church. In his eyes the natural world was God's temple, filled with His glory.[6]

Deeply concerned about Muir's condition, Carr sought ways to draw his thoughts from his affliction to focus on nature and botanical studies—nature as a source of relation and of healing. Muir confided to Carr that he could have died on the spot because he felt he did not have the heart to look at flowers again with such limited sight. She reminded him God had given him the "eye within the eye, to see in all natural objects the realized ideas of His mind." Both Muir and Carr believed the injury had meaning and purpose for his life. She assured him God would surely place him where his work was, fully recognizing him "as one baptized of Nature and the Spirit." Carr encouraged Muir to have a description of Yosemite Valley read to him. She was always looking to extend his knowledge of God's landscape. Muir had read a description of the Valley at some point during the previous year and thought of it often.

Muir's eye would never be perfect, but his sight was restored. He "bade adieu" to mechanical inventions, devoted his life to the study of the inventions of God, and headed home to Portage, Wisconsin, with his young friend Merrill Moores, the eleven-year-old nephew of Catherine Merrill. Muir and Moores traveled through the center of Illinois and botanized one week on the prairie about seven miles southwest of Pecatonia, where Muir gathered a bouquet of prairie grasses and sedges. He expected to be in Madison, Wisconsin, in three weeks. He wrote that though a cloud covered his right eye, when he gazed over the widest landscapes he was not always aware of its presence.

Muir remained in Wisconsin during the summer, botanized in Portage, and visited the Carrs and Butlers in Madison. Based on an observation of Increase I. Lapham, pioneering Wisconsin conservationist, Carr knew of the abundance of *Aspidium fragrans* in the Wisconsin dells. She wrote to Muir in mid-August regarding the possibility of his finding *Aspidiums* for a friend in Troy. By the end of the month Muir's plans for a walking tour of the southern states had solidified.

Doomed to be carried into wilderness, Muir wrote to Carr from Indianapolis that he wished he knew where he was going. He crossed from Jeffersonville on the Indiana-Kentucky line and walked through Louisville. Beyond the city he found a road going south, reached a woods, spread out his map, and traced a route south and east toward Florida. Near Burkesville, Kentucky, having walked 170 miles from Louisville, he wrote Carr that the beauty of the trees cut into his memory. How dearly he thought she would appreciate the valleys of verdure and masses of trees. His plan was to continue south-southeast through Kingston and Madisonville, Tennessee, then down through Blairsville and Gainesville, Georgia, to Florida, then to Cuba and South America.

Nature, wildness, and the least trodden way compensated for loneliness, though Muir sought the support and advice of Carr along his path. In attempting to provide a kindred connection for Muir, Carr gave him directions to the home of Ada Brooks, the sister of Walter R. Brooks, who lived near Savannah. Carr wrote to Miss Brooks on September 14 to introduce Muir and announce he was botanizing through the South. Muir passed through the Cumberland Mountains, descended the eastern slope, forded the Emory River, passed through Kingston, and on September 14 walked into the Smoky Mountains. On September 23 he passed out of the mountains, into the Georgia savanna, and entered a region of unfamiliar plant life. He arrived in Savannah on October 8, though he never stopped to meet Ada Brooks. In Savannah he expected to receive a parcel of money from his brother. Without funds he was forced to wander until he found a retreat in Bonaventure

Cemetery, where he stayed among the live oaks and slept upon the graves among the tombs. From the cemetery he wrote to Carr about the life he found there—living waters, birds, insects, and trees—a favored field of God's clearest light and life. When money arrived Muir left Savannah by schooner for Florida.[7]

Muir's encounter with alligators in Florida evoked the principles of Lamartine's stonemason, who believed God existed by reason that everything that surrounded him instructed the eyes and the soul. The idea of God entered the stonemason's eyes with the first ray of light, entered into his spirit with his first reflection, entered his heart with his first emotion. With everything the stonemason saw, whether star, insect, leaf, or grain of sand, he raised the question, "Who was it that made thee?" He considered as his neighbors humans, animals, trees, and plants, for whom he never felt hatred. In "this world where God has placed us... to live in peace and unity," he felt all things were related to humanity in body and soul. He felt a foolish tenderness "for all the rest of creation, especially for all those living creatures of other species, who live beside us on the earth, who see the same sun, who breathe the same air, who drink the same water, who are formed of the same flesh under other forms, and who appear truly less perfect members, less well-endowed by our common father, but still members of the great family of God." Not content feeling this tenderness and compassion only for animals who moved about, who felt and had intelligence suited to their condition, he felt tenderness also for trees, flowers, and mosses that did not move from their place and did not appear to think, but lived and died around him on the earth. Muir shared these sentiments. He was certain alligators were happy in the place to which they were assigned by the "great Creator." As fierce and cruel as they appeared to humans, Muir knew they were beautiful in the eyes of God. As God's children—unfallen and undepraved—they were deserving of reverence. God heard their cries, cared for them, and provided their daily food.[8]

Weak with malarial fever, Muir wrote to Carr from Cedar Key. While he convalesced and planned his trip to South America he contemplated the contrasting relation between the belief held by many that the world was made especially for humanity and his belief that each animal and plant was created to experience its own happiness. He thought humanity valued itself "as more than a small part of the one great unit of creation." The universe was incomplete without human beings; however, it was also "incomplete without the smallest transmicroscopic creature that dwells beyond our conceitful eyes and knowledge." In accord with the sentiments of the stonemason, Muir's feelings and thoughts of tenderness for God's creation were underpinned by the belief that the common dust of the earth was the source from which *Homo sapiens* and all other creatures were made (all creatures being our "earth-born companions and our fellow mortals").[9]

In January 1868 Muir booked passage to Cuba on the *Island Belle*. *For* a month he walked beaches and collected shells and plants. Though his health did not improve, he looked for a ship headed for Colombia or Venezuela from where he would travel to the headwaters of the Orinoco, then south to the Amazon. Unable to find a ship bound for South America, Muir turned north to New York to go west to California and the Yosemite Valley.

Carr's letters to Muir composed during the time he left for Canada West and traveled to the Cedar Keys are not extant. Her voice resonates in Muir's letters to her, in her letter to Ada Brooks, and in her letter to Merrill Moores written in search of Muir. Uneasy over the interruption in her correspondence to him, Carr hoped Moores had recent information as to Muir's whereabouts. Ezra Carr's resignation from the University of Wisconsin provided an opportunity for the Carrs to consider a major change in their lives. Carr wrote to Muir in May 1868 explaining their circumstance. She went east with her children to stay with her family in Castleton, Vermont, from July until October, while Ezra remained in Madison and sold the Gilman Street home and the furnishings.

As Muir traveled south, every trace of him had been beyond Carr's reach, and she felt the loss of him in her life. This was a pace and tone that would become familiar as Muir journeyed west into the Sierra and Yosemite Valley.

ɶ

Trout's Mills, near Meaford,
September 13, [*1865*]

"———" Mrs. Carr

Your precious letter with its burden of cheer and good wishes has
come to our hollow, and has done for me that work of sympathy and
encouragement which I know you kindly wished it to do. It came at a
time when much needed, for I am subject to lonesomeness at times.
Accept, then, my heartfelt gratitude—would that I could make better
return!

I am sorry over the loss of Professor Sterling's letter, for I waited and
wearied for it a long time. I have been keeping up an irregular course
of study since leaving Madison, but with no great success. I do not
believe that study, especially of the Natural Sciences, is incompatible
with ordinary attention to business; still I seem to be able to do but
one thing at a time. Since undertaking a month or two ago to invent
new machinery for our mill, my mind seems to so bury itself in the
work that I am fit for but little else; and then a lifetime is so little a
time that we die ere we get ready to live. I would like to go to college,
but then I have to say to myself, "You will die ere you can do anything else." I should like to invent useful machinery, but it comes,
"You do not wish to spend your lifetime among machines and you
will die ere you can do anything else." I should like to study medicine
that I might do my part in helping human misery, but again it comes,
"You will die ere you are ready or able to do so." How intensely I
desire to be a Humboldt! but again the chilling answer is reiterated;
but could we but live a *million* of years, then how delightful to spend
in perfect contentment so many thousand years in quiet study in
college, so many amid the grateful din of machines, as many among
human pain, so many thousand in the sweet study of Nature among
the dingles and dells of *Scotland,* and all the other less important parts
of our world! Then *perhaps* might we, with at least a show of reason,
"shuffle off this mortal coil" and look back upon our star with something of satisfaction; I should be ashamed—if shame might be in the
other world—if any of the powers, virtues, essences, etc., should ask

me for common knowledge concerning our world which I could not bestow. But away with this *aged* structure and we are back to our handful of hasty years half gone, all of course for the best did we but know all of the Creator's plan concerning us. In our higher state of existence we shall have time and intellect for study. Eternity, with perhaps the whole unlimited creation of God as our field, should satisfy us, and make us patient and trustful, while we pray with the Psalmist, "Teach us to number our days that we may apply our hearts unto wisdom."

I was struck with your remarks about our real home of stillness and peace. How little does the outer and noisy world in general know of that "real home" and real inner life! Happy indeed they who have a friend to whom they can unmask the workings of their real life, sure of sympathy and forbearance!

I sent for the book which you recommend; I have just been reading a short sketch of the life of the mother of Lamartine.

These are beautiful things you say about the humble life of our Saviour and about the trees gathering in the sunshine.

What you say respecting the littleness of the number who are called to "the pure and deep communion of the beautiful, all-loving Nature," is particularly true of the hard-working, hard-drinking, stolid Canadians. In vain is the glorious chart of God in Nature spread out for them. So many acres chopped is their motto, so they grub away amid the smoke of magnificent forest trees, black as demons and material as the soil they move upon. I often think of the Doctor's lecture upon the condition of the different races of men as controlled by physical agencies. Canada, though abounding in the elements of wealth, is too difficult to subdue to permit the first few generations to arrive at any great intellectual development. In my long rambles last summer I did not find a single person who knew anything of botany and but a few who knew the meaning of the word; and wherein lay the charm that could conduct a man who might as well be gathering mammon so many miles through these fastnesses to suffer hunger and exhaustion was with them never to be discovered. Do not these answer well to the person described by the poet in these lines?

"A primrose by the river's brim,
A yellow primrose was to him,
And nothing more."

I thank Dr. Carr for his kind remembrance of me, but still more for the good patience he had with so inept a scholar.

We remember in a peculiar way those who first give us the story of Redeeming Love from the great book of Revelation, and I shall not forget the Doctor, who first laid before me the great book of Nature, and though I have taken so little from his hand he has at least shown me where those mines of priceless knowledge lie and how to reach them. O how frequently, Mrs. Carr, when lonely and wearied, have I wished that like some hungry worm I could creep into that delightful kernel of your house, your library, with its portraits of scientific men, and so bountiful a store of their sheaves amid the blossom and verdure of your little kingdom of plants, luxuriant and happy as though holding their leaves to the open sky of the most flower-loving zone in the world!

That "sweet day" did as you wished reach our hollow, and another is with us now. The sky has the haze of autumn, and excepting the aspen not a tree has motion. Upon our enclosing wall of verdure new tints appear, the gorgeous dyes of autumn are to be plainly seen, and the forest seems to have found out that again its leaf must fade. Our stream, too, has a less cheerful sound, and as it bears its foam-bells pensively away from the shallow rapids it seems to feel that summer is past.

You propose, Mrs. Carr, an exchange of thoughts, for which I thank you very sincerely. This will be a means of pleasure and improvement which I could not have hoped ever to have been possessed of, but then here is the difficulty: I feel that I am altogether incapable of properly conducting a correspondence with one so much above me. We are, indeed, as you say, students in the same life school, but in very different classes. I am but an alpha novice in those sciences which you have studied and loved so long. If, however, you are willing in this to adopt the plan that our Saviour endeavored to beat into the stingy Israelites, *viz.*, to "give, hoping for nothing again," all will be well; and as long as your letters resemble this one before me, which you have just written, in genus, order, cohort, class, province, or kingdom, be assured that by way of reply you shall at least receive an honest "Thank you."

Tell Allie that Mr. Muir thanks him for his pretty flowers and would like to see him, also that I have a story for him which I shall tell some other time.

Please remember me to my friends, and now, hoping to receive a letter from you at least *semi-occasionally,* I remain

Yours with gratitude,
John Muir

Address Meaford, P. O.
   County Grey
   Canada West[10]

∾

Sauk City, September 24, [1865]

[*John Muir*]

This lovely Sabbath evening finds me in the delicious quiet of the country, with cow bells tinkling instead of steeple chimes, the drone and chirp of myriad insects for choral service, depending for a sermon upon the purple bluffs and flowing river.

> One lesson, Nature, let me learn of thee,
> One lesson, that in every wind is blown,
> One lesson, of two duties served in one,
> Though the loud world proclaims their enmity!
> Of Toil unsevered from Tranquility,
> Of Labor, that in still advance outgrows
> Far noisier schemes, accomplished in repose.
> Too great for haste, too high for rivalry.

I see from your letter that you suffer from that which is my most grievous burden—the pressure of Time upon Life. The scale on which our studies have been planned is indeed too large for a single life and requires Eternity. But surely it is wiser to lay the foundations deep enough for a structure that shall outlast the fleeting years.

In my private prayer book I find this petition, "Oh Lord help me to feel in my heart the leisure in which Thou dost work thy works, and teach me the secret of that Labor which is not Toil,"—a prayer for a woman whose life seems always to be used up in little trifling things, never labelled "done" and laid away as a man's may be. Then as a woman I have often to consider not the lilies only, in their perfection, but the humble honest wayside grasses and weeds, sturdily filling their places through such repeated discouragements.

I think I can sympathize in your sigh, "I shall die before I accomplish what I desire." Yes, dear friend, we have to *die* to be what we seek, to gain what we pray for, and what faith does for us is to enable us to reach out joyously into that unseen future, to *expect* it as one of the things of tomorrow.

I have thought much of you in reading lately of the life of Charles Goodyear, the "India rubber man," whose whole existence was a battle with adversity. He does not seem to have lived so near the heart of Nature or found her balms for his wounded spirit, but he was *haunted* with inventions. They tortured him, sleeping or waking, until he worked them into visible forms. A great mechanical genius is a wonderful gift, something one should hold in trust for mankind, a kind of seal and private mark which God has placed upon souls especially his own. For all these must look into the far future for their rewards; many to whom the world owes civilization, advancement, freedom from the rank materialism of want, sleep in nameless graves, and others reap what they sowed. But they are still the blessed workers working on through other hands while they truly rest from their labors and sorrows.

Madison, Sunday evening

I wish you were here in the "kernel" of the house. It looks very pleasant, especially with the wind howling without. I would give you your choice between talking and singing. I have built up two very pretty miniature Wardian cases which are filled with mosses, ferns and lichens, all growing very nicely. You would help me to contrive a tiny fountain if you should see them, then they would be perfect. They *rest* me when I am tired, and I think you might contrive a little comfort for yourself by piling up some pretty lichen covered stones on an old

plate and dropping soil among them. Plant therein a few mosses
which want nothing but shade and water to make them grow. There
is a very gay butterfly sporting about them while I write, and in the
window a bundle of twigs with large chrysalides which I look to for
a supply of their winged blossoms in the dreary season.

I have a hope of going out upon a farm near Madison with my
boys and bringing them up in the healthy exercise of all their faculties
upon a farm. I think Dr. Carr would be proud of sleek cattle and
waving harvests that had the seal of his ownership upon them, while
the return wave of the war has flooded Madison with so much wickedness that I long to be out of sight of it and gives us a reason for making
the change.

We shall not go very far, and you will find us easily.

Dear Mr. Muir, I was very much gratified by your excellent letter,
to which this is a very poor return. Your little friends are all well. I
will not keep this longer in the hope of finding leisure to fill it, for my
hands are at present full of work. Believe in my cordial and constant
interest in all that concerns you, and that I have a pleasant way of
associating you with my highest and purest enjoyments. Dr. Carr
sends his best regards, and I am,

Always your friend,
Jeanne Carr[11]

∾

"The Hollow," January 21, 1866

Dear Mrs. Carr

Your last, written in the delicious quiet of a Sabbath in the country,
has been received and read a good many times. I was interested with
the description you draw of your sermon. You speak of such services
like one who appreciated and relished them. But although the page of
Nature is so replete with divine truth, it is silent concerning the fall of
man and the wonders of Redeeming Love. Might she not have been
made to speak as clearly and eloquently of these things as she now
does of the character and attributes of God? It may be a bad symptom,
but I will confess that I take more intense delight from reading the

power and *goodness* of God from "the things which are made" than
from the Bible. The two books, however, harmonize beautifully, and
contain enough of divine truth for the study of all eternity. It is so
much easier for us to employ our faculties upon these beautiful tangible forms than to exercise a simple, humble living faith such as you
so well describe as enabling us to reach out joyfully into the future to
expect what is promised as a thing of tomorrow.

I wish, Mrs. Carr, that I could see your mosses and ferns and
lichens. I am sure that you must be happier than anybody else. You
have so much less of winter than others; your parlor garden is verdant
and in bloom all the year.

I took your hint and procured ten or twelve species of moss all in
fruit, also a club-moss, a fern, and some liverworts and lichens. I have
also a box of thyme. I would go a long way to see your herbarium,
more especially your ferns and mosses. These two are by far the most
interesting of all the natural orders to me. The shaded hills and glens
of Canada are richly ornamented with these lovely plants. *Aspidium
spinulosum* is common everywhere, so also is *A. marginale, A. aculeatum, A. lonchitis,* and *Asplenium acrostichoides* are also abundant in
many places. I found specimens of most of the other *Aspidiums,* but
those I have mentioned are more common. *Cystopteris bulbifera*
grows in every arborvitae shade in company with the beautiful and
fragrant *Linnaea borealis. Botrychium lunarioides* is a common fern
in many parts of Canada. *Osmunda regalis* is far less common here
than in Wisconsin. I found it in only two localities. Six *claytoniana*
only in one place near the Niagara Falls. The delicate *Adiantum*
trembles upon every hillside. *Struthiopteris germanica* grows to a
great height in open places in arborvitae and black ash swamps.
Camptosorus rhizophyllus and *Scolopendrium officinarum* I found in
but one place, amid the wet limestone rocks of Owen Sound. There
are many species of sedge common here which I do not remember
having seen in Wisconsin. *Calypso borealis* is a lovely plant found in
a few places in dark hemlock woods. But this is an endless thing; I
may as well stop here.

I have been very busy of late making practical machinery. I like
my work exceedingly well, but would prefer inventions which would

require some artistic as well as mechanical skill. I invented and put in operation a few days ago an attachment for a self-acting lathe, which has increased its capacity at least one third. We are now using it to turn broom-handles, and as these useful articles may now be made cheaper, and as cleanliness is one of the cardinal virtues, I congratulate myself in having done something like a true philanthropist for the real good of mankind in general. What say you? I have also invented a machine for making rake-teeth, and another for boring for them and driving them, and still another for making the bows, still another used in making the handles, still another for bending them, so that rakes may now be made nearly as fast again. Farmers will be able to produce grain at a lower rate, the poor get more bread to eat. Here is more philanthropy; is it not? I sometimes feel as though I was losing time here, but I am at least receiving my first lessons in practical mechanics, and as one of the firm here is a millwright, and as I am permitted to make as many machines as I please and to remodel those now in use, the school is a pretty good one.

I wish that Allie and Henry B. could come to see me every day, there are no children in our family here, and I miss them very much. They would like to see the machinery, and I could turn wooden balls and tops, rake-bows before being bent would make excellent canes, and if they should need crutches broom-handles and rake-handles would answer. I have not heard from Henry for a long time. I suppose that this evening finds you in your pleasant library amid books and plants and butterflies. Are you really successful in keeping happy, sportive "winged blossoms" in such weather as this?

One of the finest snowstorms is raging now; the roaring wind thick with snow rushes cruelly through the desolate trees. Our rapid stream that so short a time ago shone and twinkled in the hazy air bearing away the nuts and painted leaves of autumn is now making a doleful noise as it gropes its way doubtfully and sulkily amid heaps of snow and broken ice.

The weather here is unusually cold. How do matters stand at the University? Can it be that the Doctor is really going to become practical farmer? He will have time to compose excellent lectures while following the plow and harrow or when shearing his sheep.

I thank you for your long, good letter. Those who are in a lonely place and far from home know how to appreciate a friendly letter. Remember me to the Doctor and to all my friends and believe me

Yours with gratitude,

John Muir[12]

∽

Madison, October 12, [1866]

Dear Mr. Muir

No, dear John Muir, little Henry's letter has made me feel how much I have lost in letting you alone so many months, and I have done injustice to my own heart in not telling you how really sorry I was for the misfortune that took you out of the Canada woods. Somehow I thought you were a picture fitly framed in that wild picturesque region—did you not feel more at home with the nature there than in the human element now surrounding you?

I like to think of you either in the good old mother's arms or where man's work is the work of the ages.

But I see that you are lonely—and I know it is not well for you. I write you to ask you to come here this fall before nature puts on her winter clothes, and make me (us) a good long visit, renew your old intimacies with children and books, and make new friendships with grown people and with the plants I have to show you. I have studied the *Fungi* this year—just enough to be completely bewitched with their beauty. Their perishable nature adds to their interest for me— it allies them to the clouds, to the morning and evening light, to all things made "for beauty only." The long continued rains have produced them in unusual luxuriance and perfection, and I am daily mourning that I cannot "abide" with them for a few days in their chosen haunts. I suppose the region about your old home is even richer than this in the "little children" of the vegetable world.

We have had a bitter disappointment in the University. The Legislature of last winter voted to unite the Agricultural Grant and that to the University in a common fund for the support of an Institution which under the old name should be reorganized to cover the ground of both. We had a new Board of Regents appointed, and their first effort was to obtain a President. They finally agreed in appointing Professor Paul A. Chadbourne of Williams College, a very eminent scientific man, one of the first botanists in the country. The Massachusetts State Republican committee had also appointed him to represent them (with others) at the late Republican convention in Philadelphia.

He did not go, but had hardly arrived *here* when our democratic papers came out in a series of articles against him, and he was so disgusted with the prospect of a political quarrel that he refused to stay with us. In consequence the Faculty was not reorganized, and the institution is practically suspended. We hope they may open it early in October, but there is no certainty. A larger number than ever before had applied for rooms, and many have gone away.

I suppose you have in Indiana the advantage of access to a good library. I suppose you have before this found my beautiful book, *The Stonemason of Saint Point,* and what did you think of it? And did you ever find *Calypso* for yourself in the North woods?

I have a great many questions to ask you, and I trust there is a time coming for them all. You do not know how we hold you in our memories as one apart from all other students in your power of insight into Nature, and the simplicity of your love for her. I think you would love her as well if she did not turn mill wheels or grind anybody's grist. Besides, I like you for your individualized acceptance of religious truth and feel a deep sympathy in it. We are truly your friends, dear John, come to us *freely* and try whether it will help the loneliness, and come and see us this fall or any time when you can.

Yours most sincerely,
Jeanne Carr[13]

∾

Osgood & Smith
[*October, 1866*]

[*Mrs. Carr*]
[Beginning of letter missing]

I have not before sent these feelings and thoughts to anybody, but I know that I am speaking to one who by long and deep communion with Nature understands them, and can tell me what is true or false and unworthy in my experiences.

The ease with which you have read my mind from hints taken from letters to my child friends gives me confidence to write.

Thank you for the compliment of the great picture-frame. That is at least *one* invention that I should not have discovered,—but the picture is but an insect, an animalcule. I have stood by a majestic pine, witnessing its high branches waving "in sign of worship" or in converse with the spirit of the storms of autumn, till I forgot my very existence, and thought myself unworthy to be made a leaf of such a tree.

What work do you use in the study of the *Fungi*? and where can I get a copy? I think of your description of these "little children of the vegetable kingdom" whenever I meet any of them. I am busy with the mosses and liverworts, but find difficulty in procuring a suitable lens. Here is a specimen of *Climacium americanum,* a common moss here but seldom in fruit.

I am sorry to hear of your loss at the University of so valuable a man from such a cause. I hope that the wheels of your institution are again in motion.

I have not yet, I am sorry to say, found *The Stonemason of Saint Point,* though I have sought for it a good deal. By whom is it published?

Please remember me to my friends. I often wish myself near the Doctor with my difficulties in science. Tell Allie Mr. Muir does not forget him.

[*John Muir*][14]

ॐ

Madison, December 16, 1866

Dear John Muir

This is a very gray, chilly and *unlovely Sabbath* (those words do not look nicely together), and I have been up on the mountain side with Claude to worship under the huge stone cross. I was glad to hear from you—glad to know you found the *Calypso*. I think you deserved to find it, you are such a true lover of Nature. I want to know you, dear friend, many years hence when you shall have a true deep love *for art,* also. I do not think you ever would feel as warm an interest in works of art as in Natural objects, but the great sculptures—they would charm you. Mr. T. B. [*Thomas Buchanan*] Reads [*sic*] pictures have a wonderful natural charm. I wish you could see some of them.

I have been so very busy of late that I have read nothing new. I want to go to Chicago soon to see some new works on Natural History which we shall never be able to afford to buy. When I see them I will write to you about them.

The University has very good attendance, but we are still without a President. Professor Butler and family are well. Mr. Murdock, the tragedian and reader, has been staying with us for the last four months with two daughters. Colonel McMysin, the State Superintendent, is also a member of our family so I have not much time for reading or for my *herbal*. Allie sends love and little Henry, and Dr. Carr wishes to be remembered.

> Your friend truly,
> Jeanne Carr

I send you my copy of *The Stonemason,* by mail. When you have kept it as long as you wish you may return it to me in the same way. I thank you for the *Climacium* and should be glad to get a few more of the same.

> J. C. C.[15]

∽

For the *Boston Recorder.* THE CALYPSO BOREALIS. Botanical Enthusiasm. From Prof. J. D. Butler

A young Wisconsin gatherer of simples seems not a whit behind Thoreau as a scrutinizer and votary of nature. During the last season but one, he explored the flora of Canada,—playing the pedestrian from Lake Superior to Niagara, setting out with primroses which come before the swallow dares, and take the winds of March with beauty, nor tiring till black fronts hid the last of the flowers.

Having thus exhausted his ill-filled purse, he betook himself to the first mechanical toil that fell in his way. All naturalists will love to read what he wrote a friend who had inquired of him concerning that rarest as well as most fantastic and fairy-like of the orchid family—

the *Calypso borealis,* which is, being interpreted, the "hider of the north"—a name strangely descriptive of its nature. Who of us outsiders can fail to envy him his esoteric raptures in his close communion with virgin nature? as well as to wish with all the heart that ours were such a vision and faculty divine, and that for us also culture or genius had added a precious seeing to the eye, transforming every weed to a flower, and transfiguring every flower with seven-fold beauty? But hear the inspired pilgrim.

He writes: I did find Calypso—but only once, far in the depths of the very wildest of Canadian dark woods, near those high, cold, moss-covered swamps where most of the peninsular streams of Canada West take their rise.

For several days in June I had been forcing my way through woods that seemed to become more and more dense, and among bogs more and more difficult to cross, when, one warm afternoon, after descending a hillside covered with huge half-dead hemlocks, I crossed an ice-cold stream, and espied two specimens of Calypso. There, upon an open plat of yellow moss, near an immense rotten log, were these little plants, so pure.

They were alone. Not a vine was near, not a blade of grass, nor a bush. Nor were there any birds or insects, for great blocks of ice lay screened from the summer's sun by deep beds of moss, and chilled the water. They were indeed alone, for the dull ignoble hemlocks were not companions, nor was the nearer arbor-vitae, with its root-like pendulous branches decaying confusedly on the wet, cold ground.

I never before saw a plant so full of life; so perfectly spiritual, it seemed pure enough for the throne of its Creator. I felt as if I were in the presence of superior beings who loved me and beckoned me to come. I sat down beside them and wept for joy. Could angels in their better land show us a more beautiful plant? How good is our Heavenly Father in granting us such friends as are these plant-creatures, filling us wherever we go with pleasure so deep, so pure, so endless.

I cannot understand the nature of the curse, "Thorns and thistles shall it bring forth to thee." Is our world indeed the worse for this "thistly curse?" Are not all plants beautiful? or in some way useful? Would not the world suffer by the banishment of a single weed? The curse must be within ourselves. Give me this keen relish for simple pleasures, and he that will may monopolize the lust of the flesh, the lust of the eye, the pride of the life,—yea, all pomps and marvels of the world.[16]

∾

Madison, March 15, [*1867*]

Dear John

I grieve, as your sister might, at this news which has come today— that God has been leading you into the darkness, and long to be able to minister to your comfort while the burden of pain and weakness and loneliness is to be borne. What can I do, now, while you are so far from us but whisper some of those sweet promises which fasten the soul to the source of Light and Life? And you have these treasures laid up, so I do not know how to be useful to you in this extremity— except just to speak the words of hope and faith and courage of which my heart is full. It *is* hard, dear friend—it seems cruel, but let us look away beyond the suffering of the present. Let us *believe* that nothing is without meaning and purpose which comes from the Father's hand. And let us try to emulate the courage and fortitude of those brave thousands, who have lately sacrificed so much of the beauty and joy of life, and yet go cheerfully on with what is left. And do not let us despair of beautiful and joyous days to come. I am glad to feel that you will see more with one visual organ than most persons could with half a dozen. Dr. Carr says, even that eye must not be resigned as worthless until the best skill and largest experience have pronounced it so, for even the aqueous humor may be restored.

So my precious soldier boy, I put out my hands to ward off the consequences of the blow which struck you. You are in hospital and have to lie still and be preached to, have to let women cover your bed with tracts and wash your face when you don't want it washed. And while they are fussing about, dear, I will hurry up the *Hepaticas* and the violets, and they will tell you a good many things which I do not care to say at second hand or through an interpreter. And then you will come here and we will be eyes for you. The Cordilleras and the Amazon will stay in their places, they are waiting—have waited thousands of years to be set to music—the Queen of the Antilles will be as beautiful in her next year's green as now. You will take a richer

heart and a clearer mind with which to interpret them for this
retirement.   *eye injury*

Dear John, I have often in my heart wondered what God was training you for. He gave you the eye within the eye, to see in all natural
objects the realized ideas of His mind. He gave you pure tastes and the
steady preference of whatsoever is most lovely and excellent. He has
made you a more individualized existence than is common, and by your
very nature and organization removed you from common temptations.
Perhaps He only wants you to love and to speak of Him. Perhaps He
will not let you be a naturalist but calls you by this suffering away
from that pleasant path to speak to other souls those messages of His
your soul has heard. Do not be anxious about it. He will surely place
you where your work is. Do I seem to speak over-confidently? Dear
friend, my recognition of you from the first was just this—"one of
His beloved." When you are disposed to look hopelessly outward you
may think, "Mrs. Carr believes fully in me. She would while there was
enough left of my body to hold my soul." And you may think too that
she does not pity half as much as she loves you.

Did you get *The Stonemason* about Christmas? Mrs. Merrill says
there is another John Muir (I don't believe a word of it though), and
that made me consider the possibility that it had fallen into other
hands. I had not your address when I directed the package, for Mr.
Butler was in here one day and carried off your letter, and without
my knowledge or consent copied and published what you said of the
Calypso in a letter of his own to the *Boston Recorder.* There is no law
against such an indelicate and outrageous abuse of the privileges of
friendship. Except the law of one's own mind—but his punishment
shall be that he never lays [a] finger on [a] letter of mine again. The
bewitching name—*Calypso,* "the concealed," was his temptation. *He*
never will find one on earth or in heaven nor anything nearer to her
than "Ladyshoes." Mrs. Merrill is a woman of sense, I guess, and may
be trusted with my anger.

And now, John, if you are good and hopeful and have some kind
soul near to read you things, I will send you some good strong sweet
words from my friend and your elder brother the priest, and a letter
he wrote me last summer after the *woods* (not from them). May you
feel the "everlasting arms" beneath your pillow, may Infinite tenderness

supply all the wants of your spirit and the needs of your life, may each of these days of trial be luminous with His Presence without whom the fairest scene is dark and sorrowful. Dr. Carr feels for you. Allie looks serious and grave at the letter which brought the news. *We* are all sorry, but I am getting a dimness in my eyes thinking of yours and must say goodnight. Make your mark now and then, dear, on these envelopes, for better or worse as you feel. I can read your "worst words" and am always,

Your loving friend,
Jeanne Carr[17]

∞

Ind[ianapolis]
April 3, [1867]

Mrs. Carr

Dear friend, You have, of course, heard of my calamity.

The sunshine and the winds are working in all the gardens of God, but *I*—I am lost.

I am shut in darkness. My hard, toil-tempered muscles have disappeared, and I am feeble and tremulous as an ever-sick woman.

Please tell the Butlers that their precious sympathy has reached me.

I have read your "Stonemason" with a great deal of pleasure. I send it with this and will write my thoughts upon it when I can.

My friends here are kind beyond what I can tell and do much to shorten my immense blank days.

I send no apology for so doleful a note because I feel, Mrs. Carr, that you will appreciate my feelings.

Most cordially,
J. Muir[18]

∞

[Indianapolis]
Sunday, April 6, [1867]

Mrs. Carr, Dear friend

Your precious letter of the 15th reached me last night. By accident it was nearly lost.

I cannot tell you, Mrs. Carr, how much I appreciate your sympathy and all of these kind thoughts of cheer and substantial consolation which you have stored for me in this letter.

I am much better than when I wrote you; can now sit up about all day and in a room partly lighted.

Your Doctor says, "The aqueous humor may be restored." How? By nature or by art?

The position of my wound will be seen in this figure.

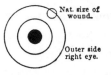

Nat. size of wound.
Outer side right eye.

The eye is pierced just where the cornea meets the sclerotic coating. I do not know the depth of the wound or its exact direction. Sight was completely gone from the injured eye for the first few days, and my physician said it would be ever gone, but I was surprised to find that on the fourth or fifth day I could see a little with it. Sight continued to increase for a few days, but for the last three weeks it has not perceptibly increased or diminished.

I called in a Dr. Parvin lately, said to be a very skillful oculist and of large experience both here and in Europe. He said that he thought the iris permanently injured; that the crystalline lens was not injured; that, of course, my two eyes would not work together; and that on the whole my chances of distinct vision were not good. But the bare possibility of anything like full sight is now my outstanding hope. When the wound was made about one third of a teaspoonful of fluid like the white of an egg flowed out upon my fingers,—aqueous fluid, I suppose. The eye has not yet lost its natural appearance.

I can *see* sufficiently well with it to avoid the furniture, etc., in walking through a room. Can almost, in full light, recognize some of my friends but cannot distinguish one letter from another of common type. I would like to hear Dr. Carr's opinion of my case.

When I received my blow I could not feel any pain or faintness because the tremendous thought glared full on me that my *right eye* was lost. I could gladly have died on the spot, because I did not feel that I could have heart to look at any flower again. But this is not so, for I wish to try some cloudy day to walk to the woods, where I am sure some of spring's sweet fresh-born are waiting.

I believe with you that "nothing is without meaning and purpose that comes from a Father's hand," but during these dark weeks I could not feel this, and, as for courage and fortitude, scarce the shadows of these virtues were left me. The shock upon my nervous system made me weak in mind as a child. But enough of woe.

When I can walk to where fruited specimens of *Climacium* are, I will send you as many as you wish.

I must close. I thank you all again for your kindness. I cannot make sentences that will tell how much I feel indebted to you.

Please remember me to all my friends.

You will write soon. I can read my letters now. Please send them in care of Osgood & Smith.

Cordially,

J. Muir

[*John Muir*][19]

∾

Madison, April 6, 1867

Dear John Muir

I was very glad to get your bit of a note last night and should have been gladder if your note had been longer! I felt sure on looking at the direction that you had "peeked out" of that good eye to write it and before I "peeked in," to see what you would say for yourself, I allowed myself to hope the bad one had got itself mended. You have no idea how much disagreeable weather, how much mud and misery you have been kept out of for the last four weeks. The earth does not look as if it had so much as the memory of a flower in it. The only sign of spring we have seen is a company of blackbirds, who have been going through their Sunday exercises on Mr. Van Slyke's roof, and their guttural note, 'Kluck 'tsee, 'Kluck 'tsee, is musical because we have waited for it more than six months. You see I am bent on congratulating you! You may be sure your beloved flowers will stay away until you are ready to look for them. And you must not prolong their days of patient waiting—they are waiting even as you are.

To be a little more serious, dear John, (sick folks need not expect to have sense talked to them), I believe fully that Nature needs us and waits for us just as we do for her. My best beloved friend says, "There are spiritual existences which the material forms of nature clothe and conceal. I had a fancy that there is a universe of spiritual bodies and forms of which the material plant and animal are the exact counterparts in the physical world—that there is a preexistent spiritual body for every moss, lichen, and plant of every kind; growth is an actual clothing upon of themselves by these spiritual beings. They gather from nature its substances to make themselves a garment exactly fitting their persons, and go through the process of life (as we see it), for the sake of adding the pleasures of activity to the sweet habitude of being. The delicate *Calopogon,* the pure white lily look up at me with a smile of recognition, pleased with their success and say, 'I am here. I have got into the world. I wanted to know how the sunshine felt, and what it would be to feel around me the elements of a material world, and I think—*in the summer*—it is beautiful!' So the poor things get a relation to us and our life which will make them nearer and dearer when they and we all are spiritual bodies again."

So he says, this dear soul who wrote the prayer I sent you once. I thought of this, John, when I witnessed your meeting with *Calypso.* I feel myself shaken with a strange inexplicable emotion in hearing the notes of some solitary birds—as if they called me to the silences of unknown worlds. They are the only true lovers I have known (as the flowers are your beloveds) and we shall exchange the secrets of our existence soon. Have they grief and pain also, these sinless creatures? Do they rejoice *to be gathered?*

These are Sunday thoughts enough for this time, and I am not going to tell you how sorry I am. Get well and *come and see.* I wrote you as soon as I heard of the misfortune (don't imagine it all *yours*), to the care of Miss (or Mrs?) Merrill. Thank you for the *Climacium.* Your muscles deserve to rest, and this may make a *doctor* of you, making you sympathetic with the *nervous.* The Butlers, and all of us, speak often of you.

Jeanne Carr

Allie sends his special love.[20]

∾

Madison, April 15, [*1867*]

Dear friend

I was very glad indeed to get your last and the most welcome news that you could see a little with the injured eye. Dr. Carr thinks the liquid you refer to was only a part of the humor—for the unshrunken appearance of the eye indicates that some must remain. Your physician will of course know best. Dr. E. L. Holmes of the Rush Medical College, Chicago, Dr. Carr thinks the best oculist he knows anything about in the west. He says he does not see why if the integrity of vision is not destroyed, in a perfectly healthy bodily condition the wasted humor should not in time be restored. Still he has too little experience to feel certain. Dr. Hobbins says the deposition of fibrin ought to be prevented, and that to secure this you need to take calomel. But at this distance there is no use in entering into particulars. Only an examination of the eye can determine. A nephew of Dr. Carr's last fall ran a pitchfork into his right eye (a little back of your wound) and for some days Dr. Hobbins thought it doubtful about his seeing. Now, after six months' rest, you cannot detect any difference and the vision is not much affected. Dr. Hobbins says you can train the left eye to do the other's work.

Yesterday the tolling bells and half hour cannon and flags at half mast testified [*to*] the people's grief over the unforgotten dead. Two years ago I lay, it was thought, at the point of death. I felt that I could see that other world, and I was sure that my days in the woods were over. I was such a wreck of myself when I began to creep feebly around the house, and here I am with years of work in me yet. Who knows but we shall see South America yet? He who weaveth the fate of nations and the destinies of the individual will surely lead us, who consciously accept and desire His guidance.

Yesterday Dr. Carr brought home two beautiful books, *The World before the Deluge* and *The Vegetable World* by Louis Figuier, and I said of the latter, "John Muir will enjoy overlooking this." Oh John, if we do get a living man to preside over this University we can make these grounds very beautiful. You will gather seeds for us in South America, and we will have a *Conservatory Fund* and by and by we will appoint John Muir F. R. B. S. Bot. Professor and director of the grounds, and he shall have a little study in the greenhouses and live like dear old Linnaeus—won't it be nice? All this if you don't make a minister.

Do you know Spanish? You ought to be picking up a little Spanish if you mean to traverse the beautiful lands. I do believe you will yet carry out your plans.

You ought not to write much. I felt guilty to see how much you had written to me. *Dielytra* just peeping out of the ground. Robins, blue-birds, fill the air with music. Can you not be permitted to sit or lie in the sun with your head protected? It would do you good to bask. The dear old Mother will heal you fast when you get upon her lap once more.

[*John*] Henry is having his first vest made, Mr. Muir. Not many years to long coats and neckties! Henry is making money, too, by carrying papers, but his riches do not spoil him. Allie is more of a baby, he is our youngling, and we like to keep him so—he is busy now planning a house to put ladybirds in. It is a trial to me to have only forty-eight rods of ground to scratch in and I only content myself by saying, "Well maybe I will yet preempt a small planet." Get some good friend to read you a description of the Yosemite Valley, and try to realize what God's landscape gardening is. Of this house of our Father! I would like to know all its mansions—and often to meet and compare notes with you, who love it with the same fervent love.

> Goodmorning,
> J. C. C.
> [*Jeanne C. Carr*]

Dr. Carr and the Butlers and all send love.[21]

∾

[*April, 1867*]

[*Mrs. Carr*]

[Beginning of letter missing]

I have been *groping* among the flowers a good deal lately. Our trees are not in leaf, but the leaves, as Mrs. Browning would say, are "scarce long enough for waving." The dear little conservative spring mosses have elevated their capsules on their smooth shining shafts, and stand side by side in full stature, and full fashion, every ornament and covering carefully numbered and painted and sculptured as were those of their Adams and Eves, every cowl properly plaited, and drawn far enough down, every hood with the proper dainty slant, their fashions never changing because ever best.

Tell Allie that I would be very glad to have him send me an *Anemone nemorosa* and *A. nuttalliana*. They do not grow here. I wish he and Henry could visit me on Saturdays as they used to do.

The poor eye is much better. I could read a letter with it. I believe that sight is increasing. I have nearly an eye and a half left.

I feel, if possible, more anxious to travel than ever.

I read a description of the Yosemite Valley last year and thought of it most every day since. You know my tastes better than any one else. I am, most gratefully,

John Muir[22]

ॐ

[*Madison, April, 1867*]

Dear John Muir

I am *mad* and mourning today, and this is my trouble. Sunday, the blessed Easter Sunday, I was happy in the resurrection of the earth, in tune with all the new life. As a gentle April rain was falling at evening, I put out my house plants to be washed and beautified in it. It was raining—of course it would not freeze! Monday morning, six inches of snow. My great geraniums, my flowing *Salvias* and tea roses, *all ruined*, even the ivy blackened and for the present spoiled. I was so excited trying to save and restore them that I did not at first feel the desolation of a flowerless home as I do now.

Then I put your big trouble alongside of my little one, and put a brave face on it, and hung the naked ropes of ivy around the "kernel of the house." There will be a few new leaves when you get able to see them.

Here's a letter from the good priest who puts a pleasant prophecy in it, and I put it in for you. You will return it please, because I keep every pleasant word of this dear soul who has passed through your sorrow, *the stonemason's sorrow*—whose life is all love and service like Claude's.

When he is dead these precious leaves of his life will be a sweet inheritance for some related soul to possess. You see, dear John, he recognizes you as one baptized of Nature and the Spirit. I hope you are better. Let me know.

Your friend,

Jeanne Carr[23]

ᐁ

Indianapolis, May 2, 1867

Dear friend Mrs. Carr

I am sorry and surprised to hear of the cruel fate of *your plants.*

I have never seen so happy flowers in any other home. They lived with you so cheerfully and confidingly, and felt so sure of receiving from you sympathy and tenderness in all their sorrows.

How could they grow cold and colder and die without *your* knowing? They must have called you. Could any bedroom be so remote you could not hear? I am very sorry, Mrs. Carr, for you and them. Can your loss be repaired? Will not other flowers lose confidence in you and live like those of other people, sickly and mute, half in, half out, of the body?

No snow fell here Easter evening, but a few wet flakes are falling here and there *today.*

Thank you for sending the prophecy of that loving naturalist of yours. It is indeed a pleasant one, but my faith concerning its complete fulfillment is weak. I do not know who your other doctor is, but I am sure that when in the Yosemite Valley and following the Pacific coast I would obtain a great deal of geology from Doctor Carr, and from yourself and that I should win the secret of many a weed's plain heart.

I am overestimated by your friend. He places me in company far too honorable, but if we meet in the fields of the sunny South I shall certainly speak to him.

Tell him, Mrs. Carr, in your next how thankful I am for his sympathy. He is one who can sympathize in full. I feel sorry for his like misfortune and am indebted to him through you for many good and noble thoughts.

A little messenger met me with your letter of April 8th when I was on my way to the woods for the first time. I read it upon a moss-clad fallen tree. You only of my friends congratulated me on my happiness in having avoided the misery and mud of March, but for the serious part of your letter, the kind of life which our plant friends have, and their relation to us, I do not know what to think of it. I must write of this some other time.

In this first walk I found *Erigenia,* which here is ever first, and sweet little violets, and *Sanguinaria,* and *Isopyrum* too, and *Thalictrum anemonoides* were almost ready to venture their faces to the sky. The red maple was in full flower glory; the leaves below and the mosses were bright with its fallen scarlet blossoms. And the elm too was in flower and the earliest willows. All this when your fields had scarce the *memory* of a flower left in them.

I will not try to tell you how much I enjoyed in this walk after four weeks in bed. You can *feel* it.

[*John Muir*]24

∾

Indianapolis, June 9, 1867

Dear friend Mrs. Carr

I have been looking over your letters and am sorry that so many of them are unanswered. My debt to you has been increasing very rapidly of late, and I don't think it can ever be paid.

I am not well enough to work, and I cannot sit still; I have been reading and botanizing for some weeks, and I find that for such work I am not very much disabled. I leave this city for home tomorrow accompanied by Merrill Moores, a little friend of mine eleven years of age. We will go to Decatur, Ill., thence northward through the wide prairies, botanizing a few weeks by the way. We hope to spend a few days in Madison, and I promise myself a great deal of pleasure.

I hope to go South towards the end of summer, and as this will be a journey that I know very little about, I hope to profit by your counsel before setting out.

I am very happy with the thought of so soon seeing my Madison friends, and Madison, and the plants of Madison, and yours.

I am thankful that this affliction has drawn me to the sweet fields rather than from them.

Give my love to Allie and Henry and all my friends.

Yours most cordially,
John Muir

Roses with us are now in their grandest splendor.

My address for five or six weeks from this date will be Portage City, Wis.[25]

∾

[Portage City, August, 1867]

Dear friend Mrs. Carr

I am now with the loved of home. I received your kind letter on my arrival in Portage four weeks ago. I have delayed writing that I might be able to state when I could be in Madison. I have never seen *Arethusa* nor *Aspidium fragrans,* but I know many a meadow where *Calopogon* finds home. With us it is now in the plenitude of glory. *Camptosorus* is not here, but I can easily procure you a specimen from the rocks of Owen Sound, Canada. It is there very abundant, so also is *Scolopendrium.* Have you a living specimen of this last fern? Please tell me particularly about the sending or bringing *Calopogon* or any other of our plants you wish for. I have no skill whatever in the matter.

I am enjoying myself exceedingly. The dear flowers of Wisconsin are incomparably more numerous than those of Canada or Indiana. With what fervid, unspeakable joy did I welcome those flowers that I have loved so long! Hundreds grow in the full light of our opening that I have not seen since leaving home. In company with my little friend [*Merrill Moores*] I visited Muir's Lake. We approached it by a ravine in the principal hills that belong to it. We emerged from the low leafy oaks, and it came in full view all unchanged, sparkling and clear, with its edging of rushes and lilies. And there, too, was the meadow, with its brook and willows, and all the well-known nooks of its winding border where many a moss and fern find home. I held these poor eyes to the dear scene and it reached me once more in its fullest glory.

We visited my millpond, a very Lilliputian affair upon a branch creek from springs in the meadow. After leaving the dam my stream flows underground a few yards. The opening of this dark way is extremely beautiful. I wish you could see it. It is hung with a slender meadow sedge whose flowing tapered leaves have just sufficient stiffness to make them arch with inimitable beauty as they reach down to welcome the water to the light. This, I think, is one of Nature's finest pieces most delicately finished and composed of just this quiet flowing water, sedge, and summer light.

I wish you could see the ferns of this neighborhood. We have some of the finest assemblies imaginable. There is a little grassy lakelet about half a mile from here, shaded and sheltered by a dense growth of small oaks. Just where those oaks meet the marginal sedges of the lake is a circle of ferns, a perfect brotherhood of the three *Osmundas,*—*regalis, claytoniana,* and *cinnamomea.* Of the three, *claytoniana* is the most stately and luxuriant. I never saw such lordly, magnificent clumps before. Their average height is not less than 3½ or 4 feet. I measured several fronds that exceeded 5,—one, 5 feet 9 inches. This palace home gave no evidence of having ever been trampled upon. I do wish you could meet them. This is my favorite fern. I'm sorry it does not grow in Scotland. Had Hugh Miller seen it there, he would not have called *regalis* the prince of British ferns. I think that I have seen specimens of the Ostrich fern in some places of Canada which might rival my *Osmunda* in height, but not in beauty and sublimity.

I was anxious to see Illinois prairies on my way home; so we went to Decatur, or near the center of the State, thence north by Rockford and Janesville. I botanized one week on the prairie about seven miles southwest of Pecatonia. I gathered the most beautiful bouquet there that I ever saw. I seldom make bouquets. I never saw but very few that I thought were at all beautiful. I was anxious to know the grasses and sedges of the Illinois prairies and also their comparative abundance; so I walked one hundred yards in a straight line, gathering at each step that grass or sedge nearest my foot, placing them one by one in

my left hand as I walked along, without looking at them or entertaining
the remotest idea of making a bouquet. At the end of this measured
walk my handful, of course, consisted of one hundred plants *arranged
in Nature's own way* as regards kind, comparative numbers, and size.
I looked at my grass bouquet by chance—was startled—held it at
arms length *in sight of its own near and distant scenery and companion
flowers*—my discovery was complete and I was delighted beyond
measure with the new and extreme beauty. Here it is:—

	(Of *Koeleria cristata*	55
	(" *Agrostis scabra*	29
	(" *Panicum clandestinum*	7
Gram'	(" " *depauperatum*	1
	(" *Stipa spartea*	1
	(" *Poa alsodes*	1
	(" " *pratensis*	1
	(" *Carex panicea*	1
Cyp'	(" " *novae-angliae*	1

The extremely fine and diffuse purple *Agrostis* contrasted most
divinely with the taller, strict, taper-finished *Koeleria*. The long-awned
single *Stipa* too and *P. clandestinum,* with their broad ovate leaves
and purple muffy pistils, played an important part; so also did the
cylindrical spikes of the sedges. All were just in place; every leaf
had its proper taper and texture and exact measure of green. Only
P. pratensis seemed out of place, and as might be expected it proved
to be an intruder, belonging to a field or bouquet in Europe. Can it
be that a single flower or weed or grass in all these prairies occupies
a chance position? Can it be that the folding or curvature of a single
leaf is wrong or undetermined in these gardens that God is keeping?

The most microscopic portions of plants are beautiful in themselves, and these are beautiful combined into individuals, and undoubtedly all are woven with equal care into one harmonious, beautiful
whole.

I have the analysis of two other handfuls of prairie plants which
I will show you another time.

We hope to be in Madison in about three weeks.

To me all plants are more precious than before. My poor eye is not better or worse. A cloud is over it, but in gazing over the widest landscapes I am not always sensible of its presence.

My love to Allie and Henry Butler and all my friends, please tell the Butlers when we are coming. Their invitation is prior to yours, but your houses are not widely separated. I mean to write again before leaving home. You will then have all my news and I will have only to listen.

Most cordially,
John Muir[26]

∽

Madison, August 14, 1867

My dear Mr. Muir

I came home from Chicago last week sick and am only just ready to return to my usual ways. The ferns I wrote of I want for a friend in Troy—*Aspidium fragrans,* if I can get them. Mr. Lapham tells me they are abundant at Kilburn and about the Dells. I care less for anything else. The *Calopogon* you can pack in a little wet moss, but do not take any trouble about them. I have some now, and we will confer about more when you come. If we were nearer to *Port Hope,* I would ask you to bring me a couple of roots of your favorite *Osmunda,* but I fear we shall not be here long enough to make it worthwhile.

I will not write more now, except to say that I enjoyed your letter very much. You must come right here with your friend, for the Butlers have a house full of summer boarders. If you can without inconvenience tuck in a root of each *Osmunda,* you may do so and oblige,

Your friend,
Jeanne Carr

Do not go off anywhere after the *Aspidium,* but if you come across [*it*] secure some for me. I generally get an old box or basket, tie the fronds closely to a stick and pack tight in moss. I can pack a great many in a long narrow box or in a long basket, but I can pack nearly as well in a bundle with some willow sticks around to prevent the fronds from being broken.

J. C. C.[27]

∾

Indianapolis, August 30, 1867

Dear friend Mrs. Carr

We are safely in Indianapolis. I am not going to write a letter, I only want to thank you and the Doctor and all of the boys for the enjoyments of the pleasant botanical week we spent with you.

We saw, as the steam hurried us on, that the grand harvest of Compositae would be no failure this year. It is rapidly receiving its purple and gold in generous measure from the precious light of these days.

I could not but notice how well appearances in the vicinity of Chicago agreed with Lesquereux's theory of the formation of prairies. We spent about five hours in Chicago. I did not find many flowers in her tumultuous streets; only a few grassy plants of wheat and two or three species of weeds,—amaranth, purslane, carpetweed, etc,—the weeds, I suppose, for man to walk upon, the wheat to feed him. I saw some green algae, but no mosses. I expected to see some of the latter on wet walls and in seams on the pavement, but I suppose that the manufacturers' smoke and the terrible noise is too great for the hardiest of them.

I wish I knew where I was going. Doomed to be "carried of the spirit into the wilderness," I suppose. I wish I could be more moderate in my desires, but I cannot, and so there is no rest. Is not your experience the same as this?

I feel myself deeply indebted to you all for your great and varied kindness,—not any the less if from stupidity and sleepiness I forgot on leaving to express it.

Farewell.
J. Muir
[*John Muir*][28]

∾

Among the Hills of Bear Creek,
seven miles southeast of
Burkesville, Kentucky,
September 9, [*1867*]

Dear friend Mrs. Carr

I left Indianapolis last Monday and have reached this point by a long, weary, round-about walk. I walked from Louisville a distance of 170 miles, and my feet are sore, but I am paid for all my toil a thousand times over.

The sun has been among the treetops for more than an hour, and the dew is nearly all taken back, and the shade in these hill basins is creeping away into the unbroken strongholds of the grand old forests.

I have enjoyed the trees and scenery of Kentucky exceedingly. How shall I ever tell of the miles and miles of beauty that has been flowing into me in such measure? These lofty curving ranks of bobbing, swelling hills, these concealed valleys of fathomless verdure, and these lordly trees with the nursing sunlight glancing in their leaves upon the outlines of the magnificent masses of shade embosomed among their wide branches,—these are cut into my memory to go with me forever.

I often thought as I went along how dearly Mrs. Carr would appreciate all this. I have thought of many things I wished to ask you about when with you. I hope to see you all again some time when my tongue and memory are in better order. I have much to ask the Doctor about the geology of Kentucky.

I have seen many caves, Mammoth among the rest. I found two... ferns at the last. My love to Allie and all.

> Very cordially yours,
> John Muir

I am in the woods on a hilltop with my back against a moss-clad log. I wish you could see my last evening's bedroom.

My route will be through Kingston and Madisonville, Tennessee, and through Blairsville and Gainesville, Georgia. Please write me at Gainesville. I am terribly hungry. I hardly dare to think of home and friends.

I was a few miles south of Louisville when I planned my journey. I spread out my map under a tree and made up my mind to go through Kentucky, Tennessee, and Georgia to Florida, thence to Cuba, thence to some part of South America, but it will be only a hasty walk. I am thankful, however, for so much.

I will be glad to receive any advice from you. I am very ignorant of all things pertaining to this journey.

Again farewell.

J. Muir

[*John Muir*]

My love to the Butlers. I am sorry I could not see John Spooner before leaving Madison.[29]

ॐ

Madison, Wisconsin, September 14, 1867

Dear Ada [*Brooks*]

This is my dear friend John Muir, whom your brother already knows and loves for my sake, as you both will one day for his own. He is botanizing through the South. I hope he may not be too late to compare notes with you and am yours lovingly always,

Jeanne Carr[30]

ॐ

September–October, 1867

[*Mrs. Carr*]

[Fragment of letter]

I gazed at this peerless avenue as one newly arrived from another planet, without a past or a future, alive only to the presence of the most adorned and living of the tree companies I have ever beheld. Bonaventure is called a graveyard, but its accidental graves are powerless to influence the imagination in such a depth of life. The rippling of living waters, the songs of birds, the cordial rejoicing of busy insects, the calm grandeur of the forest, make it rather one of the Lord's elect and favored fields of clearest light and life. Few people have considered the natural beauty of death. Let a child grow up in nature, beholding her beautiful and harmonious blendings of death and life; their joyous, inseparable unity, and Death will be stingless indeed to him.

[*John Muir*][31]

∾

Cedar Keys, [*Florida*]
November 8, [*1867*]

Dear Mrs. Carr

I am just creeping about getting plants and strength after my fever.
I wrote you a long time ago, but retained the letter, hoping to be able
soon to tell you where you might write. Your letter arrived in Gainesville just a few minutes before I did. Somehow your letters always
come when most needed. I felt and enjoyed what you said of souls
and solitudes, also that "All of Nature being yet found in man." I
shall long for a letter from you. Will you please write me a long letter?
Perhaps it will be safer to send it to New Orleans, La. I shall have to
go there for a boat to South America. I do not yet know which point
in South America I had better go to. What do you say? My means
being limited, I cannot stay long anywhere. I would gladly do anything
I could for Mr. Warren, but I fear my time will be too short to effect
much.

I did not see Miss Brooks, because I found she was 130 miles from
Savannah. I passed the Bostwich plantation and could not conveniently
go back. I am very sorry about the mistake.

I have written little, but you will excuse me. I am wearied.

My most cordial love to all.

[*John Muir*][32]

∾

Madison, Wisconsin,
May 10, 1868

Mr. Merrill Moores
Dear Sir

I am very uneasy over the interruption of my correspondence with
John Muir. Some time in the fall I received a line from him at Cedar
Keys, Florida, telling me that he was sick there and asking me to write
to an address which he gave me. I immediately complied, and before
my letter could have reached him received a second asking me to
direct to New Orleans where he was intending to go. To the latter
place I sent a long letter filled with everything which I thought would

interest him, and since then have only heard through Henry Butler, and he does not know where to direct a letter in reply.

You see my letter is of an old date. I began it and then tried to get word from some of Muir's relatives in this state. No answer having come to my inquiries in that quarter, I must trouble you for any information you possess, in the hope that it will be more recent. I enclose a word to Muir which I will ask you to direct for me in case you know where a letter would reach him.

We remember your visit to us with pleasure. I wish you could come again. I feel a kind of kinship to all young men who love the plants. My boys send their kindest remembrance to you, and I am

Your friend, truly,
Jeanne C. Carr[33]

∾

Madison, May 25, [1868]

Dear John

I feel your presence and sympathy in all the gladness of the opening season, but I also feel very keenly the loss of you in my life. I meant to keep such even step with you through all the journey which I prayed might be a blessed one, and before I knew I lost every track and trace of you. This is strange, because I wrote exactly as you directed both to Cedar Keys and to New Orleans.

I am not a little heavy hearted about you, what have the tropic weeks done to our dear pilgrim youth?

Tomorrow I am going off into the woodsiest of our woods with Thure Kumlein to find *Arethusa,* and (God willing) *Calypso*—a journey of a hundred miles by rail, wagon and on foot for just two of "our Father's children." Dear John, how *rich* you must be by this time.

I only write a word now, so uncertain is it if any word will reach you. But I want to know when you are coming back? If you should touch home soil at New York, I want you to come and see me in *Vermont* where I am going to spend the summer. I shall be in Castleton, Rutland County, after the 4th of July, until October, probably, and I want to see you very very much. My old father and brother know you and will make you welcome.

Dr. Carr has left the University. We shall keep our Madison home for the present, and wherever our tent is pitched it will be very easy to hang up a curtain for you. All send love and I am,

Always your friend,

Jeanne C. Carr[34]

PART TWO

1868–1869

*Fate and flowers have carried me to
California, and I have reveled and
luxuriated amid its plants and
mountains nearly four months.*

John Muir

Among God's Elect in
California and Parables
of Wilderness

JOHN MUIR BOARDED A SCHOONER LOADED WITH ORANGES AND
sailed from Cuba to New York in early January 1868. In New York he
boarded a steamer en route to Panama, crossed the Isthmus of Panama,
and arrived in San Francisco aboard the *Nebraska* in March. He and
Joseph Chilwell, a shipboard companion, crossed the bay on the Oakland ferry, left the train at East Oakland, and walked up the Santa
Clara Valley. They passed through San Jose and Gilroy, then crossed
the Diablo Mountains by the Pacheco Pass. From there Muir obtained
his first view of the San Joaquin Valley and the Sierra. Descending the
pass, they waded through a bed of golden Compositae, the "floweriest
piece of world" through which Muir ever walked. After crossing the
San Joaquin River at Hill's Ferry, they followed the Merced River from
Snelling by way of Coulterville, a small mining town in the Mariposa
foothills, passed through Deer Flat and Crane Flat, and entered Yosemite
Valley. Muir sketched, explored the falls, and collected plants. Cooled
by the mountain winds and the crystal water, he was cured of fever.

Muir and Chilwell returned to the San Joaquin Valley and harvested
grain at Hopeton. After the harvest Chilwell departed. Muir worked
for several months breaking horses, determined to set out again for
Yosemite as soon as he earned enough money to journey farther into
the mountains. During the next five months he tended sheep for John
Connel, "Smoky Jack."

Fate and flowers carried Muir to California. Jeanne Carr was pleas-
antly surprised to hear from him after a long silence. She wrote to Muir
about the changes in her life. Ezra, who frequently had been involved in
academic controversy at the University of Wisconsin, was dismissed from
the faculty when the regents appointed a new president. After Jeanne left
Madison to spend the summer in Castleton, Vermont, with her family,

Ezra sold their Gilman Street home. The Carrs considered three pro-
posals. They would stay in the East, move to California, or go to Buenos
Aires (tempted by Domingo Sarmineto's call for recruits to engage in
the educational development of Argentina). The news of the opening of
the University of California in Oakland precipitated their decision to
move to California. Nelson Carr, Ezra's younger brother, formerly of
Milton, Wisconsin, and now an agriculturalist in southern California,
was surely an incentive for the Carrs to move to California. No doubt
they were also swayed by California's agricultural opportunities, climate,
and scenery. Jeanne described an article in the *San Francisco Bulletin,*
"An Eden In California," as the turning point in her decision to live
and die in California. Advertisements hailed California as the land of
certain freedom and cosmopolitanism, as a place of personal independence and equality, as a hopeful and self-reliant environment filled with
large-heartedness. These qualities appealed to the Carrs, who were independent social reformers. Living in California would also provide
Jeanne the obvious close proximity to Muir.

In October the Carrs left Vermont, arrived in New York, and
boarded the steamer *Montana* bound for Panama, where they boarded
the steamer *Alaska* for the twenty-three-day voyage to San Francisco.
Carr delighted in the excursion, met homeward-bound Californians,
and saw two active volcanoes. In the wake of the 1868 earthquake, the
streets of San Francisco were littered with debris, and hotels and boarding houses were crowded. The Carrs continued on to Los Angeles. In
southern California they met Pio Pico, the former Californio governor,
and William Wolfskill and Don Benito Wilson, both early settlers. They
drove past sheep pastures, over tracks through the flowering sod to the
San Gabriel Mission. In articles written for the *Western Farmer* Carr
described the region as new and close to the great central cauldron
where islands and continents were made. She noted the present and
prospective viticulture as an example of land stewardship dependent on
the opening of railroads.[1]

Muir rejoiced in Carr's move to California. She, of all people, understood his motives and happiness. He encouraged her to prepare for her
"Yosemite baptism," where she would read for herself the glorious lessons of sky, plain, and mountain God wrote for her. Though she would
miss the plants of the Vermont hills, Muir knew she would make new

friends in the *Cassiopes,* laurels, mosses, and ferns. In San Mateo Carr waited for God to choose in which of His mansions she and her family would reside. There she taught botany at a girls' school and prepared for her trip to Yosemite Valley. Two letters from Muir outlined the journey from Stockton by stage and from Mariposa Grove by horse to the Valley. He looked forward to another baptism in the Yosemite temple with Carr's blessed company. Camping out in the Valley she would alight like a bird in beautiful groves.

Carr had some camping experience. During the summer of 1868 while visiting her family in Castleton she, her son Allie, and her two nephews, Fred and Eno, camped in a ravine near the birch-bark shanty of James Hope, a painter-friend of Carr's who lived in Castleton. They built a fireplace of slate stone and beds of hemlock boughs, and stayed a week. Camping in Yosemite Valley would be different from camping in a ravine in Vermont. Muir recommended a light tent of cotton sheeting, a strong dress, sturdy shoes, a supply of paper for pressing plants, and drawing material. The estimated cost for a ten-day journey from Stockton to Yosemite was $75.00 per person. Each additional day spent in the Valley would add approximately $3.00. Carr's party would be provided with an experienced guide and sure-footed horses accustomed to the journey. Muir hoped Dr. Carr would accompany her, and he anticipated meeting them in the Valley. He planned on arriving several days beforehand if by the first of June Carr wrote to him as to the date they would leave Stockton. The register at Hutchings's Hotel would be the means by which each would know the other had arrived in the Valley. As a guest Carr was required to sign the register. Whether Muir's name preceded Carr's is unknown. Muir was certain the mountains knew of Carr's pending arrival, and he thanked God for His goodness in turning her face toward the mountain temples. Carr set out for the Valley in June, first stopping to visit the coastal redwoods where she cried out against the wickedness of sawing them into lumber.

Captivated by nature and drawn to "preach Nature like an apostle," Muir was determined to continue to witness to nature's activities. To accomplish this he followed four other shepherds and a flock of sheep eastward into the Sierra summer pastures in early June. The sheep were the property of Pat Delaney, a neighbor of "Smoky Jack." As shepherd Muir explored and studied the mountains. He wrote to Carr that by the middle of the month, with the flock settled in their new home, he would have two weeks in which to ramble with her. Carr's letter to Muir noting her day of departure from Stockton did not reach him in time for them to meet in Yosemite. Not less than eight letters traveled in search of him. Muir responded on July 11 from five miles west of Yosemite Valley. Much later Carr pointed out that there were two locations with the name Black, one near Coulterville, the other in the Valley. Her letter had been directed to the wrong Black's.[2]

God would provide the time and place in which Carr and Muir would enjoy communion in Yosemite; in the meantime Carr sojourned in Yosemite alone. The experience deepened her conviction that it was only from the Great Mother Nature that she learned of God's love. At Hatch's Hotel she heard singing streams, breathed aromatic pines, and touched velvety grass. There she boarded a stage to Clark's Hotel on the southern route into the Valley. Carr adjusted her eyes to an ever increasing grandeur of ferns, pines, rocks, canyons, and mountain masses. In Mariposa Grove, five miles from Clark's beneath the Sequoia "Grizzly Giant," she collected her first snow-plant, *Sarcodes sanguinea,* and cradled it in the crown of her hat. Spotting a clump of lilies, she cut into the soil and secured six plants that she looped together and draped over her shoulder for safe keeping. She rode bareheaded with hands encumbered six miles on horseback down steep pitches without clinging to the pommel of her saddle for fear she would crush the flowers. With hat in hand and draped in lilies Carr rode into Clark's and the disapproving glance of Miss Dorothea Dix, who was seated in a rocking chair on the veranda. Dix was traveling in the same party as Carr. From Clark's Carr rode a mule in a divided skirt on the Mariposa Trail twenty-five miles into the Valley. Traveling in range of a party of San Francisco teachers, Carr thought of herself as alone with the entire planet to herself.

The journey through thick woods brought Carr to Inspiration Point. Overpowered by the view, six miles above the Valley floor, she was removed from her mule by the guide. Tears did not relieve her. She crouched under a boulder, shut her eyes to the vision, and sailed through space. Yosemite was the visible proof of Carr's invisible faith. Stretched before her was God's sublime creation. In the Valley she was touched by the inexplicable power of the divine. She rode up the South Fork

Canyon to Vernal and Nevada Falls, took a trip to Glacier Point, and probably rode to Mirror Lake. In the transept of the cathedral, whose columns were mighty pines, whose walls and spires were rocks three thousand feet high, whose floor was a mosaic of strange and lovely flowers, Carr rode along on Mucho, the mule. While in the Valley she befriended James M. Hutchings, the proprietor of Hutchings's Hotel (who had moved to the Valley in 1864), his wife, Elvira, and their children, Florence (Floy), whom Muir and Carr referred to as "Squirrel," and Gertrude (Cosie), and James Lamon, a Virginian who came to California from Texas in 1851, found his way into the Valley in 1857, planted an orchard opposite Half Dome in 1859, and became a permanent resident in the Valley in 1862.[3]

Carr and Muir believed they were among God's elect and shared affinities that united them to the rest of nature. Comprised of a small unique group, the few elect who were privy to nature as the language of God and to mountains as prophets, witnessed the grandeur of Yosemite as an endless revelation that guided them to a spiritual relationship with wilderness beyond the common tourist's regard. To those who worshipped in the Valley Carr wrote, "the guarded entrances and gateways to this sacred place are set as if to break the step of hasty and profane feet." Wilderness solitude initiated divine fellowship in which their eyes opened to the spiritual intimations of nature and focused on the spiritual meaning and message of God's Word. God's cipher-writing in wilderness provided literal symbols of salvation displayed upon mountains, by rivers, and in meadows and canyons. Congregants saw parables in nature equal to the parables in scripture, and in the Valley and upon the mountains they were drawn nearer to God.[4]

Carr had entered the Valley to see its beauty with Muir's eyes to help her and regretted he was not there. She would have stayed to search for him, but Ezra, who was offered a professorship at the University of California, required her counsel; she had to return home. In Muir's footsteps Carr walked Yosemite paths. Upon the bridge between Vernal and Nevada Falls she left him a message, "The Lord bless thee and keep thee." She wished this always for Muir.

During the summer of 1869 Carr and Muir did not meet in Yosemite; however, in July Muir through some inexplicable means was seized with the certainty that James Butler was below in the Valley. Having received a letter from Butler stating that he would be in California, perhaps Muir had made a mental note anticipating his visit to the Valley. Muir clambered down from North Dome where he had been sketching. At Hutchings's Hotel he located Butler's name in the register and found him and his party at the bridge between Vernal and Nevada Falls. Carr was annoyed by Butler's good fortune. Later, she wrote, "It made me so *mad* that *he* should have found you! mad at both of you."[5]

Carr recorded her experience in the Valley in an article that appeared in the *Californian,* later clipped and filed in her scrapbook. Among the pine columns and rock walls and spires she heard the vesper service of the cascades and met Jehovah face to face. Yosemite was a gateway into the spiritual world, and while there she daily turned her eyes toward the great white throne in the High Sierra, believing that when she had drunk the beauty she would be tuned to its sublime lessons of purity, constancy, and endurance.

The Carrs moved to Oakland following Ezra's appointment to the University of California as Professor of Agriculture, Agricultural Chemistry, and Horticulture. They resided in the commodious rectory of St. Paul's Church on the corner of 11th Street and Webster, a long "L" shape extended off the rear of the church, across from the university.

When Muir's obligation to Delaney and his flock ended in September, he planned to return to the Valley and the mountains. No other place attracted him like what he called Godful wilderness. Never before had he beheld divine mingling of cloud and mountain where the most delicate and decorated ferns and shrubs marked his path and where *Cassiope* whispered to him from the Tuolumne River. In October he hoped to spend the winter in the higher mountain storms. By mid-November he was climbing through the foothills on his way back to Yosemite Valley. Carr invited him to stay in Oakland, to rest and refit for new expeditions. Muir promised to bring her Sequoia cones in spring. Cloistered for the winter in the Valley, Muir feasted in God's mountain house and wandered among falls and rapids. He studied the slopes and curves, met a delicate congregation of *Adiantum,* and believed he had gone to heaven.

Near Snelling, Merced Co.,
California,
July 26, 1868

Dear friend Mrs. Carr

I have had the pleasure of but one letter since leaving home from you. That I received at Gainesville, Georgia.

I have not received a letter from any source since leaving Florida, and of course I am very lonesome and hunger terribly for the communion of friends. I will remain here eight or nine months and hope to hear from all my friends.

Fate and flowers have carried me to California, and I have reveled and luxuriated amid its plants and mountains nearly four months. I am well again, I came to life in the cool winds and crystal waters of the mountains, and, were it not for a thought now and then of loneliness and isolation, the pleasure of my existence would be complete.

I have forgotten whether I wrote you from Cuba or not. I spent four happy weeks there in January and February.

I saw only a very little of the grandeur of Panama, for my health was still in wreck, and I did not venture to wait the arrival of another steamer. I had but half a day to collect specimens. The Isthmus train rushed on with cruel speed through the gorgeous Eden of vines and palms, and I could only gaze from the car platform and weep and pray that the Lord would some day give me strength to see it better.

After a delightful sail among the scenery of the sea I arrived in San Francisco in April and struck out at once into the country. I followed the Diablo foothills along the San Jose Valley to Gilroy, thence over the Diablo Mountains to [the] valley of the San Joaquin by the Pacheco pass, thence down the valley opposite the mouth of the Merced River, thence across the San Joaquin, and up into the Sierra Nevada to the mammoth trees of Mariposa and the glorious *Yosemite*, thence down the Merced to this place.

The goodness of the weather as I journeyed towards Pacheco was beyond all praise and description, fragrant and mellow and bright. The air was perfectly delicious, sweet enough for the breath of angels;

every draught of it gave a separate and distinct piece of pleasure. I do not believe that Adam and Eve ever tasted better in their balmiest nook.

The last of the Coast Range foothills were in near view all the way to Gilroy. Their union with the Valley is by curves and slopes of inimitable beauty, and they were robed with the greenest grass and richest light I ever beheld, and colored and shaded with millions of flowers of every hue, chiefly of purple and golden yellow; and hundreds of crystal rills joined songs with the larks, filling all the Valley with music like a sea, making it an Eden from end to end.

The scenery, too, and all of Nature in the pass is fairly enchanting,— strange and beautiful mountain ferns, low in the dark canyons and high upon the rocky, sunlit peaks, banks of blooming shrubs, and sprinklings and gatherings of . . . flowers, precious and pure as ever enjoyed the sweets of a mountain home. And oh, what streams are there! beaming, glancing, each with music of its own, singing as they go in the shadow and light, onward upon their lovely changing pathways to the sea; and hills rise over hills, and mountains over mountains, heaving, waving, swelling, in most glorious, overpowering, unreadable majesty; and when at last, stricken and faint like a crushed insect, you hope to escape from all the terrible grandeur of these mountain powers, other fountains, other oceans break forth before you, for there, in clear view, over heaps and rows of foothills is laid a grand, smooth outspread plain, watered by a river, and another range of peaky snow-capped mountains a hundred miles in the distance. That plain is the valley of the San Joaquin, and those mountains are the great Sierra Nevadas. The valley of the San Joaquin is the floweriest piece of world I ever walked, one vast level, even flower-bed, a sheet of flowers, a smooth sea ruffled a little by the tree fringing of the river and here and there of smaller cross streams from the mountains. Florida is indeed a land of flowers, but for every flower creature that dwells in its most delightsome places more than a hundred are living here. Here, here is Florida. Here they are not sprinkled apart with grass between, as in our prairies, but grasses are sprinkled in the flowers; not, as in Cuba, flowers piled upon flowers heaped and gathered into deep, glowing masses, but side by side, flower to flower, petal to petal, touching but not entwined, branches weaving past and past each other, but free and separate, one smooth garment, mosses next the ground, grasses above, petaled flowers between.

Before studying the flowers of this valley, and their sky and all of the furniture and sounds and adornments of their home, one can scarce believe that their vast assemblies are permanent, but rather that, actuated by some plant purpose, they had convened from every plain, and mountain, and meadow of their kingdom, and that the different coloring of patches, acres, and miles marked the bounds of the various tribe and family encampments. And now just stop and see what I gathered from a square yard opposite the Merced. I have no books and cannot give specific names:—

Orders	Open flowers	Species
Compositae	132,125	2 yellow, 3305 heads
Leguminosae	2,620	2 purple and white
Scrophulariaceae	169	1 purple
Umbelliferae	620	1 yellow
Geraniaceae	22	1 purple
Rubiaceae	40	1 white
————	85	Natural order unknown
————	60	Plants unflowered
Polemoniaceae	407	2 purple
Gramineae	29,830	3 stems about 700; spikelets 10,700
Miscellaneous	1,000,000	2 purples, *Dicranum* & *Fumaria*
Total of open flowers	165,912	
" " flowers in bud,	100,000	
" " withered,	40,000	
" " natural orders,	9–11	
" " species,	16–17	
" " mosses,	1,000,000	

The yellow of these Compositae is extremely deep and rich and bossy, as though the sun had filled their petals with a portion of his very self. It exceeds the purple of all the others in superficial quantity forty or fifty times their whole amount, but to an observer who first looks downward and then takes a more distant view, the yellow gradually fades and purple predominates because nearly all of the purple flowers are higher. In depth the purple stratum is about ten or twelve inches, the yellow seven or eight, and second purple of mosses one.

I'm sorry my page is done. I have not told anything. I thought of you, Mrs. Carr, when I was in the glorious Yosemite and of the prophecy of "the Priest" that you would see it and worship there with your Doctor and Priest and I [sic]. It is by far the grandest of all the special temples of Nature I was ever permitted to enter. It must be the *sanctum sanctorum* of the Sierras, and I trust that you will all be led to it.

Remember me to the Doctor. I hope he has the pleasure of sowing in good and honest hearts the glorious truth of science to which he has devoted his life. Give my love to all your boys and my little [Henry] Butler.

> Adieu.
> J. Muir
> [John Muir][6]

ꝏ

> Castleton, Vermont,
> August 31, 1868

My dear, dear friend

You can hardly imagine the delight which filled my heart and eyes at the welcome sight of your handwriting after this long silence. I had worried not a little and had tried in every possible way to get word of and recover you. I had as week after week went by, begun to feel that the probabilities were only too strong that the fever which prostrated you so greatly had finally conquered your slight strength. I was indeed heavy hearted. Here in my old Vermont home with James Hope, a fellow-countryman of yours and my friend for a quarter of a century, I have talked of you, asked for you, mourned you, until they rejoice with me that the lost is found. Your letter came last evening. Dr. Carr was here to enjoy it with me. Ned and Allie are here also. The other boys are in Wisconsin.

Now I will tell you about ourselves. Dr. Carr resigned in the University in the winter. In May I decided to spend the summer in Vermont. I left in June expecting a St. Louis family to occupy our house until October. But I had not been away two weeks when Dr. Carr sold out—house, furniture, everything but books and pictures,—and came on east, after attending the meeting of the Scientific Association at Chicago. We are now considering an invitation to stay in an eastern institution and balancing it against the desire to settle in California. I am decidedly in favor of the latter, on account of climate and for the sake of the boys who are too young to go into business away from home. We have also a possible opening at Buenos Aires, South America, which deserves consideration. We shall know *very soon*, and I will write you again what we determine to do. If we live in California I wish to go where there is lovely scenery and a mild climate. I know the flowers will *never* be so dear as my *Linnaeas* and *Calypsos*. I shall find, I always do, *sweet* souls, pure souls, in which I can *almost* see the Father's face. I shall not *lose* any that I leave. Dear John, it would seem blessed to me to find you if I go. I hope we may settle near each other. And if we go to South America I wish to call you out there. Your faculty of invention would be invaluable to others and to yourself.

Last winter was especially rich in Madison. I wrote you at length of our visit from Paul Du Chaillu, the African traveller, "the Gorilla man," from M. Sarmiento, the Minister to our Government from the Argentine Confederation, and last, best and sweetest of all, from *Ole Bull,* the great Norwegian violinist who *made one day* an eternity of delight to me and through many evenings led me out on waves of harmony, beyond the regions of time and toil. Of men he is the Royalist I have known, of spirits one of the purest, of artists the incomparable. And so when Nature is locked in fetters of ice—her music hushed—there comes to me a foretaste of the life above and beyond, of deep and rich communion, and in all these hours, these joys, you are somehow mixed as if you had a place in them. I believe you have. The company of "the Elect" is not so large that we may not easily count them that are in it. I have had great delight, too, in these summer hours. You never knew this mountain land. I am told it is like Scotland only fresher and greener. Four miles from this place there is a deep ravine between mountains nearly 2000 feet above the level of the elevated plateau on which the village lies. This ravine is slate rock, is filled with great granite boulders, trunks of fallen trees, banks of *Sphagnum,*

Madotheca, Hypnea, all manner of rich mosses and liverworts creeping over rocks and decaying logs. One spot of peculiar loveliness—a bowl of pure water worn in soft gray slate, is the out-door studio of my friend [*James*] Hope, whose pictures rival Mr. [*Frederic*] Church's in their fidelity to the truth of nature. The June day in which I found him there after these nine years of absence, after the year of bloodshed in which his life had been mixed, I shall never forget. A friend had taken me in his wagon along the Rutland road within a mile of the glen. I did not know the way, but a bee could not have taken a straighter line than I did to him—across fragrant pasture land, through a hill forest of hemlock and beech, down the steep banks, over great boulders, up the bed of the singing rivulet. *There he sat,* his easel of white birch poles holding a lovely painting, and I seated myself on a bank among the thick ferns and watched him at his work. He sang and so did a hermit thrush perched in a moose maple over his head. He had grown *bald and gray;* he was repeating to himself some lines of Emerson's "Woodnotes." "What he has nobody wants. What he had, he hides, not vaunts." I took up the lines and went on, tuning my voice down to his, and then the dear old fellow looked round, moved along on his seat and beckoned me to come. I seated myself beside him, and he kept on a half-hour or so touching in the lights on his picture, the thrush singing all the time, *you know how*! By and by Hope laid aside his palette and put his arm round me. "Jenny, I have waited *twenty-seven* years for this day with you!" "You could afford to," I said, "for you and I are not made of the perishing elements." And then we spoke soul to soul of the lessons we had learned, the glories our eyes *have* seen, and the fullness of life to which we aspire. We had our dinner in one lovely spot, our supper in another. I went into the little room made of a dozen half-grown hemlocks and carpeted with *Hypnum splendens* where my friend prays (his prayers are almost all praises, I find).

Well, I had to leave him, but the next week my brother's wife went with me and we spent two days there. The week after I took my two little nephews, Fred and Eno, and Allie, my own boy. We put up a tent close by Hope's birch bark shanty on the edge of the ravine, made a fireplace of slate stones, beds of hemlock boughs, and stayed a long beautiful week. My sister came up with her lovely music friend from Boston, in whom I found an excellent botanist, and we had a *noel* among mosses and ferns and music of wild birds and splendor of mountain scenery. The week after that Dr. Carr came, caught the *infection* of our delight and took me to Llumer, a wild cascade some forty miles north, among the real mountains, for those about Castleton are only "spores." Charlie Sanderson, the aforesaid music friend was our guide and from that we came back to find western friends and to go over it all with them. So the summer has been *steeped* in out-of-door delight, and yet almost daily I have said, "If I *knew* that it were well with you the days would be brighter." Because you see, dear John, it was to South America you were bent, and I thought of noxious hateful things, of miasmas that would poison and ants that would devour and leave no trace of you—not so much as a paper to tell when you perished. *Thank God* for the good news.

There has been a vast development of material wealth in this state since I left it, through the opening of innumerable quarries of marble and slate. It is wonderful to see the hills opened and leaf by leaf of the rocky strata unfolded, to see the iron horse steaming through these quiet valleys and hear the accents of many foreign tongues. So I see how soon there will be one great nationality, *one great family,* where so lately were many opposed and conflicting nations. *There are enough to work at this furnace of politics*—let us remain as we are *meek students* of the beautiful laws—all they can do is to further the plans of God; we can worship and adore for our portion.

Dr. Carr is not less glad than I am to know of your welfare and congratulates you on the restoration of your health. I hope we shall see you in Pacific lands before the end of the year. Direct your letters to *Castleton,* Rutland County, Vermont, care Dr. H. F. Smith, and they will be forwarded to me without much delay.

I have a great deal to say, but *this* day was all appropriated before your letter came in *as a wedge*! So I must say goodbye. Know by these tokens how unwillingly we lost you and believe us,

Always your friends,
E. S. and Jeanne Carr[7]
[*Ezra S.*]

ᕔ

Address:

Hopeton, Merced Co., California

> At a sheep ranch between the
> Tuolumne and Stanislaus rivers,
> November 1, [*1868*]

Dear friend Mrs. Carr

I was extremely glad to receive yet one more of your ever welcome letters. It found me two weeks ago. I rode over to Hopeton to seek for letters. I had to pass through a bed of Compositae two or three miles in diameter. They were in the glow of full prime, forming a lake of the purest Compositae gold I ever beheld. Some single plants had upwards of three thousand heads. Their petal-surface exceeded their leaf-surface thirty or forty times. Because of the constancy of the winds all these flowers faced in one direction (southeast), and I thought, as I gazed upon myriads of joyous plant beings clothed in rosy golden light, What would *old Linnaeus* or Mrs. Carr say to this?

I was sorry to think of the loss of your letters, but it is just what might be expected from the wretched mail arrangements of the South.

I am not surprised to hear of your leaving Madison and am anxious to know where your lot will be cast. If you go to South America soon, I shall hope to meet you, and if you should decide to seek the shores of the Pacific in California before the end of the year, I shall find you and be glad to make another visit to the Yosemite with your Doctor and Priest, according to the old plan. I know the way up the rocks to the falls, and I know too the abode of many a precious mountain fern. I gathered plenty for you, but you must see them at home. Not an angel could tell a tithe of these glories.

If you make your home in California, I know from experience how keenly you will feel the absence of the *special* flowers you love. No others can fill their places; Heaven itself would not answer without *Calypso* and *Linnaea*.

I think that you will find in California just what you desire in climate and scenery, for both are so varied. March is the springtime of the plains, April the summer, and May the autumn. The other months are dry and wet winter, uniting with each other, and with the other seasons by splices and overlappings of very simple and very intricate kinds. I rode across the seasons in going to the Yosemite last spring. I started from the Joaquin in the last week of May. All the plain flowers, so lately fresh in the power of full beauty, were dead. Their parched leaves crisped and fell to powder beneath my feet, as though they had been "cast into the oven." And they had not, like the plants of our West, weeks and months to grow old in, but they died ere they could fade, standing together holding out their branches erect and green as life. But they did not die too soon; they lived a whole life and stored away abundance of future life-principle in the seed.

After riding for two days in this autumn I found summer again in the higher foothills. Flower petals were spread confidingly open, the grasses waved their branches all bright and gay in the colors of healthy prime, and the winds and streams were cool. Forty or fifty miles further into the mountains, I came to spring. The leaves on the oak were small and drooping, and they still retained their first tintings of crimson and purple, and the wrinkles of their bud folds were distinct as if newly opened, and all along the rims of cool brooks and mild sloping places thousands of gentle mountain flowers were tasting life for the first time.

A few miles farther "onward and upward" I found the edge of winter. Scarce a grass could be seen. The last of the lilies and spring violets were left below; the winter scales were still shut upon the buds of the dwarf oaks and alders; the grand Nevada pines waved solemnly to cold, loud winds among rushing, changing stormclouds. Soon my horse was plunging in snow ten feet in depth, the sky became darker and more terrible, many-voiced mountain winds swept the pines, speaking the dread language of the cold north, snow began to fall, and in less than a week from the burning plains of the San Joaquin autumn was lost in the blinding snows of mountain winter.

Descending these higher mountains towards the Yosemite, the snow gradually disappeared from the pines and the sky, tender leaves unfolded less and less doubtfully, lilies and violets appeared again, and I once more found spring in the grand Valley. Thus meet and blend the seasons of these mountains and plains, beautiful in their joinings as those of lake and land or of the bands of the rainbow. The room is full of talking men; I cannot write, and I only attempt to scrawl this note to thank you for all the good news and good thoughts and friendly wishes and remembrances you send.

My kindest wishes to the Doctor. I am sure you will be directed by Providence to the place where you will best serve the end of existence. My love to all your family.

Ever yours most cordially,
J.M.
[*John Muir*][8]

∽

Near Snellings, Merced Co.,
[*California*],
February 24, 1869

Dear Mrs. Carr

Your two California notes from San Francisco and San Mateo reached me last evening, and I rejoice at the glad tidings they bring of your arrival in this magnificent land. I have thought of you hundreds of times in my seasons of deepest joy, amid the flower purple and gold of the plains, the fern fields in gorge and canyon, the sacred waters, tree columns, and the eternal unnameable sublimities of the mountains. Of all my friends you are the only one that understands my motives and enjoyments. Only a few weeks ago a true and liberal-minded friend sent me a large sheetful of terrible blue-steel orthodoxy, calling me from clouds and flowers to the practical walks of politics and philanthropy. Mrs. Carr, thought I, never lectured thus. I am glad, indeed, that you are here to read for yourself these glorious lessons of sky and plain and mountain, which no mortal power can ever speak. I thought when in the Yosemite Valley last spring that the Lord had written things there that you would be allowed to read some time.

I have not made a single friend in California, and you may be sure I strode home last evening from the post office feeling rich indeed. As soon as I hear of your finding a home, I shall begin a plan of visiting you. I have frequently seen favorable reports upon the silk-culture in California. The climate of Los Angeles is said to be well tempered for

the peculiar requirements of the business as any in the world. I think
that you have brought your boys to the right field for the planting. I
doubt if in all the world man's comforts and necessities can be more
easily and abundantly supplied than in California. I have often wished
the Doctor near me in my rambles among the rocks. Pure science is a
most unmarketable commodity in California. Conspicuous, energetic,
unmixed materialism rules supreme in all classes. Prof. Whitney, as
you are aware, was accused of heresy while conducting the State
survey, because in his reports he devoted some space to fossils and
other equally dead and un-Californian objects instead of columns of
discovered and measured mines.

I am engaged at present in the very important and patriarchal
business of sheep. I am a gentle shepherd. The gray box in which I
reside is distant about seven miles northeast from Hopeton, two miles
north of Snellings. The Merced pours past me on the south from the
Yosemite; smooth, domey hills and the tree fringe of the Tuolumne
bound me on the north; the lordly Sierras join sky and plain on the
east; and the far coast mountains on the west. My mutton family of
eighteen hundred range over about ten square miles, and I have
abundant opportunities for reading and botanizing. I shall be here for
about two weeks, then I shall be engaged in shearing sheep between
the Tuolumne and Stanislaus from the San Joaquin to the Sierra
foothills for about two months. I will be in California until next
November, when I mean to start for South America.

I received your Castleton letter and wrote you in November. I
suppose you left Vermont before my letter had time to reach you. You
must prepare for your Yosemite baptism in June.

Here is a sweet little flower that I have just found among the rocks
of the brook that waters Twenty-Hill Hollow. Its anthers are curiously
united in pairs and form stars upon its breast. The calyx seems to
have been judged too plain and green to accompany the splendid
corolla, and so is left behind among the leaves. I first met this plant
among the Sierra Nevadas. There are five or six species. For beauty
and simplicity they might be allowed to dwell within sight of *Calypso*.
There are about twenty plants in flower in the gardens of my daily
walks. The first was born in January. I give them more attention than
I give the dirty mongrel creatures of my flock, that are about half

made by God and half by man. I have not yet discovered the poetical part of a shepherd's duties.

Spring will soon arrive to the plants of Madison, and surely they will miss you. In Yosemite you will find *Cassiopes* and laurels and azaleas, and luxuriant mosses and ferns, but I know that even these can never take the place of the long-loved ones of your Vermont hills.

Forgive me this long writing. I know that you are in a fever of joy from the beauty pouring upon you; nevertheless you seem so near I can hardly stop.

My most cordial regards to the Doctor. Californians do not deserve such as he.

A lawyer by the name of Wigonton or Wigleton, a graduate of Madison, resides in Snellings. I suppose you know him.

I am your friend,
John Muir[9]

∞

San Mateo, March 28, 1869

Dear John Muir

The "Lord is risen indeed." The Universe is singing anew the Easter song of the ages, sung long before "the visible church" had an existence,—the sweet assurance to all the future that *God* is in His world. My thoughts are unto you ward, dear Shepherd, and there is no other soul with whom I would prefer to keep this spotless day sacred to the holiest memories and hopes. I have not been to church to see the crosses of white callas and the wreaths of spirea and myrtle—nor yet upon the hills, but the day has nevertheless been blessed—and I doubt not the blessedness has reached and filled you also. Dr. Carr came down from the city and both the boys have been spending Sunday with us. Tomorrow Dr. Carr will leave and spend several weeks in the mines at Virginia City and, perhaps, as far as White Pine. I shall remain here for the next two months, and then as far as my own plans and purposes can "prepare" we shall be ready for the Yosemite trip whenever it can be arranged.

My days here "go on" in a girls' school where I teach a class of thirty in Botany, and am of a little use in other ways to the friend who insists upon making a home for us until we have one of our own. I begin to feel the *homeless* influences of California interfering with my plans, but I have learned to feel willing to have Our Father choose in which of the many mansions He will have me abide.

How do you study Botany without any work which includes many of these plants? *I study the flowers.* I am "drunk" with their gorgeous colors and rich profusion. Last week I thought I found a treasure in a snowy white "forget-me-not," I should think either a Heliotrope or *Myosotis*—now they carpet the roadsides. The California *Dodecatheon* pleased me. Ned, who rode across from Mission San Jose Friday, says he rode through miles of *Dodecatheon meadia.* I have not seen *D. meadia* here. Some of the *Portulacas* are interesting to the colorist. We shall have a *festival* here of one of our Literary Societies the last of April. (I shall send you the Programme.) Should it not interfere too much with your plans and work I wish you could come about that time. There will be nothing to offer in the way of performance but the event will be sure to fix me and I am rather uncertain between San Francisco and San Jose. You and I are of those who must leave the spiritual laws to bring us together as they surely will—if not next week or next year—in some better, riper time. I hear your voice in the undertones of life, it does not matter about your home or family, whether they are biped or quadruped. But *you must be social. John,* you must *make friends among the materialists,* lest your highest pleasures taken selfishly become impure. Only at moments am I permitted to be alone with my mind. I could envy you your solitude, but there may be too much of it. I find my truest society among the most and the *least* cultured. To every soul God gives some precious special grace, to the nettle its color, the thistle its fine firmness of growth. While we read their secret, dear Shepherd, we may keep our own and not throw our pearls away.

Perhaps I am getting too "preachy," so we'll sing a hymn together and good night. With Dr. Carr's love and the boys,

J. C. C.

[*Jeanne C. Carr*]

Direct to San Mateo. Your letter was forwarded from Los Angeles.[10]

∾

Seven miles north from Snellings,
May 16, 1869

Dear friend,

The thoughts of again meeting with you and with the mountains make me scarce able to hold my pen. If you can let me know by the first of June when you will leave Stockton, I will meet you in the very Valley itself. When the grass of the plains is dead, most owners of sheep drive their flocks to the pastures green of the mountains, and as my soul is athirst for mountain things, I have engaged to take charge of a flock all summer between the head waters of the Tuolumne and Yosemite, within a few hours' walk of the Valley. For the next two weeks I will be at Hopeton. Some time in the first week of June, I will start from this place (Patrick Delaney's ranch) for the mountains. By the middle of June or a little later we will have our flock settled in the new home, and, having made special arrangements for a two weeks' ramble with you, I will then be ready and free. Any time, say between the 20th of June and the 15th of July, will suit me. I intended to enjoy another baptism in the sanctuaries of Yosemite, whether with companions of like passions or alone. Surely, then, my cup will be full when blessed with such company.

Last May I made the trip on horseback, going by Coulterville and returning by Mariposa. A passable carriage-road reached about twelve miles beyond Coulterville; the rest of the distance to the Valley was crossed only by a narrow trail. On the Mariposa route a point is reached twelve or fourteen miles beyond Mariposa by carriages; the rest of the journey, about forty miles, must be made on horseback. Tourists are generally advised to go one way and return the other, that as much as possible may be seen, but I think that more is seen by going and returning by the same route, because all of the magnitudes of the mountains are so great that unless seen and submitted to a good long time they are not seen or felt at all.

I think that you had better take the Mariposa route, for the grandest grove of sequoias ever discovered is upon it, and it is much the best route in many respects. You can reach Mariposa direct from Stockton by stage. At Mariposa you can procure saddle-horses and all necessary supplies,—provisions, cooking utensils, etc. Provisions can also be obtained at "Clark's" and in the Valley. Clark's Hotel is midway between the Valley and Mariposa. It would be far more pleasant to camp out—to alight like birds in beautiful groves of your own choosing—than to travel by rule and make forced marches to fixed points of common resort and common confusion.

You will require a light tent made of cotton sheeting, also a strong dress and strong pair of shoes for rock service. You will, of course, bring a good supply of paper for plants. I suppose, too, that you will all bring a supply of drawing-material, but I hardly think that drawing will be done. People admitted to heaven would most likely "wonder and adore" for at least two weeks before sketching its scenery, and I don't think that you will sketch Yosemite any sooner.

Here is, I think, a fair estimate of the cost of the round trip from Stockton, allowing, say ten days from time of departure from Mariposa till arrival at same point. Stage fare and way expenses to and from Mariposa, say $40.00; saddle horse, $20.00; provisions, cooking utensils, etc. $15.00; total, direct expense for one person, $75.00. Each additional day spent in the Valley would cost about $3.00. If you and all the members of your company are good riders, and there is among you one or two men practical travelers, and you could purchase, or hire, horses at a reasonable rate in San Jose or Gilroy, you could cross the Coast Range via the Pacheco Pass or Livermore Valley, thence direct to the Yosemite across the Joaquin and up the Merced, passing through Hopeton and Snellings. This kind of a trip would be less costly, and you would enjoy it, but unless your company was all composed of the same kind of material it would not answer.

I hope the Doctor will come too. I want to see him and ask him a great many questions.

There is a kind of hotel in the Valley, but it is incomparably better to choose your own camp among the rocks and waterfalls. The time of highest water in the Valley varies very much in different seasons. Last year it was highest about the end of June. I think, perhaps, the falls would be seen to as good advantage towards the end of June as at another time, and at any rate there will be a thousand times more of grandeur than any person can absorb.

Here, then, in a word is the plan which I propose: That you take the stage at Stockton for Mariposa. At Mariposa you procure saddle-horses and one pack-animal for your tent, blankets, provisions, etc., (a guide will be furnished by the keeper of the livery-stable to take charge of the horses), and that I meet you in the Valley, which I can do without difficulty provided you send me word by the first of June what day you will set out from Stockton. Address to Hopeton.

When you arrive in the Valley, please register your name at Mr. Hutchings' hotel. I will do the same. If you should wish to reach me by letter after I have started with the sheep to the mountains, you may perhaps do so by addressing to Coulterville.

When you write, state whether you will visit the big trees on your way to the Valley or whether you will do so on your return.

I bid you good-bye, thanking the Lord for the hope of seeing you and for his goodness to you in turning your face towards his most holy mansion of the mountains.

[*John Muir*][11]

Hopeton, May 20, 1869

Dear friend Mrs. Carr,

I forgot to state in my last concerning the Yosemite that I did not receive yours until many days after its arrival, as I was shearing sheep a considerable distance from here in the foothills, and the postmaster, not knowing where I was, could not forward it; but I will remain here until the lst of June, or possibly a few days later, and will receive any letters arriving for me at once either in Snelling or Hopeton.

The grove of sequoias is only six miles from the Yosemite trail, about midway between Mariposa and the Valley. The trail leading to the grove leaves the Yosemite trail at Mr. Clark's, where you can obtain all necessary directions, etc. It is not many years since this grove was discovered. The sequoias so often described and so well known throughout the world belong to the Calaveras grove. The Mariposa grove has a much larger number of trees than the Calaveras, and it is in all the majesty and grandeur of nature undisturbed.

You will likely make the journey from Mariposa to the Valley in two days. No member of your company need be afraid of this mountain ride, as you will be provided with sure-footed horses accustomed to the journey and an experienced guide.

Most persons visiting the Sequoia grove spend only a few hours in it and depart without seeing a single tree, for the chiefest glories of these mountain kings are wholly invisible to hasty or careless observers. I hope you may be able to spend a good long time in worship amid the glorious columns of this mountain temple. I fancy they are aware of your coming and are waiting. I fondly hope that nothing will occur to prevent your coming. I will endeavor to reach the Valley a day or so before you. The night air of the mountains is very cold. You will require plenty of warm blankets.

I am sorry that the Doctor has been so suddenly smothered up in business. If he and the priest were in the company according to the *prophecy* our joy would be full.

I am in a perfect tingle with the memories of a year ago and with anticipation glowing bright with all that I love.

Farewell, John Muir

I received your letter containing "The Song of Nature" by Emerson and derived a great deal of pleasure from it.

J. M.

[*John Muir*][12]

∽

Five miles west of Yosemite,
July 11, 1869

Dear Mrs. Carr

I need not try to tell you how sorely I am pained by this bitter disappointment. Your Mariposa note of June 22 did not reach Black's until July 3d, and I did not receive it until the 6th.

I met a shepherd a few miles from here yesterday who told me that a letter from Yosemite for me was at Harding's Mills. I have not yet received it. No dependence can be placed upon the motions of letters in the mountains, and I feared this result on my not receiving anything definite concerning your time of leaving Stockton before I left the plains. I wish now that I had not been entangled with sheep at all but that I had remained among post-offices and joined your party at Snellings.

Thus far all of my deepest, purest enjoyments have been taken in solitude, and the fate seems hard that has hindered me from sharing Yosemite with you.

We are camped this evening among a bundle of the Merced's crystal arteries, which have just gone far enough from their silent fountain to be full of lakelets and lilies[?], and the bleating of our flock can neither confuse nor hush the thousand notes of their celestial song. The sun has set, and these glorious shafts of the spruce and pine shoot higher and higher as the darkness comes on. I must say good night while bonds of Nature's sweetest influences are about me in these sacred mountain halls, and I know that every chord of your being has throbbed and tingled with the same mysterious powers when you were here. Farewell. I am glad to know that you have been allowed to bathe your existence in God's glorious Sierra Nevadas and sorry that I could not meet you.

John Muir

A few miles north of Yosemite,
July 13th

We are camped this afternoon upon the bank of the stream that falls into the Valley opposite Hutchings' hotel (Yosemite Falls). We are perhaps three miles from the Valley.

This Yosemite stream is flowing rapidly here in a small flowery meadow, not meandering like a meadow stream but going straight on with ripples and rapids. It derives its waters from a basin corresponding in every respect with its own sublimity and loneliness.

July 17th. We are now camped in a splendid grove of spruce only one mile from Yosemite wall. The stream that goes spraying past us in the rocks reaches the Valley by that canyon between the Yosemite Falls and the North Dome. I left my companions in charge of the sheep for the last three days and have had a most heavenly piece of life among the domes and falls and rocks of the north side and upper end of the Valley.

Yesterday I found the stream that flows through Crystal Lake past the South Dome and followed it three miles among cascades and rapids to the dome. Were you at the top or bottom of the upper Yosemite Falls? Were you at the top of the Nevada Falls? Were you in that *Adiantum* cave by the Vernal Falls? Have you had any view of the Valley excepting from the Mariposa Trail? How long were you in Sequoia Grove?

We will, perhaps, be here about two weeks; then we will go to the "big meadows" twelve miles towards the summit, where we will remain until we start for the plains some time near the end of September. The kind of meeting you have had with Yosemite answers well enough for most people, but it will not do for you. When will you return to the mountains?

I had a letter from Professor Butler a short time ago, saying that he would probably visit California this month in company with a man of war.

Remember me to the Doctor and to Allie and Ned. Please send me a letter by the middle of September to Snellings. I have no hope of hearing from you after we start for the Big Meadows.

[*John Muir*][13]

∾

Yosemite, Wednesday evening,
July 30, [*1869*]

Dear John Muir

I have looked for you daily and hourly since coming into these heavenly places and regret more than you possibly can (until the pressure of forty years living and loving shall have deepened and widened your heart), that you were not present with me in these joys. Not less than eight letters and notes are travelling around in search of you, and having up to this moment followed your directions as nearly as I could, I can only simply acquiesce in the *inevitable* and go away without seeing you until in God's own time and way we are once more permitted to enjoy face to face communion.

All that I have seen only deepens the conviction that it is only from our Great Mother that we really learn the lessons of our Father's love for us.

We are not going to leave California at present and very likely may find a congenial home and work here. You will know all our plans as soon as they are settled. Do not feel disappointed; I expected to find a dear teacher in you who have revelled in this glory so long.

Always your friend,
Jeanne Carr

Later,

A man who has just come in from Crane's flat says you are *verily* in there, somewhere on "Pat Delaney's range." As he also says that he knows you and that you sheared sheep for him, I think I will place a little confidence in what he says,—Mr. Hatch's information that you had passed there last Thursday with a drove of sheep. "A young man, a *Scotchman,* some of the other drivers said," made me confident of overtaking you. I passed many droves. I sent a letter to Ostrander's, stopped and left a line at Empire Camp, arrived here, sent letters by parties going out Sunday to Harding's and by Coulterville. Now, dear John, I should go out and hunt you up tomorrow and stay here another week but for this—a day or two before I left Dr. Carr was tendered a professorship in the University by the Executive Committee. He must reach a decision before the 6th when the formal appointments will be made, and he wished me to be back before that time that we might consult together. You see how necessary it is for me to leave. I would not have come in for two weeks but for the hope of seeing all this beauty in its hour of prime with your eyes to help me. I have trodden these paths in your footsteps. We will talk of it all ere long. Oh the divine blessed harmonics I have *heard,* even more than I have seen in these days. There are some *beautiful people* here who will go out your way. (I return by Mariposa as I came in, as all my fares are paid and some of my things left at Clark's and Hatch's.) Dr. and Mrs. Elliott of St. Louis and Miss Dix, the philanthropist, are here. I came in with a party of teachers and owe much to their kindness. I have left only one word for you on the bridge between the Vernal and Nevada fall, "The Lord bless thee and keep thee," and this I wish always.

[Jeanne C. Carr][14]

༃

Oakland, California,
September 28, 1869

Dear John Muir

I make one more half desperate attempt to recover you "in time,"
having gone to housekeeping and having a place to which to welcome
and in which [to] keep you. You will report yourself accordingly at
Oakland, Webster Street, near corner of 11th, "Tarlton's house." I am
awfully homesick, had just as soon die and go to the woods as not,
but the Dr. and the boys might miss me, and I won't. Besides, I want
to see you again. I have room for all your plants. Prof. Butler has been
here and gone to [the] Sandwich Islands, and I am, as ever,

Your friend,
Jeanne Carr[15]

༃

Two miles below La Grange,
October 3, 1869

[*Mrs. Carr*]

My summer in the third heaven of the Sierras is past. I am again in
the smooth open world of plains. I received three of your eight notes,
which for mountain correspondence is about as might be expected. I
learned by a San Francisco newspaper that Dr. Carr had accepted a
professorship in the University, and Prof. Butler told me about a
month ago that he had gone to Madison to fetch his cabinet, etc.
Therefore I know that you are making a fixed home and that you will
yet see the mountains and the Joaquin plains. We were camped within
a mile or two of the Yosemite north wall for three weeks. I used to go
to the North Dome or Yosemite Falls most every day to sketch and
listen to the waters. One day I went down into the Valley by the
canyon opposite Hutchings and found Prof. Butler near the bridge
between the Vernal and Nevada falls. He was in company with Gen.
Alvord. He was in the Valley only a few hours, his time being
controlled by the General's military clock, and I am pretty sure that he
saw just about nothing.

I am glad that the world does not miss me and that all of my days with the Lord and his works are uncounted and unmeasured. I found the guide who was with you. He said that you wished me to gather some cones for you. I hope to see you soon in San Francisco and will fetch you specimens of those which grow higher than you have been. I am sorry that you were so short a time in the Valley, but you will go again and remain a month or two. I would like to spend a winter there to see the storms. We spent most of the summer on the south fork of the Tuolumne near Castle and Cathedral peaks, and oh, how unspeakable the glories of these higher mountains. You have not yet caught a glimpse of the Sierra Nevadas. You must go to Mono by the Bloody Canyon pass. I will not try to write the grandeur I have seen all summer but I will copy you the notes of one day from my journal.

Sept. 2nd. Amount of cloudiness .08. Sky red evening and morning, not usual crimson glow but separate clouds colored and anchored in dense massive mountain forms. One red, bluffy cap is placed upon Castle Peak and its companion to the south, but the smooth cone tower of the castle is seen peering out over the top. Tiger Peak has a cloud cap also of the grandest proportion and colors, and the extensive field of clustered towers and peaks and domes where is stored the treasures of snow belonging to the Merced and Tuolumne and Joaquin is embosomed in bossy clouds of white. The grand Sierra Cathedral is overshadowed like Sinai. Never before beheld such divine mingling of cloud and mountain. Had a delightful walk upon the north wall. Ascended by a deep narrow passage cut in the granite. Its borders are splendidly decorated with ferns and blooming shrubs. The most delicate of plantlets in the gush and ardor of full bloom in places called desolate and gloomy, where the dwarfed and crumpled pines are felled with hail and rocks and wintry snows; but as frail flowers of human kind are protected by the hand of God, blooming joyfully through a long beautiful life in places and times that are strewn with the wrecks of the powerful and the great, so in these far mountains, where are the treasures of snow and storms, live in safety and innocence these sweet, tender children of the plants. Had looked long and well for

Cassiope, but in all my long excursions failed to find its
dwelling-places and began to fear that we would never meet,
but had presentiment of finding it today, and as I passed a rock-
shelf after reaching the great gathered heaps of everlasting
snow, something seemed to whisper "*Cassiope, Cassiope.*"
That name was "driven in upon me," as Calvinists say, and,
looking around, behold the long-looked-for mountain child!

Farewell! I do not care to write much because you seem so near. I
hope that you will all be very happy in your new home and not feel
too sorely the separation from the loved places and people of
Wisconsin.

Remember me to the Doctor and to all of your boys.

I am most cordially,

Your friend,
John Muir[16]

ℳ

Oakland, Alameda County,
Corner 11th and Webster Streets,
October, [*1869*]

Dear John Muir

Yours of October 3 just received. [*I*] think you must have another
from me by this [*time*], as I wrote directing to Snellings about the date
of yours.

I hope you will consider *this your home* on the Pacific and come
home not for a meager visit, but to stay and *refit* for new expeditions,
and rest, and delight us all with what you have seen and experienced.
It is a humble home, more so than any we have known, but we are
very glad to be together and once more in the family life and to it you
are urged to come as one of us, by your

Sincere friends,
E. S. and Jeanne Carr
[*Ezra S.*]

Prof. Butler *darted* in upon the day we moved into this house,
returning from the Sandwich Islands [*Hawaiian Islands*], was dry as
a chip, darted in again four or five days later and preached a dry old
sermon in Brayton Hall and has gone back to tell of Mauna Loa and

the Liberty Cap to his winter audiences. It made me so *mad* that *he* should have found you! mad at both of you. It was *Cunningham* you saw. I think Cunningham pitied me in my disappointment. Anyway, he tried to pacify me with promises of cones and things. Mrs. Hutchings said she would send me some bulbs of *Lilium californicum*. I wish she would do herself up in a package and come here and bring "Squirrel." Come along, dear John, and we will talk it all over. Bring your plants, your trunks, your *staff and scrip* if you wish. Dr. Carr will find room to store your things with his, should it please you.

I expect I have lost my clusters of Sequoia cones. I had some good ones, but they have disappeared. I wanted Cunningham to send me some with fresh seeds that I could make grow.[17]

∾

La Grange, November 15, 1869

Dear Friends Mrs. and Dr. Carr

I thank you most heartily for the very kind invitation you send me. I could enjoy a blink of rest in your new home with a relish that only those can know who have suffered solitary banishment for so many years, but I must return to the mountains, to Yosemite. I am told that the winter storms there will not be easily borne, but I am bewitched, enchanted, and tomorrow I must start for the great temple to listen to the winter songs and sermons preached and sung only there.

The plains here are green already and the upper mountains have the pearly whiteness of their first snows.

Farewell. I will bring you some cones in the spring. I hope that you enjoy your labor in your new sphere.

My love to all your family, and I am

Yours most cordially,
John Muir[18]

∾

Yosemite, December 6, 1869

Dear friend Mrs. Carr

I am feasting in the Lord's mountain house, and what pen may write my blessings? I am going to dwell here all winter magnificently

"Snowbound." Just think of the grandeur of a mountain winter in Yosemite! Would that you could enjoy it also!

I read your word in pencil upon the bridge below the Nevada, and I thank you for it most devoutly. No one or all of the Lord's blessings can enable me to exist without a friend indeed.

There is no snow in the Valley. The ground is covered with the brown and yellow leaves of the oak and maple, and their crisping and rustling makes me think of the groves of Madison. I have been wandering about among the falls and rapids, studying the grand instruments of slopes and curves and echoing caves upon which those divine harmonies are played. Only a thin flossy veil sways and bends over Yosemite now, and Pohono is a web of waving mist. New songs are sung, forming parts of the one grand anthem composed and written "in the beginning."

Most of the flowers are dead. Only a few are blooming in summer nooks on the north side rocks. You remember that delightful fernery by the ladders. Well, I discovered a garden meeting of *Adiantum* far more delicate and luxuriant than those of the ladders. They are in a cove or covelette between the upper and lower Yosemite Falls. They are the most delicate and graceful plant creatures I ever beheld, waving themselves in lines of the most refined of heaven's beauty to the music of the water. The motion of purple dulses in pools left by the tide on the sea-coast of Scotland was the only memory that was stirred by these spiritual ferns. You speak of dying and going to the woods; I am dead and gone to heaven.

An Indian comes to the Valley once a month upon snowshoes. He brings the mail, and so I shall hope to hear from you. Address to Yosemite, via Big Oak Flat, care of Mr. Hutchings.

[*John Muir*][19]

PART THREE

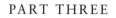

1870

*In all my wanderings through
Nature's beauty, whether it be
among the ferns at my cabin door
or in the high meadows and peaks
or amid the spray and music of
waterfalls, you are the first to meet
me and I often speak to you as
verily present in the flesh.*

John Muir

Wishing You Were Here

JOHN MUIR PREPARED TO SPEND THE WINTER IN YOSEMITE VALLEY. He and a friend, Harry Randall, left the Sierra foothills at French Bar on November 16, 1869, and advanced slowly to the Valley, walking through late flowers and passing pines and firs, maples and black oaks. Muir and Randall found employment in the Valley working for James M. Hutchings at Hutchings's Hotel, where they constructed a sawmill, built cottages and an addition to the hotel, and installed wooden partitions to replace the bed sheets that divided the guest rooms. They also guided guests and tended livestock. Randall helped Muir build a small cottage of sugar-pine shingles on the eastern bank of Yosemite Creek beneath the great falls between Hutchings's cottage and sawmill. There they lived while they took meals with the Hutchings family at the hotel.

Supported by his work for Hutchings, Muir studied nature in the Valley and in the surrounding mountains. In mid-December he saw his first Yosemite snow. While he feasted in God's mountain house, Carr reminisced about Nevada Falls, Florence (Squirrel) Hutchings, and the warmth of the pines and the fir trees from her home in Oakland. She wished she were in the Valley. Muir wished even more that she were there. As he settled into his impractical aimless life in communion with nature, he maintained a correspondence with Carr. From Oakland she directed letters to him and sent a trail of prominent friends and acquaintances to meet him in the Valley, where they heard the words of John Muir, evangelist, who proclaimed the gospel of the wilderness and the mountains. Carr also hoped relations with kindred minds would mellow Muir toward society. Among the friends she sent to Muir was J. B. McChesney, Superintendent of Schools in Oakland. Muir led him to Sunnyside Bench, a ledge Muir named that stood nearly five hundred feet above the floor of the Valley. Having approached by Indian Canyon and behind the Upper Yosemite Fall, there Muir and McChesney spent a night baptized in the spray of the falls.

Carr's devotion to Muir was nurtured in part by her devotion to David Douglas, the Scottish botanist-explorer for whom the Douglas Fir tree was named. Douglas discovered over fifty trees and shrubs and over one hundred herbaceous plants while he traveled, frequently with only a dog or a guide, in the eastern United States and in the Pacific Northwest. Carr romanticized his explorations and fused them with her botanical excursions in Castleton, Vermont, where she was born in 1825, attended seminary, and as a child collected an herbarium of her own. She referred to Douglas as a "Poet-Naturalist," venerated him as if he were a saint, and hoped to follow in his footsteps. Muir embodied the spirit of Douglas and upon him also Carr conferred the title "Poet-Naturalist."[1]

Carr drew upon Muir as a surrogate naturalist and explored wilderness vicariously through him as she often was unable to break free from the mills of society that kept her far away from Yosemite Valley. Muir's private immersion and ascetic pilgrimage were accessible to her through his letters, in which he shared his nature observations, the spiritual presence he encountered in nature, and the spirituality he cultivated in the wilderness. Muir assured Carr that she was included in his pathless meanderings in nature's beauty. His letters enriched her faith and her hope that she would some day lead a similar life. Carr, however, seldom accepted the vicarious nature of Muir's ramblings with grace. Often during the summer of 1870 while he traveled with her friends she remained entangled in responsibilities and company that left her longing to break free and join him.

While Carr struggled to liberate herself from obligations in order to journey to Yosemite, Muir basked in the glory of communion with nature and encountered solitude beyond the influx of friends and tourists. The summer of 1870 would be the first he would spend in the Valley and at times he was lonely and longed for Carr, though Elvira Hutchings was in the Valley and they had become friends while James Hutchings traveled to Washington, D.C., to seek compensation for his homestead claim and land improvements. The Yosemite Grant of June 1864 established by the United States Congress to protect Yosemite Valley and Mariposa Big Tree Grove invalidated Hutchings's land claim. During his absence Muir, who was lonely, and Elvira, who was unhappy in her marriage, were drawn together by her extraordinary views of spiritual matters. With two hundred years of Puritan ancestry behind her, it is doubtful Elvira would have accepted any advances Muir might have made. And for Muir, then thirty-two, a romantic involvement with Elvira would have been morally impossible given her marriage to Hutchings.

When Hutchings returned in late May 1870, Elvira confessed that she had shared details of their marriage with Muir. Muir and Hutchings did not like one another, and this may have deepened the rift between them. Muir thought Hutchings was unfair in his dealings with him, and Hutchings was jealous of Muir's popularity with celebrity guests. Both men were building reputations by publicizing Yosemite Valley and each believed the Valley was his own preserve. By the end of the year Hutchings requested Muir's cabin for his sister and Muir left his position at Hutchings's Hotel.

During the summer Carr broke away from the domestic and social moorings of Oakland and departed for a picnic in the Sierra with a company of eastern horticulturalists led by Marshall P. Wilder, Charles Downing (elder brother of Andrew Jackson Downing, landscape architect), George H. Ellwanger, and Patrick Barry (of the Ellwanger and Barry Nursery, Rochester, New York). Barry noted their itinerary in a pocket diary: a visit with Dr. John Strentzel in Alhambra on July 5, a trip to Oakland the following day (perhaps to visit with the Carrs), and a departure for Stockton on July 9 to start for the Calaveras Grove. Carr wrote to Muir to watch for the party. She did not accompany them into the Valley. According to Barry's diary, the group reached the "Big Trees" on the evening of July 10, stayed all night, started back the following day, returned to Stockton on July 12 and to Oakland on July 15. Barry's notations suggest the Carrs and Strentzels were acquainted in 1870. Louie Wanda Strentzel was then twenty-three.[2]

Carr, who had introduced Muir to the writings of Walter R. Brooks in 1868, sent him some of Brooks's papers in 1870. Brooks had given them to her while he traveled in Palestine and Carr selected some to forward to Muir, who referred to them while traveling with Ralph Waldo Emerson in Yosemite Valley in May 1871. Muir wrote to tell Carr that he found the letters filled with spice and poetry and expressive of his own feelings toward nature.

Carr also sent other friends to visit Muir during the summer of 1870. Among them were Judge Gilbert Winslow Colby of Benicia; Mark

Hopkins, President of Williams College; Frank H. Shapleigh, a Boston landscape painter; Mrs. Robert C. Waterston, the daughter of Josiah Quincy, the sixteenth president of Harvard College; and Theresa Yelverton, Viscountess Avonmore, who Muir noted was writing a Yosemite novel in which he and Florence Hutchings figured prominently. Yelverton, who supported herself as a travel writer, became somewhat enchanted by Muir while in the Valley. Her novel, *Zanita: A Tale of the Yo-semite,* published in 1872, portrayed the landscape of life in the Valley and featured its residents and guests.[3]

In July Joseph Le Conte, a professor of geology at the University of California, Professor Frank Soule, Jr., and eight of Le Conte's students set out to visit Yosemite Valley, the High Sierra, Mono Lake and the volcanoes in the vicinity, and Lake Tahoe. Carr hoped Le Conte would travel with her to the Valley. She wrote to Muir in July that she was disappointed Le Conte was traveling with his university boys. On August 5 the excursion party met Muir at Hutchings's sawmill. Le Conte noted Muir was a gentleman of rare intelligence and original mind with a vast knowledge of botany. Muir rambled with them for ten days.

Le Conte, Soule, the students, and Muir camped at Tenaya Creek, on the western side of Bridal Veil meadow, at Eagle Point, and at Lake Tenaya. They climbed to the meadows of the South Tuolumne, camped at the foot of Mount Dana, worshipped upon Dana, walked among the flowers and cascades of Bloody Canyon, camped at the lake, and rode to the volcanic cone nearest the lake, where Muir left the party as they headed north to Tahoe. Muir was well acquainted with the mountains and with glacial evidence, and his knowledge persuaded Le Conte to agree with him that glaciers had been active in the Valley's formation. Le Conte was among the first to support Muir's theory on the formation of Yosemite Valley. Overall and in light of Muir's position as a sawyer for Hutchings, Le Conte too was enamored by Muir's intellect and ability. Le Conte assumed a role in *Zanita* through Yelverton, who took on the guise of "Mrs. Brown," the wife of a professor of geology in a California college with whom she traveled on geological excursions.[4]

In October Ned Carr sailed for South America, joining an American colonization scheme, the Bolivian Commercial and Colonization Company, promoted by A. D. Piper of San Francisco. Piper received a concession from the Brazilian and Peruvian governments for the navigation of the waters of the upper Amazon and a grant of millions of acres on the Purus in the Department of Beni. To facilitate colonization Piper hired recruits and collected supplies in Boston and Providence. Carr encouraged Muir to consider joining the venture; it would provide inexpensive passage to the heart of the Andes. Muir, however, chose instead to remain in the Valley, where he drank the juice of Sequoia that rendered him a methodless wanderer in the Sierra. The expedition would fail the following May.

In November and December Muir wrote to Carr, whom he considered a prophet in the concerns of his outside life, and questioned why she sought his release from Yosemite and from California when his soul wallowed in California light. Carr always sought to broaden Muir's experience of both wilderness and society. Though he was less than malleable, she planted new themes and new landscapes hoping they might take root from time to time. When Hutchings required Muir's cabin for his sister, Muir with a renewed sense of homelessness considered leaving for South America. Loose notes that required organizing and the fact that Hutchings owed him money delayed further decision making. Muir found quarters within sight and hearing of the Tuolumne River on smooth level ground. There he spent the winter.

~

Oakland, January 22, 1870

Dear John Muir

I think of you as far too blessed to need words from the lower world, and yet I meant to send many and oft repeated greetings to your winter quarters. I think with delight of how the winter home looks, of little brown "Squirrel" in the glow of the firelight, of the long walks, and readings, and thinkings—the morning tintings of the rocks, the comforting warmth of the pines and firs. (I never *felt* as warm as in the pine woods in winter.) Well, I could wish I were there, but the dear ones would miss me, and I have not exhausted the beauty my soul stored up last year. Sunday Mr. Ackerson was here, my friend with whom I went to the Redwoods, and yesterday I lunched with one of our Yosemite party, and I overheard Dr. Carr say to some of the ladies that he would probably go to Yosemite himself next summer. Mrs. Brummage of Bear Valley was talking it all over the other day, and I think I shall know how to go another time, with more economy of time, fatigue, and money. I shall buy my mule and keep clear of company, though really I had nothing to complain of before. I only mean to say that I will make my allowance carry me farther another time.

My winter delight is in studying *Palms,* from books of course, but I have had a good time over Rumphius' "Flora Javonensis." Those orchids! Those *Calami!*—the heart of the world is in that mysterious *Eastern* Archipelago. Don't you want to see *Oreodoxa regia*? and those wonderful *Hoyas*? I dream and dream what I shall say to them.

John Muir, I wish I *could* tell you how full of God his Universe seemed when I stood on that little bridge by the Nevada fall. I never was *interfused* with the interior life of things as that day. A thousand years even as one day—and the people I knew in the bygone ages so shadowy and unreal. After we returned to Hutchings I walked in the gloaming....

[Remainder of letter missing]

[*Jeanne C. Carr*][5]

∾

Yosemite, April 5, 1870

Dear Mrs. Carr

I wish you were here today, for our rocks are again decked with deep snow. Two days ago a big gray cloud collared Barometer Dome. The vast booming column of the upper falls was swayed like a shred of loose mist by broken pieces of storm that struck it suddenly, occasionally bending it backwards to the very top of the cliff, making it hang sometimes more than a minute like an inverted bow edged with comets. A cloud upon the dome and these ever varying rockings and bendings of the falls are sure storm signs, but yesterday morning's sky was clear, and the sun poured the usual quantity of the balmiest spring sunshine into the blue ether of our Valley gulf, but ere long ragged lumps of cloud began to appear all along the Valley-rim, coming gradually into closer ranks, and rising higher like rock additions to the walls. From the top of the cloud-banks fleecy fingers arched out from both sides and met over the middle of the meadows, gradually thickening and blackening, until at night big, confident snowflakes began to fall. We thought that the last snow-harvest had been withered and reaped long ago by the glowing sun, for the bluebirds and robins sang spring, and so also did the bland, unsteady winds, and the brown meadow opposite the house was spotted here and there with blue violets. *Carex* spikes were shooting up through the dead leaves, and the cherry and briar rose were unfolding their leaves, and besides these spring wrote many a sweet mark and word that I cannot tell; but snow fell all the hours of today in cold winter earnest, and now at evening there rests upon rocks, trees, and weeds as full and ripe a harvest of snow flowers as I ever beheld in the stormiest, most opaque days of midwinter.

April 13

About twelve inches of snow fell in that last snowstorm. It disappeared as suddenly as it came, snatched away hastily almost before it had time to melt, as if a mistake had been made in allowing it to come here at all.

A week of spring days bright in every hour, without a stain or thought of the storm, came in glorious colors, giving still greater pledges

of happy life to every living creature of the spring, but a loud, energetic
snowstorm possessed every hour of yesterday. Every tree and broken
weed bloomed yet once more; all summer distinctions were leveled off;
all plants and the very rocks and streams were equally polypetalous.

This morning winter had everything in the Valley. The snow drifted
about in the frosty wind like meal, and the falls were muffled in thick
sheets of frozen spray. Thus do winter and spring leap into the Valley
by turns, each remaining long enough to form a small season or climate
of its own, or going and coming squarely in a single day. Whitney says
that the bottom has fallen out of the rocks here (which I most devoutly
disbelieve). Well, the bottom frequently falls out of these winter
clouds and climates. It is seldom that any long transition slant exists
between dark and bright days in this narrow world of rocks.

I know that you are enchanted with the April loveliness of your new
home. You enjoy the most precious kind of sunshine, and by this time
flower-patches cover the hills about Oakland like colored clouds. I
would like to visit these broad outspread blotches of social flowers that
are so characteristic of your hills, but far rather would I see and feel
the flowers that are now at Fountain Lake and the lakes of Madison.

Mrs. Hutchings thought of sending you a bulb of the California
lily by mail but found it too large. She wishes to be remembered to
you. Your Squirrel is very happy. She is a rare creature.

I hope to see you and the Doctor soon in the Valley. I have a great
deal to say to you which I will not try to write. Remember me most
cordially to the Doctor and to Allie and all the boys. I am much
obliged to you for those botanical notes, etc., and I am ever most

Cordially yours,

John Muir

Here is a moss with a globular capsule and a squinted, cowl-
shaped calyptra. Do you know it?[6]

∾

Yosemite, May 17, [1870]

[Mrs. Carr]

Our valley is just gushing, throbbing full of open, absorbable
beauty, and I feel that I must tell you about it. I am lonely among my
enjoyments; the Valley is full of visitors, but I have no one to talk to.

The season that is with us now is about what corresponds to full-fledged spring in Wisconsin. The oaks are in full leaf and have shoots long enough to bend over and move in the wind. The good old bracken is waist-high already, and almost all of the rock ferns have their outermost fronds unrolled. Spring is in full power and is steadily reaching higher like a shadow and will soon reach the topmost horizon of rocks. The buds of the poplar opened on the 19th of last month, those of the oaks on the 24th.

May 1st was a fine, hopeful, healthful, cool, bright day with plenty of the fragrance of new leaves and flowers and of the music of bugs and birds. From the 5th to 14th was extremely warm, the thermometer averaging about 85 degrees at noon in shade. Craggy banks of cumuli became common about Starr King and the Dome. Flowers came in troops. The upper snows melted very fast, raising the falls to their highest pitch of glory. The waters of the Yosemite Fall no longer float softly and downily like hanks of spent rockets but shoot at once to the bottom with tremendous energy. There is at least ten times the amount of water in the Valley that there was when you were here.

In crossing the Valley we had to sail in the boat. The river paid but little attention to its banks, flowing over the meadow in great river-like sheets. But last Sunday, 15th, was a dark day; the rich streams of heat and light were withheld; the thermometer fell suddenly to 35 degrees, and down among the verdant banks of new leaves, and groves of half-open ferns, and thick settlements of confident flowers, came heavy snow in big, blinding flakes, coming down with a steady gait and taking their places gracefully upon shrinking leaves and petals as if they were doing exactly right. The whole day was snowy and stormy like a piece of early winter. Snow fell also on the 16th. A good many of the ferns and delicate flowers are killed.

There are about fifty visitors in the Valley at present. When are you and the Doctor coming? Mr. Hutchings has not yet returned from Washington, and so I will be here all summer. I have not heard from you since January.

I had a letter the other day from Prof. Butler. He has been glancing and twinkling about among the towns of all the States at a most unsubstantial velocity.

Did you see the gold of the Joaquin plains this spring? There is a later gold in October which you must see, that of *Hemizonia virgata*.

Remember me warmly to Dr. Carr and all the boys, and I remain always

> Most cordially yours,
> John Muir

Yosemite
via Big Oak Flat[7]

∾

> Oakland, May 28, [*1870*]

Dear John Muir

I have answered all thy letters, and some of them have been quite long and though hurriedly written were too full of what I find no one else wants, to be lost. I am longing, yea, *pining* for the pines, for the sweet house of life in which you live, and not less to see what manner of man you are becoming, left entirely to Nature's teaching and discipline. Mr. Carlton, who writes the enclosed and is a friend worth knowing, ought to go to the Valley this year, but fears he cannot. *Mr. McChesney*, one of the teachers in Oakland, is going up soon with a camping out party of gentlemen. I like him very much. Mr. Stone of his party, a teacher also, is something of a mineralogist, perhaps geologist, but as dry as a chip or California dust. I could spend eternity in a field of wild oats more delightfully than in a world full of such men, however virtuous and useful. Will I get to you this summer? Not unless my beloved should take a sudden inspiration or be drawn into some of the *eastern* parties soon to be here. I may as well say I will not do this unless *God palpably sends me.* I wait for His voice. So much of the life I lead is not mine—in no sense mine. I am ground over and over in these mills of society, and so made a sharer in some divine purpose of *use.* It is so easy to work, to give, to spend, and be spent. I look up o' nights ere I sleep to the distant wondrous world we shall explore together, with hardly a wish for Ole's music or your dear wildernesses or the sympathy of kindred eyes which see and ears which hear. It all seems so *sure,* so *near,* at times I am a part of the soul of things. It is easy in these moods to defer *my* soul's appropriate joys. At other times I hunger and thirst for the *harmonies* of sound, color, motion, which are your daily food, for the society of the elect, as I never did for any worldly good.

I have had a great pleasure lately in a visit with George B. Emerson, who is one of the oldest Massachusetts teachers, and the author of an excellent work on the trees of Massachusetts, published more than forty years ago. He came to this coast with Dr. Jacob Bigelow, one of the oldest doctors in the country and author of Bigelow's botany, an excellent work long gone out of print. Mrs. Bigelow was along; the three, all over eighty years of age, went to Calaveras but were dissuaded from entering the Valley. I tried to make Mr. Emerson reconsider his resolution not to attempt the longer journey by telling him that when he appeared at the Heavenly gates the angels would send him back to visit the Yosemite—no admission there for a tree lover who had not been true to the end. The enthusiasm of the old men was charming. I wanted them to go to the Valley so that you could see them. Mr. Lapham of Wisconsin has been out here, and we had a day together among the plants. An *Agave americana* in one of the gardens here is sending up a blossom stem, now about thirty feet in height. The plant is very magnificent. There is much to enjoy in the garden botany of this region. My friend Mrs. Daggett is travelling with her husband in Northern Africa. [*She*] says she found near Algiers, a botanic garden far surpassing any in Europe. I want to send you her letters but fear they would be lost. I am truly glad you are to stay with Mr. Hutchings. I think you might be of great use and congenial to one another. Did I ever tell you how in secret I hope he may substantiate his claim, though it seems a pity that any *ownership* of that spot should exist. I should like to have Mr. Hutchings stay there during his and my lifetime—but I would have no roads made. Everyone should *earn the right* to enter it. Write as often as you can. Your letters keep up my faith that I shall lead just such a life sometime. The boys are all at home just now and send their regards; the Dr. also.

> Your friend,
> Jeanne Carr[8]

∿

Yosemite, Sunday, May 29, 1870

Dear friend

I received your "apology" two days ago and ran my eyes hastily over it three or four lines at a time to find the place that would say you were coming, but you *"fear"* that you cannot come at all, and only "hope" that the Doctor may; but I shall continue to look for you nevertheless. The Chicago party you speak of were here and away again before your letter arrived. All sorts of human stuff is being poured into our Valley this year, and the blank, fleshly apathy with which most of it comes in contact with the rock and water spirits of the place is most amazing. I do not wonder that the thought of such people being here, Mrs. Carr, makes you "mad," but after all, Mrs. Carr, they are about harmless. They climb sprawlingly to their saddles like overgrown frogs pulling themselves up a stream-bank through the bent sedges, ride up the Valley with about as much emotion as the horses they ride upon, and comfortable when they have "done it all," and long for the safety and flatness of their proper homes.

In your first letter to the Valley you complain of the desecrating influences of the fashionable hordes about to visit here, and say that you mean to come only once more and "into the beyond." I am pretty sure that you are wrong in saying and feeling so, for the tide of visitors will float slowly about the *bottom* of the Valley as a harmless scum, collecting in hotel and saloon eddies, leaving the rocks and falls eloquent as ever and instinct with imperishable beauty and greatness. And recollect that the top of the Valley is more than half way to real heaven, and the Lord has many mansions away in the Sierra equal in power and glory to Yosemite, though not quite so open, and I venture to say that you may yet see the Valley many times both in and out of the body.

I am glad you are going to the coast mountains to sleep on Diablo,—Angelo ere this. I am sure that you will be lifted above all the effects of your material work. There is a precious natural charm in sleeping under the open starry sky. You will have a very perfect view of the Joaquin Valley and the snowy, pearly wall of the Sierra Nevada. I lay for weeks last summer upon a bed of pine leaves at the edge of a daisy gentian meadow in full view of Mt. Dana.

Mrs. Hutchings says that the lily bulbs were so far advanced in their growth when she dug some to send you that they could not be packed without being broken, but I am going to be here all summer, and I know where the grandest plantation of these lilies grows, and I will box up as many of them as you wish, together with as many other Yosemite things as you may ask for and send them out to you before the pack train makes its last trip. I know the *Spiraea* you speak of. It is abundant all around the top of the Valley and on the rocks at Lake Tenaya and reaches almost to the very summit about Mt. Dana. There is also a purple one very abundant on the fringe meadows of Yosemite Creek, a mile or two back from the brink of the Falls. Of course it will be a source of keen pleasure to me to procure you anything you may desire. I should like to see that grand *Agave*. I saw some in Cuba but they did not exceed twenty-five or thirty feet in height.

I have thought of a walk in the wild gardens of Honolulu, and now that you speak of my going there it becomes very probable, as you seem to understand me better than I do myself. I have no square idea about the time I shall get myself away from here. I shall at least stay till you come. I fear that the *Agave* will be in the spirit world ere that time. You say that I ought to have such a place as you saw in the gardens of that mile and a half of climate. Well, I think those lemon and orange groves would do, perhaps, to make a living, but for a garden I should not have anything less than a piece of pure nature. I was reading Thoreau's *Maine Woods* a short time ago. As described by him, these woods are exactly like those of Canada West. How I long to meet *Linnaea* and *Chiogenes hispidula* once more! I would rather see these two children of the evergreen woods than all the twenty-seven species of palm that Agassiz met on the Amazons.

These summer days "go on" calmly and evenly. Scarce a mark of the frost and snow of the 15th is visible. The brackens are four or five feet high already. The earliest azaleas have opened, and the whole crop of bulbs is ready to burst. The river does not overflow its banks now, but it is exactly brim-full. The thermometer averages about 75 degrees at noon. We have sunshine every morning from a bright blue sky. Ranges of cumuli appear towards the summits with great regularity every day about 11 o'clock, making a splendid background for the South Dome. In a few hours these clouds disappear and give up the sky to sunny evening.

Mr. Hutchings arrived here from Washington a week ago. There are sixty or seventy visitors here at present.

I have received only two letters from you this winter and spring, dated Jan. 22nd and May 7th.

I kissed your untamed one [*Floy Hutchings*] for you. She wishes that she knew the way to Oakland that she might come to you.

Remember me to the Doctor and all your boys and to your little Allie. I remain ever

Yours most cordially,

J. Muir[9]

∾

Oakland, Sunday, [*July 10, 1870*]

Dear John

I've just been at the "howling" point all this afternoon having spent some hours with Mr. McClure, who gave me a detailed account of the upper Fall expedition, and coming back I met the University boys who are going in company with Prof. Joseph Le Conte. Now I had felt that Providence was saving L. C. to go with me, and I feel abused by the arrangement. It was so exactly the thing for us to have gone in company and Miss Graham, a member of his family, also wished to go, and both were willing to wait—so I thought it would all come right at last. But it won't, and now let me tell you that the Prof. is gold seven times refined, i.e. in geological science, in botanical (general), in music, in landscape love, in poetry, in self-forgetfulness, in adoration—*a Christian soul.*

I like Soule as well as I can one I have seen only once out of a ballroom, and young Phelps I like very much. He is a good student and librarian of the Oakland Library.

I suppose my friends the Boston horticulturists are not in the Valley. They are aged, some of them, and expected to stop at Calaveras. If you see Dr. and Mrs. Waterston, give her the enclosed. I expect they have gone "into the beyond," and I *wish*, no I don't, for here's my *Calopogon* from the Hamilton swamps and word that the *Brookses*

will come to California before very long! If they don't come before
you leave the Valley I shall not keep them company.

There is no body in the world I should be as glad to see as yourself. It is delight to hear Mr. McChesney talk about you. He is gold,
too. Oh, for a run in that tamarack swamp near Lake Kosh Ronony
with you. In some lazy hour you may read these letters, you know the
mood in which they were written. When Mr. Brooks went to Palestine
he left his private papers in my care, and I found these among them.
As they are his property you may keep and return them sometime.
[Letter may be incomplete.]

> [*Jeanne C. Carr*][10]

∾

> Oakland, California,
> Corner 11th and Webster Streets,
> July 10, 1870

Dear Mrs. Waterston

A letter received some weeks since from Charles Sanderson sent
me at once to San Francisco in search of you. I heard that you had left
and only last Friday of your temporary absence—my first informant
stating that you had returned to Boston. I trust it is not too late for us
to meet.

Should this find you in the Yosemite Valley, on your return from
the High Sierra, I wish it might make you acquainted with one who is
as substance to the shadow of whatever is lovely and of good report
our friend Charlie is. Dear Charles! so like a disembodied spirit, so
kindred to the shining ones, here in the lower world has never been
able to show what he is. My friend of the Yosemite has kept so close
to Nature that her blood, her health, her spicy aromatic flavor fills
him, and he knows all your paths. He is of Scotch descent—his name
is John Muir, and he is with Mr. Hutchings. You will find the rest of
him for yourself. It is a grief and a triumph of self-denial that I am not
this moment in the glorious Valley, where it would be most pleasant
to meet you. I shall hope to see you on your return.

Meanwhile I am,

> Yours most sincerely,
> Jeanne C. Carr[11]

∾

Yosemite, July 29, [*1870*]

My dear friend Mrs. Carr

I am very, very blessed. The Valley is full of people but they do not annoy me. I revolve in pathless places and in higher rocks than *the world* and his ribbony wife can reach. Had I not been blunted by hard work in the mill and crazed by Sabbath raids among the high places of this heaven, I would have written you long since. I have spent every Sabbath for the last two months in the spirit world, screaming among the peaks and outside meadows like a negro Methodist in revival time, and every intervening clump of week-days in trying to fix down and assimilate my shapeless harvests of revealed glory into the spirit and into the common earth of my existence; and I am rich, rich beyond measure, not in rectangular blocks of sifted knowledge or in thin sheets of beauty hung picture-like about "the walls of memory," but in unselected atmospheres of terrestrial glory diffused evenly throughout my whole substance.

Your Brooksian letters I have read with a great deal of interest, they are so full of the spice and poetry of unmingled nature, and in many places they express my own present feelings very fully. Quoting from your Forest Glen, "without anxiety and without expectation all my days come and go *mixed* with such sweetness to every sense," and again, "I don't know anything of time and but little of space." "My whole being seemed to open to the sun." All this I do most comprehensively appreciate and am just beginning to know how fully congenial you are. Would that you could share my mountain enjoyments! In all my wanderings through Nature's beauty, whether it be among the ferns at my cabin door or in the high meadows and peaks or amid the spray and music of waterfalls, you are the first to meet me and I often speak to you as verily present in the flesh.

Last Sabbath I was baptized in the irised foam of the Vernal and in the divine snow of Nevada, and you were there also and stood in real presence by the sheet of joyous rapids below the bridge.

I am glad to know that McClure and McChesney have told you of our night with upper Yosemite. Oh, what a world is there I passed! No, I *had* another night there two weeks ago, entering as far within

the veil amid equal glory, together with Mr. Frank Shapleigh of
Boston. Mr. Shapleigh is an artist and I like him. He has been here six
weeks and has just left for home. I told him to see you and to show
you his paintings. He is acquainted with Charles Sanderson and Mrs.
Waterston. Mrs. Waterston left the Valley before your letter reached
me, but one morning about sunrise an old lady came to the mill and
asked me if I was the man who was so fond of flowers, and we had a
very earnest, unceremonious chat about the Valley and about "the
beyond." She is made of better stuff than most of the people of that
heathen town of Boston, and so also is Shapleigh.

Mrs. Yelverton is here and is going to stop a good while. Mrs.
Waterston told her to find me, and we are pretty well acquainted now.
She told me the other day that she was going to write a Yosemite
novel and that Squirrel and I were going into it. I was glad to find that
she knew you. I have not seen Prof. Le Conte. Perhaps he is stopping
at one of the other hotels.

Has Mrs. Rapley or Mr. Colby told you about our camping in the
spruce woods on the south rim of the Valley and of our walk at
daybreak to the top of the Sentinel Dome to see the sun rise out of the
crown peaks of beyond?

About a week ago at daybreak I started up the mountain near
Glacier Point to see Pohono in its upper woods and to study the kind
of life it lived up there. I had a glorious day and reached my cabin at
daylight by walking all night. Oh, what a night among those moon
shadows! It was one o'clock A.M., when I reached the top of the
Cathedral Rocks,—a most glorious twenty-two hours of life amid
nameless peaks and meadows and the upper cataracts of Pohono.

Mr. Hutchings told me next morning that I had done two or three
days' climbing in one and that I was shortening my life, but I had a
whole lifetime of enjoyment and I care but little for the arithmetical
length of my days. I can hardly realize that I have not yet seen you
here.

I thank you for sending me so many friends, but I am waiting for
you. I am going up the mountain soon to see your lily garden at the
top of Indian Canyon.

"Let the Pacific islands lie."

My love to Allie and all your boys and to the Doctor. Tell him that
I have been tracing glaciers in all the principal canyons towards the
summit.

>   Ever thine,
>   J. Muir
>   [*John Muir*][12]

ᴔ

>   [*Yosemite, August 7, 1870*]

[*Mrs. Carr*]

[First section of letter cut]

...whether my best home will be in Yosemite or with you or up in
the high snow in a strong cabin where I will be wholly with my work
beyond the possibilities of an interruption.

Tomorrow we set out for the Lyell Glacier in company with Le
Conte and his boys. We will be with them four or five days when they
will go on Monoward for Tahoe. I mean to set some stakes in a dozen
glaciers and gather some arithmetic for clothing my thoughts.

I hope you will not allow old H[*utchings*] or his picture agent,
Houseworth, to so gobble and bewool poor Agassiz that I will not
see him.

Remember me always to the Doctor and the boys and to Mrs.
Moore, and I am
ever yours,

>   John Muir

I will return to the Valley in about a week, if I don't get over-deep
in a crevass.

Later. Yours of Monday evening has just come. I am glad your boy
is so soon to feel mother home and its blessings. I hope to meet [*John*]
Torrey, although I will push iceward as before, but may get back in
time. I will enjoy Agassiz, and Tyndall even more. I'm sorry for poor
Stoddard. Tell him to come.

I'll see Mrs. H[*utchings*], perhaps, this evening and deliver your
message.

>   Farewell.
>   [*John Muir*][13]

◌

Yosemite, August 20, [*1870*]

Dear friend Mrs. Carr

I have just returned from a ten days' ramble with Prof. Le Conte
and his students in the beyond, and, oh, we have had a most glorious
season of terrestrial grace. I do wish I could ramble ten days of equal
size in very heaven, that I could compare its scenery with that of
Bloody Canyon and the Tuolumne Meadows and Lake Tenaya and
Mt. Dana. Our first camp after leaving the Valley was at Eagle Point,
overlooking the Valley on the north side, from which a much better
general view of the Valley and the high crest of the Sierra beyond is
obtained than from Inspiration Point. There we watched the long
shadows of sunset upon the living map at our feet, and, in the later
darkness half silvered by the moon, went far out of human cares and
human civilization. Our next camp was at Lake Tenaya, one of the
countless multitudes of starry gems that make this topmost mountain
land to sparkle like a sky. After moonrise Le Conte and I walked to
the lake-shore and climbed upon a big sofa-shaped rock that stood
islet-like a little way out in the shallow water, and here we found
another bounteous throne of earthly grace, and I doubt if John in
Patmos saw grander visions than we. And you were remembered there
and we cordially wished you with us. Our next sweet home was upon
the velvet gentian meadows of the South Tuolumne. Here we feasted
upon soda and burnt ashy cakes and stood an hour in a frigid rain
with our limbs bent forward like Lombardy poplars in a gale, but ere
sunset the black cloud departed, our shins were straightened at a
glowing fire, we forgot the cold and all about half-raw mutton and
alkaline cakes, the grossest of our earthly coils was shaken off, and
ere the last slant sunbeams left the dripping meadow and spiry mountain peaks we were again in the third alpine heaven and saw and
heard things equal in glory to the purest and best of Yosemite itself.
Our next camp was beneath a big gray rock at the foot of Mt. Dana.
Here we had another rainstorm, which drove us beneath our rock,
where we lay in complicated confusion, our forty limbs woven into a
knotty piece of tissue compact as felt.

Next day we worshipped upon high places on the brown cone of
Dana and returned to our rock. Next day walked among the flowers

and cascades of Bloody Canyon and camped at the lake. Rode next day to the volcanic cone nearest to the lake, and bade farewell to the party and climbed to the highest crater in the whole range south of the Mono Lake. Well, I shall not try to tell you anything, as it is unnecessary. Prof. Le Conte, whose company I enjoyed exceedingly, will tell you all. Ask him in particular to tell you about our camp-meeting on the Tenaya rock. I will send you a few choice mountain plant children by Mrs. Yelverton. If there is anything in particular that you want, let me know. Mrs. Yelverton will not leave the Valley for some weeks, and you have time to write. I am

Ever your friend,
J. M.
[John Muir][14]

∽

Oakland, October 2, [1870]

Dear John Muir

I write as usual with the whip of neglected things suspended over me, but I must tell you that Ned has gone to South America—sails from Boston this week (probably on Tuesday), to join the Bolivian Commercial and Colonization Company, Mr. A. D. Piper of San Francisco, President. Two years ago one Col. Church, well-known in Washington circles, got a grant or concession from Brazilian and Bolivian governments for the navigation of the waters of the upper Amazon, and Mr. A. D. Piper then at LaPaz and in the favor with the authorities, induced them to make a formal grant of sixty millions of acres on the Purus in what is known as the Department of Beni—for American colonization.

They have been slowly and carefully collecting their colony, made up mostly in Boston and Providence, have purchased a good steamer, take out a cargo (private owners), and will bring back Peruvian bark, cocoa, etc. They intend to make trips every two months. Ned went with Mrs. Piper, wife of the President, and one Mr. Barry, an old Californian family from Monroe, Wisconsin, who is employed by the company to select farming lands. Expense $100, from Boston to *Herndar City* on the Purus, found—time, inside of 4 weeks, to Para (mouth of Amazon), 10–12 days, 1000 miles steaming on Amazon, 800 on Purus about ten more. John Turner (the boy who put his pick into the chloride at Eberhardt or Keystone mine), and young Beckley, formerly from Madison, are the only persons I know of going from there this trip. John goes to explore the gold fields of the Beni.

I told Mrs. Piper (who goes to mother these two hundred young men, with a good German woman for nurse and another for seamstress) of John Muir's qualifications to bless such a colony, that he could invent anything from a churn to a cherub, and she thought maybe you would like to go *to the Andes* for scenery!

Soule, or somebody, has said you were really coming down. If so, we can talk things over. You will get first of all cheap and comfortable passage to the heart of the Andes. If you join the company (no pledges are required of you), you have 320 acres of land which you can locate anywhere on the grant not reserved for school purposes. I see from the *Sacramento Union* what an evening you had at Mirror Lake. Oh dear, dear! Give my love to Mrs. Yelverton and Hutchings. Lots of Madison people here now, Mr. and Mrs. Proudfit, Mrs. Williams and daughter you may have seen. *We* are very busy eating our way through the County Fairs, but I take time to covet your walks and think of you very often. Waterstons gone within the week, after one of the most considered and profitable summers I have known tourists to take. John is South Ameriky also, Al happy with nine birds and a rabbit. We need a little squirrel in this house.

Jeanne Carr[15]

∾

Squirrelville, Sequoia Co.,
Nut-Time, [*Autumn, 1870*]

Dear Mrs. Carr

Do behold the King in his glory, King Sequoia! Behold! Behold! seems all I can say. Some time ago I left all for Sequoia and have been and am at his feet, fasting and praying for light, for is he not the greatest light in the woods, in the world? Where are such columns of sunshine, tangible, accessible, terrestrialized? Well may I fast, not from bread, but from business, book-making, duty-going, and other trifles, and great is my reward already for the manly, treely sacrifice. What giant truths since coming to Gigantea, what magnificent clusters of Sequoic *becauses*. From here I cannot recite you one, for you are down a thousand fathoms deep in dark political quagg, not a burr-length less. But I'm in the woods, woods, woods, and they are in *me-ee-ee*. The King tree and I have sworn eternal love—sworn it without swearing, and I've taken the sacrament with Douglas squirrel, drank Sequoia wine, Sequoia blood, and with its rosy purple drops I am writing this woody gospel letter.

I never before knew the virtue of Sequoia juice. Seen with sun-beams in it, its color is the most royal of all royal purples. No wonder the Indians instinctively drink it for they know not what. I wish I was so drunk with Sequoical that I could preach the green brown woods to all the juiceless world, descending from this divine wilderness like a John [*the*] Baptist, eating Douglas squirrels and wild honey or wild anything, crying, Repent, for the Kingdom of Sequoia is at hand!

There is balm in these leafy Gileads,—pungent burrs and living King-juice for all defrauded civilization; for sick grangers and politicians; no need of Salt rivers. Sick or successful, come suck Sequoia and be saved.

Douglas squirrel is so pervaded with rosin and burr juice his flesh can scarce be eaten even by mountaineers—no wonder he is so charged with magnetism! One of the little lions ran across my feet the other day as I lay resting under a fir, and the effect was a thrill like a battery shock. I would eat him no matter how rosiny for the lightning he holds. I wish I could eat wilder things. Think of the grouse with balsam-scented crop stored with spruce buds, the wild sheep full of glacier meadow grass and daisies azure, and the bear burly and brown as Sequoia, eating pine-burrs and wasps stings and all; then think of the soft lightningless poultice-like pap reeking upon town tables. No wonder cheeks and legs become flabby and fungoid! I wish I were wilder, and so, bless Sequoia, I will be. There is at least a punky spark in my heart and it may blaze in this autumn gold, fanned by the King. Some of my grandfathers must have been born on a Muirland for there is heather in me, and tinctures of bog juices, that send me to *Cassiope,* and oozing through all my veins impel me unhaltingly through endless glacier meadows, seemingly the deeper and danker the better.

See Sequoia aspiring in the upper skies, every summit modeled in fine cycloidal curves as if pressed into unseen moulds, every bole warm in the mellow amber sun. How truly godful in mien! I was talking the other day with a duchess and was struck with the grand bow with which she bade me goodbye and thanked me for the glaciers I gave her, but this forenoon King Sequoia bowed to me down in the grove as I stood gazing and the highbred gestures of the lady seemed rude by contrast.

There goes Squirrel Douglas, the master-spirit of the tree-top. It has just occurred to me how his belly is buffy brown and his back silver gray. Ever since the first Adam of his race saw trees and burrs, his belly has been rubbing upon buff bark, and his back has been combed with silver needles. Would that some of you wise—terribly wise—social scientists might discover some method of living as true to nature as the buff people of the woods, running as free as the winds and waters among the burrs and filbert thickets of these leafy, mothery woods.

The sun is set and the star candles are being lighted to show me and Douglas squirrel to bed. Therefore, my Carr, goodnight. You say, "When are you coming down?" Ask the Lord—Lord Sequoia.

[*John Muir*][16]

∾

Tuolumne River, two miles below
La Grange,
November 4, [*1870*]

Dear friend Mrs. Carr

Yours of October 2 reached me a few days since. The Amazon and Andes have been in all my thoughts for many years, and I am sure that I shall meet them some day ere I die, or become settled and civilized and useful. I am obliged to you for all this information. I have studied many paths and plans for the interior of South America, but none so easy and sure ever appeared as this of your letter. I thought of landing at Guayaquil and crossing the mountains to the Amazon, floating to Para, subsisting on berries and quinine, but to steam along the palmy shores with company and comforts is perhaps more practical though not so pleasant. Hawthorne says that steam spiritualizes travel, but I think that it squarely degrades and materializes travel. However, flies and fevers have to be considered in this case. I am glad that Ned has gone. The woods of the Purus will be a grand place for the growth of men. It must be that I am going soon, for you have shown me the way. People say that my wanderings are very mazy and methodless, but they are all known to you in some way before I think of them. You are a prophet in the concerns of my little outside life, and pray, what says the spirit about my final escape from Yosemite? You saw me at these rock altars years ago, and I think I shall remain among them until you take me away. I reached this place last month by following the Merced out of the Valley and through all its canyons to the plains above Snelling,—a most glorious walk.

I intended returning to the Valley ere this, but Mr. Delaney, the man with whom I am stopping at present, would not allow me to leave before I had plowed his field, and so I will not be likely to see Yosemite again before January, when I shall have a grand journey over the snow.

Mrs. Yelverton told me before I started upon my river explorations that she would likely be in Oakland in two weeks, and so I made up a package for you of lily bulbs, cones, ferns, etc., but she wrote me a few days ago that she was still in the Valley.

I find that a portion of my specimens collected in the last two years and left at this place and Hopeton are not very well cared for, and I have concluded to send them to you.

I will ship them in a few days by express, and I will be down myself perhaps in about a year. If there is anything in these specimens that the Doctor can make use of in his lectures, tell him to do so freely, of course.

The purple of these plains and of this whole round sky is very impressively glorious after a year in the deep rocks. People all through-out this section are beginning to hear of Dr. Carr. He accomplishes a wonderful amount of work.

My love to Allie and to the Doctor, and I am ever most

Cordially yours,

John Muir

Address to *Snelling* for the next few months.[17]

∾

Near La Grange, California,
December 22, [1870]

Dear Mrs. Carr

It is so long since I have heard from you that I begin to think you have sent a letter to Yosemite. I am feeling lonely again, and require a word from you.

Some time ago Mr. Hutchings wrote me saying that he would require my shingle cabin for his sister, and so I am homeless again. I expected to pass the winter there, writing, sketching, etc., and in making exploratory raids back over the mountains in the snow, but Mr. Hutchings jumping my nest after expressly promising to keep it for me, has broken my pleasant lot of plans, and I am at work making new ones. Were it not that Mr. Hutchings owes me money and that I have a lot of loose notes and outline sketches to work up I should set out for South America at once. As it is, I shall very likely remain where I am for a few months and return to the mountains in the spring. I wish in particular to trace some of the upper Yosemite streams farther and more carefully than I have yet done, and I *shall* dip yet once more into the fathomless grandeur of the Valley.

I am in comfortable quarters at present within sight and hearing of the Tuolumne, on a smooth level once the bottom of a shallow lake-like expansion of the river where it leaves the slates.

Evening purple on the mountains seen through an ample gap up the Tuolumne is of terrestrial beauty, the purest and best. The sheet gold of the plain compositae will soon be lighted in the sun days of spring, deepening and glowing yet brighter as it spreads away over the sphered and fluted rock-waves of this old ocean bed. You must not fail to see the April gold of the Joaquin.

I send herewith a letter to Mrs. Yelverton in your care, as you will be likely to know where she is. I have just received a letter which she left for me at Snelling, giving an account of her fearful perils in the snow. It seems strange to me that I should not have known and felt her anguish in that terrible night, even at this distance. She told me that I ought to wait and guide her out, and I feel a kind of guiltiness in not doing so.

Since writing the above yours of Nov. 19th is received, directed to the "Tuolumne River, etc." You are "glad that I am kindly disposed towards South America *but* a year is a long time," etc. *But* to me a Yosemite year is a very little measure of time, or rather, a measureless and formless mass of time which can in no manner be geometrically or arithmetically dealt with. *But,* Mrs. Carr, why do you wish to cut me from California and graft me among the groves of the Purus. Please write the reason. This Pacific sunshine is hard to leave. If souls are allowed to go a rapping and visiting where they please I think that unbodied I will be found wallowing in California light.

If the bulbs were lost I will procure some more for you, if you do not send me up the Amazon before next fall.

[*John Muir*][18]

PART FOUR

1871–1872

*Keep your mind untrammelled and
pure. Go unfrictioned, unmeasured,
and God give you the true meaning
and interpretation of his mountains.*

Jeanne Carr

Writing the Truth About Yosemite

IN JANUARY JAMES HUTCHINGS, UNABLE TO FIND A SAWYER WITH Muir's skill, asked Muir to return to the mill. Muir agreed to work for Hutchings. Having forfeited his cottage, he built a room, a "hang-bird's hang-nest," under the gable at the north end of the sawmill. Muir wrote to Carr that he was once more in the glory of the Valley and committed himself to what he called a less than useful life studying Yosemite's living glaciers. Surely he could be spared for this experiment, following his instincts, interpreting the rocks, and learning from the floods, storms, and avalanches. Glaciers became his teachers. He sought the "heart of the world."

Part of what drove Muir was a natural baptism behind the upper Yosemite Fall at Sunnyside Bench. In April he went there to spend a night in prayer. As he gazed in a trance-like state while on the narrow rock shelf, a torrent of water struck him. Crouching low, holding his breath, and anchoring himself to the rock, Muir managed to jump behind ice wedged in the wall. Too wet to remain there, he climbed down and wrote to Carr about the blessing he received, about spiritual affinities, and about relations to rock and to water. Drawn into the family of nature, he found himself separated from the profane world and graced by the power of the mountains. He expected Carr would visit him during the summer of 1871, and he set aside mid-July for rambling with her.

While Muir waited for Carr, Ralph Waldo Emerson, James Bradley Thayer, and a group of ten explorers left Boston by train and arrived in California in the spring of 1871. Emerson, who had befriended the Carrs while on a lecture circuit that took him to Madison, Wisconsin, was unable to visit them in Oakland on his way to the Valley because Jeanne Carr was busy with commencement at a San Mateo school where she taught botany. Carr wrote to Emerson, who was sixty-eight, about Muir, who was thirty-three, and trusted they would meet in the Valley.

A letter from Carr to Muir noted that Emerson would be in the Valley in a few days.

Emerson and his companions stayed at Leigid's Hotel on the Yosemite floor, where from the veranda they gazed across the Valley. Emerson remarked that Yosemite exceeded the brag about it. They climbed to Casa Nevada, perched on rocks below Nevada Falls, and returned in the late afternoon to sit on the porch and discuss philosophy. Too shy to approach Emerson, Muir sent a note entreating him to extend his stay in the Valley to experience closer communion and join him in a month's worship with nature beyond Yosemite. In response Emerson and Thayer rode to Hutchings's Mill, where they found Muir. Impressed with Muir, his hang-nest, his herbarium and sketches, and his discipleship and enthusiasm, Emerson visited him daily for "fine, clear talk." Muir proposed a camping trip into the heart of the mountains. The most, however, that Muir could expect was to accompany Emerson and his party on their way out of the Valley to Clark's Station (now known as Wawona) on the condition that Emerson camp one night with him in Mariposa Grove.

Emerson's excitement at camping out with Muir was dampened by Thayer and others who feared for Emerson's health and safety and squelched the plan. They directed Emerson to Galen Clark's hostelry, though Muir was certain the fresh air and pine boughs were better for him than carpet dust. That evening Emerson spoke few words, perhaps thinking about the years that tempered his body and spirit, that forced him to abandon a night under the Sequoia with Muir. The following morning the party rode to Mariposa Grove, where Emerson and Muir walked together in silent communion. At Clark's request Emerson chose and named a Sequoia. He called it "Samoset," after an eastern sachem. At three o'clock the group departed. Emerson rode in the rear of the party to look back upon Muir as he stood alone on the edge of the forest.[1]

Emerson stopped briefly in Oakland on his way to San Francisco to see Carr. A dense fog crept into Oakland that night and in confusion he stumbled to the back door of her home by mistake. Having heard the commotion, Carr found Emerson standing wrapped tightly in his cloak. He declined her invitation to visit as he had to follow his wife and daughter who had already taken the ferry to San Francisco, but he did not want to pass Oakland without thanking her for the letter to Muir.

Emerson was delighted with the conversation he and Muir shared in the Valley; and Carr was pleased that Emerson confirmed Muir's exceptional spirit. Muir had mentioned Brooks to Emerson, and Emerson asked Carr for more information about Brooks and his ideas on nature.

Muir wrote several letters to Emerson and sent plant specimens to him. In February 1872 Emerson responded that he had been unable to write sooner. A short list of great names Emerson kept entitled "My Men" included John Muir, whose name was the last on the list. Muir thought of Emerson as a Sequoia, the most sequoia-like soul he ever met.

While Carr's botany class put up plants in herbariums, she wrote to Muir. Lewis Francis, the president of the University of Vermont at Burlington, was in the Valley. He was, according to Carr, not among the elect. Guiding uninitiated tourists like Francis disturbed Carr, and she pitied Muir if this became his full-time occupation. If forced to hear insults directed toward nature she was certain she would pitch the culprits off a cliff. Carr's belief in election grew out of Calvinism, eight generations of Puritan ancestors, and a childhood of Sabbaths spent at the Castleton Congregational Church, where between Sunday services she wandered among her forebears' graves adjacent to the church. At the root of her understanding of election was predestination, and in the complex of Christian tradition and nature religion nature was illuminated in the spirit, the flesh, and the intellect of the beholder. This was not something one could obtain but something delivered by God through grace. Carr called the elect by different names: the beautiful ones, the immortals, nature's truest and most devoted disciples, refined gold. The titles all meant the same thing. Election gave the beholders access to the true meaning of nature (the revelation of God in His works) and privileged them to receive this message through an act of communion in God's holy temple—the mountains and Yosemite Valley. For the uninitiated Carr sought reform.

Ezra Carr's position at the University of California enabled the Carrs to expand their educational and agricultural reform objectives intended to dignify labor with knowledge and enrich it with thought. They were committed to technical and agricultural education that provided true and noble opportunities for the working class. Jeanne sought to expand female literacy and vocational education as a means to prepare women for their role in society. Together the Carrs endeavored to develop a practical curriculum at the University of California that emphasized agricultural and mechanical training rather than a liberal education.[2]

Letters and visits to Muir in the Valley continued to knit together the elect. A note from Carr to Muir introduced Henry [Harry] Edwards, who according to her was one of nature's devoted disciples. Edwards visited Muir in the Valley in July. An actor whose avocation was entomology, Edwards possessed what was regarded as one of the finest private collections of butterflies and beetles in the world. Muir collected butterflies for Edwards in the High Sierra and provided him with rare species unknown in the Valley. In a letter Edwards wrote to Muir in August he noted that Carr delivered a small box of butterflies Muir had found for him. The box contained four species of butterflies new to Edwards's collection and two that were new to entomology (a bright crimson copper one from Cathedral Peak and a small bluish one). Edwards thanked Muir for the gifts from the mountains. He hoped Muir would find truth through his labors for his own satisfaction and for the recognition of kindred spirits. In 1881 Edwards named the butterfly *Thecla muiri* after Muir.[3]

A letter of good will and confirmation of good works written by Mrs. Robert C. Waterston to Jeanne Carr in July mentioned receipt of several letters Muir sent to Carr. Carr often shared Muir's letters with others. His words had a gospel-like effect on Waterston, and her response assured Carr that all she saw in Muir was true. Fellowship among the elect called for witnessing, testimonials the external response, and peace the ultimate goal. External confirmation was benevolent, however; Muir was expecting a visit from Carr. He was dazed when she wrote she could not get away from Oakland. Escape from the power of the mountains was impossible for him, and he faced the loneliness that accompanied him on his mountain walk later that year. In early September, however, John Daniel Runkle, president of the Massachusetts Institute of Technology, traveled for five days with Muir through canyons to the névés beneath the summits and into the mountains. Runkle was convinced of the truth of Muir's glacial theory and urged him to draft his glacial system of Yosemite for the Boston Academy. Writing would validate Muir's work. Muir, however, regarded writing for publication as something that kept him from the study of nature. He discussed his ambivalence about writing with Carr. His friends badgered him to write. What did she think he should do? With clarity and vision Carr began to apply pressure to Muir's genius. She advised him to use coarse lined paper and a broad pen and begin.

Muir explored the upper tributaries of the Cascade and Tamarac streams and the basin of Yosemite Creek in October. During his ramblings in the Yosemite high country he discovered a living glacier at Red Mountain in the Merced group where a silted stream, "glacial mud," was suspended from a large field of blue ice. From letters written to friends he pieced together an article that he submitted to Horace Greeley's *New York Daily Tribune.* "Yosemite Glaciers: The Ice Streams of the Great Valley, Their Progress and Present Condition. Scenes Among the Glaciers Beds. (From an Occasional Correspondent of the Tribune.) Yosemite Valley, Cal., September 28, 1871," was published on December 5. For that which temporarily deterred him from the empirical study of nature Muir earned two hundred dollars.

Muir's ambition was to provide truth about Yosemite Valley; but his article initiated a controversy between him and Josiah Whitney, State Geologist of California, who believed Yosemite was the result of prehistoric cataclysmic fall. Muir's theory did not prove to be entirely correct; however, ice was a primary agent in the creation of the Valley. Muir consulted Louis Agassiz's hypothesis that stated there had been one Ice Age that swept over the northern continents in support of his evidence that Sierra glaciers were remnants of that glaciation. The glaciers Muir studied were actually generated by climatic conditions in the Sierra. They were independent glaciers. Whitney was nonetheless wrong.

In the heart of the mountains while he studied glaciers and rocks, Muir found a small lake hidden away. He called it Shadow Lake. Caught in a snowstorm on Mount Lyell, he retreated to the lake and stayed the night by a boulder. He fashioned bark snowshoes and three days later skipped over the snow back to the Valley, where problems with Hutchings persisted. Muir wrote to Carr that he would have no further dealings with Hutchings, whose quarrel with Muir seemed to be over the time he spent away from the sawmill chasing glaciers and guiding the many friends sent to him by Carr and others. Muir confessed that he felt Hutchings had used him shabbily, attempting to hold back wages, and he left the sawmill to spend the winter as a caretaker at Black's Hotel. In his cabin at Black's he began to write. On New Year's Day 1872 he prepared "cascade jubilee," thoughts on a mid-December storm, a manuscript he sent to Carr with a December/January letter. He asked her to edit it, cut off rough edges, and wedge in good words. "Yosemite in Winter" appeared in the *New York Daily Tribune* in January.

∾

Yosemite, [*Spring, 1871*]

My dear friend Mrs. Carr

"The Spirit" has again led me into the wilderness, in opposition to all counter attractions, and I am once more in the glory of the Yosemite.

Your very cordial invitation to your home reached me as I was preparing to ascend and my whole being was possessed with visions of snowy forests of the pine and spruce, and of mountain spires beyond, pearly and half transparent, reaching into heavens blue not purer than themselves.

In company with another young fellow whom I persuaded to walk, I left the plains just as the first gold sheets were being outspread. My first plan was to follow the Tuolumne upward as I had followed the Merced downward, and, after reaching Hetch Hetchy Valley, which has about the same altitude as Yosemite, and spending a week or so in sketching and examining its falls and rocks, to cross the high mountains past the west end of the Hoffman Range and go down into Yosemite by Indian Canyon, passing thus a glorious month with the mountains and all their snows and crystal brightness, and all the nameless glories of their magnificent winter; but my plan went agley. I lost a week's sleep by the pain of a sore hand, and I became unconfident in my strength when measured against weeks of wading in snow up to my neck. Therefore I reluctantly concluded to push directly for the Valley and Tamarac.

Our journey was just a week in length, including one day of rest in the Crane's Flat Cabin. Some of our nights were cold, and we were hungry once or twice. We crossed the snow-line on the flank of Pilot Peak Ridge six or eight miles below Crane's Flat. From Crane's Flat to [*the*] brim of the Valley the snow was about five feet in depth, and as it was not frozen or compacted in any way we of course had a splendid season of wading.

I wish that you could have seen the edge of the snow-cloud which hovered, oh, so soothingly, down to the grand Pilot Peak brows, discharging its heaven-begotten snows with such unmistakable gentleness and moving perhaps with conscious love from pine to pine as if bestowing separate and independent blessings upon each. In a few hours we climbed under and into this glorious storm-cloud. What a harvest of crystal flowers and what wind songs were gathered from the spiry firs and the long fringy arms of the Lambert pine! We could not see far before us in the storm, which lasted until some time in the night, but as I was familiar with the general map of the mountain we had no difficulty in finding our way.

Crane's Flat Cabin was buried, and we had to grope about for the door. After making a fire with some cedar rails, I went out to watch the coming-on of the darkness, which was most impressively sublime. Next morning was every way the purest creation I ever beheld. The little flat, spot-like in the massive spiring woods, was in splendid vesture of universal white, upon which the grand forest-edge was minutely repeated and covered with a close sheet of snow flowers.

Some mosses grow luxuriantly upon the dead generations of their own species. The common snow flowers belong to the sky and in storms are blown about like ripe petals in an orchard. They settle on the ground, the bottom of the atmospheric sea, like mud or leaves in a lake, and upon this soil, this field of broken sky flowers, grows a luxuriant carpet of crystal vegetation complete and ripe in a single night.

I never before knew that these mountain snow plants were so variable and abundant, forming such bushy clumps and thickets and palmy, ferny groves. Wading waist-deep, I had a fine opportunity for observing them, but they shrink from human breath,—not the only flowers which do so,—evidently not made for man, neither the flowers composing the snow which came drifting down to us broken and dead, nor the more beautiful crystals which vegetate upon them. A great many storms have come to these mountains since I passed them, and they can hardly be less than ten feet; at the altitude of Tamarac still more.

The weather here is balmy now, and the falls are glorious. Three weeks ago the thermometer at sunrise stood at 12 degrees.

I have repaired the mill and dam, and the stream is in no danger of drying up and is more dammed than ever.

Today has been cloudy and rainy. Tissiack and Starr King are grandly dipped in white cloud.

I sent you my plants by express. I am sorry that my Yosemite specimens are not with the others.

I left a few notes with Mrs. Yelverton when I left the Valley in the fall. I wish that you would ask her, if you should see her, where she left it, as Mrs. Hutchings does not know.

I shall be happy to join [*Charles Warren*] Stoddard in anything whatever. Mrs. H[*utchings*] had a letter from him lately, part of which she read to me. And now, Mrs. Carr, you must see the upper mountains and meadows back of Yosemite. You have seen nothing as yet, and I will guide you a whole summer if you wish. I am very happy here and cannot break for the Andes just yet.

Squirrel is at my knee. She says, "Tell Mrs. Carr to come here tomorrow and tell her to bring her little boy when she comes." If you will come, she says that she will guide you to the falls and give you lots of flowers. Mrs. H[*utchings*] tells me to say that she has received a very kind letter from you, which she will answer. Sends thus her kindest regards. If she can find a chance, she will send bulbs of lily by mail.

I have been nearly blind since I crossed the snow.

Give my kindest regards to all your homeful and to my friends.

I am always

> Yours most cordially,
> J. M.
> [*John Muir*][4]

∾

> Midnight [*Yosemite*],
> [*April 3, 1871*]

O Mrs. Carr, that you could be here to mingle in this night moon glory! I am in the Upper Yosemite Falls and can hardly calm to write, but, from my first baptism an hour ago, you have been so present that I must try to fix you a written thought.

In the afternoon I came up the mountain here with a blanket and a piece of bread to spend the night in prayer among the spouts of the fall. But now what can I say more than wish again that you might expose your soul to the rays of this heaven?

Silver from the moon illumines this glorious creation which we term falls and has laid a magnificent double prismatic bow at its base. The tissue of the falls is delicately filmed on the outside like the substance of spent clouds, and the stars shine dimly through it. In the solid shafted body of the falls is a vast number of passing caves, black and deep, with close white convolving spray for sills and shooting comet shoots above and down their sides like lime crystals in a cave, and every atom of the magnificent being, from the thin silvery crest that does not dim the stars to the inner arrowy hardened shafts that strike onward like thunderbolts in sound and energy, all is life and spirit, every bolt and spray feels the hand of God. O the music that is blessing me now! The sun of last week has given the grandest notes of all the yearly anthem . . . than you might read the glory that I cannot write. The notes of this nights song echo in every fibre and all the grandeur of form is engraved not in sheet perspective.

I said that I was going to stop here until morning and pray a whole blessed night with the falls and the moon, but I am too wet and must go down. An hour or two ago I went out somehow on a little seam that extends along the wall behind the falls. I suppose I was in a trance, but I can positively say that I was in the body, for it is sorely battered and wetted. As I was gazing past the thin edge of the fall and away through beneath the column to the brow of the rock, some heavy splashes of water struck me, driven hard against the wall. Suddenly I was darkened; down came a section of the outside tissue composed of spent comets. I crouched low, holding my breath, and, anchored to some angular flakes of rock, took my baptism with moderately good faith.

When I dared to look up after the swaying column admitted light, I pounced behind a piece of ice which was wedged tight in the wall, and I no longer feared being washed off, and steady moonbeams slanting past the arching meteors gave me confidence to escape to this snug place where McChesney and I slept one night, where I had a fire to dry my socks. This rock shelf extending behind the falls is about five hundred feet above the base of the fall on the perpendicular rock-face.

How little do we know of ourselves, of our profoundest attractions and repulsions, of our spiritual affinities! How interesting does man become, considered in his relations to the spirit of this rock and water! How significant does every atom of our world become amid the influences of those beings unseen, spiritual, angelic mountaineers that so throng these pure mansions of crystal foam and purple granite!

I cannot refrain from speaking to this little bush at my side and to the spray-drops that come to my paper and to the individual sands of the slope I am sitting upon. Ruskin says that the idea of foulness is essentially connected with what he calls dead unorganized matter. How cordially I disbelieve him tonight! and were he to dwell awhile among the powers of these mountains, he would forget all dictionary differences between the clean and the unclean and he would lose all memory and meaning of the diabolical, sin-begotten term, *foulness*.

Well, I must go down. I am disregarding all of the Doctor's physiology in sitting here in this universal moisture.

Farewell to you and to all the beings about us! I shall have a glorious walk down the mountains in this thin white light, over the open brows grayed with *Selaginella* and through the thick black shadow caves in the live oaks all stuck full of snowy lances of moonlight.

[*John Muir*][5]

ℚ

Yosemite, April 15, [*1871*]

Dear friend

Your note of Feb. 14th with tidings of your sorrow has just reached me. You know that you have my innermost sympathy and I am glad to see that you so healthily and happily look upon Death.

My own views concerning death have changed very much since I walked with Nature and I almost think of copying some thoughts for you from my notebook.

Mrs. Hutchings and I were speaking of death sorrows some time ago. She said that in her opinion those were the happiest who possessed the greatest number of large griefs. I wish that *you* were with us among these mountain powers, we would go to a shadowy place and have a glorious mingling of death thoughts, but I will not try to write. Farewell.

Ever your friend,
John Muir[6]

∽

[*Oakland*], May 1, [*1871*]

Dear John

I think you have another letter from me than the February one to which this is an answer—but never mind—they are all alike stupid and soulless. Thanks for yours. I am feeling as glad for you as possible since Mr. Emerson will be in the Valley in a few days—and in your hands I hope and trust, the dear old singer in the places where we have sung his song. I have not seen him yet, but shall after his return. Have been so driven with work and company no spiritual influence could be felt. Else I could have gone straight to him with my eyes shut.

There are doctors enough in San Francisco this week to physic the universe, and my particular doctor is lost in them. So lost that although he is going "'forinst" Diablo this week to lecture—won't take me with him.

Dry, windy, dusty—your *moonlight* letter was a beam from the upper sky—I take it out into the cool dewy moonlights—where the large oaks are looking their beautifullest and sitting down upon a root think it over! I suppose if you are gone over the fall, John, some button or rag would have told the story, but I should have felt that you were safe and always to be found in those parts—I wish the Government would make you Life Guardian of the Valley, and perhaps they will when Galen Clark dies.

Oh, we have a delightful letter from Ned—dear fellow, the expedition went pretty much to pieces before they reached Manaos, but Jack Turner and the pluckiest ones go on and are in sight of the Andes. We shall go, I am sure of it. Last Sunday I had a visit from Prof. Esmark, the Scandinavian Agassiz, a dear old naturalist at home with snakes and tarantulas. Mrs. T. with five children in her flossy mud house was making preparations for a trip to Christiania. Are you in the mill? I shall send Mr. Emerson a note to you—or about you. Am off to San Mateo this P.M. where I have a class in Botany. I find when I get up the canyons where *Aquilegia* is, that I feel Vermonty and comforted. My love to Mrs. Hutchings and the children. And I am always,

Your friend,

Jeanne Carr[7]

∾

Yosemite Valley,
Monday night, [*May 8, 1871*]

Mr. R. W. Emerson

Dear Sir

I received today a letter from Mrs. Professor Ezra Carr of Oakland, California stating that you were in the Valley and that she expected to see you on your return. Also she promised that she would write you here and send you to me. I was delighted at the thought of meeting you but have just learned that you contemplate leaving the Valley in a day or two.

Now Mr. Emerson I do most cordially protest against your going away so soon, and so also I am sure do all your instincts and affinities. I trust that you will not "outweary their yearnings." Do not thus drift away with the mob while the Spirits of these rocks and waters hail you after long waiting as their kinsman and persuade you to closer communion.

But now if fate or one of those mongrel and misshapen organizations called parties compel you to leave for the present, I shall hope for some other fullness of time to come for you.

If you will call at Mr. Hutchings' mill I will give you as many of Yosemite and high Sierra plants as you wish as specimens.

I invite you join me in a months worship with Nature in the high temples of the great Sierra crown beyond our holy Yosemite. It will cost you nothing save the time and very little of that for you will be mostly in Eternity.

And now once more, in the name of Mounts Dana and Gibbs of the grand glacial hieroglyphics of Toulumne Meadows and Bloody canyon, in the name of a hundred glacial lakes of a hundred glacial daisy gentian meadows. In the name of a hundred cascades that barbarous visitors never see. In the name of the grand upper forests of *Picea amabilis* and *P. grandis,* and in the name of all the spirit creatures of these rocks and of this whole spiritual atmosphere. Do not leave us now with most cordial regards I am yours in Nature

John Muir[8]

∾

[*San Mateo*], May 16, [*1871*]

Dear John Muir

Coming in last night from a hard day's work in examining classes at the Girls' High School, who should I find but Mr. Emerson, and of course you know the rest. How weariness fled and my delight was full, you do not need to be told. But if there is any joy of angels to be had in the flesh, it is that of finding your soul "confirmed in its faith through the soul of another." And so, dear friend, my joy *in you* was full, and I laugh to think how they go up to the mountains, the beautiful ones, to find *you* in the confessional, the only soul I know whom the mountains fully own and bless.

Mr. Emerson says he wants to know Mr. Brooks more than ever since seeing you—I have laid up in my heart so much that he told me of his trip, never have I heard him so delightful in conversation, his silver speech flowed on and on and it was hard to remember engagements, as we both were compelled to do.

I wait to talk with you about it. There are *more people* Yosemite bound, among them Mr. and Mrs. *Libby,* friends of mine and of McChesneys. Mc having spoken of you with great enthusiasm they asked me for a letter to you.
[Remainder of letter lost]

[*Jeanne C. Carr*][9]

∾

San Mateo, May 24, [*1871*]

Dear John Muir

My botanical class are all sitting around me busy in putting up their plants, but as this is "silent hour" I can get in a little conversation with you. Your two good letters were mailed at the same time, and I found not one but many crumbs of comfort therein. I have already written you of Mr. Emerson's enthusiasm for the Valley and for yourself.

I see among the newspaper arrivals that of the President of the University of Vermont at Burlington, *Lewis Francis,* who will doubtless appear among the mob of visitors and is better worth than most who go—though not one of the initiated. I pity you in my inmost heart, if you do make guiding a business—for even here I feel as if some one were calling my mother bad names when I meet the returning squadrons and hear their comments upon the trip. If I were forced to hear her insulted to her face I should be pitching people over those cliffs—and giving them the only impressions possible to such.

Yes, my friend, I know the long Astronomy will bring the ages of peace and perfectness—and I can wait, am of the waiting kind—but the unnaturalness of my sorrow wears into me deeper and deeper. I hate to be obliged *to reason* myself into comforting assurances. I *feel* that the education we are getting is at too awful a price to him through whom it has come, if I were only sure it lay in the *line of his promotion* I would be *joyful*. The American Institute, New York City, have written Dr. Carr to make arrangements for an extensive exhibition of California products at their annual fair in the fall. We hope to accomplish it. I wish to have sections of woods, cones, etc. and Mr. Hutchings told the writer of the letter that he knew of a tree very near a stream from which a fine Sequoia section could be obtained. I wish you would ascertain where it is and what the cost of obtaining such a section would be.

If there was time I would make a collection of California flowers, putting them up in an attractive form. It is dry and flowerless here. My girls made good collections for six weeks, and their volumes were charming. I might have made a fine show of Boraginaceae and Compositae had I known I should need them.

Next week I go to Sacramento to attend a school anniversary, taking Benicia on my way. After that a short pause. Dr. Carr's vacation will come July 9th (if it comes at all) so there is no prospect of his getting into the Valley earlier. If I can ride up with Allie I shall not wait for him.

Meanwhile tell the beloved creatures whose blood I feel in all my veins—creatures of the Rocks, the Waters, the Woods, the Meadows, those short-lived beings of a day, and the Immortals, Mrs. H[*utchings*] and Squirrel (the little "half and half") that their true lover burns toward them in longing and desire.

As for you, John, the Ages to come have lives on lives for us to enjoy in company, and it will be so easy to be *nourished* and *trans-*

ported that of all that we need take no thought. So out of this world of vehicles and victuals, I send you greeting, as in that I shall send you grace.

Jeanne Carr[10]

∾

[Yosemite], Thursday eve., June 22,
[1871]

Dear friend Mrs. Carr

Amid all Yosemite things there is this constant thought—your early coming.

I hope to see the mill-race dry in one or two weeks when I will be ready for the high Sierra and hope that you will be ready about that time for a month of rambling, a month containing a greater number of days than was ever heard of in rhyme or reason.

I expect to be free from this confounded mill about the first or second week of next month, and you must be here to go with me to a thousand places that I wish to show you. A little Scotch photographer will go with us to procure some sun pictures, but he will not mar our enjoyments. You will require one pack animal to carry a small light tent, and blankets, bread, etc. You can obtain all necessary provisions here.

Mr. Libby is to purchase a few small articles for me, perhaps you can bring them in.

Now, Mrs. Carr, come. A thousand voices are calling from many a forest and stream and meadow of the grand Sierra crown. Bring your Doctor and Allie if you possibly can, and any of your other friends if you cannot possibly help it.

We will have a season of unmeasured bliss, and I am stupid with the whole prospect.

I spoke to Mr. Hutchings about the section of Sequoia, and he said that he knew nothing whatever about the matter, which statement is doubtless entirely correct. I then wrote to Galen Clark, and he informed me that a section fourteen feet in length by about fifteen or twenty in dia. was cut from the Fresno grove last year and hauled to Stockton at an expense of about $2500.00. The Fresno grove can be reached by wagon, and a section procured at less expense than from the Mariposa or Calaveras groves. Of the section taken from the Fresno grove last season, only the bark and a small portion of the wood was taken, in small numbered sections like staves.

The Libby party left the Valley Tuesday morning. I was sorry to see them go so soon. I liked most of the party, especially Mrs. and Mr. Libby and perhaps Mrs. Hoyt and Miss Birmingham. Tell Libby that I am very sorry that I did not run away from the mill and go with them to Eagle Point and Mt. Hoffman.

I seldom see Mrs. Hutchings now, but I know that she would like to go with us. I fear she will not get away. She spends her spare moments in painting Yosemite flowers.

I shall be nervously anxious about our ramble until I verily behold you here. Remember me to the Doctor and Allie and all my friends. I wish Le Conte could come.

If you see Mrs. Yelverton before you start for the Valley I wish you would ask her about a notebook that I left with her last fall and which I have not since heard of.

[*John Muir*][11]

Oakland, June 30, [*1871*]

My dear John

In our lower world Mr. [*Henry*] Edwards, who brings you this note, is accounted one of Nature's truest and most devoted disciples. You will take pleasure in introducing him to your heavenly bugs and butterflies, and the winged dragons that hover over those hot breathing springs "in the beyond." I do not know how long he proposes to sojourn there, but make the most of the time, for he has the keys to the Kingdom.

And I am always

Your friend,
Jeanne C. Carr

That little bug who inhabits the "slew" between Hutchings and the mill (and which we once needed a skiff to pass over) is probably waiting for Mr. Edwards. *Found in grass roots.*

J. C. C.[12]

∾

71 Chester Square, Boston,
July 10, 1871

Dear Mrs Carr

On my return a few days ago from a journey I found a letter
directed by you, and containing two letters from Mr. Muir to yourself.
I searched in vain for any word from yourself, and as the letter was
postmarked "Boston" I presume you gave them hurriedly to some
friend on his way here. I thank you much for the privilege of reading
these letters—they are poems of great and exquisite beauty—worthy
to be written out of a heart whose close communion with nature
springs to a perfect love.

> Too near to God for doubt or fear,
> He shares the eternal calm.

It is delightful to me to know that there is such a soul among those
wonderful "sky ceiled rocks," amid those great visions, the great
white throne of the Central Dome.

> I feel His glory who could make a world,
> Yet in the lost depth of the wilderness
> Leave not a flower unfinished.

What rest, what perfect trust, we ought to feel in such a Father of
Nature, Soul, and Spirit.

I trust such healing wings have closed around your wounded spirit
and carried you up to the serene heights of Peace. You can hardly
resist the call to the Yosemite. How I wish I could join you there, with
Mr. Muir for a guide. I am glad he met Mr. Emerson. I only wonder
how Mr. E[merson]. could resist camping out under the Great Trees.

A year has passed since we were at the Yosemite—a year—it
seems hardly a day. I have a picture of the Sentinel Rock, hanging
opposite my room. It is by Mr. Shapleigh, who was in the Valley
with us. I chose it from all his sketches and call it my Rock. It is
indeed the Rock which is higher than I, and typifies many things

spiritual and eternal, while recalling the great original at whose foot we dwelt.

I should like to keep Mr. Muir's letters until I hear from you again, so do not enclose them—they are safe and much prized.

Mr. Waterston and I have just returned from a five weeks' trip to the Green Mountains, where we have enjoyed ourselves very highly. We spent a day or two to Brandon, but unfortunately Charlie Sanderson had not arrived at his cottage. We walked to it and looked in at the window and saw white muslin curtains, a print of Beethoven and other tokens of its master's pure and peaceful soul. I slipped a card under the door and took a rosebud from a bush near it. A note from Perabo tells me he is just going to join C. S. there. I met Mrs. Mary Parkman this spring and spoke to her of my having seen you in California. She did not know where you were residing. She desired me to give you her kind regards and remembered with interest your kindness and regard for her husband. Mr. Waterston met Ole Bull one evening at a Club where he seemed very bright and happy—the baby must seem like a grandchild to him, as indeed it should be.

We returned from the closing exercises of the schools, as Mr. Waterston is on the committee and we have just entertained at our house the graduating class of the Everett School—55 girls—a rose garden of girls they looked in their white muslins. How does your University and various interests progress? Mr. Waterston had a very interesting letter from Mr. Bacon lately, who writes many pleasant things. I wish Oakland was not three thousand miles off!

So they sentenced Mrs. Fair—it was more than I expected. If anyone deserves capital punishment it would seem to be in such a case, and yet—well, God knows how to deal with sinners better than we do.

Mrs. Howison is out of town. I saw her bright face just before we all went away. Hoping to hear from you soon, we send many best loves. I go this week to Newport to stay with my sister, but our letters are sent here.

> Ever yours,
> C. L. W[aterston]
> [Mrs. Robert C. Waterston][13]

∿

Yosemite, August 13, [*1871*]

Dear friend,

I was so stunned and dazed by your last that I have not been able to write anything. I was sure that you were coming, and you cannot come; and Mr. King, the artist, left me the other day and I am done with Hutchings, and I am lonely. Well it must be wait, for although there is no common human reason why I should not see you and civilization in Oakland, I cannot escape from the powers of the mountains. I shall tie some flour and a blanket behind my saddle and return to the Mono region and try to decide some questions that require undisturbed thought. There I will stalk about on the summit slates of Dana and Gibbs and Lyell, reading new chapters of glacial manuscript and more if I can. Then, perhaps, I will follow the Tuolumne down to the Hetch Hetchy Yosemite; then, perhaps, follow every Yosemite stream back to its smallest source in the mountains of the Lyell group and the Cathedral group and the Obelisk and Mt. Hoffman. This will, perhaps, be my work until the coming of the winter snows, when I will probably find a sheltered rock nook where I can make a nest of leaves and mosses and doze until spring.

I expect to be entirely alone in these mountain walks, and, notwithstanding the glorious portion of daily bread which my soul will receive in these fields where only the footprints of God are seen, the gloamin' will be lonely, but I will cheerfully pay the price of friendship and *all* besides.

I suppose that you have seen Mr. King, who kindly carried some [*butter*]flies for Mr. Edwards. I thought you would easily see him or let him know that you had his specimens. I collected most of them upon Mt. Hoffman, but was so busy in assisting Reilly that I could not do much in butterflies. Hereafter I shall be entirely free.

The purples and yellows begin to come in the green of our groves, and the rocks have the autumn haze, and the water songs are at their lowest hushings; young birds are big as old ones; and is it true that these are Bryant's Melancholy Days? I don't know, I will not think, but I will go above these brooding days to the higher, brighter mountains.

Farewell.

Cordially ever yours,
John Muir

I shall hope to hear from you soon. I will come down some of the Valley canyons occasionally for letters.

I am sorry that you are so laden with University cares. I think that you and the Doctor do more than your share.

Do you know anything about this Liebig's extract of meat? I would like to carry a year's provisions in the form of condensed bread and meat, and I have been thinking perhaps all that I want is in the market.[14]

∾

Yosemite, September 8, [*1871*]

Dearest friend Mrs. Carr

I am sorry that King made you uneasy about me. He does not understand me as you do, and you must not heed him so much. He thinks that I am melancholy and above all that I require polishing. I feel sure that if you were here to see how happy I am and how ardently I am seeking a knowledge of the rocks, you could not call me away but would gladly let me go with only God and his written rocks to guide me. You would not think of calling me to make machines or a home, or of rubbing me against other minds, or of setting me up for measurement. No, dear friend, you would say: "Keep your mind untrammelled and pure. Go unfrictioned, unmeasured, and God give you the true meaning and interpretation of his mountains."

You know that for the last three years I have been ploddingly making observations about this Valley and the high mountain region to the east of it, drifting broodingly about and taking in every natural lesson that I was fitted to absorb. In particular the great Valley has always kept a place in my mind. How did the Lord make it? What tools did He use? How did He apply them and when? I considered the sky above it and all of its opening canyons, and studied the forces that came in by every door that I saw standing open, but I could get no light. Then I said: "You are attempting what is not possible for you to accomplish. Yosemite is the *end* of the grand chapter; if you would learn to read it, go commence at the beginning." Then I went above to the alphabet valleys of the summits, comparing canyon with canyon, with all their varieties of rock-structure and cleavage and the comparative size and slope of the glaciers and waters which they contained; also the grand congregations of rock-creations was present to me, and I studied their forms and sculpture. I soon had a key to every Yosemite rock and perpendicular and sloping wall. The grandeur of these forces and their glorious results overpower me and inhabit my whole being. Waking or sleeping, I have no rest. In dreams I read blurred sheets of glacial writing, or follow lines of cleavage, or struggle with the difficulties of some extraordinary rock-form. Now it is clear that woe is me if I do not drown this tendency towards nervous prostration by constant labor in working up the details of this whole question. I have been down from the upper rocks only three days and am hungry for exercise already.

Prof. [*John Daniel*] Runkle, president of the Boston Institute of Technology, was here last week, and I preached my glacial theory to him for five days, taking him into the canyon of the Valley and up among the grand glacier wombs and pathways of the summit. He was fully convinced of the truth of my readings and urged me to write out the glacial system of Yosemite and its tributaries for the Boston Academy of Science. I told him that I meant to write my thoughts for my own use and that I would send him the manuscript, and if he and his wise scientific brothers thought it of sufficient interest they might publish it.

He is going to send me some instruments, and I mean to go over all the glacier basins carefully, working until driven down by the snow. In winter I can make my drawings and maps and write out notes. So you see that for a year or two I will be very busy. I have settled with Hutchings and have no dealings with him now.

I think that next spring I will have to guide a month or two for pocket money, although I do not like the work. I suppose I might live for one or two seasons without work. I have five hundred dollars here, and I have been sending home money to my sisters and brothers,— perhaps about twelve or fifteen hundred dollars,—and a man in Canada owes me three or four hundred dollars more, which I suppose I could get if I was in need, but you know that the Scotch do not like to spend their last dollar. Some of my friends are badgering me to write for some of the magazines, and I am almost tempted to try it, only I am afraid that this would distract my mind from my work more than the distasteful and depressing labor of the mill or of guiding. What do you think about it?

Suppose I should give some of the journals my first thoughts about this glacier work as I go along and afterwards gather them and press them for the Boston wise; or will it be better to hold my wheesh [*silence*] and say it all at a breath? You see how practical I have become and how fully I have burdened you with my little affairs.

Perhaps you will ask, "What plan are you going to pursue in your work?" Well, here it is,—the only book I ever have invented. First I will describe each glacier with its tributaries separately, then describe the rocks and hills and mountains *over* which they have flowed or *past* which they have flowed, endeavoring to prove that all of the various forms which those rocks now have are the necessary result of the ice action in connection with their structure and cleavage, etc. Also the different kinds of canyons and lake-basins and meadows which they have made. Then, armed with this data, I will come down to the Yosemite, where all my ice has come, and prove that each dome and brow and wall and every grace and spire and brother is the necessary result of the delicately balanced blows of well-directed and combined glaciers against the parent rocks which contained them, only thinly carved and moulded in some instances by the subsequent action of water, etc.

Libby sent me Tyndall's new book, and I have looked hastily over it. It is an Alpine mixture of very pleasant taste, and I wish I could enjoy reading and talking it with you. I expect Mrs. H[*utchings*] will accompany her husband to the East this winter, and there will not be one left with whom I can exchange a thought. Mrs. H[*utchings*] is going to leave me out all the books I want, and Runkle is going to send me Darwin. These, with my notes and maps, will fill my winter hours, if my eyes do not fail, and, now that you see my whole position, I think that you would not call me to the excitements and distracting novelties of civilization.

The bread question is very troublesome. I will eat anything you think will suit me. Send up either by express to Big Oak Flat or by any other chance, and I will remit the money required in any way you like.

My love to all and more thanks than I can write for your constant
kindness.

[*John Muir*][15]

∾

Yosemite, September or October,
1871

Dear friend Mrs. Carr,

I am again upon the bottom meadow of Yosemite after a most
intensely interesting bath among the outer mountains. I have been
exploring the upper tributaries of the Cascade and Tamarac streams.
And in particular all of the basin of the Yosemite Creek. The present
basin of every stream which enters the Valley on the north side was
formerly filled with ice, which also flowed into the Valley, although
the ancient ice basins did not always correspond with the present
water basins because glaciers can flow up hill. The *whole* of the north
wall of the Valley was covered with an unbroken flow of ice, with
perhaps the single exception of the crest of Eagle Cliff, and though
the book of glaciers gradually dims as we go lower on the range, yet I
fully believe that future investigation will show that, in the earlier ages
of Sierra Nevada ice, vast glaciers flowed to the foot of the range east
of Yosemite and also north and south at an elevation of 9000 feet. The
glacier basins are almost unchanged, and I believe that ice was the
agent by which all of the present rocks receive their special forms. More
of this some other day. Would that I could have you here or in any
wild place where I can think and speak! Would you not be thoroughly
iced? You would not find in me one unglacial thought. Come, and I
will tell you how El Capitan and Tissiack were fashioned. I will most
likely live at Black's Hotel this winter in charge of the premises, and
before next spring I will have an independent cabin built, with a
special Carr corner where you and the Doctor can come and stay all
summer; also I will have a tent so that we can camp and receive night
blessings when we choose, and then I will have horses enough so that
we can go to the upper temples also. I wish you could see Lake Tenaya.
It is one of the most perfectly and richly spiritual places in the moun-

tains, and I would like to preempt there. Somehow I should feel like leaving home in going to Hetch Hetchy. Besides, there is room there for many other claims, and it soon will fill with coarse homesteads, but as the winter is so severe at Lake Tenaya, very few will care to live there. Hetch Hetchy is about four thousand feet above sea, while Lake Tenaya is eight. I have been living in these mountains in so haunting, soaring, floating a way that it seems strange to cast any kind of an anchor. All is so equal in glory, so ocean-like, that to choose one place above another is like drawing dividing lines in the sky. I think I answered your last with respect to remaining here in the winter. I can do much of this ice work in the quiet, and the whole subject is purely physical, so that I can get but little from books. All depends upon the goodness of one's eyes. No scientific book in the world can tell me how this Yosemite granite is put together or how it has been taken down. Patient observation and constant brooding above the rocks, lying upon them for years as the ice did, is the way to arrive at the truths which are graven so lavishly upon them.

Would that I knew what good prayers I could say or good deeds I could do, so that ravens would bring me bread and venison for the next two years! Then would I get some tough gray clothes the color of granite, so no one could see or find me but yourself. Then would I reproduce the ancient ice-rivers and watch their workings and dwell with them. I go again to my lessons tomorrow morning. Some snow fell, and bye-and-bye I must tell you about it.

If poor good Melancholic Cowper had been here yesterday morning, here is just what he would have sung:—

> The rocks have been washed, just washed in a shower
> Which winds in their faces conveyed.
> The plentiful cloudlets bemuffled their brows
> Or lay on their beautiful heads.
>
> But cold sighed the winds in the fir trees above
> And down on the pine trees below,
> For the rain that came laving and washing in love
> Was followed, alas, by a snow.

Which, being unmetaphored and prosed into sense, means that yesterday morning a strong southeast wind, cooled among the highest snows of the Sierra, drove back the warm northwest winds from the hot San Joaquin plains and burning foothill woods, and piled up a jagged cloud addition to our Valley walls. Soon those white clouds began to darken and to reach out long filmy edges which, uniting over the Valley, made a close, dark ceiling. Then came rain, unsteady at first, now a heavy gush, then a sprinkling halt, as if the clouds so long out of practice had forgotten something, but after half an hour of experimental pouring and sprinkling there came an earnest, steady, well-controlled rain.

On the mountain the rain soon turned to snow and some half-melted flakes reached the bottom of the Valley. This morning Starr King and Tissiack and all the upper Valley are white.

Did I tell you in my last that I had settled up with Hutchings. He used me very shabbily trying to keep back part of my wages. If I am about the Valley hotels at all next summer I shall stop at Blacks. . . . [Sentence erased]

> Ever devoutly your friend,
> John Muir[16]

∞

> Yosemite, December 11, 1871

Dear Mrs. Carr

We are snowbound and your letter of Nov. lst came two days ago. I sympathize with you for the loss of your brown Japanese, but I am glad to know that you found so much of pure human goodness in the life of your scholar. The whole world is enriched, beautified by a stratum—an atmosphere—of Godlike souls, and it is ignorance alone that banks human love into narrow gutter channels and stagnant pools, making it selfish and impure when it should be boundless as air and light, blending with all the world, keeping sight of our impartial Father who is the fountain sun of all the love that is rayed down to earth. But glaciers, dear friend—ice is only another form of terrestrial love. I am astonished to hear you speak so unbelievingly of God's glorious crystal glaciers. "They are only pests," and you think them wrong in temperature, and they live in "horrible times" and you don't care to hear about them "only that they made instruments of Yosemite music." You speak heresy for once, and deserve a dip in Methodist Tophet, or Vesuvius at least.

I have just been sending ice to Le Conte, and snow to McChesney and I have nothing left but hailstones for you, but I don't know how to send them—to speak them. You confuse me. You have taught me here and encouraged me to read the mountains. Now you will not listen, next summer you will be converted—*you will be iced then.*

I have been up Nevada to the top of Lyell and found a living glacier, but you don't want that; and I have been in Hetch Hetchy and the canyon above, and I was going to tell you the beauty there; but it is all ice-born beauty, and too cold for you; and I was going to tell about the making of the South Dome, but ice did that too; and about the hundred lakes that I found, but the ice made them every one; and I had some groves to speak about—groves of surpassing loveliness in *new* pathless Yosemites, but they all grew upon glacial drift,—and I have nothing to send but what is frozen or freezable.

You like the music instruments that glaciers made, but no songs were so grand as those of the glaciers themselves, no falls so lofty as those which poured from brows, and chasmed mountains of pure dark ice. Glaciers *made* the mountains and ground corn for all the flowers, and the forests of silver fir, made smooth paths for human feet until the sacred Sierras have become the most approachable of mountains. Glaciers came down from heaven, and they are angels with folded wings, white wings of snowy bloom, locked hand in hand the little spirits did nobly; the primary mountain waves, unvital granite, were soon carved to beauty. They bared the lordly domes and fashioned the clustering spires; smoothed godlike mountain brows, and shaped lake cups for crystal waters; wove myriads of mazy canyons, and spread them out like lace. They remembered the loud-songed rivers and every tinkling rill. The busy snowflakes saw all the coming flowers, and the grand predestined forests. They said, "We will crack this rock for *Cassiope* where she may sway her tiny urns. Here we'll smooth a plat for green mosses, and round a bank for bryanthus bells." Thus labored the willing flake-souls linked in close congregations of ice, breaking rock food for the pines, as a bird crumbles bread

for her young, spiced with dust of garnets and zircons and many a
nameless gem; and when food was gathered for the forests and all
their elected life, when every rock form was finished, every monument
raised, the willing messengers, unwearied, unwasted, heard God's
"well done" from heaven calling them back to their homes in the sky.

January 8, 1872

Dear Friend

   We are gloriously snowbound. One storm has filled half of last
month, and it is snowing again—would that you could behold its
beauty! I half expected another glacial period, but I will not say
anything about ice until you become wiser, but I send you a cascade
jubilee which you will relish more than anybody else. I have tried to
put it in form for publication, and if you can rasp off the rougher
angles and wedge in a few slippery words between bad splices perhaps
it may be sufficiently civilized for *Overland* or *Atlantic*. But I always
felt a chill come over my fingers when a calm place in the storm
allowed me to think of it. Also I have been sorry for one of our bears
and I think you will sympathize with me. At least I confide my dead
friend to your keeping, and you may print what you like. Heavens! if
you only had been here in the flood.

[*John Muir*][17]

∾

Oakland, December 31, [*1871*]

Dear John

   I have been a victim to the worst weather I have ever known in
California—neuralgic pains *got hold of my face,* but all the more time
have I lying around good for nothing to think "why don't he write." I
sent you a box in October and sent you Yelverton's papers in the
magazines and book soon after, and have written, and you must be
dead and the Lord has buried you. I would write you if there was a
feeling uppermost that you would receive my letters. I do not think it
strange because we are cut off from nearer places. How wonderful
things must be in these stormy days with you. The only really enjoyable
day I have had in a month was one with Prof. Bolander on the Berkeley

hills—and that was cold enough to freeze one's marrow. No letters from the east beyond Chicago—all is at a deadlock. Mr. Stone comes in now and then, McChesney is as good, genial and industrious as ever, means to go a bugging in Japan one day. Le Conte is cogitating the Cosmos. The Libbys, I rarely see. That Mrs. Hoyt, who was with them, is Dr. Kellogg's friend. I expect that blessed old soul has been washed off from his eyrie on Jones Street—a queer place it was in dry weather. Harry [*Henry*] Edwards and his wife spent last Sunday with us. Professor Marsh made us a flying visit. This is all the news I know.

Akin to the scenes in which you were bred the winter glory, the flowers of the snow, are but a great exaltation of what was familiar and dear. I seem to see nothing very familiar or dear. I have been shut in the house so long that everything is very stale to me. I really meant to spend the holidays on the *Summit* just for the glory and uplifting. Then this storm came. I never knew such a mean looking and feeling storm. It sounds like *money* falling on the roof. Thanksgiving day I went over into Sunol Valley to see John [*Henry Carr*]. Found him ploughing—cheeks red, eyes *so* blue. He did not expect me. "How do you do, Ole Carson?" (His hair is so light he looks just like a Norwegian.) The smile that broke over his face was the pleasantest thing I have seen this winter.

The Geological Survey is in rather a dubious position before the Legislature. Have you seen the bills for *Forest Master,* and the Yosemite road bill. How glad I shall be when a narrow gauge road is built into the Valley (think of my beginning that word with a little v!—almost as bad as the Wisconsin lawyer who began the greatest of monosyllables with a little j), for that will bring you out of it. A good old Wisconsin "nature feller" has just settled in Seattle; he says the wildernesses beyond are unexplored save by Indians—there be also waterfalls. I have been lying, I find, on these back pages—all owing to this infernal weather.

[*Jeanne Carr*][18]

PART FIVE

1872

Do not accuse me of intentionally keeping the best wine of kindred and related spirits till the last of your season's feast.

Jeanne C. Carr

Up into Mountain Light,
Down into Town Dark

MUIR'S DECISION TO PUBLISH HIS ESSAYS WAS HIS OWN. HE WAS "NO mush of concession" in any matter, and this was no exception. Though he spoke of having no literary ambition, Muir sensed that writing would provide a course of independence and the freedom for him to engage in rambles in and beyond Yosemite. During his excursions into wilderness he kept a journal, the source of letters to friends and the fountainhead of his essays. What he wrote, how he wrote, and where his essays were published was, however, dependent on friends during the first years of his writing career. Among his friends he relied the most on Jeanne Carr. From her he asked for guidance. Carr's role in shaping his career cannot be overemphasized. He sent his manuscripts to her for revising and following her meticulous editing (the piecing together in some cases of frayed bits of letters), she sent his essays to publishers.

In January Carr began in earnest to draw Muir deeper into the public sphere. She sent a personal letter along with his manuscript to the editor of the *Overland Monthly* requesting that Muir's essay be published. The following month Ezra Carr delivered Muir's manuscript "Jubilee of the Waters" to the *Overland,* where it was published three months later as "Yosemite Valley in Flood." Before the end of the year the *Overland* published two additional essays. By 1873 Muir was referred to as their leading contributor. Carr sent Muir's "glacier letter" to Emerson for publication in the *Atlantic Monthly*; and she asked Muir to prepare his Yosemite journal for publication and requested that he write about humans as well as about nature, wilderness, mountains, and ice. Sometimes Carr directed Muir's letters and essays without his knowledge or she informed him after they had been sent to publishers for consideration. Encouraged by the success of his *Tribune* articles, Muir found this period germinal for his writing. His observations coalesced in rough form from within the Valley and, prodded and polished by Carr, who lived in Oakland, Muir's essays entered the public sphere.

Carr filled her letters to Muir with nature observations not only out of her own love of botany but as a way of sharpening Muir's skills, observations, and style. The *Hepaticas* were preparing for spring and the rain greened the *Hypnum* beds. Carr's painter-friend, James Hope, who lived in Castleton, Vermont, once told her she had such an affinity for nature and plants that she had once been made of moss. Carr drew her friends from both nature and from society and counted among them the literati and cultural elite. Among them were Charles Warren Stoddard, a long-time resident of San Francisco and an author and poet, and Theresa Yelverton, author of *Zanita: A Tale of the Yo-semite.* Most of the friends Muir invited to join him in the Valley were Carr's friends. In February he summoned Stoddard to a vagabond ramble, and while Muir waited for Yelverton's book and articles to arrive, he encouraged Carr to commit to a trip to the Valley. Muir had in fact invited so many friends that he told Carr he would have to save a slice of his season, one, two, or three months, for her, Ezra, and Allie.[1]

Muir transformed his wilderness rambles into tracts, into nature propaganda. The core of "Twenty Hill Hollow" he sent to Carr to mend for publication. In April the article appeared in the *Overland Monthly.* The essay urged lovers of the truth and beauty of wilderness to consider a trip to Twenty Hill Hollow in Merced County, where a baptism in nature would prepare them for communion in Yosemite Valley. In the Hollow they would bathe in spirit-beams, lose consciousness of their own separate existence, blend into the landscape, and become part of nature.

Carr experienced nature and wilderness as a release from the cadre of people, places, and ideas that consumed her daily life. She whizzed around like a hummingbird, drawing friends and purposes together in a web, each person linked in a chain of cultural being intended to create order and perpetuate truth. In late February she visited Albert Bierstadt, the landscape painter, and Albert Kellogg, the physician and first botanist resident in California who began in early 1852 the study of the Sequoia. Carr delighted in the personalities and accomplishments of her friends, whom she nurtured as an extension of herself.

On March 26 Muir was awakened by an earthquake. Eagle Rock on the south wall of Yosemite gave way and crashed two thousand feet to the Valley floor. Muir delighted in the formation of a mountain talus and in rock voice and common motion set in place by the noble earth-quake storm. As fellow residents fled the Valley, Muir raced to the boulders. He waited for Carr and modified their plan to "mingle... two or three nights" up in the full-moon light with the Godful music on Sunnyside Bench. The threat of a future earthquake required consideration. When Carr arrived they would spend an afternoon behind the Yosemite falls.[2]

While Muir planned Carr's visit to the Valley, she wrote to him about her plans to move to Berkeley. The University of California was located in Oakland and the Carrs resided in the Episcopal rectory nearby. In early 1872 the university received a building appropriation that resulted in the relocation of the campus and faculty housing to Berkeley. The construction of their home in Berkeley was something the Carrs looked forward to. They prepared for their move while Muir built a shanty near James Lamon's cabin on the sunny north side of the Valley at the base of the Royal Arches. There Muir waited for the Carrs and Merrill Moores. Muir's letter to Carr described the Valley white with snow. The mountains were thick with snow that would melt slowly and fill the falls with long loud music. Muir also waited for Albert Kellogg, whom he expected that spring.

Muir rejoiced at Carr's pending visit. She would be in the Valley with her friends the Daggetts from Chicago. It was not soon enough for him. Yosemite was too far away from her "hard-crusted cares." Muir and Carr would share spring and she would listen to his stories about ice, in which he found increasing rewards of truth. Muir suggested that Carr and the Daggetts travel by way of Clark's Station, spend a day or two in Mariposa Grove, then go on to Sentinel Dome and Glacier Point, and down into the Valley. They could enter the Valley by Little Yosemite and Nevada and Vernal Falls or by Indian Falls on the north side of the Valley. Carr did not accompany the Daggetts on their trip into the Valley. That summer her friends from Oakland, Mr. and Mrs. J. P. Moore, also visited Muir. Muir and Mrs. Moore traveled to Hetch Hetchy together and returned in early July. During their rambles in grassy meadows and spangled rivers Carr was often remembered.

Merrill Moores, who had hiked with Muir in Wisconsin and was now sixteen, arrived to spend the summer in Yosemite with Muir. He traveled on the railroad, bought a horse in San Francisco, took a boat to Stockton, and rode to Black's Hotel, where he met Muir. Muir encouraged Carr to permit Allie to join them, but he did not. Muir and Moores spent July planting stakes across the glacier near the top of Mount Lyell to measure the glacial flow.

Later that month Carr wrote to Muir to announce the arrival of Asa Gray, the Harvard botanist, with whom she had spoken about Muir and with whom Muir had already corresponded. Muir and Gray spent a week together in and above the Valley while Moores took care of their horses. Gray, like Emerson and John D. Runkle, president of the Massachusetts Institute of Technology, encouraged Muir to go east to teach. Too long wild, Muir did not want to burn in the furnace of education. Instead he wrote to Carr that he was approaching a "fruiting-time" in his mountain work and he hoped to see her to discuss his writing. Following his trip to the Valley, Gray and his wife visited Carr in late July. They spent a Sabbath in the Redwoods, traveled to an extinct forest, and to the trunk of a Sequoia led by Henry Gibbons, a friend of Carr's and a prominent San Francisco physician and member of the faculty of the Cooper Medical School. Carr wrote to Muir, wishing he had been with them to take the spare seat in the carriage.

Carr expected to travel to Yosemite at some point during 1872. With Ned Carr returning from South America sick with a fever contracted while working on the Amazon, she directed her energy toward her son's pending arrival and his health and deferred the beauty of the Valley and the pleasure of Muir's company until 1873. Muir hoped she and Ned would accompany him that fall on easier excursions in and around the Valley. He was certain the healing waters of the mountains would restore Ned's health as they had restored his in 1868. Carr's response must have surprised Muir. She urged him to leave Yosemite in the fall and live with her, Ezra, and the Carr children over the winter. Mrs. Moore wrote to Muir in early August. She and Carr had spoken at length about Muir and agreed he should leave the Valley and spend the winter in Oakland. Carr thought he could write, study, and visit with friends while ways opened for his departure to South America. Perhaps Yosemite might not be his permanent home. God would show him that places and people dear to him were only tents in the night, nomadic abodes from which he would move on. Carr's responsibilities repeatedly took her from family and friends. She had left Castleton, Vermont, for Madison, Wisconsin, and Madison for Oakland. Soon she would be in Berkeley. She often missed her Vermont plant-friends. Gaps were filled with new relations and old kindred spirits lingered in her heart though miles away. God would teach Muir the cost of the choices he was making as He had taught Carr. Muir responded in August that he was learning to live close to the lives of friends without seeing them. He was referring to his friend Jeanne Carr.

If Carr could not visit him in Yosemite, Muir thought he might leave the Valley and travel to Oakland late in the year to study the coast and the coastal ranges. His plan was to return to winter in the Valley or in a deep canyon among the glacial summits where he would write. At present, however, he was engaged in the study of glaciers, which was soon to be interrupted by Louis Agassiz's arrival in San Francisco. If Ezra Carr had visited Yosemite that year it would have been with Agassiz; however, Agassiz was too ill to travel. Carr and Joseph Le Conte urged Muir to visit him in San Francisco. Muir wanted to meet Agassiz. Perhaps the thought of speeding down into town life was overwhelming, the adjustment too great. Muir, who had just returned from a fifteen-day ramble in the basins of the Illilouette and Pohono, quickly departed for the summit glaciers to study canyons and examine the stakes he had planted in the ice in July with Moores. He would not leave his studies during the harvest of rocks while the season drew to a close. As a result Muir and Agassiz never met.

At the close of the summer Muir traveled north of the Valley into the Tuolumne River Canyon and Hetch Hetchy Valley. Certain that Hetch Hetchy was created by glacial erosion, he sought further evidence to support his claim. Stakes he planted in August, he read in October. The ice-masses possessed true glacial motion.

Details about Carr's familial responsibilities crept into her letters to Muir. In early September her son John Henry returned from an expedition with nothing more than the clothes he was wearing. Carr nursed Mrs. Moore and Harry Edwards, who suffered from inflammatory rheumatism. Carr and Muir also corresponded about a lecture Le Conte delivered on the glaciers of the High Sierra. Had Le Conte credited Muir for his discoveries? In early October Muir wrote that he knew nothing about Le Conte's glacier lecture though he was confident Le Conte drew all he knew of the Sierra glaciers from him. Muir assumed he would credit him. Le Conte did not. Muir recognized that his research was not protected from theft. Professor Samuel Kneeland, Secretary of the Massachusetts Institute of Technology, gathered letters Muir sent to Runkle and his *Tribune* article on glaciers and hashed them into a lecture he delivered to the Boston Society of Natural History. Muir received little credit. Although Kneeland's paper may have drawn considerable attention to Muir's explorations and views, Muir wrote to Carr that such meanness worked permanent evil on Kneeland. By correlation Muir implied it would do the same for Le Conte.[3]

A quick visit to Oakland late in the year and his return to winter in the Valley or the mountains suited Muir. He would have a chance to see and talk with Carr. The thought of wintering in Oakland among the human impurities of town life, however, repulsed him. In the meantime he set out on a ten-day trip in the summit region in the headwaters of the Tuolumne among the peaks of Lyell and McClure. Returning to his cabin below the Royal Arches, he and Moores set out again, this time with three artists, William Keith, a Scotsman and a landscape painter of repute (with whom Muir developed a close friendship); Benoni Irwin (whom Carr commissioned to sketch Muir in his hay rope suspenders); and a Mr. Ross (a plumber with artistic talent). They had arrived in the Valley with a letter of introduction from Carr. Together the group traveled along the upper Tuolumne River toward its headwaters, where Muir promised a wealth of landscapes and left the artists to sketch in Lyell Canyon while he set off to climb Mount Ritter, one of the highest peaks in the Sierra. Muir made the first recorded ascent of Mount Ritter. Later in the month he, Moores, and Le Conte climbed to the top of Clouds Rest. Shortly thereafter Moores left the Valley for Oregon and Muir and Le Conte started for Mono Lake.

Encouraged by Jeanne Carr, William Keith, Mrs. J. P. Moore, Joseph Le Conte, and J. B. McChesney, Muir arrived in Oakland in December for a brief visit. Drawn to town life by well-meaning friends, he found it difficult to reconcile society's demands. It mattered little that both Carr and Emerson impressed upon him society's claim on his life. In Oakland he was entertained by those well-meaning friends. The Carrs, McChesneys, Le Contes, and Keiths accompanied him across the Bay to visit libraries, museums, galleries, and editorial offices in San Francisco. He met Carr's friends Edward Rowland Sill, poet and educator;

Ina Donna Coolbrith, poet; Charles Warren Stoddard, author, poet, and traveler; and Benjamin P. Avery, the editor of the *Overland Monthly.* Muir sat for a photographic portrait in the San Francisco studio of Rulofson. After two weeks he fled from the mountain of municipal confusion back to the safety of the wilderness. He boarded a train and when he reached Turlock sped over the fields through miles of *Hemizonia* and *Eriogonum* to Hopeton, looking toward the mountains. He passed Coulterville and headed toward the Valley.[4]

Muir set out immediately to clear away the effects of dead pavement and city air, having lost "the tone and tune of the rocks." On December 25 he wrote to Carr that memories of Oakland were worn by the waves of winter in Yosemite though he felt her everlasting love, believing their friendship kindled like a planet burning along its own path. Carr responded that Muir needed to abandon letter writing, a profane act that detracted from his divine mission. Silence would spread between Muir and Carr, who sacrificed their correspondence to Muir's purpose. Muir confessed that bookmaking frightened him. Words were difficult to fashion, though the spark that ignited the direction his relation with the profane world would take was clear, strong, and true.

⌒

Editor Overland

Dear Sir

Mr. Emerson urged me last summer to put my monthly bulletins from the Yosemite which come in private letters from our friend and pupil *John Muir* before the public. In accordance with my request, this last letter is in readiness for the printers use. Mr. Muir has been in the Valley for three years, studying it as no other instructed person has ever done, he is as modest as he is gifted, and utterly devoid of literary ambition.

I offer this paper to the *Overland* on my own responsibility, if accepted please notify me, and if not return as early as possible to

Mrs. E. S. Carr

[*Jeanne C. Carr*][5]

⌒

Oakland, February 4, 1872

Dear John

The rain falls so gently, I seem to feel the ferns uncoiling, the social companies of pulsatilla whispering to each other *just* under ground, "The morning is near," *Hepaticas* getting ready for their leap into the arms of Spring, under its influence. Just such a rain as fills every moss urn in our northern woods and makes the *Hypnum* beds so green, so green.

Strange, isn't it, that those woods, that beech trunks and hemlock thickets should seem so much more spiritual than any creature of this occidental world. [*James*] Hope used to say, when for the fiftieth time my hand would go *smoothing* a patch of moss in Forest Glen, as one strokes a cat or caresses an animal, "You were made out of all these things." I believe it is true. I am so possessed at times with the memory of their life, the life I lived with them once when we were rained on and even so glad. If you had written me your glory, glacial letter then, dear John, I couldn't have answered it—no more can I in this intermediate state, but I should have liked to feel your footstep!

It is beautiful, though, that we can understand each other—while in such singular apartness, you dwelling in the house of forces, becoming *elemental* yourself through sympathy, and I living only among such forms of these as are charged with personality. I now and then touch a subtle thread of analogy, which enables me to recognize these humans in the ages agone, in their cast-off forms, and then I can guess what it is to live in Eternity.

My spirit was converted by your lovely sermon, but my flesh isn't, and when your track is from lands of snow to lands of sun, only then shall I be able to follow you. I sent you a reprint of Ned's letter which you will understand it was a joy and a relief to get. And now he is probably at "Santa Cruz de la Sierra," where he can see the Southern cross, and the eternal snows, and the ever-ascending smoke from the great planetary censers which swing day and night in that grandest of temples. What a world of poetry there is in those Spanish names, both of sense and sound. I hope Ned's temporal discomforts will not blind him to the wonders through which he is passing. He is too young by a dozen years to get the full benefit of such an experience, but you can see from the letter, which I copied word for word, how much manliness it has bred in him.

Charles Stoddard is about starting for the Navigator Islands [*Samoa*], there to soak and steep himself in all savagery; too lean to be made a dainty for their Gods, we may expect he will return fattened for the literary shambles. He says he "pines to know John Muir." I think I should enjoy seeing you together.

Dr. Carr took the "Jubilee of the Waters" to the *Overland*. I expect it will be out next month. I did not think it best to offer the Bear Story for the same, and Charlie S[*toddard*] thought I ought to send it east. I would not send [*it*] until there was a prospect of its going through in six months or so, consequently it lies in my desk. We were all (some twenty of us) delighted with both papers, *but my letter is the best of all.* I wish to get a chance to read it to Clarence King, who is "so near to yet so far" that he seems to elude my touch.

Perhaps if you should try very hard to make me, and I transpare myself, I *could* see your new heavens and new earth! I challenge it, and am yours always,

J. C. C.

[*Jeanne C. Carr*]⁶

ᘗ

Yosemite Valley, February 13, 1872

Dear friend Mrs. Carr

Your latest letter is dated December 31st. I see that some of your letters are missing. I received the box and ate the berries and Liebig's extract long ago and told you all about it, but Mrs. Yelverton's book and magazine articles I have not yet seen. Perhaps they may come next mail. How did you send them? I sympathize with your face and your great sorrows, but you will bathe in the fountain of light, life, and love of our mountains and be healed. And here I wish to say that when you and Al and the Doctor come, I wish to be completely free. Therefore let me know that you will certainly come and *when*. I will gladly cut off a slice of my season's time however thick—the thicker the better—and lay it aside for you. I am in the habit of asking so many to *come, come, come* to the mountain baptisms that there is danger of having others on my hands when you come, which must not be. I will mark off one or two or three months of bare, dutiless time for our blessed selves or the few good and loyal ones that you may choose. Therefore, at the expense even of breaking a dozen of civilization's laws and fences, I want you to *come*. For the high Sierra the months of July, August, and September are best.

As for your Asiatic sayings, I would gladly creep into the Vale of Cashmere or any other groove upon our blessed star. I feel my poverty in general knowledge and will travel some day. You need not think that I feel Yosemite to be all in all, but more of this when you come.

I am going to send you with this a few facts and thoughts that I gathered concerning Twenty Hill Hollow, which I want to publish, if you think you can mend them and make them into a lawful article fit for *outsiders*. Plant gold is fading from California faster than did her placer gold, and I wanted to save the memory of that which is laid upon Twenty Hills.

Also I will send you some thoughts that I happened to get for poor persecuted, twice-damned Coyote. If you think anybody will believe them, have them published. Last mail I sent you some manuscript about bears and storms, which you will believe if no one else will. An account of my preliminary rambles among the glacier beds was published in the *Daily Tribune* of New York, Dec. 9th. Have you seen it? If you have, call old Mr. Stebbins's attention to it. He will read with pleasure. Where is the old friend? I have not heard from him for a long time. Remember me to the Doctor and the boys and all my old friends.

Yours, etc.,
John Muir[7]

∾

Yosemite Valley, February 20,
[*1872*]

Dear Stoddard

I have been claiming you for a friend for a long time. Although a few miles of air has separated us, Mrs. Carr has mirrored you up here many times and our mutual friend Mrs. Hutchings has said many a loving word for you, and last spring Mr. Emerson asked me many questions concerning you and spoke of verses you had sent him, in a way that made me hope that you had a song to sing grander than any you have yet conceived. In this way I have learned to know you. I am cordially glad to feel that you are coming nearer.

You hope that you will not "disappoint me." The danger of being disappointed is all on your own side. Don't believe one half that Mrs. Carr says. I am only a piece of jagged human mist drifting about these rocks and waters, Heaven only knows how or wherefore.

Hitherto I have walked alone. I shall rejoice in you as companion but remember that in that case "a vagabond shalt thou be." Moreover, you must not hope that I can teach you, I am only a baby slowly learning my mountain alphabet. But I can freely promise that

Nature will do great things for you. I know little of men yet I venture to say that half our best teachers are manufactured,—so ground and pressed in the mills of culture that God cannot play a single tune upon them.

I am glad to learn my friend that you have not yet submitted yourself to any of the mouldy laws of literature—that your spiritual affinities are still alive and unsatisfied. Come then to the mountains and bathe in fountain Love. Stand upon our Domes and let spirit winds blow through you and you will sing effortless as an Eolian harp.

You will enjoy the ocean. There is but little difference between land and sea. Heavens! What glorious storm nights you will have among phosphorescent foam.

May God be good to you. Lave your existence in the Beauty and Love of those Isles of the Sea. Keep your heart pure and it shall be like a silvered plate printed with God in a thousand forms.

Ever your friend

John Muir[8]

∾

[*Oakland, Late February, 1872?*]

[*John Muir*]

[Fragment of letter]

...[*com*]missioners? I should like you to have absolute control of some place in that region where the elect might resort in the evil times coming when the Valley will be thronged with the baser sort. Inform yourself of everything pertinent to this subject.

I shall try to see [*Albert*] Bierstadt in a day or two. I've a notion that he means to paint some winter landscape in the mountains.

Went to see Dr. Kellogg Saturday. *Such* a house as I found him in, just like the inside of a haystack. We will have a day together, some-where. I told him I wanted [*him*] to go to the Valley with us. He said he could not go this year, has never been; has an arrangement to live one season there with Duncan.

Jos. Le Conte lunched with me and read your letter. Said he was about persuaded to relinquish the Columbia and go to you. I wish he had and we had started the next day. We talked an hour about *the discovery,* appreciated it, and *your rapture,* and throbbed in tune. *Wait,* my friend, until you stand in the Cordilleras and Alps and see how the handwriting all corresponds, and then your anthem shall be sung.

Have a letter from South America today, but not from our dear boy. I enclose Mrs. Waterston's last, you see how true the spiritual laws are, and so we will love God and one another and go to sleep.

Your friend anear and afar,

Jeanne C. Carr[9]

∾

[*San Mateo, February 26, 1872*]

[*John Muir*]

[Fragment of letter]

I shall put your glacial letter to me with the one to Le Conte into shape and send to Mr. Emerson, asking him to get it published in the *Atlantic.* You are not to know anything about it—Let it take its chances.

But my mind is made up on one "point." All this fugitiveness is going to be gathered up, lest you should die like Moses in the mountains and God should bury you where "no man knoweth." I copied every word of your old Journal. It looks pretty and reads well. You have only to continue it and make the "Yosemite Year Book," painting in your inimitable way, the march of the Seasons there.

Try your pen on some of the humans, too. Get sketches at least. I think it would be a beautiful book. Then you will put your scientific convictions into clear-cut crystalline prose for other uses.

I have not broached the money question with Mr. Carmany; will set Mr. Benton upon that if any smallness should manifest itself.

March 3d

Our good minister, Mr. Hamilton, is ill and Dr. Carr preached today, Mr. Benton doing the praying. The lecture was upon the *Identities of Faith,* with readings from Hindoo [*sic*] scriptures and from Paul and others in our own—and the prayers were excellent and fitted to the occasion. It was a very uncommon thing all through and seemed [*to*] open a window into some minds. Excuse these accidental half sheets. Dr. Carr sends love, and Allie, and

I am always your friend,

J. C. C.

[*Jeanne C. Carr*][10]

∾

Yosemite Valley, March 16, [*1872*]

Dear Mrs. Carr

Yours of Feb. 26 reached me today and as I have a chance to send you a hasty line by an Indian who is going to Mariposa I would say that I fear you are giving yourself far too much trouble about those little fragments. If they or any other small pieces that chance to the end of my pen give you and the Doctor any pleasure I am well paid. Very few friends besides will care for them. If you conclude to publish "Twenty Hill Hollow" I want you to correct my statement that the Lark of the Hollow and the Eastern lark are identical in species. They are so similar in size, color, and gestures, that I took them to be the same, although there is a marked difference in their songs. According to Dr. Newberry the Cal. meadow lark is *Sturnella neglecta* instead of *S. ludoviciana.*

You don't understand my reference to Ruskin's "Moderation." Don't you remember that he speaks in some of his books about the attributes of Nature, "Repose," "Moderation," etc. He says many true and beautiful things of Repose, but weak and uninspired things concerning Moderation, telling us most solemnly that Nature is never immoderate! and that if he had the power and the paint he would have "Moderation" brushed in big capitals upon all the doors and lintels of art factories and manufactories of the whole world!! etc., etc., as near as I can recollect. The heavy masonry of the Sierra seems immoderate to some.

I am astonished at your copying those dry tattered notes. People speak of writing with one foot in the grave. I wrote most of those winter notes with one foot in bed while stupid with the weariness of

Hutchings' logs. I'm not going to die until done with my glaciers. As for that glacier which you propose to construct out of your letter and Le Conte's, I cannot see how a balanced unit can be made from such material.

I had a letter from Emerson the other day of which I told you in another letter. He prophesies in the same dialect that you are accustomed to use, that I shall one day go to the Atlantic Coast. He knows nothing of my present ice work. I read your Hindu extracts with much interest. I am glad to know by you and Emerson and others living and dead that my unconditional surrender to Nature has produced exactly what you have foreseen—that drifting without human charts through light and dark, calm and storm, I have come to so glorious an ocean. But more of this by and by.

As for that idea of Mountain Models, I told Runkle last fall that a model in plaster of paris of a section of the Sierra reaching to the summits, including Yosemite would do more to convince people of the truth of our glacial theory of the formation of the Valley and of canyons in general than volumes of rocky argument; because magnitudes are so great only very partial views are obtained. He agreed with me and promised to send me a box with plaster for a model three or four feet long, and instruments, barometer, level, etc., but it has not come.

I am in no hurry. I want to see all the world. I am going to be down about the Golden Gate looking for a mouth to a portion of my ice. I answered two others of yours dated 4th and 8th of Feb., but the letter is still here. I will risk only this with Lo.

Farewell, with love to all,

[John Muir]

I have material for some outline glacier maps, but as I had no barometer last fall I have no definite depths of canyons or heights. If you think they would be worth presenting to the wise Congress of next summer I will send them. Emerson told me, hurry done with the mountains. I don't see how he knows I am meddling with them. Have you told him? He says I may go East with Agassiz. I will not be done here for several years. I am glad to know that the Doctor preaches. I think I might be admitted to his church.[11]

∾

New Sentinel Hotel,
Yosemite Valley, [*April, 1872*]

[*Mrs. Carr*]

Sunday night I was up in the moon among the lumined spray of the upper Falls. The lunar bows were glorious and the music Godful as ever. You will yet mingle amid the forms and voices of this peerless fall.

I wanted to have you spend two or three nights up there in full moon and planned a small hut for you, but since the boisterous waving of the rocks the danger seems forbidding at least for you. We can go up there in the afternoon, spend an hour or two, and return.

I had a grand ramble in the deep snow outside the Valley and discovered one beautiful truth concerning snow-structure and three concerning the forms of forest trees.

These earthquakes have made me immensely rich. I had long been aware of the life and gentle tenderness of the rocks, and, instead of walking upon them as unfeeling surfaces, began to regard them as a transparent sky. Now they have spoken with audible voice and pulsed with common motion. This very instant, just as my pen reached "and" on the third line above, my cabin creaked with a sharp shock and the oil waved in my lamp.

We had several shocks last night. I would like to go somewhere on the west South American coast to study earthquakes. I think I could invent some experimental apparatus whereby their complicated phenomena could be separated and read, but I have some years of ice on hand. 'T is most ennobling to find and feel that we are constructed with reference to these noble storms, so as to draw unspeakable enjoyment from them. Are we not rich when our six-foot column of substance sponges up heaven above and earth beneath into its pores? Aye, we have chambers in us the right shape for earthquakes. Churches and the schools lisp limpingly, painfully, of man's capabilities, possibilities, and fussy developing nostrums of duties, but if the human flock, together with their Rev.'s and double L-D shepherds, would go wild themselves, they would discover without Euclid that the solid contents of a human soul is the whole world.

Our streams are fast obtaining their highest power; warm nights and days are making the high mountain snow into snow avalanches and snow-falls; violets, blue, white, and yellow, abound; butterflies [*flit*] through the meadows; and mirror shadows reveal new heavens and new earths everywhere.

Remember me to the Doctor and all the boys and to McChesney and the brotherhood.

Cordially,

J. Muir[12]

∾

San Mateo, April 9, 1872

Dear John

Yours of . . . received, giving notice of house building. Had I written you a week ago as I was on the point of doing the letter would have pleased you more than this will. For in the meantime a building appropriation for the University of $300,000, makes the Berkeley residence nearer to our hopes, and involves large plans which will require no little oversight. It is impossible to tell whether Dr. Carr will be loosened at all this summer, and I write to say that you must not let your plans be affected by ours.

My friends the Daggetts of Chicago will be here about the first of May to stay three months—to Yosemite of course, perhaps to Shasta later. I shall expect to accompany them until something comes to make it impossible. They spent the winter year before last in Northern Africa—last year in Greece and Palestine. Mrs. D[*aggett*] is an excellent botanist, deep hearted towards all nature. He is a pure piece of human nobleness. Well the rest you will find out for yourself. They are of my dearest ones, and thoughts of such a summer as may be among the possibilities keeps me awake when I should sleep.

If I take them into the Valley what route should I choose? Mr. Benton thinks from Clark to [*the*] top of Sentinel Dome one day, then back to Inspiration Point. I like the *education* of the senses gained by. . . . [Remainder of letter lost]

[*Jeanne C. Carr*][13]

∾

New Sentinel Hotel,
Yosemite Valley, April 23, 1872

Dear Mrs. Carr

Yours of Apr. 9th and 15th, containing Ned's canoe and colonization adventures came tonight. I feel that you are coming and I will not
hear any words of preparatory consolation for the unsupposable case
of your non-appearance. Come by way of Clark's and spend a whole
day or two in the Sequoia, thence to Sentinel Dome and Glacier Point.
From thence swoop to our meadows and groves *direct* by a trail now
in course of construction which will be completed by the time the
snow melts. This new trail will be best in scenery and safety of five
which enter the Valley. It leads from Glacier Point down the face of
the mountain by an easy grade to a point back of Leidig's Hotel and
has over half a dozen inspiration points.

I hear that Mr. Peregoy intends building a hotel at Glacier Point.
If he does, you should halt there for the night after leaving Clark's. If
not, then stop at the present "Peregoy's," five or six miles south of the
Valley at the Westfall Meadows—built since your visit. You might
easily ride from Clark's to the Valley in a day, but a day among the
silver firs and another about the glories of the Valley-rim and settings
is a "sma' request."

The snow is deep this year, and the regular Mariposa Trail leading
to Glacier Point, etc., will not be open before June. The Mariposa
travel of May and perhaps a week or so of June will enter the Valley
from Clark's by a sort of sneaking trail along the river canyon below
the snow, but you must not come that way.

You may also enter the Valley via Little Yosemite and Nevada and
Vernal Falls by a trail constructed last season; also by Indian Falls on
the north side of the Valley by a trail now nearly completed. This last
is a noble entrance but perhaps not equal to the first. Whatever way
you come, we will travel all of those up and down, and bear in mind
that you must go among the summits in July or August. Bring no
friends that will not go to these fountains beyond or are uncastoffable.
Calm thinkers like your Doctor, who first led me with science, and Le
Conte are the kinds of souls fit for the formation of human clouds

adapted to this mountain sky. Nevertheless, I will rejoice beyond measure though you come as a comet tailed with a whole misty town.

Ned is a brave fellow. God bless him unspeakably and feed him with his own South American self.

I shall be most happy to know your Daggetts or anything that you call dear.

Goodnight and love to all.

I have not seen any of my *Tribune* letters, though I have written five or six. Send copy if you can.

J. M.
[*John Muir*][14]

○◦

Yosemite Valley,
May 12, 1872

Dear Mrs. Carr

The plants from Mrs. Yelverton which you kindly forwarded, are here. I have been writing a dozen letters but my pen slips wholly frictionless only to a few.

I wish you here in this morning beauty, away from and out of your hard-crusted cares. Glorious light fills our bath gorge today and you would speedily melt in the Godful flux.

It is the time of leaves, and they are falling from the sun covering all the meadows and trees flake by flake like a bounteous grace of snow. Clouds of plant color—they are a revelation—a Thus-saith-the Lord of color, given in songs of summer leaves off from the whirling sun.

I know how intensely you love this purple and yellow and green— these warm sun-songs of color, but I must edge in a kind word for ice. Glaciers are paper-manufacturers and they pulped these mountains and made the meadowy sheets on which this leaf-music is written.

Are you pluming for our mountain better-land? I was on Cloud's Rest yesterday and enjoyed a very vigorous snow-storm. Did you not hear a shout? Three avalanches of ice and snow started from the summit of Cloud's Rest ridge, one after the other in glorious gestures and boomings. I was within a few yards of them.

It will probably be late in June before we can get out among the summits. Snow is very abundant. Nevada and Vernal and the strip of glory between were in gush of spirit life when I passed yesterday.

My love to all.

John Muir

My studies have increasing rewards of truth and I will seek to be true to them although all the rest of the world of Beauty besides these mountains burn and nebulize back to star smoke.[15]

∾

New Sentinel Hotel,
Yosemite Valley, May 31, 1872

Dear Mrs. Carr

Yours announcing the Joaquin and the Daggetts and *more* is here. I care not when you come, so that you come calm and timeful. I will try to compel myself down to you in August, but these years and ages among snows and rocks have made me far more unfit for the usages of civilization than you appreciate. My nerves' strings shrink at the prospect, even at this distance. But if by diving to that slimy town sea-bottom I can touch Huxley and Tyndall and mount again with you to calm months in the Sierras, I will draw a long breath and splash into your fearful muds.

I would rather have you in September and October than at any other time, but a few weeks of this white water would be very glorious. Merrill Moores, who was with me in Wisconsin and at your Madison home, will be here soon to spend a good big block of a while with me. Why can't you let Allie join him?

For the last week our Valley has been a lake and my shanty is in flood. But the walls about us are white this morning with snow, which has checked the free life of our torrents, and the meadows will soon be walkable again. The snow fell last night and this morning. The falls will sing loud and long this year, and the mountains are fat in thick snow that the sun will find hard to fry.

Your other letter telling of John and sheep came a few days ago. You ought not to gray yourself away among these ghaunt [sic] and morbid philanthropies.

[Portion of letter erased] I am sorry that I was ... of ... only ... speak ... house with unwearied kindness. ... You must know her better when you come. Her health is improving since. ... The Doctor [*Carr*] is killing himself with overwork. Tell him to run away. A month here would be no loss to any of his works.

Ever yours,
John Muir

Tell Kellogg that there is one here who will be ready to welcome him in all kinds of times and weathers. When he comes here, he will come to his own, "His are the mountains and the valleys his."[16]

ᴄᴡ

[*Yosemite, Spring, 1872*]

[*Mrs. Carr*]

[Letter cut]

... upward into light to the very heart of the sun and downward miles deep among Holy Ghosts of glaciers and seas of mountain domes.

... I had a letter from Emerson. He judges me and my loose drifting voyages as kindly as yourself. The compliments of you two are enough to spoil one, but I fancy that he, like you, considers that I am so mountain-tanned and storm-beaten I may bear it. I owe all of my best friends to you. A prophecy in this letter of Emerson's recalled one of yours sent me when growing at the bottom of a mossy maple hollow in the Canada woods, that I would one day be with you, Doctor, and Priest in Yosemite. Emerson prophesies in similar dialect that I will one day go to him and "*better men*" in New England, or something to that effect. I feel like objecting in popular slang that I can't see it. I shall indeed go gladly to the "Atlantic Coast" as he prophesies, but only to see him and the Glacier Ghosts of the North. Runkle wants to make a teacher of me, but I have been too long wild, too befogged to burn well in their patent, high-heated, educational furnaces.

[Paragraph cut]

I had a good letter from Le Conte. He evidently doesn't [*know*] what to think of the huge lumps of ice that I sent him. I don't wonder at his cautious withholding of judgment. When my mountain mother first told me the tale I could hardly dare to believe either, and kept saying "what?" like a child half awake.

Farewell. My love to the Doctor and the boys. I hope the Doctor [*Carr*] will run away from his enormous bundles of duty and rest a summer with the mountains. I have a great deal to ask him. I have begun to build my cabin. You will have a *home* in Yosemite.

Ever thine,
J. Muir[17]

∾

New Sentinel Hotel, Yosemite
Valley,
July 6, 1872

Dear Mrs. Carr

Yours of Tuesday evening telling me of our Daggetts and Ned and Merrill Moores has come, and so has the lamp and the book. I have not yet tried the lamp, but it is splendid in shape and shines grand as gold. The Lyell is just what I wanted.

I think that your measure of the Daggetts is exactly right—as good as civilized people can be. They have grown to the top of town culture and have sent out some shoots half gropingly into the spirit sky.

I am very glad to know that Ned is growing strong. Perhaps we may see South America together yet. I hope to see you come to your own of mountain fountains soon. Perhaps Mrs. Hutchings may go with us. You live so fully in my own life that I cannot realize that I have not yet seen you here; a year or two of waiting seems nothing.

Possibly I may be down on your coast this fall or next, for I want to see what relations the coast and coast mountains have to the Sierras. Also I want to go north and south along this range and then among the basins and ranges eastward. My subject is expanding at a most unfollowable pace. I could write something with data already harvested, but I am not satisfied.

I have just returned from Hetch Hetchy with Mrs. Moore. Of course we had a glory and a fun—the two articles in about parallel columns of equal size. Meadows grassed and lilies head-high, spangled river-reaches, and currentless pools, cascades countless and unpaintable in form and whiteness, groves that heaven all the Valley. You were with us in all our joy and you will come again.

I am a little weary and half inclined to truantism from mobs however blessed, in some unfindable grove. I start in a few minutes for Clouds' Rest with Mr. and Mrs. Moore. I like Mrs. Moore and Mr. [*Moore*] first-rate.

My love to the Doctor and all the boys. I hope for Merrill daily. I am

> Ever your friend,
> J. Muir
> [*John Muir*][18]

ॐ

> New Sentinel Hotel, Yosemite
> Valley,
> July 14, 1872

Dear Mrs. Carr

Yours announcing Dr. [*Asa*] Gray is received. I have great longing for Gray, whom I feel to be a great, progressive, unlimited man like Darwin and Huxley and Tyndall. I will be most glad to meet him. You are unweariable in your kindness to me, and you helm my fate more than all the world beside.

I am approaching a kind of fruiting-time in this mountain work and I want very much to see you. All say *write,* but I don't know how or what, and besides I want to see North and South and the midland basins and the seacoast and all the lake-basins and the canyons, also the alps of every country and the continental glaciers of Greenland, before I write the book we have been speaking of; and all this will require a dozen years or twenty, and money. The question is what will I write now, etc. I have learned the alphabet of ice and mountain structure here, and I think I can read fast in other countries. I would let others write what I have read here, but that they make so damnable a hash of it and ruin so glorious a unit.

I miss the [*J. P.*] Moores because they were so cordial and kind to me. Mrs. Moore believes in ice and can preach it too. I wish you

could bring Whitney and her together and tell me the fight. Mrs.
M[oore] made the most sensible visit to our mountains of all the
comers I have known. Mr. Moore is a man who thinks, and he took
to this mountain structure like a pointer to partridges.

I am glad your Ned is growing strong; then we will yet meet this
summer in Yosemite places. Talk to Mrs. Moore about Hetch Hetchy,
etc. She knows it all from Hog Ranch to highest sea-wave cascades,
and higher, yet higher.

I ought not to fun away letter space in speaking to you. I am
weary and impractical and fit for nothing serious until I am tuned and
toned by a few weeks of calm.

Farewell. I will see you and we will plan work and ease and days
of holy mountain rest. Remember me to Ned and all the boys and to
the Doctor, who ought to come hither with you.

Ever thine,
John Muir[19]

∾

[Oakland], Saturday night, [July,
1872]

Dear John

You know so well both how great and how rare the joy is of
finding a voice for one's best thoughts and an answer to one's hardest
questions, that I need not tell you how I enjoyed Prof. Gray's visit
today, nor how I wish you could take the spare seat in the carriage
and go with us to enjoy a Sunday in the Redwoods. Isn't he the
gloriousest old boy, and was it not good to find your tramping
machine matched at last by one in equal running order? Dr. Henry
Gibbons, one of my friends that you must know, is going with us as a
guide to the extinct forest, and to the trunk of the tree thirty four feet
in diameter which when standing could be seen so far out at sea that
it was the guide-post to mariners. You and I will go there by and by.

Now that the Grays have returned I feel almost that I have been in
the Valley. Three or four days ago we had a letter from Ned who said
he was not gaining any in flesh, and that he felt a good deal discouraged
about himself. We have written for him to come home by slow and

easy stages. My brother who lives in Michigan will go to Vermont and take Ned home with him. A day will take him from there to Madison or Chicago and thence he will have good company, for he will wait for it. I shall not think of any pleasuring for myself this year, and you must tell Mrs. Hutchings, who will help you to understand it, that I could not enjoy the Valley even with half my heart upon my boy. Thank God this is so far from being hard, that I know the deferred pleasure is only deferred.

Mr. and Mrs. Daggett write so warmly of you, John. You are a real Harry Wadsworth fellow, and the pulses of your rich life are felt afar off. And this is what you are going to do. After the harvest time is over, and the last bird plucked (I wish I could see some of your game birds, all that I see are sacred storks and ibises), you will pack up all your duds, ready to leave [*Yosemite*] two or more years, take your best horse and ride forth some clear September morning.

You will live with us, and your horse at Moore's (near by), whenever you are not exploring the coast range. We will have some choice side trips, and Ned will be eating his way to complete recovery, so that I can leave him for a week or so without uneasiness. You will pass the winter here, and meanwhile ways will open for you to go to South America.

You will write up all your settled convictions, and put your cruder reflections in the form of notes and queries, not without scientific worth, and securing to yourself any advantage there may be in *priority* of observation. So writing and studying and visiting, the months will pass swiftly until your Valley home is filled again with color and song.

Perhaps it will not be your home again. God will teach you, as He has taught me, that the dear places and the dearer souls are but tents of a night; we must move on and leave them, though it cost heartbreaks. Not those who cling to you, but those who walk apart yet ever with you are your true companions.

Dr. Carr will stay here yet longer on account of University changes, but I hope will not be prevented from taking a long rest.

Tuesday eve. I go in the morning to Sunol, near Pleasanton, where a sister-in-law is very ill. Shall be nurse and housekeeper for some days, perhaps longer. Goodbye to all projects for the present. Dr. Jos.

Le Conte will be in the Valley soon. If Dr. Carr comes at all it will be with the Agassiz and Hill persuasion.

More hereafter. Adios

J. C. C.

[*Jeanne C. Carr*]

Mrs. Moore complained of herself for not having written you when I saw her today. She was feeling out o'sorts—her splendid mana flowing free, en sacque, she wished herself in the wilds again.[20]

∾

Yosemite Valley, July 27, 1872

Dear Mrs. Carr

I want to see you. I want to speak about my studies, which are growing broader and broader and spreading away to all countries without any clear horizon anywhere.

I will go over all this Yosemite region this fall and write it up in some form or other. Will you be here to accompany me in my easier excursions?

I have a good horse for you and will get a tub and plenty of meal and tea, and you will keep house in very old style and you can bring whom you please.

I've had a very noble time with [*Asa*] Gray, who, though brooded and breaded by Hutchings, gave most of his time to me. I was sorry that his time was so meanly measured and bounded. He is a most cordial lover of purity and truth, but the angular factiness of his pursuits has kept him at too cold a distance from the spirit world.

I know that Mrs. Moore has given you ice in abundance, though even Yosemite glaciers might melt in the warmth of her laughter and sunshine. She handles glacier periods like an Agassiz and has discovered a Hetch Hetchy period that is her own. Don't you believe all she tells you about the walk and the dark and the dust of Indian Canyon.

I want to get Daggett's address.

I will begin my long mountain excursion soon, for the snow is mostly gone from the high meadows.

I have been guiding a few parties and will take a few more if they are of the right kind, but I want my mind kept free and sensitive to all influences excepting human business.

I have ten horses, but another man takes charge of them, and I am all free.

I need to talk with you more than ever before. Mrs. Hutchings is always kind to me, and the clearness of her views on all spiritual things is very extraordinary. She appreciates your friendship very keenly, and I am glad to think you will soon know each other better. Her little Cosie (Gertrude) is as pure a piece of sunbeam as ever was condensed to human form.

Hoping that Ned will be able to come here to the mountain waters for perfect healing and that you will also find leisure for the satisfying of your thirst for beauty, I remain ever

Your friend,
John Muir

My love to Doctor and all the boys.[21]

ॐ

Oakland, California,
August 4, 1872

My dear Mr. Muir

At last I have an hour to myself and we will have a little chat. Ever since my return the house has been full of visitors, too busy and too full to think of writing, though I found letters waiting for me. Yet this is the first I've written.

Mr. Moore has gone to church and taken McChesney with him, and the quiet of the house is delicious. I would love to be with you in that glorious country this beautiful morning, but yet I can enjoy it here and do. For two weeks after our return the fog was dreadful and how sorry I was that I did not stay longer, but now the weather is charming and I am more contented. We had a good trip home, for the hills had a new interest and told their stories in plainer language and with clearer voices. You must certainly follow up your ice streams, I saw much that looked as if the Pacific had swallowed them up. But yet many things bothered me, things that would give you no trouble, I'm sure, for you know I'm "only a baby" yet in this thing. What good long talks your dear Mrs. Carr and I have had all about you, and she thinks as I and all your friends do—that you ought to come

down this fall to the Coast Range—for a look around, if no more—
before you go farther in your studies. What a sincere unselfish friend
you have in her! It is lovely to see such a pure affection, so true, and
yet so clear sighted, for—mind you—she sees your shortcomings too!
Ah! this is a glorious woman!

How about your coming down, let me tell you what we are going
to do, and see if you can't time your movements to harmonize with
ours. About the first of October we shall go up to the ranch for a
month—can't you manage to go with us? What long tramps we will
have! and what good times "on fresh fields and pastures new." What
do you say? Say yes, and I will arrange the trip so that it will be right,
no mutton-heads shall trouble us, be sure!

Apropos. I have seen our H. H. [Hetch Hetchy] party only once.
Mr. Smith called and I like him so much. He is looking forward to the
Tamalpais trip with you. The bill from Bayley was about $65.00—I
think he must have become ashamed of the first estimate and reduced
it to about what he thought we would stand. Even then he seemed in
doubt about it and wanted to know if we thought it too much! Ah,
Nature puts her sign manual on some people, only we don't take the
trouble to read it. The Cheneys—that is all, but Robert and Mr. C.
have gone East but Annie and two uncles are coming back next
month. I think they will conclude to live here. Mr. C. has been gaining in health ever since his return. He dined here yesterday and I
never saw him looking better. He talked of you and wished to be
remembered in this letter, and said many kind things of you, for he
admires you. And by the way, so did Annie, but that I'll reserve to
tease you with when I see you. "Any young man who don't improve
his opportunities, etc." you know the rest!

Mrs. Carr is not at home just now, unless she returned last night.
A sister-in-law has been sick and she went down to see her some days
ago. So the Professor brought up a letter from you night before last
for me to read. Thanks, many thanks, for your kindly memories of
me, and all my botherings, which were neither few nor far between.
I fully appreciate your forbearance, for I know I'm inclined to be
lawless at times, and the glorious freedom of the mountains bewitched
me, but keep my memory green, for a while anyhow.

O didn't I hear from Mrs. Carr all about Dr. Gray and what a good rich time you had? didn't I think of you every day, for I knew when he went up, and didn't I enjoy it all with you in fancy? *Of course I did.*

Now, see here. I've filled this sheet full and said very little of what I intended to say, for instance about the possibility of Mrs. Carr going up to the beautiful valley this fall. She thinks it out of the question, and that you'd better come down, and a dozen other things I wanted to say. Just room for Mr. Moore's love but not for mine, for remember that no one takes a warmer interest in you or your studies or sympathizes more fully in all your hopes and aspirations or believes more fully in you or has a warmer, cozier place in her heart for you than

Your friend,

M. R. Moore

[*Mrs. J. P. Moore*]

Remember me kindly to Mrs. Hutchings.[22]

Yosemite Valley, August 5, 1872

Dear Mrs. Carr

Your letter telling me to catch my best glacier birds and come to you and the coast mountains only makes me the more anxious to see you, and if you cannot come up, I will have to come down, if only for a talk. My birds are flying everywhere,—into all mountains and plains, of all climes and times,—and some are ducks in the sea, and I scarce know what to do about it. I must see the coast ranges and the coast, but I was thinking that a month or so might answer for the present, and then, instead of spending the winter in town, I would hide in Yosemite and write; or I thought I would pack up some meal and dried plums to some deep wind-sheltered canyon back among the glaciers of the summits, and write there, and be ready to catch any whisper of ice and snow in these highest storms.

You anticipate all the bends and falls and rapids and cascades of my mountain life, and I know that you say truly about my companions being those who live with me in the same sky, whether in reach of hand or only of spiritual contact, which is the most real contact of all.

I am learning to live close to the lives of my friends without ever seeing them. No miles of any measurement can separate your soul from mine.

[Paragraphs cut]

Farewell. I'm glad you are to get your Ned again. The fever will soon cool out from his veins in the breath of California.

The Valley is full of sun, but glorious Sierras are piled above the South Dome and Starr King. I mean the bossy cumuli that are daily upheaved at this season, making a cloud period yet grander than the rock-sculpturing, Yosemite-making, forest-planting glacial period.

Yesterday we had our first midday shower. The pines waved gloriously at its approach, the woodpeckers beat about as if alarmed, but the hummingbird moths thought the cloud shadows belonged to evening and came down to eat among the mints. All the firs and rocks of Starr King were bathily dripped before the Valley was vouchsafed a single drop.

After the splendid blessing, the afternoon was veiled in calm clouds, and one of intensely beautiful pattern and gorgeously *irised* was stationed over Eagle Rock at the sunset.

Farewell. I'll see you with my common eyes, and touch you with these very writing fingers ere long.

Remember me cordially to Mrs. Moore and Mr. and all your family, and I am as ever

Your friend,
John Muir[23]

ॐ

Yosemite Valley,
August 28, 1872

Dear Mrs. Carr

My horse and bread, etc., are ready for upward. I returned three days ago from Mts. Lyell, McClure, and Hoffman. I spent three days on a glacier up there, planting stakes, etc. This time I go to the Merced group, one of whose mountains shelters a glacier. I will go over all the lakes and moraines, etc., there. Will be gone a week or two or so.

Hutch[*ings*] wants to go with me to "help me"!! but I will, etc., etc.

Ink cannot tell the glow that lights me at this moment in turning to the mountains. I feel strong to leap Yosemite walls at a bound. Hotels and human impurity will be far below. I will fuse in spirit skies. I will touch naked God.

Farewell, or come meet in ghost between Red Mountain and Black on the star-sparkled ice.

Love to all thine and to Moores and Stoddard.

[*John Muir*][24]

ᘯ

Yosemite Valley, September 13, 1872

Dear Mrs. Carr

Yours of Aug. 23rd is received. Le Conte writes me that Agassiz will not come to the Valley.

I just got down last evening from a fifteen-day ramble in the basins of Illilouette and Pohono, and start again in an hour for the summit glaciers to see some canyons and to examine the stakes I planted in the ice a month ago.

I would like to come down to see Agassiz, but now is my harvest of rocks and I cannot spare the time.

I shall work in the outer mountains incessantly until the coming of the snow... your ferns, etc.

[Remainder of letter cut]

Love to all,

[John Muir][25]

ᘯ

[*Oakland, September, 1872?*]

[*John Muir*]

[Fragment of letter]

I took your Hetch Hetchy love to her today and read her the letter, she lying with her head in ice could enjoy and appreciate it. I have not read her any of your more recent letters for reasons. Sunday I went from Mrs. Moore's bedside to Harry Edwards', who has been brought over here for a change. Saw Harry eat his first meal in ten weeks, his feet tied up in a woolen rug, and his hands about twice their natural size—just able to go through a feeble game of knife and fork. He is still a great sufferer from inflammatory rheumatism.

Allie and I walked out last night under the stars. Dr. Carr was in Sacramento. Ned delayeth his coming. John got back from his expedition with the clothes on his back, "nothing more," and looking all through the heavenly host not one was baleful, not one evil. Faint as the music of far off brooks in my green hills I heard,

> For God is God, my darling,
> Of the night as well as the day.

Let the days shorten, let winter and grief draw nigh our dwelling: every mark of the Rock's old torture is fair in the aftertime?

They all send their love, the sick and well, and give mine to Mrs. Hutchings.

Did you see that Dr. Jo. Le Conte lectures on Monday evening week on the glaciers of the High Sierras, "advancing many new and interesting theories." Dr. Carr wondered if they were credited to their proper origin. We did not hear the lecture, which will be published.

Always yours,
J. C. C.
[Jeanne C. Carr][26]

∾

Oakland, September 24, [1872?]

My dear John

Yours of the 18th and one of older date are before me. I sent to Agassiz the one you enclosed. Either that or something from the papers (*New York Tribune* clippings) excited him to say with great warmth, "Muir was studying to greater purpose and with greater results than any one else has done." Le Conte told me he spoke of your work with enthusiasm.

Perhaps you saw the poetic welcome to him from the *Bulletin*. I suppose Mrs. H[utchings] cuts and clips the news which belongs to you and gives it to you assorted when you descend to such things.

I have not given Charlie [*Stoddard*] one of your messages. First, he has not been to see me and I had no chance—he does not like to have me call on him at his father's, and I don't write to anyone if I can possibly avoid it. Then he is engaged to read or recite one of his own poems at Harry Edwards' benefit Thursday evening and he ought to do his best, for Harry Edwards and his wife have been the true and the tried to Charlie. Then one cannot say that you will not hasten down and have one talk with Agassiz who prolongs his stay, and in case he feels himself bettering may do so until you come. Let Charlie's visit pass for this fall. He is miserably morbid and the mood would not be likely to yield to your ministrations. He is a real lover at last, and I think....

[Remainder of letter lost]

[*Jeanne C. Carr*][27]

∾

[*Autumn, 1872*]

[*Mrs. Carr*]

[Beginning of letter missing]

The bottom portion of the foregoing section, with perpendicular sides is here about two feet in depth and was cut by the water. The Nevada here *never was* more than four or five feet deep and all of the bank records of all the upper streams say the same thing of the absence of great floods.

The entire region above Yosemite and as far down as the bottoms of Yosemite has scarcely been touched by any other denudation than that of ice. Perhaps all of the post glacial denudation of every kind would not average an inch in depth for the whole region.

Yosemite and Hetch Hetchy are lake basins filled with sand and the matter of moraines washed from the upper canyons. The Yosemite ice in escaping from the Yosemite basin was compelled to flow upward a considerable height on both sides of the bottom walls of the Valley. The canyon below the Valley is very crooked and very narrow and the

Yosemite glacier flowed across all of its crooks, and high above its walls without paying any compliance to it, thus the light lines show the direction of the ice-current.

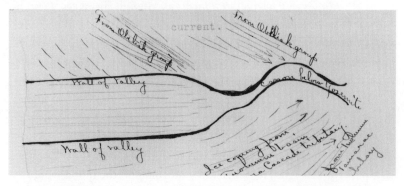

In going up any of the principal Yosemite streams lakes in all stages of decay are found in great abundance regularly becoming younger until we reach the almost countless gems of the summits with scarce an inch of *Carex* upon their shallow sandy borders, and with their bottoms still bright with the polish of ice. Upon the Nevada and its branches there are not fewer than a hundred of these glacial lakes from a mile to a hundred yards in diameter, with countless glistening pondlets not much larger than moons.

All of the grand fir forests about the Valley are planted upon moraines and from any of the mountain tops, the shape and extent of the neighboring moraines may always be surely determined by the firs growing upon them.

Some pines will grow upon shallow sand and crumbling granite, but those luxuriant forests of the silver firs are always upon a generous bed of glacial drift. I discovered a moraine with smooth pebbles upon a shoulder of the South Dome, and upon every part of the Yosemite upper and lower walls.

I am surprised to find that *water* has had so little to do with mountain structure here. Whitney says that there is no proof that glaciers ever flowed in this valley, yet its walls have not been eroded to the depth of an inch since the ice left it, and glacial action is glaringly apparent many miles below the Valley.

[Paragraph missing]

[John Muir][28]

∾

Oakland, October 2, [*1872*]

My dear Muir

When you know Mr. [*Benoni*] Irwin and Mr. [*William*] Keith to whom this will introduce you, do not accuse me of intentionally keeping the best wine of kindred and related spirits till the last of your season's feast.

You will know them by their coming so late, as of the order of the autumn leaves, and feed them with the year's ripe fruit; perhaps with an appetizer of snow and ice. Melt and fuse your spirits in the great Nature baptism in which all Art and Science inspirations are born and replenished. Eyes that can see are not common, even in your Himmelslande.

The Agassizes, God bless them, go today, taking some of your glacierest letters, and the slip from *New York Tribune* containing "A Glacier's Death," for reading on the way. I send a package Dr. Gray sent you with his love. I had two lovely little letters from him, and what do you think, *thirty* species of living sempervirens from every uplifted land, Alps, Pyrenees, Ural—some not larger than a shirt button. When I am rich you shall have a set for studs. Mrs. Moore is bettering, sends love to you, Mr. M. also. Ned *has come, has come.* By and by I shall know if Ned is here. I fancy I see the spell of those great solitudes upon him. He does not talk much, but with appreciation of the land so far away when I think of his returning to it.

I commission Mr. Irwin to sketch you in your hay rope suspenders, etc., against the day when you are famous and carry all the letters of the alphabet as a tail to your literary kites. Goodbye. Love these good and true souls, and artists as well, as does your

Friend,

Jeanne C. Carr

The second volume of Lyell has come. Shall I send it?[29]

∾

Yosemite Valley,

October 8, 1872

Dear Mrs. Carr

Here we are again, and here is your letter of Sept. 24th. I got down last evening, and boo! was I not weary after pushing through the rough upper half of the great Tuolumne Canyon? I have climbed more than twenty-four thousand feet in these ten days, three times to the top of the glacieret of Mt. Hoffman, and once to Mts. Lyell and McClure. I have bagged a quantity of Tuolumne rocks sufficient to build a dozen Yosemites; strips of cascades longer than ever, lacy or smooth and white as pressed snow; a glacier basin with ten glassy lakes set all near together like eggs in a nest; then El Capitan and a couple of Tissiacks, canyons glorious with yellows and reds of mountain maple and aspen and honeysuckle and ash and new indescribable music immeasurable from strange waters and winds, and glaciers, too, flowing and grinding, alive as any on earth. Shall I pull you out some? Here is a clean, white-skinned glacier from the back of McClure with glassy emerald flesh and singing crystal blood all bright and pure as a sky, yet handling mud and stone like a navvy, building moraines like a plodding Irishman. Here is a cascade two hundred feet wide, half a mile long, glancing this way and that, filled with bounce and dance and joyous hurrah, yet earnest as tempest, and singing like angels loose on a frolic from heaven; and here are more cascades and more, broad and flat like clouds and fringed like flowing hair, with occasional falls erect as pines, and lakes like glowing eyes; and here are visions and dreams, and a splendid set of ghosts, too many for ink and narrow paper.

I have not heard anything concerning Le Conte's glacier lecture, but he seems to have drawn all he knows of Sierra glaciers and new theories concerning them so directly from here that I cannot think that he will claim discovery, etc. If he does, I will not be made poorer.

Professor [*Samuel*] Kneeland, Secretary Boston Institute of Technology, gathered some letters I sent to Runkle and that *Tribune* letter, and hashed them into a compost called a paper for the Boston Historical Society, and gave me credit for all of the smaller sayings and doings and stole the broadest truth to himself. I have the proof-sheets of "The Paper" and will show them to you some time. But all of such meanness can work no permanent evil to any one except the dealer.

As for the living "Glaciers of the Sierras," here is what I have learned concerning them. You will have the first chance to steal, for I have just concluded my experiments on them for the season and have not yet cast them at any of the great professors, or presidents.

One of the yellow days of last October, when I was among the mountains of the "Merced Group," following the footprints of the ancient glaciers that once flowed grandly from their ample fountains, reading what I could of their history as written in moraines and canyons and lakes and carved rocks, I came upon a small stream that was carrying mud I had not before seen. In a calm place where the stream widened I collected some of this mud and observed that it was entirely mineral in composition and fine as flour, like the mud from a fine-grit grindstone. Before I had time to reason I said, Glacier mud, mountain meal.

Then I observed that this muddy stream issued from a bank of fresh quarried stones and dirt that was sixty or seventy feet in height. This I at once took to be a moraine. In climbing to the top of it I was struck with the steepness of its slope and with its raw, unsettled, plantless, newborn appearance. The slightest touch started blocks of red and black slate, followed by a rattling train of smaller stones and sand and a cloud of the dry dust of mud, the whole moraine being as free from lichens and weather stains as if dug from the mountain that very day.

When I had scrambled to the top of the moraine, I saw what seemed a huge snow-bank four or five hundred yards in length by half a mile in width. Imbedded in its stained and furrowed surface were stones and dirt like that of which the moraine was built. Dirt-stained lines curved across the snow-bank from side to side, and when I observed that these curved lines coincided with the curved moraine and that the stones and dirt were most abundant near the bottom of the bank, I shouted, "A living glacier." These bent dirt lines show that the ice is flowing in its different parts with unequal velocity, and these embedded stones are journeying down to be built into the moraine, and they gradually become more abundant as they approach the moraine because there the motion is slower.

On traversing my new-found glacier, I came to a crevass, down a wide and jagged portion of which I succeeded in making my way, and discovered that my so-called *snow-bank* was clear green ice, and, comparing the form of the basin which it occupied with similar adjacent basins that were empty, I was led to the opinion that this glacier was several hundred feet in depth.

Then I went to the "snow-banks" of Mts. Lyell and McClure and believed that they also were true glaciers and that a dozen other snow-banks seen from the summit of Mt. Lyell crouching in shadow were glaciers, living as any in the world and busily engaged in completing that vast work of mountain-making, accomplished by their giant relatives now dead, which, united and continuous, covered all the range from summit to sea like a sky.

But although I was myself fully satisfied concerning the real nature of these ice- masses. I found that my friends regarded my deductions and statements with distrust, therefore I determined to collect proofs of the common measured arithmetical kind.

On the 21st of Aug. last I planted five stakes in the glacier of Mt. McClure, which is situated east of Yosemite Valley, near the summit of the range. Four of these stakes were extended across the glacier in a straight line, from the east side to a point near the middle of the glacier. The first stake was planted about 25 yds. from the east bank of the glacier. The second 94 yards, the third, 152, and the fourth, 223 yards. The positions of these stakes were determined by sighting across from bank to bank past a plumbline made of a stone and a black horse-hair.

On observing my stakes on the 6th of Oct., or in 46 days after being planted, I found that stake No. 1 had been carried down stream 11 inches; No. 2, 18 inches; No. 3, 34; No. 4, 47 inches. As stake No. 4 was near the middle of the glacier, perhaps it was not far from the point of maximum velocity, 47 inches in 46 days, or 1 inch per day. Stake No. 5 was planted about midway between the head of the glacier and stake No. 4. Its motion I found to be in 46 days 40 inches.

Thus these ice-masses are seen to possess the true glacial motion. Their surfaces are striped with bent dirt bands. Their surfaces are bulged and undulated by inequalities in the bottom of their basins, causing an upward and downward swedging corresponding to the horizontal swedging as indicated by the curved dirt bands.

The McClure Glacier is about one half mile in length and about the same in width at the broadest place. It is crevassed on the south-east corner. The crevass runs about southwest and northeast and is several hundred yards in length. Its width is nowhere more than one foot.

The Mt. Lyell glacier, separated from that of McClure by a narrow crest, is about a mile in width by a mile in length.

I have planted stakes in the glacier of Red Mountain also but have not yet observed them.

The Sierras adjacent to the Yosemite Valley are composed of slabs of granite set on edge at right angles to the direction of the range, or about N 30 degrees E, S 30 degrees W. Also lines of cleavage cross these, running nearly parallel with the main range. Also the granite of this region has a horizontal cleavage or stratification. The first mentioned of these lines have the fullest development, and give direction and character to many valleys and canyons and determine the principal features of many rock forms. No matter how hard and domed and homogeneous the granite may be, it still possesses these lines of cleavage, which require only simple conditions of moisture, time, etc. for their development. But I am not ready to discuss the origin of these planes of cleavage which make this granite so easily denudable, nor their full significance with regard to mountain structure in general. I will only say here that oftentimes the granite contained between two of these N 30 degree E planes is softer than that outside and has been denuded, leaving vertical walls as determined by the direction of the cleavage, thus giving rise to those narrow slotted canyons called "Devil's slides," "Devil's lanes," "Devil's gateways," etc.

In many places in the higher portions of the Sierra these slotted canyons are filled with "snow," which I thought might prove to be ice—might prove to be living glaciers still engaged in cutting into the mountains like endless saws.

To decide this question on the 23d of August last I set two stakes in the narrow slot glacier of Mt. Hoffman, marking their position by sighting across from wall to wall, as I did on the McClure glacier, but on visiting them a month afterwards I found that they had been melted out, and I was unable to decide anything with any considerable degree of accuracy.

On the 4th of October last I stretched a small trout-line [sic] across the glacier, fastening both ends in the solid banks, which at this place were only 16 feet apart. I set a short inflexible stake in the ice so as just to touch the tightly drawn line, by which means I was enabled to measure the flow of the glacier with great exactness. Examining this stake in 24 hours after setting it, I found that it had been carried down about 3/16 of an inch. At the end of four days I again examined it, and found that the whole downward motion was 3/16 of an inch, showing that the flow of this glacieret was perfectly regular.

In accounting for these narrow lane canyons so common here, I had always referred them to ice action in connection with special conditions of cleavage, and I was gratified to find that their formation was still going on. This Hoffman glacieret is about 1000 feet long by 15 to 30 feet wide, and perhaps about 100 feet deep in deepest places.

Now then, Mrs. Carr, I must hasten back to the mountains. I'll go tomorrow.

[*John Muir*][30]

ை

[*Yosemite, October, 1872*]

[*Mrs. Carr*]

I'm going to take your painter boys with me into one of my best sanctums on your recommendation for holiness.

Emerson has sent me a profound little book styled "The Growth of the Mind," by Reed. Do you know it? It is full of the fountain truth.

I'm glad your boys are safely back. Perhaps Ned and I may try that Andes field together.

I would write to Mrs. Moore but will wait until she is better. Tell her the cascades and mountains of upper Hetch Hetch Hetch Hetch!!

I hope I may see you a few days soon. I had a pretty letter from old Dr. [*John*] Torrey, and from Gray I have heard three or four times. I am ever

Cordially yours,
John Muir

Send Lyell if you have good chance.[31]

[Remainder of postscript missing]

∾

Yosemite, October 14, [*1872*]

Dear Mrs. Carr

I cannot hear from you. There are some souls, perhaps, that are never tired, that ever go steadily glad, always tuneful and songful like mountain water. Not so, weary, hungry me. This second time I come from the rocks for fresh supplies of the two breads, but I find but one. I cannot hear from you. My last weeks were spent among the canyons of the Hoffman range and the Cathedral Peak group east of Lake Tenaya. All gloriously rich in the written truths which I am seeking. I will now go to the wide, ragged tributaries of Illilouette and to Pohono, after which I will mope about among the rim canyons and rock forms of the Valley as the weather permits.

Perhaps I have not yet answered all of your last long pages. Here is a quotation from Tyndall concerning the nature and origin of his intense mountain enjoyments. He reaches far and near for a theory of his delight in the mountains, going among the accidents of his own boyhood and those of his remotest fathers, but surely this must be all wrong, and, instead of groping away backwards among the various grades of grandfathers, he should explore the most primary properties of man. Perhaps we owe "the pleasurable emotions which fine land-scape makes in us" to a cause as radical as that which makes a magnet pulse to the two poles. I think that one of the *properties* of that com-pound which we call man is that when exposed to the rays of mountain beauty it glows with *joy*. I don't know who of all my ancestry are to blame, but my attractions and repulsions are badly balanced tonight and I will not try to say any more, excepting farewell and love to you all.

John Muir[32]

∾

Yosemite Valley, December 25, 1872

Dear Mrs. Carr

My memories of that far off country of Oakland are already dim as if worn by the waves of a hundred winters, but your self-sacrificing everlasting love burns clear to my eye as a naked sun.

For you, my friend, I could sing thanks and praise on a thousand pages but you know my gratitude better than any song can tell and I need not sound a single note. The light of our friendship requires no adjustment—like a planet, it will burn along its own path without our care, for all of the clean love that the world contains is divine, and circles around God as stars around their sun!

You told me I ought to abandon letter writing, and I see plainly enough that you are right in this, because my correspondence has gone on increasing year by year and has become far too bulky and miscellaneous in its character, and consumes too much of my time. Therefore I mean to take your advice and allow broad acres of silence to spread between my letters, however much of self-denial may be demanded.

Bookmaking frightens me, because it demands so much artificialness and retrograding. Somehow, up here in these fountain skies I feel like a flake of glass through which light passes, but which, conscious of the inexhaustibleness of its sun fountain, cares not whether its passing light coins itself into other forms or goes unchanged—neither charcoaled nor diamonded! Moreover, I find that though I have a few thoughts entangled in the fibres of my mind, I possess no words into which I can shape them. You tell me that I must be patient and reach out and grope in lexicon granaries for the words I want. But if some loquacious angel were to touch my lips with literary fire, bestowing every word of Webster, I would scarce thank him for the gift, because most of the words of the English language are made of mud, for muddy purposes, while those invented to contain spiritual matter are doubtful and unfixed in capacity and form, as wind-ridden mist-rags.

These mountain fires that glow in one's blood are free to all, but I cannot find the chemistry that may press them unimpaired into booksellers' bricks. True, with that august instrument, the English language, in the manufacture of which so many brains have been broken, I can proclaim to you that moonshine is glorious and nice, and sunshine more glorious and nicer, that winds rage, and waters roar, and that in "terrible times" glaciers guttered the mountains with their hard cold snouts. This is about the limit of what I feel capable of doing for the public—the moiling, squirming, fog-breathing public. But for my few friends I can do more because they already know the mountain harmonies and can catch the tones I gather for them though written in a few harsh and gravelly sentences. Here you demand an account of work accomplished for either friends or public, well this is all. Next morning after reaching Turlock I sped afoot over the stubble fields and through miles of brown *Hemizonia* and purple *Eriogonum,* to Hopeton, conscious of but little more than that the great town was behind and beneath me, and the mountains above and before me. Next day pushed on through the oaks and chaparral of the foothills— next passed Coulterville and ascended the first great mountain step upon which grows the sugar pine. Here I slackened my pace for I drank the spicy rosiny wind and was at home; never did pine trees seem so dear. How sweet was their breath and their song, and how grandly they winnowed the sky, and how I tingled my fingers among their tassels, and rubbed my feet among the fallen needles and burrs.

I had a grand greeting of Yosemite rocks, never did they appear so lovable or more willing to speak to me as to a friend. But though I bathed in the bright river and sauntered on the meadows and rustled in the brown ferns and prayed with the pines, I was still uneasy as if tainted with the sticky sky of your town. Therefore I determined to run out to the higher mountains. "The days are sunful," I said, and though it is now winter there will be but little danger and a sudden storm will not prevent me from forcing my way back to the Valley and will do me the good I seek. Next morning after this decision I rolled up a pair of blankets and set out up the Canyon of Tenaya caring little about the quantity of bread I carried, for I said that a fast and a storm and a difficult canyon is just the medicine I require to heal me of all this town heaviness.

The distance from Mirror Lake up the Tenaya Canyon to Lake Tenaya is about ten miles and the scenery all the way is not a whit less glorious than that of Yosemite. Indeed this Tenaya Canyon is a fork of Yosemite which shallows gradually until within a mile and a half of Lake Tenaya. For about a mile above Mirror Lake the Canyon bottom is flat and level and is grandly forested with fir and Douglas Spruce and *Libocedrus.* This forest is growing upon the filled in portion of the Mirror Lake basin. At the head of these lake groves is the Tenaya falls about 80 feet high. For about 30 yards above the brink of the fall the stream rushes in rapids down a flat open granite pavement inclined at an angle of 18 degrees. This sheet of rapids which in high water is 75 feet wide is varied by three parallel grooves running parallel with the stream. They have been formed by the action of the water on soft seams. And as these grooves are variable in width and slightly sinuous and rounded boulders are wedged firmly in narrow places, they compel the swift water to leap and arch and scatter itself in crystals in most unanticipatable [*sic*] methods. Thus the whole stream in descending this incline is beaten into foam and broidered with endless variety of living forms before it reaches the brink. When it leaps down 80 feet into a sort-of cross gorge and flows out at bottom at right angles to its general course somewhat like the Victoria Falls on the Zambezi.

The glory of this fall is the abundance of luxuriant groviness about it and mingling with it. Its white waters issue from a tangle of evergreen trees and shrubs and ferns and mosses and flow through a tangle into a tangle. Ferns, tall woodwardian and gentle floating maidenhairs and emerald mosses in sheltered coves ever wet with mealy spray are precious and luxuriant fringes of maidenhair and thickets of the tall *Woodwardia*.

John Muir[33]

Jeanne C. Carr, 1843. Courtesy of the
Archives at the Pasadena Historical
Museum.

Ezra S. Carr, Madison, Wisconsin, 1857.
Courtesy of the State Historical Society
of Wisconsin.

Dr. James D. Butler in his library at 518
Wisconsin Avenue, Madison, Wisconsin,
1894. Courtesy of the State Historical
Society of Wisconsin.

The Reverend Dr. Walter R. Brooks, c. 1877.
Muth & Hill Portrait and Landscape Photographers, Hamilton, New York. Courtesy of
Colgate University, Case Library Special
Collections.

Carr house at 114 Gilman Street, Madison,
Wisconsin, that Muir frequently visited.
Courtesy of Bonnie Johanna Gisel.

Edward C. Carr, son of Jeanne C. and Ezra S. Carr, c. 1866. Courtesy of the Archives at the Pasadena Historical Museum.

John Henry Carr, son of Jeanne C. and Ezra S. Carr, c. 1874. Courtesy of the Huntington Library.

Ezra S. Carr, Jr., son of Jeanne C. and Ezra S. Carr, 1870. Courtesy of the Archives at the Pasadena Historical Museum.

Albert [Allie] Lee Carr, c. 1880s. Courtesy of the Archives at the Pasadena Historical Museum.

View of Castleton, Vermont, where Jeanne
Carr was born, attended school, and married
Ezra Slocum Carr. Oil on canvas. Painted by
James Hope, Castleton, Vermont, 1873.
Courtesy of the Castleton Historical Society.

Hutchings Hotel, Yosemite Valley, c. 1870s.
Stereograph by Thomas Houseworth & Co.
Courtesy of the Huntington Library.

Portrait of the Hutchings family, James M.,
Gertrude (Cosie), and William M. Hutchings
in Yosemite Valley, c. 1870s. Courtesy of the
Yosemite Museum, Yosemite National Park.

Florence [Floy] [Squirrel] Hutchings, c. 1870.
Studio portrait by Thomas Houseworth.
Courtesy of the Yosemite Museum, Yosemite
National Park.

Elvira Hutchings seated in the manzanita
armchair made by James M. Hutchings,
Yosemite Valley, c. 1870s. Carte-de-Visite
attributed to James Reilly. Courtesy of the
Yosemite Museum, Yosemite National Park.

Theresa Yelverton, seated in the manzanita
armchair made by James M. Hutchings,
Yosemite Valley, c. 1870s. Carte-de-Visite by
James Reilly. Courtesy of the Yosemite
Museum, Yosemite National Park.

John Muir photographed by Rulofson in San Francisco in 1872 during his first trip out of Yosemite Valley to Oakland and San Francisco since 1869. Courtesy of the Bancroft Library, University of California, Berkeley.

Emily Pelton, c. 1875. E. C. Dwight & Co., Freeport, Illinois. Courtesy of the John Muir Papers, Holt-Atherton Department of Special Collections, University of the Pacific Libraries. Copyright 1984 Muir-Hanna Trust.

Dr. Albert Kellogg, c. 1890s. From an 1893 issue of *Zoe: A Biological Journal.*

William Keith, c. 1870s. Carleton E. Watkins Art Gallery, San Francisco. Courtesy of the Huntington Library.

"Camp on Tenaya Creek above Mirror Lake,
Yo Semite (Mrs. Carr, John Muir, Dr. Kellogg,
William Keith, and Allie Carr), July 1873."
(Allie Carr is seated on the rock.) Sketch by
A. L. Carr, 1873. Courtesy of the Archives at
the Pasadena Historical Museum.

"Our Companions."
Sketch by Jeanne C. Carr,
c. 1873. Courtesy of the
Archives at the Pasadena
Historical Museum.

"Our Gondola. Mrs.
Carr and John Muir."
Sketch by Jeanne C. Carr,
c. 1873. Courtesy of the
Archives at the Pasadena
Historical Museum.

Shadow Lake ~ headwaters of Merced River. 15 miles above Yo Semite. (see reverse side) 1873.

"Shadow Lake, Headwaters of Merced River, 15 miles above Yosemite, 1873." Sketch by Jeanne C. Carr, 1873. Courtesy of the Archives at the Pasadena Historical Museum.

"The first glacier seen from Merced Mountain about half way up the mountain as you ascend the river." Sketch by Jeanne C. Carr, 1873. Courtesy of the Archives at the Pasadena Historical Museum.

"Summits of Mount Dana and Mount Gibbs." Sketch by Jeanne C. Carr, c. 1873. Courtesy of the Archives at the Pasadena Historical Museum.

"Effect of Wind and Snow." Sketch by Jeanne C. Carr, c. 1873. Courtesy of the Archives at the Pasadena Historical Museum.

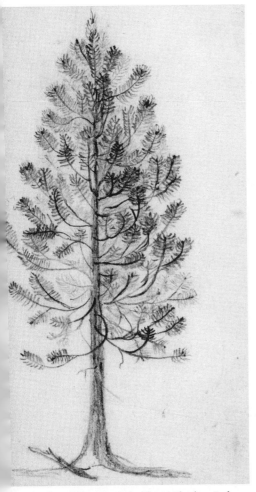

"Yellow Pine, Cascade Above Shadow Lake, July 29, 1873." Sketch by Jeanne C. Carr, 1873. Courtesy of the Archives at the Pasadena Historical Museum.

"*Juniperus occidentalis,* left bank of Merced, July 30, 1873." Sketch by Jeanne C. Carr, 1873. Courtesy of the Archives at the Pasadena Historical Museum.

"Yellow Pine, Skeleton, near camp, Muir Lake, August 2, 1873." Sketch by Jeanne C. Carr, 1873. Courtesy of the Archives at the Pasadena Historical Museum.

"Merced Banks, August 7, 1873." Sketch by Jeanne C. Carr, 1873. Courtesy of the Archives at the Pasadena Historical Museum.

"*Abies williamsonii.*" Sketch by Jeanne C. Carr. Courtesy of the Archives at the Pasadena Historical Museum.

The Lost "Leader", and effect of snow on *Abies Williamsonia*. Summit Lake Aug 17, 1873

"The lost leader and effect of snow on *Abies williamsonii,* Summit Lake, August 17, 1873." Sketch by Jeanne C. Carr, c. 1873. Courtesy of the Archives at the Pasadena Historical Museum.

Carmelita, residence of Jeanne C. and Ezra S. Carr, Pasadena, California, c. 1886. Dr. Orville H. Congar's residence at right across Colorado Street. Courtesy of the Archives at the Pasadena Historical Museum.

Carmelita, house and gardens, Pasadena, California, c. 1886. Courtesy of the Archives at the Pasadena Historical Museum.

Gardens at Carmelita, residence of Jeanne C.
and Ezra S. Carr, Pasadena, California, c.
1880s. Courtesy of the Huntington Library.

Jeanne C. and Ezra S. Carr, Carmelita,
Pasadena, California c. 1882. Courtesy of the
Archives at the Pasadena Historical Museum.

Jeanne C. Carr and Ezra S. Carr, Carmelita,
Pasadena, California, c. 1880s. Courtesy of
the Archives at the Pasadena Historical
Museum.

Jeanne C. Carr on the porch of her Kensington Street cottage, c. 1892. Courtesy of the Archives at the Pasadena Historical Museum.

Mission-style cottage on Kensington Street built by Carr after the sale of Carmelita in 1892. Courtesy of the Archives at the Pasadena Historical Museum.

Jeanne C. Carr, 1876. Carte-de-Visite by
Dunham & Lathrop, Oakland, California.
Courtesy of the State Historical Society of
Wisconsin.

Ezra S. Carr, 1888. Courtesy of the Archives
at the Pasadena Historical Museum.

Interior of the original Carmelita three-room
cottage used by Ezra S. Carr as a study, c.
1880s. Courtesy of the Archives at the Pasadena
Historical Museum.

Louie Wanda Strentzel Muir, c. 1880.
Courtesy of the State Historical Society of
Wisconsin.

Annie Wanda Muir and Helen Lillian Muir,
c. 1888. Courtesy of the Archives at the
Pasadena Historical Museum.

John Swett, left, and John
Muir on the Swett porch
at Martinez, California,
c. 1890s. Courtesy of
The Bancroft Library,
University of California,
Berkeley.

In 1909 John Muir prepared this list of
letters written to Jeanne C. Carr that he
wished expurgated in part or in whole.
Courtesy of the John Muir Papers, Holt-
Atherton Department of Special Collections,
University of the Pacific Libraries. Copyright
1984 Muir-Hanna Trust.

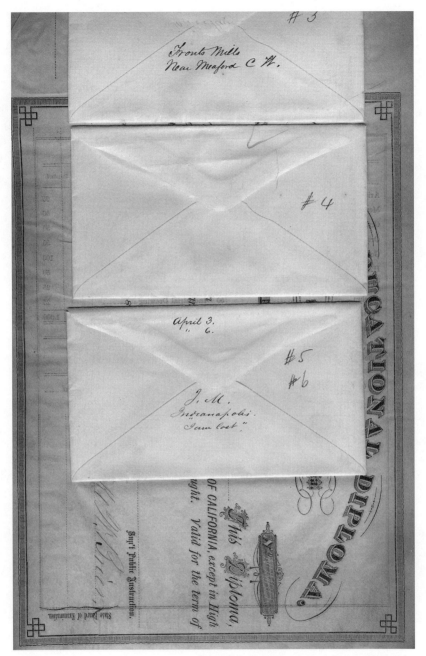

Page of Jeanne C. Carr's undated scrapbook of letters she received from John Muir. Courtesy of the John Muir Papers, Holt-Atherton Department of Special Collections, University of the Pacific Libraries. Copyright 1984 Muir-Hanna Trust.

John Muir at the home of Theodore P.
Lukens, c. 1899. Courtesy of the Huntington
Library.

John Muir, Louis Wanda Strentzel Muir,
Annie Wanda Muir, Helen Lillian Muir, and
their dog Stickeen at their home in Martinez,
California, in 1901. Photograph by C. Hart
Merriam. Courtesy of the Contra Costa
County Historical Society.

PART SIX

1873

Glad in the riches which I see
unfolded in your spirit and in all the
benedictions of sky and mountain
that fall into it, I must go into the
world which waits for your words
and bring its message.

Jeanne C. Carr

The House of God and
The Gate of Heaven

A FOUNTAIN OF LIGHT FOUND ITS WAY TO JOHN MUIR IN YOSEMITE
in 1872. The source of the beam was a St. Germain "sunrise" lamp, a
gift from Mrs. Kate N. Daggett, a friend of Jeanne Carr who had visited Muir in the Valley during the summer. He was thrilled to have the
lamp. Made by a true artist in whom Godfulness presided, its base
glowed and its green shade sparkled like a high glacier lake. Muir lit
the lamp for the first time in late December. It shed light on the letters
and essays he composed. He wrote to thank Daggett for her gift. The
light of the St. Germain lamp triggered his memory of the darkness in
which he resided in 1867 following his eye injury. Muir recalled the terrible umbra in which he died to light and lived again in a God-given
light that carried him into a new life in the spirit light that bathed the
holy mountains. The sunrise lamp clearly loosened his memories and
living in its shadow confirmed his purpose as the new year began.[1]

There are twelve extant letters from Muir to Carr written during
1873. With the exception of the first letter in the 1873 series, Carr's letters to Muir are lost. Carr's letter of February 3 described her efforts to
plant trees on the grounds of the University of California at Berkeley;
alluded to the kindred friendship shared by Carr, Muir, J. B. McChesney, and Mrs. J. P. Moore; drew Carr into a discussion with Muir and
McChesney about John Ruskin; referred to Muir's brush with death
on Mount Watkins; and mentioned a manuscript on which Carr was
working.

On the grounds of the University of California at Berkeley during
1873 Carr planted thirty species of pine trees. She confided to Muir in
her February 3 letter that the work exhausted her body but clarified her
spirit. The proper maintenance of the university grounds concerned
Carr, and a letter to the Board of Regents impressed upon them the need
to take appropriate care of the campus for posterity. In 1874 the Carrs
would request from the University additional trees for planting.[2]

Muir, McChesney, and Carr engaged in a discussion of John Ruskin's understanding of nature and mountains early in 1873. McChesney forwarded several volumes of Ruskin's *Modern Painters* to Muir, the nature of which provoked Muir into a discussion with both McChesney and Carr. Muir had never experienced Ruskin's mountain gloom. And Ruskin, who perceived nature as the "joint work of God and the devil," according to Muir, lacked faith in the "Scriptures of Nature." *Cassiope*, the purest words of love God ever lettered on mountain meadows, was not deceitful. Poisonous if eaten, the mountain heather was, however, not the work of "the devil's half of Nature." Muir, who lived with and slept with *Cassiope*'s flowers, knew she lived in "Love Divine." Likewise the barren rock, the moaning wind, and the merciless whirlpools of the mountain streams, all declared God's love. "Christianity and mountainanity" were for Muir pure streams from the same fountain.[3]

Carr may have read Muir's letter to McChesney. At the least she knew Muir came close to death in late December during his exploration of the full length of the Tenaya Canyon. As he crawled across glacier-polished Mount Watkins, a thousand feet above a gorge, he fell backwards, his head struck the granite, and he plummeted down the sheer wall of the gorge to its brink. When he regained consciousness he discovered his plunge had been blocked by bushes that grew along the edge of the precipice. In response to Muir's criticism of Ruskin, Carr suggested that had Muir died, though buried in sweet rocks, flowers, and ferns, his broken body would have been tortured by creatures. In the dichotomy Carr understood Ruskin's morbid words. There was both light and darkness, good and evil, in nature's wildness. Muir, who resided only in God's love, did not realize the terrors of wrath under which some souls abided and he could not comprehend the attraction to heaven and the understanding of hell to which Carr, herself, was drawn.[4]

Carr published "The Rural Homes of California" in February and March 1873 and "Nursery and Residence of W. F. Kelsey, Oakland, Cal." in May in the *California Horticulturist*; and a five-part series, "Flower Studies," in the *Illustrated Press* from February through July 1873. Writing was "cunning work" for Carr. Muir found literary business irksome. He endeavored to do his best, believing in the bone-heap articles some hints of God's nature beauty would be found. Muir's journals compressed his thoughts and observations and were the reservoir from which he drew the narrative style he applied to the many articles on which he was working. Carr delivered his letter to her about his exploration of Tenaya Canyon to Benjamin P. Avery, editor of the *Overland Monthly,* where it was published in April. "Hetch-Hetchy Valley" appeared in July and "Exploration of the Tuolumne Cañon" appeared in August. By the end of 1873 the *Overland Monthly* ranked Muir as their leading contributor.[5]

Carr prepared her own manuscripts for publication, edited Muir's letters and essays, and planned her visit to Yosemite. Information obtained through a brief visit with Elvira Hutchings and through letters Elvira wrote to her that she and Muir were involved in a relationship that may have crossed the boundaries of moral propriety almost precluded Carr's visit to the Valley. Elvira's description of her friendship with Muir was and remains easy to misinterpret and may have led Carr to hypothesize a liaison that had not taken place. The parameters of the relationship and the record are vague. Carr had drawn Muir and Elvira together through the study of botany grounded in the spirit all three experienced in nature in the Valley. Carr repeatedly expressed her love for Elvira and for the Hutchings children and considered them members of her kindred family. Undoubtedly she was not prepared for Elvira's letter of April 12, 1873, attesting to a growing affection for Muir.

Elvira described an awakening experience in which God's glory filled the space between her and her husband, James. She planned to faithfully prepare herself for a soulmate and confided to Carr that following her awakening she met someone Carr knew. Elvira thought he was the person for whom she waited and regardless of the temptation she expected to join him in his wanderings. A second letter dated April 17 and a third dated May 14 preceded a visit Elvira made to Carr on May 27. Initially Carr felt compelled to cancel her plans to visit Muir in the Valley for fear she would regret what she would say to him. Carr wrote to Muir regarding his poor judgment, telling him that encouraging Elvira disappointed her hopes for him. She warned Muir that if he pursued anything further he would fall below his own standards. Not above the law of duty, Carr assured Muir that by her standards his future as a naturalist and the concomitant writings that would contribute to his successful career would be sacrificed should he continue to pursue Elvira, if in fact that was what he had done. For reasons that remain unclear (they may have been put forth in Carr's June 1 letter to Muir, a letter he requested be expurgated in 1909), the incident was settled and Carr, noted botonist Albert Kellogg, and landscape painter William Keith prepared for their visit to Yosemite Valley in June.[6]

En route to Yosemite Valley Carr, her son Allie (nearly 16), Kellogg, and Keith traveled by stage to Clark's Station. A reporter for the *Elmira Gazette* (New York) described their party as "wedded to nature" and characterized Carr as a heart-absorbed worker for the advancement of women and an enthusiastic botanist. At Clark's Carr, Allie, Kellogg, and Keith pitched tents under trees by a stream and made couches of pine boughs. They traveled on foot to Mariposa Grove to study and to camp among the "Big Trees," where late in the evening they fell asleep under the trees full of moonlight. Their dreams were interrupted by Muir's shouts and whistles as he came up from the Valley to join their circle and was welcomed with oatmeal cakes and tea. Carr described the morning at Mariposa Grove as her entry into the house of God and the gate of heaven.[7]

The tenet of their rambling was to lose themselves to find life in nature that called them to a faithful "affection for trees and plants." Guided by scripture they entered into the domain of creatures so wise they lived their happy lives without defacing the primitive beauty of the earth. They chose a hymn of St. Francis of Assisi as their mantra.

> Praised be my Lord God with all his creatures! Especially our brother, the sun, who brings us the day, and who brings us the light: fair is he, and shining with a very great splendor. O Lord, he signifies to us, Thee!
>
> Praised be my Lord for our sister, the moon, and for the stars which he has set clear and lovely in the heavens!
>
> Praised be the Lord for our mother, the earth, which doth sustain and keep us, bringing forth divers fruits, and flowers of many colors and grass.
>
> Praised be the Lord for our brothers and sisters, the living creatures which Thou hast made: the birds of the air, the beasts of the field,

the fishes that inhabit the rivers and the sea. They too, are Thy children, and Thou blessest them with Thy love.

The Valley was entered in an atmosphere of faith and psalm at the height of the season. The group traveled on foot and without tents as an invitation to their brother, the sun, and their sister, the moon, and the stars, to always travel with them. Carr, Kellogg, and Keith intended to study and sketch the forests and cascades, and Muir would examine the living glaciers and snow fountains of the Tuolumne and the Merced Rivers.[8]

On June 28 Carr, Muir, Kellogg, and Keith by way of Indian Canyon headed toward Tuolumne Canyon. Allie and Manuel, a driver, accompanied them for twelve miles to Sentinel Dome and Glacier Point, down Glacier Point Trail, and into Tenaya Canyon, where they made their first camp. The plan was for Allie and Manuel to return ten days later to meet the party at Tenaya Canyon with provisions and horses. Allie sketched the group by Tenaya Creek above Mirror Lake. In a forest setting at a makeshift table Carr was depicted standing at one end of the table, while Muir, Kellogg, and Keith are on the far side of the table and Allie faced the table seated on a rock. That evening Carr and Allie slept on a flat-topped granite boulder they reached by a tree trunk fallen against it in which steps were cut.

Carr carried a tin plant case, six pairs of stockings, knives, spoons, tea, and light provisions. She wore a short skirt, an old velvet jacket, heavy mountain shoes with strong nails, and a big hat. In her leather belt she carried Allie's hatchet, a trowel, and a tin cup. Around her pack she wrapped a blanket shawl. Muir carried two blankets and provisions for two. Keith carried a pack equal to Muir's and his paints and canvases. Kellogg carried the pack he had brought to Carr's home in Oakland.

Descending from 9,400 feet over snow banks to chapparal, they entered the watershed of the melting snow that swept past them in foaming torrents. On hands and knees they crept between a snow avalanche and the rock wall against which it rested. Camp was made on the bank of the Tuolumne River; dinner consisted of canned salmon and bread. They fell asleep around a fire. Because they were unable to ford the Tuolumne River they discovered a tributary of cascades where Kellogg and Keith constructed a log bridge while Muir and Carr explored a cataract from which Muir went on to the upper section of the canyon. A day of hard climbing above Hetch Hetchy brought the party to the heart of Tuolumne Canyon.

The journey from Tenaya Canyon to Tuolumne Canyon took five days. From camp to camp they hid clothing and provisions for their return. In the cascades Muir became ill. Forced to remain an additional day with few provisions, Carr prepared stewed plums with Tuolumne water. Several hours later Muir, Kellogg, and Keith became ill. For Muir Carr prepared a wet blanket pack, piled blankets on him, and placed hot stones at his feet. The following morning they returned to their previous camp to discover that their provisions and Carr's stockings had been eaten by bears. Muir hurried on ahead to the next camp, which the bears had also ransacked. Carr, Kellogg, and Keith waited while Muir continued on to the top of the canyon. Later that evening he returned with mutton chops, lump sugar, bread, tea, and letters. With regained strength they reached Allie, Manuel, and the horses and returned to the Valley on July 10.

From Yosemite Valley Carr wrote to her husband, Ezra Carr, professor of agriculture, agricultural chemistry, and horticulture at the University of California. She described herself as the only one of the group who had not become ill or disabled by the severe exercise. Though lighter in flesh she was fresh as an ordinary tourist who returned from little trips around the Valley floor.

On July 11 Muir left the Valley for Mount Dana and Mono Lake with a party from Oakland and San Francisco that included his old Prairie du Chien friend, Emily Pelton. Pelton was the niece of the owner of the Mondell House hotel, where Muir had stayed while he worked for Norman Wiard following the exhibition of his inventions at the State Agricultural Society Fair in Madison, Wisconsin, in 1860. During Muir's absence Carr and Kellogg botanized in and around the Valley. Upon his return, he, Carr, and Kellogg departed on July 24 and moved up the Merced River along the Clouds Rest Trail to the sources of the Merced and the San Joaquin Rivers. (Keith did not join them because his wife Alice Elizabeth [Lizzie] and his son Charlie at some point entered the Valley. The Keith family proceeded with Muir and the Pelton party and then probably left Yosemite.) Carrying 150 pounds of provisions, they spent over four weeks traveling up Little Yosemite to Soda Springs, and continued on into the region of the Minarets, Cathedral Peaks, and Mount Lyell. While Carr and Kellogg botanized, Muir went on to study glaciers during rambles that lasted two to three days.

Carr, Kellogg, and Muir walked on for five days, camped in the rocky and forested river ways, and reached a log hut that had sheltered Muir in 1872. Muir set out on a fourteen-day excursion to pursue glacial studies in the area of Mount Lyell and Mount McClure, while Carr and Kellogg made their highest camp in the Merced Group, near Red Mountain [Red Peak?], at an altitude of nearly 12,000 feet, on the border of a lake dotted with twenty islands. In six weeks of wandering they saw no trace of human footsteps. Occasionally they met deer and bear. Carr described herself as traveling as easily as a spirit miles and days without an ache or weariness. She saw unspoiled and uncivilized rivers that fed no hungry mills and met the Merced and Tuolumne Rivers in regions of perpetual glacial snow and ice. The *California Farmer* hailed her as the active, wonderful wife of Professor Carr, who scaled the highest summits of the Sierra on botanical excursions and asserted women's rights by carrying her portion of provisions.[9]

The first week in September Carr returned to Oakland. She carried a portfolio of drawings completed that summer: a yellow pine and a western juniper; the effects of snow on a Williamsonia spruce near Summet Lake; Mount Dana and Mount Gibbs; the first glacier she saw from the Merced River halfway up the mountain as she ascended the river; Shadow Lake (Merced Lake) on the headwaters of the North Fork of the San Joaquin River, fifteen miles above Yosemite Valley, where a garden of lupines worshipped and turned their happy faces toward the sun, "as angels toward the Lord, opening their silver hands to receive His blessing."[10]

In Oakland the Carr family prepared for the move to their residence near the University of California's Berkeley campus. Carr was assured their home would be completed by September 1, so she limited her stay in the mountains to oversee the move. Leaving what she described to Louie Wanda Strentzel as the most delightful companions a woman ever had, Carr felt defrauded by the regent engaged in building operations for the university. She bitterly complained to Strentzel that never again would there occur such a fortunate conjunction of kindred spirits nor would she ever find herself with gentlemen whose companionship was so informative.

The five letters she received from Muir as he traveled south did not help. They described his five-week journey with Kellogg, Billy Simms, an artist, and Galen Clark, Yosemite pioneer, to the Inyo Mountains, the Kings River Canyon, the headwaters of the Kings River, and Mount Whitney.

In autumn Carr planned to meet Muir and Kellogg at Lake Tahoe, where they would continue exploring. While she remained in Oakland she wrote about her travels in the Sierra. During her sojourn nature lavished choice beauty and pure lessons and wilderness preached sublimity, patience, faith, charity, and immortality. The lessons learned did not prepare her for the event that occurred on October 23, the day her son Ezra Smith Carr, a railroad brakeman, was crushed and killed between two railroad cars in Alameda, California. Perhaps to assuage her loss and pain Carr addressed the Oakland Farming Club on the "Big Tuolumne Canyon." In late October she continued her engagements and traveled to San Jose to attend a meeting at the Normal School and to speak before the State Grange. Muir wrote from Tahoe City in November, having received news of Carr's bereavement. He sent his sympathy and prayers that God would sustain and soothe her in her grief. Even before the news of Ezra's death, Muir had sensed there was no hope of meeting her at Lake Tahoe.

Muir spent the next nine months in Oakland, where he worked on his Sierra studies for the *Overland Monthly*. He stayed with J. B. McChesney and his wife, Sarah. Life in Oakland was confining and writing was difficult. Muir could have prepared his manuscripts in Yosemite, but he left the wilderness for civilization. Perhaps, at least in part, it was to console Jeanne Carr. Muir would forever wrestle with the peace that drew him to reside in wilderness, the love that connected him to his friends, and the hope that flowed from him to the public.[11]

〜

Oakland, February 3, [*1873*]

Dear John

I enclose a letter from that dear old man, Dr. Stebbins, perhaps you already have its counterpart.

I have been having such perfect days at Berkeley, coming home exhausted in body but clarified in spirit. One night coming thus I found more of you than ever before, and have you around with me constantly since, as I am planting my pine orchard, especially. On the highest point of the grounds, but not the driest, I have put as tenderly and carefully as ever I put my babies into their cradles, the little groups of *Abies, Picea,* etc., in all thirty species of cone trees.

I hear you pitying me, but I don't care. I know the souls in abodes which I catch a glimpse of from my hilltop who will call my work blessed when they catch the piney smells, and watch the lovely growth of these. It is a pleasure, this making of soul bread for those who cannot make it for themselves, shared with Our Father who scattered it so abundantly throughout His world!

Your big thick letter blessing had to be exchanged with McChesney for his slice and with Mrs. Moore for hers, and now that I have it back again I will go over it crumb by crumb. Suppose it had been *so,* and a great sob from the Valley pines had reached me and a call had come from the soft-voiced one to find you, missing and always to be missed. If alone I had found you I would have covered you with rocks and granite-loving flowers and ferns, and Nature would have been all sweet and kindly as before. But if also I should have tracked you bruised and bleeding, broken limbed, unable to defend yourself from creatures that had tortured you, all that agony written about the place, then I should have understood many of Ruskin's pages better than you do, better than *I* do. There is a great deal of morbidness in Ruskin's writings, the traces of terrible anguish, which he has seen reflected in the tortured rocks. God has been so loving, so gentle to thee, my bairn, you cannot realize that other side, the terrors of wrath under which in natural and spiritual things some souls abide. I think I told you once that such have an awful attraction for me. To persuade and draw them to my heaven, I try to understand their hells.

But, glad that none are bereaved of you, dear, as I never shall be, glad in the riches which I see unfolded in your spirit and in all the benedictions of sky and mountain that fall into it, I must go into the world which waits for your words and bring its message. It says, *Work and Write*. The last *Silliman's Journal* has your living glaciers bodily. I think it a great compliment. I am going to stop writing *to* you that I may write of you. The big letter, under some head, must go to the many. Some cunning work has come to me, and I am going to write up the "Rural Homes of California," to be illustrated with photos. Far enough it will be from that bit of description of your "little bed room." "Do I see you, do I hear you?" It pours a flood, wetting my pine children through and through, and you are in that nasty black place under the roof a hearing it. You had better be here, and when the sky is washed you would not smell the smoke. I do wish you here.

Irwin is married and housekeeping. Nothing could be more suitable. Will'st say a word of congratulation?

We all love you, and I am,

J. C. C.
[*Jeanne C. Carr*][12]

∾

Yosemite Valley,
March 30, 1873

Dear Mrs. Carr

Your two last are received. The package of letters was picked up by a man in the Valley. There was none for thee. I have Hetch Hetchy about ready. I did not intend that Tenaya ramble for publication, but you know what is better.

I mean to write and send all kinds of game to you with hides and feathers on, for if I wait until all become one, it may be too long.

As for Le Conte's Glaciers, they will not hurt mine, but hereafter I will say my thoughts to the public in any kind of words I chance to command, for I am sure they will be better expressed in this way than in any second-hand hash, however able. Oftentimes when I am free in the wilds I discover some rare beauty in lake or cataract or mountain form and instantly seek to sketch it with my pencil, but the drawing is always enormously unlike the reality. So also in word sketches of the same beauties that are so living, so loving, so filled with warm God, there is the same infinite shortcoming. The few hard words make but a skeleton, fleshless, heartless, and when you read, the dead, bony words rattle in one's teeth. Yet I will not the less endeavor to do my poor best, believing that even these dead bone-heaps called articles will occasionally contain hints to some living souls who know how to find them.

I have not received Dr. Stebbins' letter. Give him and all my friends love from me. I sent Harry Edwards the butterflies I had lost. Did he get them? Farewell, dear, dear spiritual mother! Heaven repay your everlasting love.

John Muir[13]

∾

[*Yosemite*], April 1, 1873

Dear Mrs. Carr

Yours containing Dr. Stebbins' was received today. Some of our letters come in by Mariposa, some by Coulterville, and some by Oak Flat, causing large delays.

I expect to be able to send this out next Sunday, and with it Hetch Hetchy, which is about ready and from this time you will receive about one article a month.

This letter of yours is a very delightful one. I shall look eagerly for the rural homes.

When I know Dr. Stebbins' summer address I will write to him. He is a dear young soul, though an old man.

I am "not to write" therefore.

Farewell with love.

I will some time send you "Big Tuolumne Canyon," Ascent of Mt. Ritter, Formation of Yosemite Valley, Yosemite Lake, Other Yosemite Valleys (one, two, three, four, or more), The Lake District, Transformation of Lakes to Meadows Wet, to Meadows Dry, to Sandy Flats

Treeless, or to Sandy Flats Forested, The Glacial Period, Formation of Simple Canyons, of Compound Canyons, Description of each Glacier of Region, Origin of Sierra Forest, Distribution of Sierra Forests; a description of each of the Yosemite falls and of the basins from whence derived; Yosemite Shadows, as related to groves, meadows, and bends of the river; Avalanches, Earthquakes, Birds, Bear, etc., and "mony mair."

[John Muir][14]

∾

Yosemite Valley, April 13, 1873

Dear Mrs. Carr

Indian Tom goes out of the Valley tomorrow. With this I send you "Hetch Hetchy."

Last year I wrote a description of Hetchy and sent it to Prof. Runkle. Not having heard of it since, I thought it lost in some wastebasket, but today I received a Boston letter stating that a Hetch from my pen appeared in the *Boston Transcript* of about March 12th, 1873, which may possibly be the article in question. If so, this present H. H. will be found to contain a page or two of the same, but this is about three times as large and all rewritten, etc. That Tuolumne song of five cantos "Nature loves the Number Five" may perhaps be better out. If you think it unfit for the public, keep it to thyself. I never can keep my pen perfectly sober when it gets into the bounce and hurrah of cascades, but it never has broken into rhyme before.

Love to all and "Fare ye well, my ain Jean."

The kerchiefs have come from Bentons and a package of books from Daggett.

[John Muir][15]

∾

Yosemite Valley,
April 19, 1873

Dear Mrs. Carr

The bearer of this is my friend Mr. Black, proprietor of Black's Hotel, Yosemite. He will give you tidings of all our Valley affairs.

I sent off a letter and article for you a week ago. I find this literary business very irksome, yet I will try to learn it.

The falls respond gloriously to the ripe sunshine of these days; so do the flowers.

I hope that you will be able to send me word when you will *come*, so that I may arrange accordingly. Mr. Black will give all particulars of trails, times, etc. If Moores have not gone ranching, send Mr. Black over to their house. It will do her good. I fondly hope she is growing strong.

Love to all.

John Muir[16]

∾

Yosemite Valley,
May 15, 1873

Dear Mrs. Carr,

The robins have eaten too much breakfast this morning, and there is a grossness in their throats that will require a good deal of sunshine for its cure. The leaves of many of the plants are badly disarranged, showing that they have had a poor night's sleep. The reason of all this trouble is a snowstorm that overloaded the flowers and benumbed the butterflies, upon which the birds have breakfasted too heartily.

The grand Upper Yosemite Fall is at this moment (7 A.M.) coming with all its glorious array of fleecy comets out of a cloud that is laid along the top of the cliff, and going into a cloud that is drawn along the face of the wall about half way up. These clouds are shot through and through with sunshine, forming, with the snowy waters and fresh-washed walls, one of the most openly glorious scenes I have ever beheld. A lady on Black's piazza is quietly looking at it, sitting with arms folded in her chair. A gentleman is pointing at it with his cane, while another gentleman is speaking loudly and businessly about his "baggage." Eyes have they but they see not.

Looking up the Valley, the cloud effects are yet more lavishly glorious. Tissiack is mantled with silvery burning mists, her gray rocks appearing dimly where thinly veiled. Over the top of Washington Column the clouds are descending in a continuous stream and rising again suddenly from the bottom like spray from a waterfall. O dear! I wish you were here. I may write this cloud glory forevermore but never be able to picture it for you.

24th. With this I send No. 1 of explorations in Big Canyon. There will be two more.

[Two paragraphs cut]

I have been looking anxiously for dear Kellogg. When is he going to start?

Farewell with much love.

[*John Muir*][17]

∾

Yosemite Valley,
June 7, 1873

Dear friend Mrs. Carr

I came down last night from the Lyell Glacier, weary with walking in the snow, but I forgot my weariness and the pain of my sun-blistered face in the news of your coming.

I would like you to bring me a pair or two of green spectacles to save my eyes, as I have some weeks of hard work and exposure among the glaciers this fall. They are sore with my last journey. All of the upper mountains are yet deeply snow-clad, and the view from the top of Lyell was infinitely glorious.

Thanking God for thee, I say a short farewell.

Dr. Kellogg has not yet appeared, nor any of the other friends you speak of.

[*John Muir*][18]

∾

Yosemite Valley,
July 11, 1873

My dear husband

We returned last night from the Great Tuolumne Canyon to find letters, and to feel a little more gratitude than words will convey, for the good news. Of all our party, I was the only one who had not been ill or disabled by the severe exercise, and I feel quite as fresh today as the ordinary tourists who come in from the little trips around the Valley. We are all lighter in flesh, but I am quite sure in my own case, what has been lost in quantity is made up in quality.

I started two weeks ago today—Dr. Kellogg, Keith, Muir and Myself, each well mounted with Manuel and Allie to drive the two pack animals and return with the horses we rode. Without a trail other than the one we made, the boys were to return for us in ten days through some twelve miles of forest lying between the Yosemite Valley and the Tuolumne or rather the summit of the *divide* between the latter river and the Merced. Sunday morning Allie turned back with the guide and eight horses, and we moved on, each carrying his pack. Muir had two pairs of blankets and provisions for two, weighed some sixty...

[Pages 3–6 missing]

... for not far above we could see that the river swept the canyon wall.

Camped at four o'clock, and Muir commenced the task of cutting down a tree, a yellow pine nearly four feet in diameter and, perhaps, eighty in height. The river ran with a strong current and narrow channel at this point and a bridge we must and would make. There was only Allie's hatchet to make it with. The next morning after four hours vigorous chopping our tree fell, just as we wished, but the fall and river were too much, the great log snapped like a thread and went down stream. We crept on to find another tree with the right leaning and in threading the mazes of a tributary found a necklace of beautiful cascades. Camped at the junction of the Tuolumne and the aforesaid tributary naming this Cascade Camp.

The next morning while Muir and I explored the Tributary, Dr. Kellogg and Keith made a log bridge across, and we went on until nightfall to find just at dark an immense log felled by a natural process.

It was a *Librocedrus* tree that carried us safely over the main trunk of the river. It took another day of hard climbing to put us into the Cascades in the heart of the Canyon. The admission fee here was shoes, stockings, gloves, and all superfluous freight of clothing. Bare footed and handed we stuck to the glacier polished rocks and pulled ourselves up to the broad plane of a rock wall, that said "thus far shalt these go," but did not say how far we should *stick on*. As we had moved from camp to camp we had left clothing and provisions we thought well protected for our return. We took only a days provisions into the Cascades, consequently when Muir fell sick there and we had to lay over a day, we got hungry and hungrier and longed to get back to our base of supplies. Because these men were hungered, with butter gone—no sugar and only cracked wheat and poor coffee—the gentlemen ate heartily of plums stewed in their own juice, with a trifle of Tuolumne water for seasoning. Not many hours after my three companions behaved as if each has swallowed a glacier! I ordered for my dear Muir, a wet blanket pack, for he was in a high fever—wrung my shawl out in the river, wrapped the patient in it, piled on the blankets, put hot stones to his feet, and ate the cracked wheat which I was beginning to think anything but nutritious, feeling almost sure that I should be obliged to spend some days there.

The next morning all bettered, and we made our first days return march to find at the end all our provisions devoured by the Bears. They had gobbled up all the dried beef and chewed my stockings. Many of their tracks were on the sand around us.

Muir hurried on to the next camp, to get something for us to eat, and there also the Bears had been beforehand with us. We all felt "aching voids" and that the "things of the world were not goodies."

We could not stop to get hungrier, pushed on with only a little graham flour and salt which the Bears had not gathered. With our appetites a little assuaged with a cheese rind and some unleavened pancakes, we lay down in the stones to rest before a grand fire.

Feeling very lonesome without Muir (who had pushed up to the top of the canyon to spare anxiety to the boys at whose horse station we were already due), I dropped asleep. About half past eleven, "I heard a voice crying in the Wilderness!" *Bread, meat, sugar, letters*!! and there stood our Angel of Deliverance *laughing* over his ragged trousers and torn shoes and at our bewildered faces, for it did not seem possible that he could have returned *so soon*.

He brought us good mutton chops, lump sugar, and *tea*! These scoundrels running on four legs had eaten our tea also.

The next day we reached Allie and the horses, and our feat was accomplished. Dr. Kellogg and Keith both held out bravely. I never heard a complaining or impatient word from any of the party.

Keith has fine sketches and the Doctor and myself many plants, some rare if not new species. I will resume this Narrative when I am a little more rested.

Good night,

J. C. C.

[*Jeanne C. Carr*]

Muir brought me yours of the 3rd . . . and some other papers.[19]

∾

Clark's Station, September 13,

[*1873*]

Dear Mrs. Carr

We have just arrived from the Valley, and are now fairly off for the ice in the highest and broadest of the Sierras. Our party consists of the blessed Doctor [*Kellogg*] and Billy Simms, *Artist,* and I am so glad that the Doctor will have company when I am among the summits. We hope to have secured Clark also, a companion for me among the peaks and snow, but alack, I *must* go alone. Well, I will not complain a word, for I shall be overpaid a thousand, thousand fold. I can give you no measured idea of the time of our reaching Tahoe, but I will write always on coming to stations if such there be in the rocks or sage where letters are written.

I was surprised last evening by receiving an envelope enclosing this letter of yours and a line requesting me to read and remail it. I sealed it without reading it, thinking that it would be better for you to read it first, knowing that you could easily bring it to Tahoe if you wished me to see it.

Now for God's glorious mountains. I will miss you, yet you will more than half go. It is only that I feel that I am taking leave of you. *Farewell.* Love to all.

[*John Muir*][20]

∾

Clark's, September 15, [*1873*]

Dear Mrs. Carr

By waiting a day have got dear Galen [*Clark*] to go. The horses are ready saddled—will be off in a few minutes. Fancy Billy Paint [*Simms*] and the Doctor [*Kellogg*] alone, and Clark and I hacking steps in the high ice. Our arms are the butterfly net with which the doctor drives the mule. A six-shooter and rifle for game and Indians (Pah Utes).

Billy is joyful and innocent as ever, and more so. He says, "That was a good sketch of Mrs. Carr. It's got form to it, and she makes trees first-rate. My first wasn't as good." He has been here a day or two retouching some seven paintings that he sold some time ago. He says, "I put on some white paint for highlights like Bierstadt and Hill, but Sam (the purchaser) didn't like it, and I had to take them out." Clark takes pencil and sketch-book for the first time. Billy says, "I'll learn him. He can watch me."

My dear friend, farewell. Ere many days we will walk the meadowy streets of many a mountain heaven. I see the alpinglow [*sic*] inspiring their peaks and domes and bestowing yet more of autumn purple and gold.

To all Farewell.

John Muir

Remember me to Mrs. Moore and Keith.[21]

∾

Camp on South Fork, San Joaquin,
near divide of San Joaquin and
Kings River,
September [*27, 1873*]

Dear Mrs. Carr

We have been out nearly two weeks. Clark is going to leave us. Told me five minutes ago. Am a little nervous about it, but will of course push on alone.

We came out through the Mariposa Grove, around the head of the Chiquita Joaquin, across the canyon of the North Fork of San Joaquin, then across the canyon of Middle Fork of San Joaquin, and up the east side of the South Fork one day's journey. Then picked our wild way across the canyon of the South Fork and came up one day's journey on the west side of the canyon, where we made a camp, for four days. I was anxious to see the head fountains of this river, and started alone, Clark not feeling able to bear the fatigue involved in such a trip. I set out without blankets for a hard climb. Followed the Joaquin to its *Glaciers,* and climbed the highest mountain I could find at its head, which was either Mt. Humphreys or the mountain next South. This is a noble mountain, considerably higher than any I have before ascended. The map of the geological survey gives no detail of this wild region.

I was gone from camp four days; discovered fifteen glaciers, and Yosemite valleys "many." The view from that glorious mountain (13,500 feet high?) is not to be attempted here. Saw over into Owens River valley and all across the fountains of Kings River. I got back to camp last evening.

This morning after breakfast Clark said that he ought to be at home attending to business and could not feel justified in being away, and therefore had made up his mind to leave us, going home by way of the valley of the main Joaquin.

We will push over to the Kings River region and attempt to go down between the Middle and North Forks. Thence into the canyon of the South Fork and over the range to Owens Valley, and south to Mount Whitney if the weather holds steady, then for Tahoe, etc.

As we are groping through unexplored regions our plans may be considerably modified. I feel a little anxious about the lateness of the season. We may be at Tahoe in three or four weeks.

We had a rough time crossing the Middle Fork of the Joaquin. Brownie rolled down over the rocks, not sidewise but end over end. One of the mules rolled boulder-like in a yet more irregular fashion.

Billy went forth to sketch while I was among the glaciers, and got lost—Was 36 hours without food.

I have named a grand *wide-winged* mountain on the head of the Joaquin Mt. Emerson. Its head is high above its fellows and wings are white with ice and snow.

This is a dear bonnie morning, the sun lovingly to His precious mountain pines. The brown meadows are nightly frosted browner and the yellow aspens are losing their leaves. I wish I could write to you, but hard work near and far presses heavily and I cannot. Nature makes huge demands, yet pays a thousand thousand fold. As in all the mountains I have seen about the head of Merced and Tuolumne this region is a song of God.

On my way home yesterday afternoon I gathered you these orange leaves from a grove of one of the San Joaquin Yosemites. Little thought I that you would receive them so soon.

Remember me to the Doctor and the boys and to Mrs. and Mr. Moore and Keith. Farewell.

[*John Muir*]

Dr. Kellogg wishes to be kindly remembered.[22]

&

> Camp in dear bonnie grove where
> the pines meet the foot-hill oaks,
> About 8 or 10 miles SE from the
> confluence of the N fork of Kings
> River with the trunk,
> October 2, [*1873*]

Dear Mrs. Carr

After Clark's departure a week ago we climbed the divide between the south fork of the San Joaquin and Kings River. I scanned the vast landscape on which the ice had written wondrous things. After a short scientific feast I decided to attempt entering the valley of the west branch of the north fork, which we did, following the bottom of the valley for about 10 miles. Then we were compelled to ascend the west side of the canyon into the forest. About 6 miles farther down we made out to reenter the canyon, where there is a Yosemite valley, and by hard efforts succeeded in getting out on the opposite side and reaching the divide between the east fork and the middle fork. We then followed the top of the divide nearly to the confluence of the east fork with the trunk and crossed the main river yesterday, and are now in the pines again, over all the wildest and most impracticable portions of our journey. In descending the divide of the main Kings River we made a descent of near 7000 feet down, clear down with a vengeance, to the hot pineless foot-hills. We rose again, and it was a most grateful resurrection. Last night I watched the writing of the spirey [*sic*] pines on the sky gray with stars, and if you had been here I would have said, Look, etc.

Last eve, when the Doctor [*Kellogg*] and I were bed-building, discussing as usual the goodnesses and badnesses of boughy mountain beds, we were astonished by the appearance of two prospectors coming through the mountain rye. By them I send this note.

Today we will reach some of the Sequoias near Thomas' Mill (*vide* Map of Geological Survey), and in two or three days more will be in the canyon of the south fork of Kings River. If the weather appears tranquil when we reach the summit of the range, I may set out among the glaciers for a few days, but if otherwise I shall push hastily for the Owen's River plains and thence up to Tahoe, etc. I am working hard and shall not feel easy until I am on the other side beyond the reach of early snowstorms. Not that I fear snowstorms for myself, but the poor animals would die or suffer.

The Doctor's duster and fly-net are safe, and therefore he. Billy is in good spirits, apt to teach sketching in and out of season.

Remember me to the Doctor and the boys and Moores and Keith, etc.

> Ever yours truly,
> John Muir[23]

∞

> Independence,
> October 16, 1873

Dear Mrs. Carr

All of my season's mountain work is done. I have just come down from Mt. Whitney and the newly discovered mountain five miles northwest of Whitney, and now our journey is a simple saunter along the base of the range to Tahoe, where we will arrive about the end of the month or a few days earlier.

I have seen a good deal more of the high mountain region about the head of Kings and Kern rivers than I expected to do in so short and so late a time.

Two weeks ago I left the Doctor [*Kellogg*] and Billy in the Kings River Yosemite, and set out for Mt. Tyndall and adjacent mountains and canyons. I ascended Tyndall and ran down into the Kern River Canyon and climbed some nameless mountains between Tyndall and Whitney, and thus gained a pretty good general idea of the region. After crossing the range by the Kearsarge Pass, I again left the Doctor and Billy and pushed southward along the range and northward and up Cottonwood Creek to Mt. Whitney, then over to the Kern Canyon again and up to the new *"highest"* peak, which I did not ascend, as there was no one to attend to my horse. Thus you see I have rambled this highest portion of the Sierra pretty thoroughly, though hastily. I spent a night without fire or food in a very icy wind-storm on one of the spires of the new highest peak by some called Fisherman's Peak. That I am already quite recovered from the tremendous exposure proves that I cannot be killed in any such manner. On the day previous I climbed two mountains, making over 10,000 feet of altitude.

I saw no mountains in all this grand region that appeared at all inaccessible to a mountaineer. Give me a summer and a bunch of matches and a sack of meal, and I will climb every mountain in the region.

I have passed through Lone Pine and noted the Yosemite and local subsidences accomplished by the earthquakes. The bunchy bush Compositae of Owen's Valley are intensely glorious.

I got back from Whitney this P.M. How I shall sleep! My life rose wavelike with those lofty granite waves; now it may wearily float for a time along the smooth, flowery plain.

It seems that this new Fisherman's Peak is causing some stir in the newspapers. If I feel writeful, I will send you a sketch of the region for the *Overland*.

Love to all my friends.

Ever cordially yours,
John Muir[24]

∾

University of California,
Oakland, Cal.
October 29, 1873

Dear Louie

I received your letter only today, but should not have waited for it to thank your father for the grapes. The grapes came last Monday morning. We had a notice that they were at the express office Sat. evening too late to get them before the hour of closing. That was the day after the meeting of the Club. We distributed them immediately among the friends—and left for San Jose! where the State Grange were in convention last week, which with some doings in the Normal School, kept us all the week. The subject before the Club was Fruit Nomenclature, and I did not therefore prepare any elaborate account of my trip and occupied only half an hour—which it seems was an "appetizer" for I am requested to repeat it with amplifications for the benefit of the Oakland Library. Should this be one of a series of readings for their benefit I will let you know.

I am very much defrauded and as much provoked that I believed the promises made to us about homes at Berkeley. Dr. Merritt, who has been the principal Regent engaged in building operations, assured me that our houses would be completed by the 18th of September, just as I was starting for the mountains, and as I was far beyond post offices I felt that I must limit myself to that time and be on hand for the necessary moving. Came home alone, leaving my companions (the most delightful [a] woman ever had or will have) to spend a blissful Autumn between the head of Kings River, around Mt. Whitney, etc., and to take a horseback journey from there to Shasta, in which I could have accompanied them had I known there was no home and no moving in the case. It vexes me to read the five letters I have received since I left them and know what might have been. They have been in entirely untrodden ways—but all the time with animals, so that the fatigues were nothing to those already borne. No such fortunate conjunction of kindred spirits will ever occur again, nor shall I ever find myself with gentlemen whose companionship is so instructive. I never once felt that I was an incumbrance or restraint upon their movements.

I want you to know my John Muir, and I wish I could give him to some noble young woman "for keeps" and so take him out of the wilderness into the society of his peers. As he is coming to spend the winter with us, I hope you will meet. But [it] is awfully provoking that I cannot gather all my pets into a home which would be attractive to them, and some expression of myself. My homes hitherto have been larger and roomier bodies, expressing my individuality so well, that you would have felt acquainted with me, and with all my beloveds, had you been shut up there all by yourself. I always expected to see your mother's bonnie face by my ingleside, which does not mean a stone or a hole in the floor!

Thank the father as he should be thanked. The pretty leaves were spoiled—not so the unspoilable kindness. Loving you all dearly, we are,

> Your obliged,
> E. S. & Jeanne Carr
> [*Ezra S.*]

I am very sorry to hear the father is ailing, I trust not for long.[25]

ભ

> Tahoe City,
> November 3, [*1873*]

My Dear Friends Dr. and Mrs. Carr

I received the news of your terrible bereavement a few moments ago, and can only say that you have my heart sympathy and prayer that our Father may sustain and soothe you.

Dr. Kellogg and Billy Simms left me a week ago at Mono, going directly to Yosemite. I reached this queen of lakes, two days ago and rode down around the shore on the east side. Will continue on around up the west coast homeward through Lake and Hope valleys and over the Sierra to Yosemite by the Virginia Creek trail, or Sonora road if much snow should fall. Will reach Yosemite in about a week.

Somehow I had no hopes of meeting you here. I could not hear you or see you, yet you shared all of my highest pleasures, as I sauntered through the piney woods, pausing countless times to absorb the blue glimpses of the lake, all so heavenly clean, so terrestrial yet so

openly spiritual. I wish, my dear, dear friends, that you could share
this divine day with me here. The soul of Indian summer is brooding
this blue water, and it enters one's being as nothing else does. Tahoe is
surely not one but many. As I curve around its heads and bays and
look far out on its level sky fairly tinted and fading in pensive air, I am
reminded of all the mountain lakes I ever knew, as if this were a kind
of water heaven to which they all had come.

[Section of letter cut]

...pers that your Berkeley house was not likely to be built

...my mind to winter among Yosemite rocks again, but if

...ed better winter with you, say so in another letter directed to the
Valley and I will come.

Ever yours,

John Muir[26]

PART SEVEN

1874–1875

I care to live only to entice people to look at Nature's loveliness. My own special self is nothing.

John Muir

Inaccessible as if in a Crowd: Mountains and Agricultural Reform

JEANNE AND EZRA CARR THOUGHT AMERICANS WERE INDUSTRIOUS by nature, but for the working masses of mechanics and farmers to reach their fullest potential required daily muscular and mental effort and an education of the head and of the hand. The Carrs set out to establish a true and noble education that would undergird the work ethic and guarantee respect for America's laborers. On this issue they would not compromise. Efforts to develop a practical curriculum at the University of California that would emphasize the mechanical and agricultural arts locked the Carrs in a bitter dispute involving the university, the grangers, the Mechanics' Deliberation Assembly, the Mechanics' State Council, and the newspapers (who took sides in the controversy). The Carrs, mechanics, and grangers opposed the elitist liberal arts curriculum planned for the university under the direction of President David Coit Gilman. Ezra Carr demanded that the university provide technical instruction in the mechanical arts and increase the budget in the agricultural studies department. As a result of his demands, charges of incompetency were filed against him. When asked to resign, he refused and was dismissed in August 1874. The grangers were outraged. The following year their support helped elect Carr to the position of State Superintendent of Public Instruction in Sacramento.[1]

To improve literacy among agriculturalists, the Carrs supported the organization and administration of the Patrons of Husbandry (the California Grange). Temescal Grange, Oakland Township, Alameda County was organized on July 10, 1873, and Ezra Carr was elected to the office of "Worthy Lecturer." Later he served on the "American Finance" committee; as General Deputy, Oakland Grange, Alameda County; and as Master, Sunol Grange, Alameda County.[2]

Women played a role equal to that of men in the administration of the grange, and Jeanne Carr utilized her authority as a member of several standing committees, the "Good of the Order" and the "Arrangements of Business," to advocate for women's literacy and educational equality. Carr also served with Louie Wanda Strentzel as a member of the state board in 1877. The grange was valued by women as a training school for business, a platform for developing organizational skills, and an opportunity for usefulness.

Carr's dedication to the grange and to her family and friends consumed her. Perhaps she privately bemoaned her inability to write a book, but her silent aspirations were somehow detected by Charles Warren Stoddard, who in July asked Carr about her book writing. Stoddard thought Carr too willing and too responsible for her own good. If she were to be walled up for a time with only a window in her cell, he was certain the results would be a great single work that in the end would accomplish more good than the ten thousand little good acts she achieved daily. According to Stoddard Carr had been given the duty to cover more ground than the small things he celebrated. Muir thought Carr overworked and active in an avalanche of public calamity. He did not believe her "educational departmental institutional" work was what God wanted her to do.

The dismissal of Ezra Carr from his professorship at the University of California brought closure to the Carrs' lives in Oakland. They would spend at least part of the time between 1875 and 1880 in Sacramento. The completion of a series of articles on mountain structure, "Studies in the Sierra," for the *Overland Monthly* kept Muir at the McChesney home from December 1873 until September 1874 and ended his long period of "town dark." In his upstairs room dead bony words had rattled in his head, pale ghosts of his thoughts and observations. The words appeared to him to be hints of the realities of nature. There were endless revisions on rough inexpensive paper.

In Oakland Muir ate most meals in restaurants, was reluctant to attend parties, and preferred to dress casually in what Mrs. McChesney described as "negligee," a blue flannel shirt with a sprig of greenery, influenced perhaps by the botanist Carolus Linnaeus (1707–1778, the father of botany), who wore a sprig of green and whom Muir admired. Muir rekindled friendships with William Keith and Joseph Le Conte, and a friendship developed between Muir and John Swett, teacher, principal, State Superintendent of Schools, and a pioneer in California public education. Swett and Keith made trips from San Francisco to Oakland to visit Muir. In May 1874 the first of Muir's studies appeared in the *Overland Monthly*. An article in the series appeared each month until the last was published in January 1875.[3]

The Sierra series complete, Muir escaped from Oakland and returned to his home in the wildness of the Sierra and Yosemite Valley in September. He knew pine air far from civilization benefited him. He sought fresh animation in wilderness. He bathed in the sacred Merced stream, but there he felt like a stranger. He was certain his life in the Valley was over. Rocks and mountains did not respond to him. Muir's two letters to Carr from Yosemite described the small creatures he saw upon his return. Palimpsest-like, the tracks of grasshoppers and mice were letters etched into the ground (the dust of the rocks and the mountains). These he could still read and study. Perhaps because rocks and mountains did not respond, Muir felt drawn to ouzels and goldenrod, *Hemizonia* and butterflies, grasshoppers and mice who awakened him and reacquainted him with wilderness.

Muir's glacial eyes returned in October. He knew he was hopelessly and forever a mountaineer. His focus, however, turned from one of self-development to one of teaching others to observe nature's beauty. His intention was "to entice people to look at Nature's loveliness." Muir's feet recovered their cunning after the long months in Oakland on hard pavement. He left the Valley and traveled Shastaward, headed north along the old California-Oregon stage road taking notes for a series of letters he would write for the *San Francisco Daily Evening Bulletin*. From Norman Sisson's Hotel he wrote to Carr that when he first glimpsed Shasta he was transformed. On foot, alone, and weary, he found that the mere sight of the mountain turned his blood to wine, and he experienced no further fatigue. Wanting only mountains until he returned to civilization, Muir climbed icy Shasta on November 2. A guide, Jerome Fay, climbed with Muir to the timberline. Muir ascended the summit alone. A storm was approaching when Muir descended to camp, and he hollowed a cave, made a campfire, and snuggled beneath wool blankets to observe and write. On the fourth day of the storm Fay arrived on a horse, leading another, sent by Sisson to rescue Muir, who reluctantly rode down from camp and missed the finest effects of the storm.[4]

By December Muir had made four excursions to Shasta. A letter to Carr addressed from Sisson's Hotel noted that he was more than married to the icy mountain. He was nervous about another period of "town dark." Drawn from the mountains to write, he understood he had lived more than a common eternity not affected or diminished by civilization, cities, and well-intended friends. Leaving Shasta at the end of December, Muir traveled by stage and train to Brownsville to visit Emily Pelton, who had moved to California to live with relatives, the Knox family. From Brownsville Muir traveled along the Yuba and Feather River, explored adjacent forests, and in a wild gale climbed to the top of a one-hundred-foot spruce to experience the wild swirling praying pine. Trees, like human beings, were travelers.

Muir resided with John Swett, his wife, Mary, two grandmothers, and four children, Emily, Frank, John, and Helen, on Taylor Street in San Francisco in February 1875. He spent the spring writing about his excursions. In April Muir's essay "Wild Wool" appeared in the *Overland Monthly*. During April he also traveled to Shasta with a group from the Coast and Geodetic Survey to make barometric observations. Trapped in a sudden storm on the summit of Shasta, Muir and Jerome Fay spent the night on the mountain, taking refuge in shallow hot springs. At dawn they struggled to the timberline and reached food, fire, and sleep. Rescued by Sisson Muir was, however, lame from frostbite, battered and scarred like a log traveling down a river during a flood. Returning home from icy Shasta, Muir found himself safe in the arms of Daddy Swett. In the life Muir lived in the city he remembered he was always a mountaineer. Bound to his studies, he was swept onward in a general current that endured irresistibly.[5]

Muir's life and letters were a mixture of wilderness and civilization, nature and friends. An April letter to Carr mentioned the Strentzels' farm and a letter Louie Wanda Strentzel wrote to Carr that Carr carefully folded and sent on to Muir to read. Carr's objective, perhaps from the moment she met Louie, a graduate of Miss Atkins's Young Ladies' Seminary at Benicia (later Mills College in Oakland), was to introduce her and Muir. In 1872 she wrote to Louie, "I wish I could give him [*Muir*] to some noble woman 'for keeps' and so take him out of the wilderness into the society of his peers." A chance meeting at the Carr home in the summer of 1874 brought the Strentzels and Muir together. Dr. John Theophile Strentzel, a political exile from Poland, who was educated in medicine and horticulture, was a prominent landowner and fruit rancher in Contra Costa County. An early scientific horticulturalist, Strentzel was eager to meet Muir. Louie was twenty-seven when she met Muir, who was thirty-six.[6]

Dr. Strentzel invited Muir to his Martinez ranch, which accounts for Muir's reference to a visit to the bees and orchards in Alhambra. Three years would elapse before Muir and the Strentzels would meet again. Muir was not ready to visit the Strentzel ranch when Shasta snow-dust drew him from apple-bloom. In the meantime, though Carr's attempts to arrange further meetings between Muir and the Strentzels failed, she sought any means available to keep Louie ever present in Muir's thoughts, and thus the daintily written letter of Louie Wanda Strentzel was sent by Carr to Muir.[7]

Only one of Jeanne Carr's letters contributes to the 1874–1875 series. In Muir's letters there are few references to the tenor of Carr's life. According to Muir she was often lost in conventions, elections, and women's rights and buried beneath granger hay. Carr wrote for the *Pacific Rural Press* in 1875. Her essay "Birds and Caterpillars—A Hardshell Sermon" was an amalgamation of Carr's faith, love of nature, preservationist leanings, and educational objectives. She observed that every few years nature offered a gratuitous lesson on "the importance of preserving the divinely appointed equilibrium between the different orders of creation." Humanity in haste to get rich disturbed nature's delicate balance that then created the plagues that beggar.

While Carr may not have fulfilled her true calling, according to Stoddard and Muir, among the California grangers she was regarded as a mainspring. In May 1875 Carr addressed the grangers' picnic. She noted that the grange was founded upon charity, sympathy, and fraternity, and established credit and cooperation for and among farmers. Within it and through its efforts women found a true equality, a complete recognition of reciprocal rights and duties, and opportunities to advance toward full and complete usefulness without the limitations of narrow custom or prejudice. Accordingly grangers were the saints of God's earth, embodied the principles of universal love and good will, and were a choir acting in harmony with God's creation. The quintessential conveyance for the dissemination of education necessary to implement nature's protection was the grange, and Carr saw herself vested as a preacher to the farmers.[8]

Muir noticed Carr's grange associations and her absence in his life. He wrote to her in June that she was inaccessible to him as if in a crowd. The grange remained a viable platform for Carr's educational and agricultural objectives. Her authority and knowledge (even her exotic experience in the Sierra) enabled her to assume a leadership role within an environment where women's voices were equipoised with men's and agriculture was naturally and ideologically close to the home. The grange furnished an environment in which Carr could act upon issues, ideas, and images important both to her and to the other grangers. Her faith in the grange tethered her to a considerable public audience with whom she felt accepted and accomplished.

Carr's involvement in grange activity encouraged Muir's friendship with William Keith, who lived near the Swetts on Clay Street in San Francisco. Keith prodded Muir during his visits to the Swett home. In June Muir returned to the Valley to collect observations for literary assignments and traveled in the High Sierra with Swett, Keith, and McChesney. On the cold moraine of the trunk glacier of Yosemite Creek they camped and watched butterflies pass by on the hillside among the pines. Through miles of silver fir they rode, crossed Yosemite Creek, and camped at Lake Tenaya. Muir visited the grave of James Lamon, pioneer settler and cultivator of the Valley, who had died in the Valley in May.[9]

In July Muir traveled to the Kings River Yosemite on the South Fork and to Mount Whitney with George Bayley of San Francisco and Charles Washburn, a university student. Muir returned to the Valley at the end of July and departed in August with Brownie, his small brown mule, on a solitary exploration of the Sequoia belt. Traveling from Yosemite to the White River in Tulare County, he camped in the Upper Fresno Basin; on the Lower Fork of the San Joaquin; near South Fork, Kings River; and in a mountain garden on the South Fork of the Kaweah River.

Muir collected thoughts and observations while he traveled. The heart of nature beat around him and in him; he witnessed nature's transforming presence. All that was needed to achieve immortality was a day in the woods. Muir questioned people's inability to calmly wait to see nature unfold and then meet nature face to face. When he came upon Hyde's sawmill on the Kings-Kaweah Divide south of the Kings River on the southwestern extreme of the Kings River Sequoia belt, he wondered what human beings would do with the mountains. Hyde's, established in 1872, had obtained full possession of the forest for several miles. The mill cut two million board feet of lumber in 1875, though Muir noted that *Sequoiadendron giganteum* when felled shattered like glass, resulting in the loss of from 25 to 50 per cent of the timber. Booming and moaning like a bad ghost, Hyde's was one of five mills Muir found operating in or near the belt. Overall Muir was dismayed at how little attention was directed toward nature. No one published the accounts of nature's voice, the music of rivers, the ways of clouds.[10]

Muir intended his journey as an escape from the hooks of civilization that drew him to return to San Francisco, to Taylor Street, and to his upstairs writing room; it became, however, a purposeful examination of the relation between wilderness and humanity. The destiny of human beings appeared to be to extract wealth from nature with expediency and waste. The Sequoia, "majestic living temples, the grandest of Gothic cathedrals," who grew always where deep loaming soil holds the winter moisture all year, were seen as blocks of material to sell. Muir on the other hand saw and experienced wilderness as the counterpart to humanity. In the mountains and in the forest were health and life, rest and repose. On November 12 as he paused in his studies to reflect he shouted, "Ho, come to the Sierra forests. The King is waiting for you—King Sequoia!"[11]

Muir's autumn excursion strengthened his resolve to entice others to witness nature's beauty and the healing powers of wilderness. In November he returned to the Swetts' home on Taylor Street. He continued to struggle with his writing, preferring to tell stories. Often Swett ordered Muir to his room to write. Again Muir spent time with Keith, Le Conte, and Ina Donna Coolbrith. He was delighted to hear from Jeanne Carr that Ezra had been elected to the position of State Superintendent of Public Instruction for the State of California in October. Ezra appointed Jeanne deputy superintendent. She was among the first women in California to hold public office and the first to hold the office of Deputy Superintendent of Public Instruction.

Jeanne continued to focus on the education of women. Since most women lived in the country, her objectives were to teach them how to live nobly, happily, and healthfully through the study of pomology, forestry, floriculture, market gardening, fruit drying, silk culture, dairy farming, and the health and proper care of children. Carr hoped to provide for women what had been provided for men: land-ownership, which she believed was the basis for independence, power, and wealth. Carr would benefit from her understanding of the value of land ownership. In 1874 she contemplated purchasing orange and vine land in Pasadena among what Muir described as "the warm California angels." When she and Ezra retired from public office in 1880 they moved to southern California, to the homestead they named Carmelita.[12]

Yosemite Valley,
[September, 1874]

Dear Mrs. Carr

Here again are pine trees, and the wind, and living rock and
water. I have met two of my ouzels on one of the pebbly ripples of the
river, where I used to be with them. Most of the meadow gardens are
disenchanted and dead, yet I found a few mint spikes, and asters, and
brave sunful golden-rod, and a patch of the tiny *Mimulus* that has
two spots on each lip. The fragrance, and the color, and the form, and
the whole spiritual expression of golden-rod are hopeful and strength-
giving beyond any other flower that I know. A single spike is sufficient
to heal unbelief and melancholy.

On leaving Oakland I was so excited over my escape that of
course I forgot and left all the accounts I was to collect. No wonder
and no matter. I am beneath the grand old pine that I have heard so
often in storms, both in the night and in the day. It sings grandly now,
every needle sun-thrilled, and shining, and responding tunefully to the
azure wind.

When I left, I was in a dreamy, exhausted daze. Yet from mere
habit or instinct I tried to observe and study. From the car window
I watched the gradual transitions from muddy water, spongy tule,
marsh, and level field, as we shot up the San Jose Valley, and marked,
as best I could, the forms of the stream canyons as they opened to the
plain, and the outlines of the undulating hillocks and headlands
between. Interest increased at every mile, until it seemed unbearable
to be thrust so flyingly onward, even toward the blessed Sierras. I will
study them yet, free from time and wheels. When we turned suddenly
and dashed into the narrow mouth of the Livermore Pass, I was looking
out of the right side of the car. The window was closed on account of
the cinders and smoke from the locomotive. All at once, my eye seized
a big hard rock not a hundred yards away, every line of which is as
strictly and outspokenly glacial as any of the most alphabetic of the
high and young Sierra. That one sure glacial word thrilled and over-
joyed me more than you will ever believe. Town smokes and shadows

had not dimmed my vision, for I had passed this glacial rock twice before, without reading its meaning.

As we proceeded, the general glacialness of the range became more and more apparent, until we reached Pleasanton, where once there was a grand *mer de glace*. Here, the red sun went down in a cloudless glow, and I leaned back, happy and weary, and possessed with a life full of noble problems.

At Lathrop, we had supper and changed cars. The last of the daylight had long faded, and I sauntered away from the din, while the baggage was being transferred. The young moon hung like a sickle above the shorn wheatfields. Ursa Major pictured the Northern sky; the milky way curved sublimely through the broadcast stars, like some grand celestial moraine with planets for bowlders; and the whole night shone resplendent, adorned with that calm, imperishable beauty it has worn unchanged from the beginning.

I slept at Turlock, and, next morning, faced the Sierra, and set out through the sand on foot. The freedom I felt was exhilarating, and the burning heat, and thirst, and faintness could not make it less. Before I had walked ten miles, I was wearied and footsore, but it was real earnest work and I liked it. Any kind of simple, natural destruction is preferable to the numb, dumb apathetic deaths of a town.

Before I was out of sight of Turlock, I found a handful of the glorious *Hemizonia virgata* and a few specimens of the patient, steadfast [*Eriogonums*] that I had learned to love around the slopes of Twenty-Hill Hollow. While I stood with these old dear friends, we were joined by a lark, and in a few seconds more, Harry Edwards came flapping by with spotted wings. Just think of the completeness of that reunion: Twenty Hill Hollow *Hemizonia, Eriogonum*, Lark, butterfly and I, and lavish outflows of genuine Twenty Hill Hollow sungold. I threw down my coat and one shirt in the sand; forgetting Hopeton, and heedless that the sun was becoming hotter every minute. I was wild once more, and let my watch warn and point as it pleased. Heavy wagon loads of wheat had been hauled along the road, and the wheels had sunken deeply and left smooth, beveled furrows in the sand. Upon the slopes of these sand furrows, I soon observed a most beautiful and varied embroidery: evidently tracks of some kind. At first, I thought of mice, but I soon saw they were too light and delicate even for the tracks of these little animals. Then, a tiny lizard darted into the stubble ahead of me, and I carefully examined the track he made, but it was entirely unlike the fine print-embroidery I was studying. However, I knew that he might make very different tracks, if walking leisurely; therefore I determined to catch one and experiment. I found in Florida that lizards, however swift, are short winded; so I gave chase and soon captured a tiny gray fellow, and carried him to a smooth sand-bed where he could embroider, without getting away into grass tufts or holes. He was so wearied that he could not skim, and was compelled to walk, and I was excited with delight in seeing an exquisitely beautiful strip of embroidery about five-eighths of an inch wide, drawn out in flowing curves behind him as from a loom. The riddle was solved. I knew that mountain bowlders move in music. So also do lizards, and their written music printed by their feet (moved so swiftly as to be invisible) covers the hot sands with beauty wherever they go. But my sand embroidery-lesson was by no means finished. I speedily discovered a yet more delicate pattern on the sands, woven into that of the lizards. I examined the strange combination of bars and dots. No five-toed lizard had printed that music. I watched narrowly, down on my knees, following the strange and beautiful pattern along the wheel furrows, and out into the stubble. Occasionally, the pattern would suddenly end in a shallow pit half an inch across and an eighth of an inch deep. I was fairly puzzled, picked up my bundle and trudged discontentedly away; but my eyes were hungrily awake and I watched all the ground. At length, a gray grasshopper rattled and flew up, and the truth flashed upon me that he was the complementary embroiderer of the lizard. Then followed long, careful observation, but I never could see the grasshopper until he jumped, and after he alighted he invariably stood watching me with his legs set ready for another jump in case of danger. Nevertheless, I soon made sure that he was my man; for I found that, in jumping, he made the shallow pits I had observed at the termination of the pattern I was studying. But no matter how patiently I waited he wouldn't *walk,* while I was sufficiently near to observe—they are so nearly the color of the sand. I therefore caught one, and lifted his wing covers, and cut off about half of each wing with my penknife, and carried him to a favorable place on the sand. At first, he did nothing but jump and make dimples, but soon became weary and walked in common rhythm with all his six legs. My interest you may guess, while I watched the embroidery: the written music, laid down in a beautiful ribbonlike strip behind him. I glowed with wild joy, as if I had found a new glacier, copied specimens of the precious fabric into my note book, and strode away with my own feet sinking with a dull craunch, craunch, craunch, in the hot gray sand, glad to believe that the dark and cloudy vicissitudes of the Oakland period had not dimmed my vision in the least. Surely, Mother Nature pitied the poor boy and showed him pictures!

Happen what would, fever-thirst or sunstroke, my joy for that day was complete. Yet I was to receive still more. A train of curving tracks, with a line in the middle, next fixed my attention, and almost before I had time to make a guess concerning their author, a small hawk came shooting down vertically out of the sky, a few steps ahead of me, and picked up something in his talons. After rising thirty or forty feet overhead, he dropped it by the roadside, as if to show me what it was. I ran forward and found a little bunchy field mouse, and, at once suspected him of being embroiderer number three. After an exciting chase through stubble-heaps and weed-thickets, I wearied and captured him without being bitten, and turned him free to make his mark in a favorable sand bed. He also embroidered better than he knew, and at once claimed the authorship of the new trackwork.

I soon learned to distinguish the pretty sparrow-track from that of the magpie and the lark, with their three delicate branches and the straight scratch behind, made by the back curving claw dragged loosely like a spur of a Mexican vacquero. The cushioned, elastic feet of the hare frequently were seen mixed with the pattering, scratchy prints of the squirrels. I was now wholly trackful. I fancied I could see the air whirling in dimpled eddies from sparrow- and lark-wings, earthquake bowlders descending in a song of curves, snowflakes glinting songfully hither and thither. "The water in music the oar forsakes." The air in music the wing forsakes. All things move in music and write it. The mouse, lizard, and grasshopper sing together on the Turlock sands, sing with the morning stars.

Scarce had I begun to catch the eternal harmonies of Nature, when I heard the hearty goddamning din of the mule driver; dust whirled in the sungold, and I could see the sweltering mules leaning forward, dragging the heavily piled wheat-wagons deep sunken in the sand. My embroidery perished by the mile, but the grasshoppers never wearied, nor the gray lizards, nor the larks, and the coarse confusion of man was speedily healed.

About noon, I found a family of grangers feeding, and remembering your admonition anent my health, requested leave to join them. My head ached with fever and sunshine, and I could not dare the ancient brown bacon, or the beans and cakes, but water and splendid butter-milk came in perfect affinity and made me strong. Toward evening, after passing through miles of blooming *Hemizonia,* I reached Hopeton, on the edge of the oak fringe of the Merced. Here, all were yellow and woe-begone with malarial fever. I rested one day, spending the time in examining the remarkably flat, water-eroded Valley of the Merced, and the geological sections which it offers. In going across to the river, I had a suggestive time, breaking my way through tangles of black-berry and briar-rose, and willow. I admire delicate plants that are well prickled, and, therefore, took my scratched face and hands patiently. I bathed in the sacred stream, seeming to catch all its mountain tones while it softly murmured and rippled over the shallows of brown pebbles. The whole river, back to its icy sources, seemed to rise in clear vision with its countless cascades, and falls, and blooming meadows, and gardens. Its pine groves, too, and the winds that play them, all appeared and sounded.

In the cool of the evening, I caught Brownie and cantered across to the Tuolumne; the whole way being fragrant and golden with *Hemi-zonia.* A breeze swept in from your Golden Gate regions over the passes, and across the plains, fanning the hot ground and drooping plants, and refreshing every beast and bird and weary plodding man. It was dark before I reached my old friend Delaney, but was instantly recognized by my voice, and welcomed in the old, good, uncivilized way, not to be misunderstood.

All the region adjacent to the Tuolumne River, where it sweeps out into the plain, after its long eventful journey in the mountains, is exceedingly picturesque. Round terraced hills, brown and yellow with grasses and compositae and adorned with open groves of darkly foliaged live-oak, are grouped in a most open, tranquil manner, and laid upon a smooth, level base of purple plain; while the river bank is lined with nooks of great beauty and variety, in which the river has swept and curled, shifting from side to side, retreating and returning, as determined by floods, and the gradual erosion and removal of drift-beds formerly laid down. A few miles above here, at the village of La Grange, the wild river had made some astonishing deposits in its young days, through which it now flows with the manners of stately old age, apparently disclaiming all knowledge of them. But a thousand thousand bowlders, gathered from many a moraine, swashed and ground in pot-holes, record their history, and tell of white floods of a grandeur not easily conceived. Noble sections, nearly a hundred feet deep, are laid bare like a book, by the Mining Company. Water is drawn from the river, several miles above, and conducted by ditches and pipes, and made to play upon these deposits for the gold they contain. Thus the Tuolumne of today is compelled to unravel and lay bare its own ancient history, which is a thousandfold more important than the handfuls of gold sand it chances to contain.

I mean to return to these magnificent records in a week or two, and turn the gold disease of the La Grangers to account, in learning the grand old story of the Sierra flood period. If these hundred laborious hydraulickers were in my employ, they could not do me better service, and, all along the Sierra flank, thousands of strong arms are working for me, incited by the small golden bait. Who shall say that I am not rich?

On I went up through the purple foothills to Coulterville, where I met many hearty, shaggy mountaineers, glad to see me. Strange to say, the *Overland* "Studies" have been read and discussed in the most unlikely places. Some numbers have found their way through the Bloody Canyon pass to Mono.

In the evening, Black and I rode together up into the sugar pine forests, and through the moonlight on to his old ranch. The grand, priest-like pines held their arms above us in blessing; the wind sang songs of welcome; the cool glaciers and the running crystal fountains added their greetings. I was no longer on, but in the mountains: home again, and my pulses were filled. On and on reveling in white moon-light spangles on the streams, shadows in rock hollows and briery ravines, tree architecture on the sky, more divine than ever stars in their spires, leafy mosaic on meadow and bank. Never had the Sierra seemed so inexhaustible. Mile on mile onward in the forest through groves old and young. Pine tassels overarched and brushed both cheeks at once. The chirping of crickets only deepened the stillness. About eight o'clock, a strange mass of tones came surging and waving through the pines. "That's the death song," said Black, as he reined up his horse to listen. "Some Indian is dead." Soon, two glaring watch-fires shone red through the forest, marking the place of congregation. The fire glare and the wild wailing came with indescribable impressiveness through the still, dark woods. I listened eagerly as the weird curves of woe swelled and cadenced, now rising steep like glacial precipices, now swooping low in polished slopes. Falling bowlders, and rushing streams, and wind tones caught from rock and tree were in it. When at length we rode away, and the heaviest notes were lost in distance, I wondered that so much of mountain nature should well out from such a source. Miles away, we met Indian groups slipping through the shadows on their way to join the death wail. Farther on, a harsh grunting and growling seemed to come from the opposite bank of a brook along which we rode. "What? Hush! That's a bear," ejaculated Black, in a gruff, bearish undertone. "Yes," he said, "some rough old Bruin is sauntering this fine night, seeking some wayside sheep lost from migrating flocks." Of course, all night-sounds, otherwise unaccountable, are accredited to bears. On ascending a sloping hillock, less than a mile from the first, we heard another grunting bear, but whether or not daylight would transform our bears to pigs, may well be counted into the story.

Past Bower Cave we went and along a narrow winding trail in deep shadow. It was so dark that I had to throw the reins on Brownie's neck and trust to his skill; for I could not see the ground, and the hillside was steep. A fine, bright tributary of the Merced sang far beneath us, as we climbed higher, higher, through the hazels and dogwoods that fringed the rough, black boles of spruces and pines. We were now nearing the old camping ground of the Pilot Peak region, where I learned to know the large nodding lilies (L. *pardalinum*), so abundant along these streams, and the groups of alder-shaded cataracts, so characteristic of the North Merced Fork.

Moonlight whitened all the long fluted slopes of the opposite bank, but we rode in continuous shadow. The rush, and gurgle, and prolonged a-a-a of the stream coming up, sifting into the wind, was very impressive and solemn. It was here that you first seemed to join me. I reached up as Brownie carried me underneath a big Douglas spruce, and plucked one of its long, plumy sprays which brought you in a moment from the Oakland dead. You are more spruce than pine, though I never definitely knew it till now. Here were miles and miles of tree scripture, along the sky: a Bible that will one day be read. The beauty of its letters and sentences have burned me like fire, through all these Sierra seasons. Yet I cannot interpret their hidden thoughts. They are terrestrial expressions of sun, pure as water and snow. Heavens! listen to the wind song! I am still writing beneath that grand old pine in Black's yard; and that other companion scarcely less noble, back of which I took shelter during the earthquake, is just a few yards beyond. The shadows of their boles lie like charred logs on the gray sand; while half the yard is embroidered with their branches and leaves. There goes a woodpecker with an acorn to drive into its thick bark for winter, and well it may gather its stores, for I can myself detect winter in the wind!

Few nights of my mountain life have been more eventful than that of my ride in the woods from Coulterville, when I made my reunion with the winds and pines. It was eleven o'clock when we reached Black's ranch. I was weary, and soon died in sleep. How cool, and vital, and re-creative was the hale young mountain air! On, higher, higher, up into the holy of holies of the woods. Pure, white, lustrous clouds overshadowed the massive congregations of silver fir and pine. We entered, and a thousand living arms were waved in solemn blessing. An infinity of mountain life. How complete is the absorption of one's life into the spirit of mountain woods! No one can love or hate an enemy here, for no one can conceive of such a creature as an enemy. Nor can one have any distinctive love of friends. The dearest and best of you all seemed of no special account, mere trifles. Hazel green water, famous among mountaineers, distilled from the pores of an ancient moraine, spiced and toned in a maze of fragrant roots. Winter does not cool it, nor summer warm it. Shadows over shadows keep its fountains always cool. Moss and felted leaves guard from spring and autumn frosts; while a woolly robe of snow protects from the intenser cold of winter. Bears, deer, birds, and Indians love alike the water and the nuts of hazel green; while the pine squirrel reigns supreme and haunts its incomparable groves like a spirit. Here a grand old glacier swept over from the Tuolumne ice fountains, into the basin of the Merced, leaving the hazel-green moraine for the food of her coming trees, and the fountains of her predestined waters.

Along the Merced divide, to the ancient glacial lake-bowl of Crane's Flat, was ever fir or pine more perfect? What groves! What combinations of green and silver- gray and glowing white of glinting sunbeams! Where is leaf or limb wanting; and is this the upshot of the so-called "mountain glooms and mountain storms?" If so, is Sierra forestry aught beside an outflow of Divine Love? These round-bottomed grooves sweeping across the divide, and adown whose sides our horses canter with accelerated speed, are the pathways of ancient ice-currents, and it is just where these crushing glaciers have borne down most heavily, that the greatest loveliness of grove and forest appears.

A deep canyon filled with blue air now comes in view on the right. That is the valley of the Merced, and the highest rocks visible through the trees belong to the Yosemite Valley.

More miles of glorious forest, then out into free light and down, down, down, into the groves and meadows of Yosemite. The new wagon road has opened out some very striking views both up and down the Valley. How simple all the problems are that I studied last winter! Yet how hopeless seems the work of opening other eyes by mere words! No one will ever know the grandeur of this Sierra sculpture in its entirety, without the same study on the spot.

No one of the rocks seems to call me now, nor any of the distant mountains. Surely this Merced and Tuolumne chapter of my life is done.

I have been out on the river bank with my letters. How good and wise they seem to be! You wrote better than you know. All together they form a precious volume whose sentences are more intimately connected with my mountain work than any one will ever be able to appreciate. An ouzel came as I sat reading, alighting in the water with a delicate and graceful glint on his bosom. How pure is the morning light on the great gray wall, and how marvelous the subdued lights of the moon! The nights are wholly enchanting.

I will not try [to] tell the Valley. Yet I feel that I am a stranger here. I have been gathering you a handful of leaves. Show them to dear Keith and give some to Mrs. McChesney. They are probably the last of Yosemite that I will ever give you. I have not seen Mrs. Hutchings and hope I shall not. I will go out in a day or so. Farewell! I seem to be more really leaving you here than there. Keep these long pages, for they are a kind of memorandum of my walk after the strange Oakland epoch, and I may want to copy some of them when I have leisure.

Remember me to my friends. I trust you are not now so sorely overladen. Good-night. Keep the goldenrod and yarrow. They are auld lang syne.

Ever lovingly yours
John Muir[13]

∾

(Consider the grasshoppers how they grow & go)

Yosemite Valley,
Sunday, September 27, 1874

Dear Mrs. Carr

I have been down bathing in the Ganges. I wonder if I will ever know another river like this. After plashing and laving in the spangling crystal I swam across to examine a section of the bank and found charred bark ten feet below lake and flood deposits. In a vertical portion of the bank I discovered two small frogs of a new species each snugly nestled in a dainty nitch [sic] from whence they could look out over the water. They are not water frogs however. I swam over with them in my hand holding them aloft and when I ducked them they made a great nervous ado. I have them in my room hoping they may sing like crickets or tree frogs for me in the night.

In walking over the pebbles I received some tingling lessons about drift formations upon the soles of my feet. The wind sifted deliciously through my reviving flesh and thrilled every fiber. The afternoon sun shimmered upon the glossy poplars, bright as upon the rippled currents of the river. A thicket of tall waving goldenrods warms the south bank and the whole Valley is full of light like a lake in which one instinctively laves and winnows as if it were water.

I chased a grasshopper and finally wearied the lusty fellow and made him attempt to fly over the river into which he fell and I ran out and captured him before any of the trouts. Another larger one flew which I also succeeded in driving into the river but just as I got within arms length a trout caught him by the legs and drew him down.

I clipped the wings of the first and carried him to my room to experiment upon his habits and movements. Here is an exact copy of his walking embroidered track natural size which I got by compelling him to walk across a plateful of fine sand in my room. I showed the original track to an Indian, but he only grinned and didn't sabe. Black's Chinaman was also puzzled, and thought it must be writing. Billy Simms happened along and inquired for Kellogg and Keith. I showed him the track and he guessed it might be that of a tarantula or centipede. No. 1 in the figure is made by the middle feet No. 2 by the front feet and No. 3 by the feet of the big jumping pair. Figure 4 is made by his body and is more or less continuous according to his weariness or the depth his feet sink in the sand. The three figures at the head are copies of the track he makes in jumping. Figures 1 are made by the front pair 2 the second 3 the third and 4 by the body in crouching.

It is beautiful is it not and the track embroidery of the gray lizard is still more beautiful.

The above grasshopper in the grass is supposed to have walked once up both sides and along the bottom, and jumped thrice on the top of the page.

[*John Muir*][14]

∾

Yosemite Valley, October 7, 1874
Dear Mrs. Carr

I expected to have been among the foothill drift long ago, but the mountains fairly seized me, and, ere I knew, I was up the Merced canyon, where we were last year, past Shadow and Merced lakes and our soda springs, etc. I returned last night. Had a glorious storm, and a thousand sacred beauties that seemed yet more and more divine. I camped four nights at Shadow Lake, at the old place in the pine thickets. I have ouzel tales to tell. I was alone, and during the whole excursion, or period rather, was in a kind of calm, uncurable ecstasy. I am hopelessly and forever a mountaineer.

How glorious my studies seem, and how simple! I found out a noble truth concerning the Merced moraines that escaped me hitherto. Civilization and fever and all the morbidness that has been hooted at me has not dimmed my glacial eyes, and I care to live only to entice people to look at Nature's loveliness. My own special self is nothing. My feet have recovered their cunning. I feel myself again. Tell Keith the colors are coming to the groves.

I leave Yosemite for over the mountains to Mono and Lake Tahoe in a week, thence anywhere,—Shastaward, etc. I think I may be at Brownsville, Yuba County, where I may get a letter from you. I promised to call on Emily Pelton [*Wilson*] there.

Farewell.

John Muir

Mrs. Black has fairly mothered me. She will be down in a few weeks.[15]

Sisson's Station,
November 1, 1874

Dear Mrs. Carr.

Here is icy Shasta fifteen miles away yet at the very door. It is all close wrapt in clean young snow down to the very base, one mass of white from the dense black forest girdle at an elevation of five or six thousand feet to the very summit. The extent of its individuality is perfectly wonderful.

When I first caught sight of it over the braided folds of the Sacramento valley, I was fifty miles away and afoot, alone, and weary, yet all my blood turned to wine and I have not been weary since. Stone was to have accompanied me, but has failed of course. The last storm was severe, and all the mountains shake their heads and say impossible, etc., but you know I will meet all its icy snows lovingly.

I set out in a few minutes for the edge of the timber-line. Then upwards, if unstormy, in the early morning. If the snow proves to be mealy and loose, it is barely possible that I may be unable to urge my way through so many upward miles, as there is no intermediate camping-ground. Yet I am feverless and strong now and can spend two days with their intermediate nights in one deliberate, unstrained effort.

I am the more eager to ascend to study the mechanical conditions of the fresh snow at so great an elevation; also to obtain clear views of

the comparative quantities of lava inundation northward and southward; also general views of the channels of the ancient Shasta glaciers,
etc.; many other lesser problems, besides the fountains of the rivers
here and the living glaciers. I would like to remain a week or two and
may have to return next year in summer.

I wrote a short letter a few days ago which was printed in the
Evening Bulletin, which I suppose you have seen.

I wonder how you all are faring in your wilderness educational
departmental institutional, etc. Write me a line here in care of Sisson.
I think it will reach me on my return from icy Shasta.

Farewell.   Ever cordially yours,
                                       John Muir

Love to all,—Keith and the boys and McChesneys, etc.

Don't forward any letters from the Oakland office. I want only
mountains until my return to civilization.[16]

ᮧ

                                       [*Oakland, November, 1874*]
[*John Muir*]
[Fragment of letter]

      ...had lost *thirteen* pounds! I think he has gained some
during the last week, but there is little prospect that he will be able to
do anything this winter. John is very steady in a better position than
before, Dr. Carr lecturing before Institutes and societies, will go to Los
Angeles next month.

Dr. Kellogg called on me last week—has been invited by Secretary
Stearns to connect himself with the University as a teacher of Electro-
typing! I dare say he will accept. He was very nicely dressed, very
cordial and affectionate, did not speak of his friends in the Valley.

Mrs. Moore's sudden departure for Europe excites some comment.
There is a great excitement in business circles, and many heavy
failures. I have heard it rumored that the Moore brothers have all the
load that they can carry. I sincerely hope they may not fail, for they
have been helpful in many ways and cannot be spared from the ranks
of reliable men. The Grangers have had a blow in the failure of their
agent, but at the worst they have lost less *as a body, by two millions,*

than they would had they gone on the old business basis of selling to the wheat speculators. This fact inclines all but individual losers to keep to their former policy. It has been a wild week on change, and has buried private cares under the *avalanche of public calamities* to some extent.

You have several letters—I opened two and found they were from *General Alvord* at Washington asking for pine seeds and cones. I opened to see if they were important enough to justify a telegram, didn't know but they contained a Government appointment. The Nov. *Overland* has your article on the first page—is highly spoken of in all the papers. Your letters to me gave me great pleasure. I wish I could give you as much, but yours must be....

[Remainder of letter missing]

[*Jeanne C. Carr*][17]

ᴏᴜ

Sisson's Station,
December 9, 1874

Dear Mrs. Carr

Coming in for a sleep and rest, I was glad to receive your card. I seem to be more than married to icy Shasta.

One yellow, mellow morning six days ago, when Shasta snows were looming and blooming, I slept outside the bar-room door to gaze and was instantly drawn up over the meadows, over the forests, to the main Shasta glacier in one rushing cometic whiz, then, swooping to Shasta valley, whirled off around the base like a satellite of the grand icy sun. I have just completed my first revolution. Length of orbit, 100 miles; time, one Shasta day.

For two days and a half I had nothing in the way of food, yet suffered nothing and was finely nerved for the most delicate work of mountaineering both among crevasses and lava cliffs. Now I am sleeping and *eating*. I found some geological facts that are perfectly glorious, and botanical ones too.

I wish I could make the public be kind to Keith and his paint.

And so you contemplate vines and oranges among the warm California angels. I wish you would all go a-granging among oranges and bananas and all such blazing, red-hot fruits, for you are a species of Hindoo [sic] sun fruit yourself.

For me, I like better the huckleberries of cool glacial bogs and acid currants and benevolent, rosy, beaming apples and common Indian-summer pumpkins.

I wish you could see the holy morning's Alpen glow of Shasta.

Farewell. I'll be down into gray Oakland some time.

I am glad you are essentially independent of those commonplace plotters that have so marred your peace, eat oranges and hear the larks and wait on the sun.

Ever cordially,
John Muir

Love to all.

The letter you sent here is also received. Emily's I will get bye and bye. Love to color Keith.[18]

∽

Sisson's Station,
December 21, 1874

Dear Mrs. Carr

I have just returned from a fourth Shasta excursion and find yours of the 17th. I wish you could have been with me on Shasta's shoulder last evening in the sun glow. I was over on the head waters of the McCloud; and what a head! Think of a spring giving rise to a river! I fairly quiver with joyous exultation when I think of it. The infinity of Nature's glory in rock, cloud, and water! As soon as I beheld the McCloud upon its lower course, I knew that there must be something extraordinary in its Alpine fountains, and I shouted, "O where, my glorious river, do you come from?" Think of a spring fifty yards wide at the mouth issuing from the base of a lava bluff with wild songs, not gloomily from a dark cavy [sic] mouth, but from a world of ferns and mosses, gold and green.

I broke my way through chaparral tangle in eager vigor utterly unweariable. The dark blue stream sang solemnly with a deep voice, pooling and bowlder-dashing and an *a-a-aing* in white flashing rapids,

when suddenly I heard water notes I never had heard before. They
came from that mysterious spring. And then the Elk forest and the
Alpine glow and the sunset,—poor pen cannot tell it.

The sun this morning is at work with its blessings as if it had never
blessed before. He never wearies of revealing himself on Shasta. But in
a few hours I leave this altar and all its————.

Well, to my Father I say "Thank you" and go willingly.

I go by stage and rail to Brownsville to see Emily [*Pelton Wilson*]
and the rocks there and Yuba. Then, perhaps, a few days among the
auriferous drifts on the Tuolumne, and then to Oakland and that
book, walking across the Coast Range on the way, either through one
of the passes or over Mt. Diablo. I feel a sort of nervous fear of
another period of town dark, but I don't want to be silly about it. The
sun glow will all fade out of me and I will be deathly as Shasta in the
dark, but mornings will come, dawnings of some kind, and if not, I
have lived more than a common eternity already.

Farewell, don't *overwork*; that is not the work your Father wants.
I wish you could come a-beeing in the Shasta honey lands. Love to the
boys.

[John Muir]

[*John Muir*][19]

ೲ

Brownsville, Yuba County,
January 19, 1875

My Dear Mrs. Mother Carr, here are some of the dearest and bonniest
of our Father's bairns,—the little ones that so few care to see. I never
saw such enthusiasm in the care and breeding of mosses as Nature
manifests among these northern Sierras.

I have studied a big fruitful week among the canyons and ridges of
the Feather, and another along the Yuba River living and dead.

I have seen a dead river, a sight worth going around the world to
see. The dead rivers and dead gravels wherein lie the gold form
magnificent problems, and I feel wild and unmanageable with the
intense interest they excite, but I *will* choke myself off and finish my
glacial work and that little book of studies. I have been spending a
few fine social days with Emily [*Pelton Wilson*], but now work.

How gloriously it storms! The pines are in ecstasy, and I feel it and must go out to them. I must borrow a big coat and mingle in the storm and make some studies. Farewell. Love to all.

How are Ned and Keith? I wish Keith had been with us these Shasta and Feather River days. I have gained a thousandfold more than I hoped. Heaven send you light and the good blessings of wildness. How the rains splash and roar! and how the pines wave and pray!

[John Muir]

Emily and Mrs. Knox send love.[20]

∾

Sunday morn, [April 15, 1875]

Dear Mrs. Carr

I would like to saunter with you to the buckeye, but confess I don't feel like plashing into the middle of Miss Buckmaster's lake of lassies. I would rather revel with the bees in the bloom of Strentzel's big orchards, but in a day or two I am going to take snuff, Shasta snow-dust, and therefore cannot have either buckeye or apple bloom. I am going to the summit of Mt. Shasta sometime this week to be gone eight or ten days, and I suppose it will then be too late, for Diablo at least.

Louie's letter is a marvelous piece of scribery—almost fairy in fineness and daintiness. Keith's painting is glorious. Mrs. Harry Edwards sends love to you, while I am ever,

Yours cordially,

John Muir

All my book is in the meantime buried in Shasta snow-dust.[21]

∾

1419 Taylor St., [San Francisco],

May 4, 1875

Dear Mrs. Carr

Here I am, safe in the arms of Daddy Swett, home again from icy Shasta and richer than ever in dead-river gravel and in snowstorms and snow. The upper end of the main Sacramento Valley is entirely covered with ancient river drift, and I wandered over many square miles of it. In every pebble I could hear the sound of running water. The whole deposit is a poem whose many books and chapters form the geological Vedas of our glorious State.

I discovered a new species of hail on the summit of Shasta and experienced one of the most beautiful and most violent snowstorms imaginable.

I would have been with you ere this to tell you about it and to give you some lilies and pine tassels that I brought for you and Mrs. McChesney and Ina Coolbrith, but alack! I am battered and scarred like a log that has come down the Tuolumne in flood-time, and I am also lame with frost-nipping. Nothing serious, however, and I will be well and better than before in a few days.

I was caught in a violent snowstorm and held upon the summit of the mountain all night in my shirt-sleeves. The intense cold and the want of food and sleep made the fire of life smoulder and burn low. Nevertheless, in company with another strong mountaineer [*Jerome Fay*] I broke through six miles of frosty snow down into the timber and reached fire and food and sleep and am better than ever with all the valuable experiences. Altogether I have had a very instructive and delightful trip.

The *Bryanthus* you wanted was snow-buried, and I was too lame to dig it out for you, but I will probably go back ere long.

I'll be over in a few days or so.

[*John Muir*][22]

∾

Yosemite Valley,
June 3, 1875

Dear Mrs. Carr

Where are you? Lost in conventions, elections, women's rights and fights, and buried beneath many a load of musty granger hay. You always seem inaccessible to me, as if you were in a crowd, and even when I write, my written words seem to be heard by many that I do not like.

I wish some of your predictions given in your last may come true, like the first you made long ago. Yet somehow it seems hardly likely that you will ever be sufficiently free, for your labors multiply from year to year. Yet who knows.

I found poor [*James*] Lamon's grave, as you directed. The upper end of the Valley seems fairly silent and empty without him.

Keith got fine sketches, and I found new beauties and truths of all kinds. Mack [*McChesney*] and Swett will tell you all. I send you my buttonhole plume.

Farewell.

[*John Muir*][23]

∾

Black's Hotel, Yosemite, California,
July 31, 1875

Dear Mrs. Carr

I have just arrived from our long excursion to Mt. Whitney, all hale and happy, and find your weary plodding letter, containing things that from this rocky standpoint seem strangely mixed—things celestial and terrestrial, cultivated and wild. Your letters set one a-thinking, and yet somehow they never seem to make those problems of life clear, and I always feel glad that they do not form any part of my work, but that my lessons are simple rocks and waters and plants and humble beasts, all pure and in their places, the Man beast with all his complications being laid upon stronger shoulders.

I did not bring you down any *Sedum* roots or *Cassiope* sprays because I had not then received your letter, not that I forgot you as I passed the blessed Sierra heathers, or the *Primulas,* or the pines laden with fragrant, nutty cones. But I am more and more made to feel that my gardens and herbariums and woods are all in their places as they grow, and I know them there, and can find them when I will. Yet I ought to carry their poor dead or dying forms to those who can have no better.

The Valley is lovely, scarce more than a whit the worse for the flower-crushing feet that every summer brings. The Editorial party are awful wise. Yet I find some fine and good-looking people among them. I am not decided about my summer. I want to go with the Sequoias a month or two into all their homes from north to south, learning what I can of their conditions and prospects, their age, stature, the area they occupy, etc. But John Swett, who is brother now, papa then, orders me home to booking. Bless me, what an awful thing town duty is! I was once free as any pine-playing wind, and feel that I have still a good length of line, but alack! there seems to be a hook or two of civilization in me that I would fain pull out, yet *would not pull out*—O, O, O!!!

I suppose you are weary of saying book, book, book, and perhaps when you fear me lost in rocks and Mono deserts I will, with Scotch perverseness, do all you ask and more. All this letter is about myself, and why not when I'm the only person in all the wide world that I know anything about—Keith, the cascade, not excepted.

Fare ye well, mother quail, good betide your brood and be they and you saved from the hawks and the big ugly buzzards and cormorants—grangeal, political, right and wrongical—and I will be

> Ever truly,
> John Muir
> "Only that and nothing more."[24]

∾

> Old Yosemite Home,
> November 3, 1875

Dear Mrs. Carr

I'm delighted, in coming out of the woods, to learn that the Doctor is elected to do the work he is so well fitted for.

I've had a glorious season of forest grace, notwithstanding the hundred canyons I've crossed, and the innumerable gorges, gulches, and avalanchal corrugations.

A day or two of resting and lingering in my dear old haunts, and then down, town, work.

I'm sorry about Keith's stocks. Though of scarce any real consequence, they yet serve to perturb and spoil his best moods and works.

It seems a whole round season since I saw you, but have I not seen the King Sequoia in forest glory?

Love to all.

> John Muir[25]

*For you, beloved friend, I am always
grateful, and my heart always builds
precious hopes upon you.*

Jeanne C. Carr

In Remembrance of Yosemite: Writing a Long Old-Time Letter

EZRA CARR ASSUMED THE OFFICE OF SUPERINTENDENT OF PUBLIC Instruction for the State of California on December 4, 1875, and appointed Jeanne Carr deputy superintendent. The Carrs maintained a residence in Oakland and when in Sacramento they stayed at the Watson House on 10th Street opposite the state capitol.

Muir gave his first public lecture on glaciers and forests to the Literary Institute of Sacramento at the Congregational Church on January 25, 1876. In the past he had refused invitations to lecture. Muir admittedly had no skill as a lecturer and was uneasy about the prospect of formal presentations, but provided with a mountain landscape painted by William Keith, upon which he gazed during his talk, he forgot himself and his audience. The unconventional lecture was well received. Although there is no record of Carr attending Muir's lecture, it is fair to say that if she was in Sacramento she was present.

Muir completed his first essay on forest preservation in January. Inspired by his autumn tour of the Sequoia belt, which sharpened his awareness of the need to preserve wilderness, "God's First Temples: How Shall We Preserve Our Forests?" appeared in the *Sacramento Daily Union,* February 5. It stressed the economic results of the destruction of forests and urged legislation to preserve them.[1]

Ezra Carr delegated many of his responsibilities as superintendent to Jeanne due to his recurring rheumatism. Jeanne also taught at the Normal School in San Francisco and at Mill's Seminary, a school for young women located in the Brooklyn Hills of Oakland. She lectured throughout the state on issues related to education and continued to write articles. An important outlet for her ideas, the *California Teacher,* discontinued circulation in April 1876.

In the spring John Henry Carr was assaulted and thereafter suffered recurring violent headaches from which he found no relief. Muir expressed concern and hope that "Johnnie" had recovered and that the situation was resolved.

Traveling from Redding to Siskiyou in May, Carr attended the Siskiyou County Teachers' Institute annual session. On the way she passed the "white wonder" of Mount Shasta, lost sight of the mountain for many hours as the stage followed the McCloud, Pitt, and Sacramento Rivers, and caught one compensatory view by moonlight. The mountain had a healing effect on Carr. On May 2, after silently worshipping at Shasta's feet, she described the ride around the base of the mountain as charming, enhanced by the braided beauty of pine and fir forests and singing waters. All seekers of health and recreation she directed northward to the hospitable wilderness where wild strawberries flowered as in dreams, the forest billows rose and fell like pulsations from the living soul of the scene, and young rivers musically poured their silver floods out of the forest's stillness.[2]

Wearing a linen duster to protect her dress from ash and smoke, Carr traveled aboard the Pacific Railroad from Sacramento on her way to Philadelphia to attend the United States Centennial. Stopping in Madison, Wisconsin, she visited her former home on Gilman Street. Nearly all the wild plants she had cultivated were flourishing. To the Centennial Carr carried a book of ferns, representative of California flora, and two bound volumes of penmanship, bookkeeping, maps, and freehand drawings from the students at Crescent City School, Del Norte County, California. In Philadelphia she collected information about industrial education. Returning to Oakland in early October, Carr stopped to see the Strentzels in Alhambra. Well into the night she talked about the Centennial, the Educational Convention, and the Women's Convention, and described the colleges and universities she visited while in the east.[3]

Muir returned to the Swett residence in December and remained there until spring, working on articles. In February 1877 Jeanne Carr purchased a forty-two-acre homestead on the northeast corner of Orange Grove Avenue and Colorado Street in Pasadena. It was the land among the warm California angels she had written to Muir about in 1874 and would be a sanctuary for the Carrs following the death of John Henry Carr on April 9, 1877.

Having taken a room at the Arcade Hotel in Sacramento, John Henry, twenty-four, shot himself in the head with a Smith & Wesson revolver; death was instantaneous. Several months earlier he had attempted suicide; in April he succeeded. In response to the McChesneys, who wrote to express their sympathy, Carr replied that her days went on into profounder grief as the loss of her son sank deeper into her consciousness. His death was too sudden, appalling, needless, and cruel. He was sweet and faithful, sympathetic and sensitive. In losing him Carr mourned not what she made but what she loved. Louisiana Strentzel noted in her diary, "Did ever a mother have such trials as she."[4]

Southern California would provide a ray of hope following the death of Carr's son and the years of public service often controversial and disappointing. Ezra Carr's rheumatism hampered his productivity and, exacerbated by the death of John Henry, left him all but crippled. He was "too lame to use 'shovel or hoe.'" Muir hoped Carr would realize her plan to cultivate a substantial garden, plant orange groves, and open a school of horticultural studies for young women. He thought it a great consolation for her to look forward to tranquil seclusion. She would "dig and dibble in that mellow loam" following years of encompassing obligations.

Muir traveled among the peaks of the Wasatch Range in Utah, tracing glacial rivers as a correspondent for the *San Francisco Daily Evening Bulletin*. He made a short dash into the Highlands above Yosemite in July. Coming from the salt deserts of Utah, his spirit was replenished by the wild icy water, sweet forest, and the *Cassiope* he encountered in the Valley. Five "shaggy days" were spent in the heart of the San Gabriel Mountains, where he saw Carr's orange lands and met with Orville H. Congar, an original member of the San Gabriel Orange Grove Association, a former student of Ezra Carr, and a classmate of Muir's at the University of Wisconsin. Congar had helped Carr negotiate the purchase of her Pasadena homestead, for which she paid seventy-five dollars an acre. Returning northward, Muir rambled in the Santa Cruz woods, climbed to the summit of Mount Hamilton, and spent a week in San Jose, where he lectured to the San Jose State Normal School faculty (later San Jose State University).[5]

In early September Carr traveled to Plumas County to spend ten days in the "Garden of the Gods." From there she sent Louie Wanda

Strentzel a box of *Linnaea borealis, Cypripedium,* and *Aspidium.* Returning to Sacramento, she met with botanist Asa Gray and English botanist and curator of Kew Botanical Gardens, London, Sir Joseph Hooker, who were on their way to Mount Shasta with Muir. Hooker agreed to exchange notes with Carr on acclimatization and offered assistance with supplies for her proposed horticultural school. Muir, Gray, and Hooker stopped briefly at the Rancho Chico on the Sacramento River, where they were joined by the California pioneer General John Bidwell, his wife, Annie Kennedy Bidwell, and her sister, Sallie Kennedy. When Muir, the Bidwells, and Kennedy returned to Rancho Chico, Bidwell's carpenter built Muir a skiff christened *The Spoonbill.* From Bidwell's landing Muir floated down the Sacramento River to Sacramento. The first night he camped on an island beneath a large sycamore surrounded by busy owls and the rush of the river. Birds were abundant. Muir also camped on a low sloping bank between willows, under an arching sycamore, on a sandy bar on the edge of a growth of cottonwoods, and on a sandy cove. He reached the confluence of the Feather River on October 8, beached his *Snagjumper* (rechristened because of its efficiency in surmounting snags) in Sacramento, and took a steamer to San Francisco.[6]

In the fall Carr traveled to San Francisco, spoke before the Institute of Sonoma County in Petaluma, returned to her office in Sacramento, and made several visits to the state agricultural fair. Muir took the train to Visalia and headed for the Middle Fork of the Kings River with a young explorer, John Rigby. Upon his return to Hopeton Muir built a skiff, *Snagjumper II,* by the Merced River and on November 10 floated 250 miles down the Merced and the San Joaquin to Martinez. On November 27 he walked two miles to the Alhambra Valley and made his first visit as a naturalist to the Strentzel family to call upon the horticulturalist, Dr. John Strentzel. Muir returned to the Swett home to write and lecture and remained there until spring.

During 1877 Carr reclaimed seven acres and planted orange trees on the flat below the rise where stood their three-room rough-board-and-battened "California house," typical of pioneer homes in the Pasadena colony and elsewhere in southern California. Vines planted around the cottage grew quickly and soon engulfed the house in a web of leaves and flowers. Pines were planted during the first year so Carr could listen to them whisper as she worked. The development of Carmelita, "little grove," was for Jeanne Carr the practical application of her belief that women as well as men were able to earn a livelihood from land stewardship. Inherent in land were both spiritual and republican values. Upon God's unencumbered acres, where intelligence prevailed and contentment dwelled, Carr staked her faith in the independent, dignified, and honorable life of a farmer. The pure California sunshine was a fountain of youth and her land a garden of Eden.[7]

The development of the tract was undertaken with the help of her sons, Albert (Allie) and Edward (Ned), and Martin H. Weight, a Pasadena resident, assisted by other colonists. Nursery stock was donated by local nursery owners. Carr received gifts from friends who remembered her request for seeds, plants, and cuttings. Sir Joseph Hooker planted an English yew tree; A. T. Stratton, a friend, sent roses and proteaceae seeds; and Marshall P. Wilder, a Boston horticulturalist, sent a *Camellia*. Carr searched remote areas of the San Gabriel Mountains for scarlet gooseberries and carried in her lunch basket trees from Oakland that she cultivated in her garden. She made frequent visits to see her plan drawn to scale carried out and traversed her forty-two acres in a Studebaker wagon, gradually transforming the dusty sun-scorched sheep-run into one of the first noteworthy estates in Pasadena. Confiding to her friend, author, and special commissioner to the Mission Indians of California, Helen Hunt Jackson, Carr declared that she would "make the wilderness not only blossom but repay the cost of its blossoming." According to Jackson, Carr's effort was hardly less than "a second sight inspiration ... to a person whose only relations with nature were of the closest, and of long standing." Nothing short of an enthusiastic passion for outdoor life and for plants could have created Carmelita.[8]

Muir's first article for *Scribner's Monthly,* "The Humming-Bird of the California Water-Falls," appeared in February 1878. During the spring he visited the Strentzels. Scientific discussions with John Strentzel gave way to walks in the Alhambra hills with Louie Wanda. In June Muir remained at the Strentzels' a week working, resting, and eating cherries. He remarked to Carr that he particularly enjoyed the white bed upon which he slept. As summer approached, Muir joined the Coast and Geodetic Survey in Utah and Nevada as a correspondent for the *San Francisco Daily Evening Bulletin*. Late in the year he began work on an article on bee pastures for *Scribner's,* and Carr completed planting fourteen acres of sandy Pasadena soil in walnut trees and pomegranates. In 1879 she planted ten acres in orchard and vineyard. Muir wrote to her wondering if she would really go quietly to live in Pasadena and rest in the afternoon of her life among kin and orange leaves. He thought nothing less than an exhaustive miniature of all the leafy organisms of the planet would satisfy her aspirations for Carmelita. Muir's April 24 letter to Carr reflected the demands upon her. He thought she would have made at least one brief visit to see him. She was nearly invisible.[9]

Muir had "little real sympathy" for Carr's play-garden schemes, though he offered assistance and provided tree seeds and several redwoods, and planted a Sequoia in Carmelita. Throughout their friendship Muir and Carr would disagree ideologically and empirically on the transplanting of wild plants to a garden setting. Muir considered cultivated gardens and groves a means to profit. For him real gardens were "a piece of pure nature," found only in wilderness. Carr believed nature invited her to cooperate in the production of beauty through the cultivation of plants and trees. Wild plants enabled her to touch the beauty of the wilderness, illustrate the beauty of their place of origin, and reference the beauty of God's home. Their cultivation made them more useful in her eyes. Carr's understanding of her relation with nature was girded by her belief that by rooting herself "firmly to the earth" she had a fairer chance of rising, like the trees she planted, "into the free heavens, to endure as they endure, than in the overcrowded callings and professions." Carr's horticultural and agricultural pursuits at Carmelita were an experience through which she washed away the life she had lived in order to enter into a more favorable relation with God.[10]

At a nationwide Sunday-school convention in Yosemite Valley, Muir lectured on "The Geological Records of the Yosemite Valley Glaciers." He electrified his audience during two presentations, tours, and a campfire talk. Over one hundred people followed him up Eagle Point Trail and two hundred joined him on an excursion up the Glacier Point Trail. Muir made a brief visit to the Strentzels' ranch on the eve of his departure for Alaska. The occasion was his engagement to Louie Wanda. Muir wrote to Carr that he was going home to summer in the snow, ice, and forests of the north coast, perhaps to Alaska. He did not mention his betrothal, which remained a Strentzel family secret. Muir's trip came at a critical time in his relation with Louie. It was indicative of the future. Louie would share Muir with the wilderness and the mountains that fortified him. A letter Muir wrote to Louie from Victoria, British Columbia, asked her to be patient. In October Louie responded. She prayed the dear Lord would lead Muir from the depths of blue glacier caves and permit her to once again look upon his face. In December to her "Beloved Friend" she wrote that her heart was in all his work and she rejoiced over his gains in God's Wilds, but the price for it all in toil, hardship, and suffering was so great. Louie accepted Muir's wilderness idiosyncrasies; she did not understand them.[11]

Muir traveled with a friend, Thomas Magee of San Francisco, to British Columbia and south into Oregon. From Portland Muir sailed north on the steamship *California*. At Fort Wrangell he met the resident Presbyterian missionary, S. Hall Young, and traveled with him and frequently with a mission party of Presbyterian clergy northward along the coast on the river steamer *Cassiar* to Sitka, the Stikine River, the Fairweather Mountains, and Glacier Bay. Muir returned to Portland in January 1880. A "tangle" of lectures in Portland and business in San Francisco kept him from returning to the Alhambra Valley, the Strentzel ranch, and Louie until mid-February.

When Jeanne and Ezra Carr formally moved to Pasadena in early 1880, four hundred people were residing there. Deer came down from the mountains every few days, the trees were full of birds, and Carr's sons, Albert (Allie) and Edward (Ned), went out hunting for bear. At night coyotes howled; tarantulas crawled across the hard adobe soil and horned toads were plentiful. Windstorms whipped sand through cracks in the walls of their cottage. The Carrs became accustomed to the rough life and lived mostly outdoors, with their kitchen stove in a grove of tall bamboo trees.[12]

The marriage of John Muir and Louie Wanda Strentzel, a private affair, took place on April 14, 1880. The ceremony was performed by the Reverend J. E. Dwinell of the Sacramento Congregational Church at the Strentzel ranch amidst a rainstorm, surrounded by flowers gathered from the ranch. Twenty years of wandering had brought the forty-two-year-old Muir home to a life with Louie Wanda, who was thirty-three. Carr responded to the celebratory news of their union with the affirmation that she had long hoped that, more than fame, Muir would find the completeness that came only in living "in perfected home relations." She believed the marriage was made in heaven, foreordained from the beginning. Muir and Louie lived in the Coleman home formerly occupied by Louie's parents, who took temporary quarters while they built a Victorian mansion. Muir rented land from John Strentzel, began a career as a fruit rancher, and assisted Strentzel in the management of his 2,600-acre holdings. The interim between July and the October harvest was set aside for Muir to travel, and he departed for Alaska as a correspondent for the *San Francisco Daily Evening Bulletin*, traveling with Thomas Magee north to Victoria. From there they traveled to Fort Wrangell and joined S. Hall Young. At Sitka Magee sailed home and Muir, Young, Lot Tyeen, an Indian, his son-in-law Joe, Billy Smart, and Stickeen, a small black-white-and-tan dog, embarked on a canoe trip to Glacier Bay. Rambling on Taylor Glacier, Muir and Stickeen shared their adventure on the ice. Muir returned by steamer to Portland in September and to Alhambra in the fall. On March 25, 1881, Annie Wanda Muir was born. Muir wrote to Mary L. Swett that the Strentzel-Muir family was now five, four old lovers around one little love. Bloom-time had come and a bloom baby arrived. Not since the glacial period began were there happier people.[13]

Muir's health, however, was affected by the heavy ranch work, by the fact that he drove himself to profitable work now that he had a family to support, by his in-laws, who pressured him to curtail his wilderness chases, and by the fact that he did not have the freedom to ramble at his own pace and time in the wilderness that sustained him. Suffering with a bronchial cough and nervous indigestion, he was encouraged by Louie to go to the mountains. Muir accepted an invitation from Captain C. L. Hooper of the cutter *Corwin* to accompany an expedition in search of the lost steamer *Jeannette* that had set out on a polar expedition in 1879. In May Muir departed on the *Corwin* as a correspondent for the *San Francisco Daily Evening Bulletin*. He returned in October to harvest grapes and to greet a new neighbor. John Swett purchased the adjacent ranch and named it Hillgirt.[14]

After the cruise of the *Corwin* Muir devoted six years almost exclusively to his family and the ranch. He became a practical horticulturalist and commanded the highest market prices. No fruit jobber got the better of him in a deal. Muir converted pasturage to vineyards and orchards, refrained from agricultural experimentation, and concentrated on cash crops—pears, grapes, and cherries. He corresponded with immediate family and seldom wrote to friends, accounting for the absence of letters to Carr. Extant letters written between 1881 and 1887 included fifteen written to friends, of which one was the letter to Mary Swett regarding the birth of his daughter and another was a letter to Jeanne Carr written in 1887. Muir traveled to the mountains every summer, remained close to post offices and telegraph stations, and returned every fall for the harvest. Consumed with managing the Strentzel-Muir ranch, Muir accumulated a reserve of money for his family. His literary silence was noticed by friends and colleagues. Botanists Charles C. Parry and Albert Kellogg of the California Academy of Sciences, and Robert Underwood Johnson, on the staff at *Scribner's Monthly,* urged Muir not to abandon writing altogether.

Muir's horticultural efforts were matched by Carr's. She surrounded the entrance to Carmelita with manzanita masked by roses and the grounds with a living hedge of cypress, roses, grapes, and lime trees. More than ninety varieties of trees and grapes, strawberries, raspberries, and blackberries were planted. Carr experimented with silk culture and with fig culture, distributing over five thousand fig cuttings for cultivation on Southern California farms. Hesperian fruit, however, was difficult to grow. Unprecedented frosts during the winter of 1879–1880 destroyed nursery stock as well as five- and six-year-old trees. In 1882–1883 a late frost nipped the fruit and trees were unusually full, dwarfing the oranges and detracting from their quality. Carr wrote to the Strentzels that she and her family were shivering with cold, their orange trees were frozen, and there were no buds or blooms. When the market opened the weather was cold and rainy and there was little interest in sour fruit, which drove prices down.[15]

Carr's agrarian inclination and practical educational precepts, grounded in biblical tenets and drawn from her ancestral associations, culminated in and around Carmelita and her plans for a horticultural school for women. She endured in anticipation of her school; however, the failure of the citrus crop resulted in her abandoning her plan to provide for women a noble life and industrial independence through training in the rural arts. Helen Hunt Jackson recognized that it would be a long time before there would arise another "such prophetess and priestess combined of natures worship and work." Though Carr's personal dream remained unfulfilled, Throop Polytechnic Institute (the forerunner of Caltech) incorporated practical arts education for women in its curriculum.[16]

By the end of Pasadena's first decade in 1883 the influx of settlers had increased property values. Carr sold a three-acre lot on the corner of Fair Oaks Boulevard and Colorado Street for $6,000 and built a commodious redwood boarding house with accommodations for twenty. She planted an ornamental rose garden around a circular basin fed by a fountain in which goldfish darted in and out beneath *Victoria regia* and common pond lilies. Banana trees and Nile papyrus shaded the pool. The three-room cottage occupied by the Carrs prior to the construction of the boarding house was moved to the north edge of the grounds, where it was used by Ezra Carr as a study. To accommodate increased traffic on Colorado Street, Pasadena's main thoroughfare, the street was widened along Carmelita's south line. From the uprooted cypress hedge a rustic cabin known as "bachelor hall" was constructed. Carmelita, the first literary center in southern California, attracted many cultured visitors and guests. Actress Helena Modjeska, authors Margaret Collier Graham, Abbott Kinney, and Charles Frederick Holder, San Francisco architect Sumner W. Bugbee, and Helen Hunt Jackson all stayed at Carmelita. Carr met with a modicum of success and shipped grapes to Chicago and London. The following year there was crop failure again.[17]

Antithetical to Carr's struggle was the prosperity that governed the Strentzel-Muir ranch, except for the fact that Muir felt as contented as would a wild animal in a cage. Muir's burdens, however, were equal to Carr's. In 1884 David Galloway, Muir's brother-in-law, died of grief following the accidental drowning of his only son, George. In late August 1885 Muir was overcome with a powerful premonition that his father, Daniel Muir, was dying. Muir had not seen his father since the summer of 1867, when he departed from Hickory Hill, Wisconsin. There had been little correspondence between them in the intervening years, yet Muir felt compelled to travel back east. He stopped at Shasta and in Yellowstone on his way. He spent two weeks in Yellowstone, where he traveled with a couple, Mr. and Mrs. Alfred H. Sellers, on a 150-mile horseback and camping trip through the park. In Portage Muir gathered family members and proceeded to Kansas City, arriving on September 24 to find his father failing. Daniel Muir died on October 6.[18]

The birth of Helen (Midge) Lillian Muir on January 23, 1886, kept Muir, devoted to his frail daughter, at the Strentzel-Muir ranch for most of the next eighteen months. In spring 1887 he accepted an offer from the J. Dewing & Co., New York and San Francisco, to contribute to and edit *Picturesque California*. Muir's labored and uninspired first drafts were coequal to the difficulties Carr experienced as she wrote the four- to five-thousand-word manuscript for the chapter on Southern California. Muir suggested she pitch in and finish, not worrying about the jogs and lifts of the Cordilleras. He called it fine preaching, perhaps addressing himself as well. Muir sporadically took a room in an obscure San Francisco hotel to concentrate on his writing. *Picturesque California* was published in 1888 with contributions from both Muir and Carr.[19]

Louie persuaded Muir to join Charles C. Parry in June 1888 on a week's camping trip to Lake Tahoe, where wild roses and strawberries were plentiful and spruce and pine were not endangered by the axe. From Tahoe Muir and William Keith traveled to Oregon by Pullman car. They met Norman Sisson, proprietor of Sisson's Hotel, at the station on the flank of Mount Shasta. Washington lilies and *Spiraea* were in full bloom. Huckleberries, raspberries, and blackberries were ripe. Shasta was glorious in clouds and sun-fire. Muir and Keith departed from Sisson's Station on a train going north to Seattle, Washington. On August 9 Louie wrote to Muir as he and Keith set out via the Yellowjacket Trail, along the Nisqually River, with six men determined to climb Mount Rainier and a local postmaster as a guide. On August 14 the party began their ascent of the mountain following the Nisqually Glacier for several miles, then up the flank leading to the spur that divided the Nisqually from the Cowlitz Glacier basin. By nightfall they had reached the foot of the great rock. The following day, climbing ice-slopes and crevasses, they reached the summit. On Shasta Muir found himself once again close to nature, and he found something of his narrative voice. Walking alone in the woods, he wrote that above the woods and in the zone below the ice and snow there is quietude and freedom where sunshine sleeps on alpine gardens, young rivers flow from glacial caves, and *Eriogonums* are open to light.[20]

Muir received Louie's letter when he returned to Seattle. Noble in tone, independent in thought, and framed by her understanding of Muir's spirit, the letter was intended to set him free. He had to be himself, well and strong, fed by nature's currents. The Alaska book and the Yosemite book needed to be written. The only consideration was the welfare of their children. The ranch meant nothing if it called for the sacrifice of Muir's life and work. For Louie there was nothing more to be said. When Muir returned to Alhambra she had begun the protracted process of selling and leasing large portions of the ranch to relieve Muir's burden so he could resume writing.[21]

During 1888 Carr, a tiny withered cricket worn by years of struggle, faced her own realization. The collapse of the boom in Pasadena forced her to mortgage berry lots and other acreage. She admitted that she yielded to the necessity of a softer climate for her family and to the seductive charms of fruit growing. All forms of life were experimental, and Carr faced the serious burdens in "natural paradise," realizing forest planning and preservation, which alone made irrigation possible, were the chief factors that would lead to success in southern California.[22]

Robert Underwood Johnson, now associate editor of the *Century* (formerly *Scribner's Monthly*), arrived in San Francisco in early June 1889 to begin preparation for a series on the gold rush. He also planned to meet Muir, whom he wanted to write for the *Century*. Johnson may have sensed that he had arrived at an opportune time. A visit to the ranch was followed by an invitation to visit Yosemite. From the Valley Muir arranged a pack trip into Tuolumne Meadows, where he and Johnson camped beside Soda Springs. From there they rambled. At night by a campfire they talked. Muir spoke of the joy he found in nature and of its healing qualities. But the mountain meadows were gone, pigsties and corrals littered the Valley, and the beauty was diminished to make hayfields for horses, mules, and sheep. Only a portion of Yosemite had

been made a state park by President Abraham Lincoln in 1864. Under
the management of the Yosemite Park Commission there was wide-
spread devastation. Johnson listened and devised a plan. A national park
around the state park would protect the meadows and the headwaters
of the streams that fell into the Valley. Muir, highly skeptical, knew Californians were indifferent to the destruction of natural resources; their
love of unspoiled nature was "desperately modest." Johnson urged Muir
to write two articles for the *Century*, one portraying the natural features
of the region, the other outlining the boundaries for the proposed park.
Johnson would take the articles to Washington and lobby for passage
of a bill creating a national park. Together Muir and Johnson launched
a campaign for Yosemite National Park that collided with local entre-
preneurs and threatened to displace cattlemen, sheepherders, and lumbermen, who made free use of the land.[23]

In the summer of 1889 Muir wrote two articles for the San Francisco
Daily Evening Bulletin exposing the impediments to improving the Valley under state control and demonstrating the destruction to the surrounding region wrought by sheepherders and lumbermen. In early summer 1890 he completed the two articles Johnson had requested for the
Century. "The Treasures of the Yosemite" appeared in August and "Features of the Proposed Yosemite National Park" followed in September.
They were his first appearance in a national publication in eight years,
and the appeal would reach two hundred thousand subscribers. Both
"Treasures" and "Features" included illustrations, but whereas the first
article included images of the devastation caused by sheepherders and
lumbermen, the second illuminated the natural beauty of the region.
Both included a map of the proposed new boundaries. Muir's articles
and his recommendations for the park were critical to the success of
the Yosemite campaign.[24]

Worn with grippe, Muir departed from San Francisco on June 14
on the steamer *City of Paeblo* with "faithful hope" of recovery, wilderness being the only cure. He headed north to explore Muir Glacier and
its tributaries. In Port Townsend he boarded the *Queen*. Everywhere
and always Muir thought he was in God's eternal beauty and love. He
believed that in nature he was awake, discovered interesting things,
and reached a mark he did not seek. A new flower or waterfall drew

his attention and he stopped to study it. No places in the fields of nature were blank or barren. Every spot was covered with harvest. This time Muir's eyes were fixed on the glaciers of Glacier Bay. He returned to Martinez in September.

Opposition to the Yosemite Bill was led by John P. Irish, secretary and treasurer of the Yosemite Commission, who charged Muir and Johnson with conspiracy to defraud the state. Irish accused Muir of despoiling the Valley, logging and sawing timber at Hutchings's Mill as willingly as any lumberman. Muir was nothing but a "pseudo-naturalist." Muir publicly denied the charge in an article that appeared in the *Oakland Daily Evening Tribune,* claiming he milled only fallen timber while employed by Hutchings in the Valley. William E. Colby, William Keith, Professor William D. Armes of the University of California, and Jeanne C. Carr, who paid a visit to the editor of a San Francisco newspaper to discredit Irish, came to Muir's defense. Personal friends of Johnson introduced the bill that passed on September 30 and was signed into law by President Benjamin Harrison on October 1, 1890. Yosemite National Park surrounded the Valley, which remained a state park. The campaign for the recession of the Valley to the federal government began in 1895; that bill was signed by President Theodore Roosevelt in 1905.[25]

The celebration marking the passage of the Yosemite Bill in early October dissipated in late October, when Dr. John Strentzel died. The Muir family moved to the "Big House" to care for Louisiana Strentzel. By 1890 Pasadena's Orange Grove Avenue "millionaire's row" was lined with palatial homes. The steady growth of the colony compromised its rural character. Migration from the eastern states and the growing importance of Los Angeles as the commercial metropolis of Southern California contributed to the boom. Pasadena's growth put pressure on the agrarian aspirations of the colonists. Once-prized orange groves were sacrificed for elegant villas. Unable to compete, Carr dug up and sold many of Carmelita's trees and plants. She hoped Pasadena would at least preserve its natural resources and proposed the formation of a corporation to convert the area along the Arroyo Seco stream into a public park.[26]

The arrival of John and Margaret Muir Reid in spring 1891 brought some relief to Muir, who turned over a portion of the ranch supervision to his brother-in-law. Muir still felt he seldom accomplished real work. In

June he retreated to the South Fork Kings River with the artist Charles D. Robinson. Along the northern boundary of Grant Park Muir noted loggers were cutting many Sequoia. The number of mills along the Sequoia belt had doubled. At the foot of South Fork Kings River Valley he and Robinson entered a spacious park of pine, fir, and oak trees. Kings River had fewer meadows than Yosemite but more parks and sugar pines. Instead of Mirror Lake there was Bear Meadow. Muir returned to Martinez in mid-June. Like the sun, every god-like mountain radiated beams of beauty that touched him with a mysterious influence.

In recognition of Muir's accomplishments Carr agreed to write an essay for the *Californian* focused on his formative years in Wisconsin and in Yosemite Valley. In "John Muir," published in June 1892, she created a narrative based on Muir's letters, weaving together the highlights of his experiences and ramblings. A tribute to Muir, it was an acknowledgment of the kindred relation he and Carr shared inclusive of family and friends.[27]

Carmelita and eleven acres were sold to Simeon Reed of Portland, Oregon, in 1892. The Carrs moved to a mission-style cottage on Kensington Place. Once a major cog in the wheels that turned Pasadena, Carr, who had been a member of the Oakland Library Association, secretary of the Pasadena Free Library and Village Improvement Association, a trustee of Throop Polytechnic Institute, and a preservationist who worked to save the California missions, was no longer a social and educational leader.[28]

As Carr withdrew into herself, Muir entrenched himself with Robert Underwood Johnson, Warren Olney, a San Francisco attorney, other like-minded friends, promoters of wilderness, and intellectuals, who together formulated a defense league to protect Yosemite National Park. The first organizational meeting of the Sierra Club was held in San Francisco in late May. The club promoted the exploration and enjoyment of the Pacific mountain regions and enlisted the support and cooperation of individuals and the government in preserving the forests and other features of the Sierra. It was for Muir the crystallization of his dreams and labors to preserve and protect the wilderness through concerted effort. In February 1893 the Sierra Club stopped the bill presented by Congressman Anthony Caminetti intended to contract the boundaries of Yosemite National Park.

The defeat of the Caminetti Bill and the fact that Muir's brother-in-law John Reid and his brother David (who arrived in April following the failure of his dry-goods business in Portage) could supervise the ranch provided Muir incentive to travel with William Keith to the eastern United States and to Europe in May. Following a stop in Portage, Wisconsin, Muir visited the World's Columbian Exposition in Chicago. In New York he met the naturalist John Burroughs; the editor-in-chief of the *Century,* Richard Watson Gilder; the authors Mark Twain, Charles Dudley Warren, Rudyard Kipling, and George Washington Cable; and the electrical engineer Nikola Tesla. He also met the importing and manufacturing executive James Pinchot and his son Gifford, a student of forestry. On June 26 Muir sailed for Liverpool, stopped briefly in Edinburgh, and traveled by train to Dunbar, Scotland. He visited his boyhood home and his old school and his cousin Margaret Hay Lunam and her daughter Maggie. Over the Scottish countryside and the rock-bound shore he rambled. By mid-September Muir had traveled to Norway, the English Lake District, London, Switzerland, and Ireland. Awaiting his return to New York was a telegram from Louie urging him to go to Washington to meet with the new Secretary of the Interior, Hope Smith. Following lobbying efforts with Robert Underwood Johnson in Washington, Muir returned to Martinez in October.

Throughout most of 1894 Muir worked on his first book, *The Mountains of California,* a compilation of articles that rallied preservation sentiments. In November he sent a copy to Jeanne Carr, who enjoyed it "in sips and dips." But Carr's thoughts by then could not have been further from Muir and his success. The death of Ezra S. Carr in November 1894, was a great loss to her and marked the saddest of all her years. Muir sent condolences in January. Passing from life to life though glorious was sad. He prayed for her strength. A late December letter Carr sent to Muir mentioned George Wharton James, who wanted to meet Muir. James was to become Muir's nemesis. It was James's receipt of the Muir letters that created the stir that resulted in the publication of *Letters to a Friend* in 1915.[29]

The monotony of rain, wind, and black weather did not affect Muir as he sat at his scribble desk writing about Alaskan mountains and glaciers. Muir's second-floor study was filled with books, manuscripts, and sketches. A white marble fireplace stood opposite the door that led to the hallway. Over the mantle covered with framed photographs of friends hung William Keith's painting "The Oaks." There was a flat-topped desk by the east window at which Muir wrote. Supervision of the ranch was now a part-time activity, enabling him to apply himself to writing. As he worked on an essay about Glacier Bay in late January, a storm sent robins down from the hills. Frogs sang lustily out in the fields, and Muir caught a small screech owl who flew around his room and bumped his head against the window. The *Century* received "The Discovery of Glacier Bay" in February and published it in June.[30]

Rambling from Tahoe to Tuolumne Canyon and Hetch Hetchy Valley in July, Muir was driven from camp by hunger and met Theodore Parker Lukens, who gave him food. From Hetch Hetchy Muir entered Yosemite Valley, found his cabin, hidden like a bird's nest, walked to Royal Arches and to Hutchings's log cottage, and visited the graves of Floy (Squirrel) Hutchings and James Lamon. Muir expected to call on Carr in Pasadena after the grape harvest. There is no extant record of Muir stopping at Carmelita, but he did visit Lukens in southern California and lecture at Throop Polytechnic Institute and at the Pasadena High School late in the year.

Among the sycamores on Alhambra Creek there were thirty-one heron nests. Peach trees were blooming and buckeye would soon be in full leaf. It was spring in Alhambra Valley, Contra Costa County. Muir walked the hills with his daughters, Wanda and Helen. Tall grain waved in the wind and wild oats danced. In June while sitting at his desk Muir felt an unshakable premonition that his mother was dying in Portage, Wisconsin. When he, his sister Mary, and her daughter Helen arrived in Portage they found Anne Muir gravely ill. She rallied, and Muir traveled on to Cambridge, Massachusetts, to receive an honorary degree from Harvard, but in New York en route to Cambridge he received in a telegram the word that his mother had died in her sleep. Following the ceremony at Harvard, Muir returned to Portage.[31]

Muir joined the Forestry Commission in Chicago in July and traveled west to inspect forests. Every forest they saw was shrouded in smoke and blackened stumps. Watershed forests essential to irrigation were being logged off. Gifford Pinchot joined them in Montana. He and Muir hiked the Grand Canyon rim and camped together in a grove of pine and cedar. Leaving the party, Muir joined Henry Fairfield Osborn, the renowned paleontologist, whom Muir had met in New York in 1893, and together they traveled to Alaska. Muir returned to Oregon, rejoined the commission at Crater Lake, and returned home in the fall. The Forestry Commission report recommended immediate federal regulation to protect western timberlands, the establishment of thirteen forest reserves, and the appointment of a military force to police the reserves until a trained civilian forest bureau could be arranged. During the final days of his administration, President Grover Cleveland created thirteen new reserves totaling 21.4 million acres of western land. Cleveland's decision set off a preservation/conservation battle that would erupt during the administration of President William McKinley.

In December 1896 Carr, now seventy-one, sold her Kensington Place cottage, gathered resources, and entered the Crocker Home for Old Ladies in San Francisco. Suffering mental and physical depression, she lost short-term memory, though according to Theodore Parker Lukens her recollection of past events was perfectly clear. Muir visited Carr at some point between 1896 and 1898. It was their last contact and final exchange of thoughts. He described her as cheerfully "holding on to life with wonderful tenacity like a storm-beaten, fire-scarred Sequoia."[32]

Muir responded to the controversy over forest and land preservation in two articles. The first, "National Parks and Forest Reservations" appeared in *Harper's Weekly* on June 5, 1897; the second was published in the August *Atlantic Monthly*. Appealing to common concern, Muir's "The American Forests" evoked an image of America as a primeval forest garden felled by the steel axe that doomed every tree. Moving westward, the "invading horde of destroyers" did not rest until they reached the shore of the Pacific Ocean. Not a grove would remain in which to rest or pray. Muir proclaimed a gospel of beauty set in forest temples and heralded a brighter day rising up from a past cloaked in public indifference. Any fool could destroy trees. The duty of the government was to protect public forests. By contrast Gifford Pinchot saw forests as a resource to be engineered. He thought sheep grazing in the reserves did little if any harm. Muir was outraged. Two distinct approaches to wilderness emerged. Muir claimed wilderness preserves were a spiritual and physiological necessity. Pinchot, a strict utilitarian, viewed wilderness as a commodity.[33]

In August Muir embarked on his sixth trip to Alaska, accompanied by Charles S. Sargent, the Harvard botanist, and William M. Canby, a botanist from Wilmington, Delaware. They traveled via Banff, Alberta, the Selkirk Mountains, and the Canadian Rockies, studying trees and forest conditions. Muir returned in September to find Mrs. Strentzel critically ill. Within two weeks she was dead. From fall until spring Muir remained in Martinez advancing his claim that wilderness preserves were fountains of life. His second *Atlantic Monthly* article, "Wild Parks and Forest Reservations of the West," called for an awakening of public opinion to stop the plough and the pasture, the axe and the saw. From September until the end of November Muir traveled with his friends Charles S. Sargent and William Canby on a tour of southern forests from Tennessee to Florida. A side trip took Muir to New York, Montreal, Vermont, and Maine. When he, Sargent, and Canby arrived in Cedar Key, Muir inquired about the Hodgson family who had cared for him in 1867 when he was ill with malaria. Mr. Hodgson and his eldest son had died, but Mrs. Hodgson was living in Archer, Florida, where Muir visited her in her garden. She did not recognize him but remembered his name. Thirty-one years had passed; his visit had not been forgotten. On his journey home through southeastern California Muir noted how glad he was to see the trees on the Tehachapi Mountains.[34]

In June 1899 Edward H. Harriman, the railroad magnate, financed an expedition to Alaska aboard the steamship *George W. Elder* equipped with laboratories, a large social hall, and a smoking den. The party consisted of 126 passengers, among them Harriman, his wife, three daughters, and two sons; a group of Harriman's friends; a staff of artists and photographers; twenty-three scientists; John Muir; Charles Keeler, a young Berkeley poet; and the naturalist John Burroughs. Along the coast, bays, and islands plants were gathered, and climate, geology, and glaciers were charted. They reached Glacier Bay on June 8. The following day a two-hundred-foot iceberg discharged, making acres of floe. After one hundred years of slow invisible action, Muir noted, the ice was "free at last to speak out . . . and dance to its own thunder." Beyond Glacier Bay the itinerary included Sitka, Prince William Sound,

Cook Inlet, Unalaska, Plover Bay in Siberia, and St. Lawrence Island. The Harriman excursion ended in late July. Muir arrived in Portland on August 1. On the trip home his attention was drawn to the dry woods that seemed strange and open. Shasta was smoking, and there was little snow but for the glaciers.[35]

Muir suffered from recurring episodes of the grippe and bronchial cough. When he departed with Sargent and Canby in 1898 to survey southern forests, he was ill, and he recovered as he traveled. In February 1900 Muir again became ill with the flu and bronchitis. He did not recover until June. In August the restless urge to travel drove him and Dr. C. Hart Merriam, chief of the U.S. Biological Survey, to Lake Tahoe, Mono Lake, Bloody Canyon, Tuolumne Meadows, and Yosemite Valley. At some point before 1901, while Muir was recovering from bronchitis or perhaps traveling in Yosemite, Jeanne Carr left the Crocker Home, briefly stayed in Paso Robles, and then went to reside with Ezra Carr's brother, Elijah Melanthon Carr, on a ranch in Santa Paula, Ventura County, California.

Following the shooting death of President William McKinley in Buffalo, New York, Theodore Roosevelt became President of the United States in September 1901. An avid outdoorsman, he would during his presidency initiate unprecedented advances in the American conservation movement. Roosevelt shared many of the views on forest preservation put forth by Muir, most recently published in the September *Atlantic Monthly*. In "Hunting Big Redwoods" Muir expanded his earlier chronicle of the Sequoia belt. He stated that whereas nature kept the Sequoia safe, human agency was rapidly destroying the trees. He appealed to those who lived in the plain and were dependent on irrigation. They relied on the Sequoia, which sent living water to the lowlands through the hot dry summer. Sequoia were trees of life. Every grove cut caused a stream to dry. In November Muir published his second book, *Our National Parks,* composed of ten articles previously published in the *Atlantic Monthly.* On November 13 he wrote to Theodore Parker Lukens. Soon he would forward copies to both Lukens and his daughter Mrs. Helen Lukens Jones. Muir requested that Lukens retrieve the letters he had written to Carr beginning in 1865, unaware she had already given the letters to George Wharton James. In December

Muir again wrote Lukens, shocked to hear that Jeanne Carr, enduring dementia, was being badly treated. He hoped the news was exaggerated.[36]

Roosevelt emphasized the conservation of America's natural resources in his first message to Congress, delivered in early December 1901. As an advisor to the President Muir, however, cautiously gauged and interpreted Roosevelt's remarks. Gifford Pinchot, who assisted in the preparation of the section of the congressional message that advocated conservation, skewed the remarks toward a utilitarian perspective. Forest protection under the influence of Pinchot was drafted as a means to increase and sustain natural resources and the industries dependent on them. Wilderness was either product or waste. The application of the utilitarian conservation principles was tested in San Francisco's battle for water that resulted in the damming of Hetch Hetchy Valley, Yosemite's twin, twenty miles in a northwesterly direction from Yosemite and within the same national park reserve. To circumvent restrictions a measure was passed in Congress in February 1901 granting rights of way compatible with public interest through national parks for canals, pipelines, tunnels, or other water conduits. Reserved lands could be contracted. The damming of Hetch Hetchy Valley, which was every bit the scenic counterpart to Yosemite Valley, compromised the integrity of the national park. Muir would devote eleven years to stop the movement to dam Hetch Hetchy as a water reservoir for San Francisco. On December 19, 1913, the battle was lost and Hetch Hetchy was dammed. President Woodrow Wilson signed the Raker Bill, marking the loss of the "Tuolumne Yosemite."[37]

In mid-May 1903 Roosevelt prevailed upon Muir to accompany him on a tour of Yosemite Valley. They traveled alone and spent three days and nights camping in Mariposa Grove. After Muir returned to Martinez, he set off with Charles S. Sargent and his son Robeson on a world tour. He was gone one year. When Jeanne Carr died in Templeton on December 14, Muir was en route from Ceylon to Treemantle, Australia. The letter to Muir from Carr's brother-in-law Elijah Melanthon Carr noted, "Her last days were peaceful, she gradually sank to her rest and did not seem to suffer much pain." It is highly unlikely that Muir knew Carr had died until he was closer to home in May 1904. Carr's death was in Templeton, but according to Charles F. Saunders, who chronicled the history of Carmelita, her heart never left Carmelita. James Hope, an artist and close friend from Castleton, Vermont, once told Carr she was made of the same things as plants. It was true. Carr felt possessed at times with the memory of the life of plants and the life she once lived with them in the wilderness.[38]

∾

1419 Taylor St., San Francisco,
January 12, [*1876*]

Dear Mrs. Carr

John Swett told me how heavy a burden you were carrying of
work and sickness. I hope ere this that the Doctor has recovered from
his severe attack of rheumatism and that you have had sleep and rest.

Your description of the orange lands makes me more than ever
eager to see them,—in particular the phenomenon of a real lover of
Nature such as you mention, for one does feel so wholly alone in the
midst of this metallic, money-clinking crowd. And so you are going to
dwell down there, and how rosily you will write about it! Well, I hope
you may realize it all. Independence in quiet life must be delightful
indeed, after the battles and the burdens of these heavy years. In any
case it is a fine thing for old people who have worked and fought
through all kinds of strenuous experiences to have thoughts and
schemes so fresh and young as yours. We all hope to see you soon.

Cordially yours,
John Muir[39]

∾

1419 Taylor Street, San Francisco,
April 3, 1876

Dear Mrs. Carr

We will all be glad to see you. We all heard of the outrage committed on Johnnie and hope it might not be so serious as made to appear in the press. Mr. Swett told me the other day that he met a friend
down town who was acquainted with the Whites intimately, who gave
it as his opinion that Mr. White was insane, had a brother in the asylum,
and he was as jealous of a half-dozen other persons as of Johnnie.

If I knew Ned's boarding-house, I would visit him, for I know he
must feel terribly agitated. The last time I saw him, he was rejoicing
over Johnnie's steady manly development, like an old fond father over
some reformed son.

As for the stranded sapless condition of political geology, I care only for the fruitless work expended upon it by friends. The glaciers are not affected thereby, neither am I nor *Cassiope*.

The first meeting I had with Mr. Moore was at the lecture the other night. He seemed immeasurably astonished to find me in so anti-sequestered a condition, but in the meanwhile he is more changed than I, for he seems semi-crazy on literature, as Mrs. M[*oore*] is wholly, doubly so on paint.

I will show your letters to Mr. Swett when he comes in, who will doubtless be able to decipher the meaning of heads and tails of your bodyless sentences.

I'm sorry most of all for the destruction of the "Teachers," thus cutting off the only adequate outlet for your own thought; but hang it! let them decapitate and hang, they cannot hang *Cassiope*.

Ever yours cordially,
John Muir[40]

∾

Swett Home,
July 23, [*1877*]

Dear Mrs. Carr

I made only a short dash into the dear old Highlands above Yosemite, but all was so full of everything I love, every day seemed a measureless period. I never enjoyed the Tuolumne cataracts so much. Coming out of the sun land, the gray salt deserts of Utah, these wild ice waters sang themselves into my soul more enthusiastically than ever, and the forests' breath was sweeter, and *Cassiope* fairer than in all my first fresh contacts.

But I'm not going to tell here. I only write now to say that next Saturday I will sail to Los Angeles and spend a few weeks in getting some general views of the adjacent region, then work northward and begin a careful study of the redwoods. I will at least have time this season for the lower portion of the belt; that is, for all south of here. If you have any messages, you have time to write me. I sail at 10 A.M., or if not you may direct to Los Angeles.

I hope to see Congar, and also the spot you have selected for home. I wish you could be there in your grown fruitful groves, all rooted and grounded in the fine garden nook that I know you will make. It must be a great consolation in the midst of the fires you are compassed with to look forward to a tranquil seclusion in the South of which you are so fond.

John [*Swett*] says he may not move to Berkeley, and if not I may be here this winter, though I still feel some tendency towards another winter in some mountain ice.

It is long indeed since I had anything like a quiet talk with you. You have been going like an avalanche for many a year, and I sometimes fear you will not be able to settle into rest even in the orange groves.

I'm glad to know that the Doctor is so well. You must be pained by the shameful attacks made upon your tried friend La Grange. Farewell. Ever cordially yours,

John Muir[41]

∽

Los Angeles, Cal., August 12, 1877
Pico House

Dear Mrs. Carr

I've seen your sunny Pasadena and the patch called yours. Everything about here pleases me, and I felt sorely tempted to take Dr. Congar's advice and invest in an orange-patch myself. I feel sure you will be happy here with the Doctor and Allie among so rich a luxuriance of sunny vegetation. How you will dig and dibble in that mellow loam! I cannot think of you standing erect for a single moment, unless it be in looking away out into the dreamy west. I made a fine shaggy little five days' excursion back in the heart of the San Gabriel Mountains, and then a week of real pleasure with Congar, resurrecting the past about Madison. He has a fine little farm, fine little family, and fine cosy home.

I felt at home with Congar and at once took possession of his premises and all that in them is. We drove down through the settlements eastward and saw the best orange groves and vineyards, but the mountains I as usual met alone. Although so gray and silent and unpromising they are full of wild gardens and ferneries, and lilyries,—

some specimens ten feet high with twenty lilies big enough for bonnets. The main results I will tell you some other time, should you ever have an hour's leisure. I go north today, by rail to Newhall, thence by stage to Soledad, and on to Monterey, where I will take to the woods and feel my way in free study to San Francisco. May reach the city about the middle of next month.

Heard through your factor here that Miss Powell is worse and that you would not be down soon. I *received* your letter and postal, also the letters you thought I had lost, via one from Salt Lake for which I sent and one from Yosemite which Black forwarded.

With love to all I am ever

Yours cordially,
J. M.
[*John Muir*]⁴²

∾

1419 Taylor St., San Francisco,
September 3, [*1877*]

Dear Mrs. Carr

I have just been over at Alameda with poor dear old [*W. P.*] Gibbons [, *M.D.*]. You have seen him, and I need give no particulars. "The only thing I'm afraid of, John," he said, looking up with his old child face, "is that I shall never be able to climb the Oakland hills again." But he is so healthy and so well cared for we will be strong and hope that he will.

He spoke for an hour with characteristic unselfishness on the injustice done Dr. Kellogg in failing to recognize his long-continued devotion to science, at the botanical love-feast held here the other night. He threatens to write up the whole discreditable affair, and is very anxious to obtain from you a copy of that Gray letter to Kellogg which was not delivered.

I had a glorious ramble in the Santa Cruz woods and have found out one very interesting and picturesque fact concerning the growth of this Sequoia. I mean to devote many a long week to its study. What the upshot may be, I cannot guess, but you know I am never sent away empty. I made an excursion to the summit of Mt. Hamilton in extraordinary style, accompanied by Allen, Norton, Brawley, and all the lady professors and their friends. A curious contrast to my ordinary *still-hunting*. Spent a week at San Jose; enjoyed my visit with Allen very much. Lectured to the faculty on Methods of Study without undergoing any very great scare.

I believe I wrote you from Los Angeles about my Pasadena week. Have sent a couple of letters to the *Bulletin* from there, not yet published.

I have no inflexible plans as yet for the remaining months of the season, but Yosemite seems to place itself as a most persistent candidate for my winter. I shall soon be in flight to the Sierras or Oregon.

I seem to give up hope of ever seeing you calm again. Don't grind too hard at these Sacramento mills. Remember me to the Doctor and Allie.

Ever yours cordially,
John Muir[43]

∾

1419 Taylor Street, [San Francisco],
June 5, 1878

Dear Mrs. Carr

I'm sorry I did not see you when last in the city. I went over to Oakland, thence to Alameda to spend a week and finish an "article" with our good old Gibbons; but the house was full; then I went to Dr. Strentzel's, where I remained a week, working a little, resting a good deal and eating many fine cherries. I enjoyed most the *white* bed in which first I rested after rocking so long in the rushes of the Stockton slough. They all were as kind as ever they could possibly be, and wanted me to stop longer, but I could not find a conscientious excuse for so doing and came away somewhat sore with obligations for stopping so long. Met Mr. and Mrs. Allen there.

Swett has gone this morning to Shasta, taking Helen, and I'm terribly lonesome and homesick and will not try to stand it. Will go to the woods tomorrow. How great are your trials! I wish I could help you. May the Doctor be speedily restored to health.

Cordially yours,
John Muir[44]

∾

920 Valencia St., San Francisco,
February 18, 1879

Dear Mrs. Carr

Yesterday I sent you by mail five dollars worth of tree seeds, according to directions. They seemed fresh, and I was assured they were so. Hope they may grow as well as they can for you, and at least hint the beauty of their homes and their fathers.

I have been strongly tempted to make another visit to Southern California, but have concluded the season is too far gone.

Your letter lay at John Swett's some time, so the seeds may not reach you in time, though I suppose Allie will attend to the planting. I am glad to think of Allie as a tiller of the soil. Good luck to the boy.

I am now quartered with Mr. Upham, Payot's partner, and am well off, though the writing mood has not yet appeared. Remember me to the Congars and Allie. May you find your farm always a heaven, taking nothing of politics into it when you leave Sacramento.

I saw Mr. Moore last Sunday. His is a sad case. No heaven for him this side the mysterious one built on faith.

Cordially yours,
John Muir[45]

∾

920 Valencia St., [*San Francisco*]
April 9, 1879

Dear Mrs. Carr

I did not send the pine book to you, because I was using it in rewriting a portion of the California forest article, which will appear in *Scribner's,* May or June, and because, before it could have reached you, you were, according to your letter, to be in San Francisco and could then take it with you. It is entitled *Gordon's Pinetum,* published by Henry G. Bohn, Henrietta St., Covent Garden; Simpkin, Marshall & Co., Stationers, Hall Court; 1875; second edition. It is an "exhaustive" work, very exhausting anyhow, and contains a fine big much of little.

The summit pine of our Sierra is *P. albicaulus* of Engelmann, and the *P. flexilis* Torrey, given in this work as a synonym, is a very different tree, growing sparsely on the eastern flank of the Sierra, from Bloody Canyon southward, but very abundant on all the higher basin ranges, and on the Wahsatch and Rocky Mountains.

The orange book is, it seems, another exhaustive work. There is something admirable in the scientific nerve and aplomb manifested in the titles of these swollen volumes. How a tree book can be exhaustive when every species is ever on the wing from one form to another with infinite variety, it is not easy to see.

I have n't the least idea who Mr. Rexford is, but, if connected with the *Bulletin,* I can probably get the title of his citrus book through Mr. Williams. Will probably see him next Sunday.

The Sunday convention manager offered me a hundred dollars for two lectures on the Yosemite rocks in June. I have not yet agreed to do so, though I probably shall, as I am not going into Colorado this summer.

Excepting a day at San Jose with Allen, I have hardly been out of my room for weeks, pegging away with my quill and accomplishing little. My last efforts were on the preservation of the Sierra forests, and the wild and trampled conditions of our flora from a bee's point of view.

I want to spend the greater portion of the season up the Coast, observing ice, and may possibly find my way home in the fall to see my mother.

I wonder if you will really go quietly away South when your office term expires, and rest in the afternoon of your life among your kin and orange leaves, or, unable to get full absolution from official woman's rights' unrest, you will fight and squirm till sundown. I've seen nothing of you all these fighting years.

I suppose nothing less than an *Exhaustive* miniature of all the leafy creatures of the globe will satisfy your Pasadena aspirations. You know how little real sympathy I can give in such play-garden schemes. Still, if so inappreciative and unavailable a man as I may be of use at all, let me know.

Ever cordially yours,
John Muir[46]

∾

920 Valencia St., San Francisco,
April 24, [*1879*]

Dear Mrs. Carr

I enclose at last the name of the big orange book. Either Payot &
Co. or Gregoire & Co. will import it for Mr. Cra[?] at the price he
named, for less if intended for the library.

I thought you would have been to make at least one of your small
businesslike calls to see me ere this, but I suppose the office and
conventions and your farm leave you precious little time. Your days
all go by in little beats and bits, while you move so fast you are nearly
invisible.

Had a moment's talk with the Doctor [*Gibbons*]. Am glad he is
looking so much like himself again. The summer is coming. Don't
know how it will be spent.

Did you hear the Butlers lecture the other day? Glassy leaves tilted
at all angles.

Cordially yours,
John Muir[47]

∾

San Francisco, June 19, 1879

Dear Mrs. Carr

Good-bye. I am going home, going to my summer in the snow and
ice and forests of the north coast. Will sail tomorrow at noon on the
Dakota for Victoria and Olympia. Will then push inland and along
land. May visit Alaska.

I hope you and the Doctor may not suffer yourselves to be drawn
away into the stream of politics again. You will be far happier on your
land.

I was at the Valley. How beautiful it was! fresh and full of cool
crystal streams and blooms. Was not scared in my lectures after the
first one.

With kind regards to the Doctor and the boys. Farewell.
John Muir[48]

∾

Pasadena, Friday evening,

[*May, 1880*]

Dear Mrs. Strentzel

I ought not to write you on a Friday, or in a Fridayish mood; but tomorrow is one of our mail days, and I cannot allow it to pass without carrying to you all, and especially to John Muir, the congratulations of Dr. Congar's family, and his many friends in this region, as well as our own.

We read the news in Wednesday's *Record Union*—just a week after the wedding; as I read it aloud to the family some one reminded us of a friend whose husband was a sea-faring man; when the news of his death reached her nearly three years after the event, she said she had been a widow so long it was not proper to wear mourning. So having lost the pleasures of anticipation in Louie's case, we seem to think of John and herself as having always been mated and the event as long past. I have been accustomed to think of John as one specially beloved and cared for by the higher powers; now I know that he is, since he may call you mother. He will never know how sweet a privilege that is while you remain with us; but when the "well done" shall be spoken to you he will feel it the one great blessedness that has come after many lonely years. A man quickly comes to think of his wife as another self, and this is many men's excuse for negligence and inattention; but men hold the mother thought, the mother relation in great reverence. I am grateful to you all that you have enclosed with your love one so precious to me. It seems a suitable mating and rarely do two spirits so finely tuned strike the perfect chord.

I shall be interested in every particular which any of you may care to repeat to me. I felt like writing Dr. Strentzel that he should have telegraphed the advent of a son in the family and that mother was doing as well as could be expected.

I hope you will be on your feet this summer, and make your bairn drive you about a great deal. Let the young people take the laboring over, and you and the dear doctor rest and travel.

We have had almost continual cold weather, and an excess of rain. But the succession of fruit-flowers has made it delightful, nevertheless.

Tell Muir that *Calypso borealis* is looking exquisitely and the *Linneae* growing under an Oregon cedar in the grounds. My wee beech tree is full of tender leaves, maple and scarlet oak showing their colors. I have more than a hundred species of eastern fruit trees, most of them quite small but growing well.

Tell Louie that if I could bring her here to be bridally kissed and congratulated there should be no lack of favor in the performance. I commission John to do it for me; he does not need to be told that I rejoice in his happiness. Above fame, and far stronger than my wish to see his genius acknowledged by his peers, I have desired for him the completeness which can only come in living for others, in perfected home relations.

My sons have been out for twenty-four hours after some grizzly bears; I can look up the mountain side scarcely more than three miles in an air line, where the canyons are so nearly inaccessible that the bears have half a county to themselves. They have visited the bee ranches nightly for two or three weeks, and yesterday a regular hunt was organized.

The deer come down every few days, but no one shoots them. Our trees are full of birds. Dr. Carr is heartier and stronger than he was in Sacramento, but a good deal depressed at times from the great change—he misses the spur of daily duty.

I am too busy to get the blues, and, perhaps, lack sympathy with natures less hopeful. It is easy to rejoice with those that rejoice, and this I do most heartily tonight with the house of Muir-Strentzel. Love to John, Senior, its honored head.

Your affectionate
Jeanne C. Carr[49]

∞

Pasadena, June 3, 1880

My dear John and Louie

I should hardly have waited a formal announcement of your wedded happiness before sending my blessing directly to you, under other circumstances; but never has my life been so involved and so little under my own control.

I think of your charming home as complete now, of the dear
mother content to lie still and get well with so excellent a story-teller
always at command, of a certain comforting sense in the father's mind
that somebody will care for his beloved trees when his time for rest
arrives; more than all I hope and believe that this marriage was made
in heaven, foreordained from the beginning. I could not have been
more pleased if I had mixed the cup myself.

Dear John—Mrs. Moore is with us. She came very much broken,
is better and paints diligently many hours every day. You remember
the ranch, well, she says she has never liked any place as much save
that home in the Redwoods.

I have also two boarding pupils, all in the barn. The place is in fine
order, thanks to Ned, who turns out to be an excellent farmer. Allie is
not able to do much hard work, and Dr. Carr is too lame to use
"shovel or hoe." We shall have a fine crop of grapes, and our wee
oranges are full freighted, also cherries, currants and other things
which we were assured would not live and bear fruit. Come and see
us when you can. I suppose the true bridal trip will be to the Yosemite,
of course at the summit of the season.

If you go, please take Louie to Mrs. Black, and give her my love,
and this message, "This is the *only* woman that I ever knew, who
seemed a mate for John."

Dr. Carr and Ned send love and congratulations, and Mrs. Moore
intends to write hers.

Most affectionately yours,
Jeanne C. Carr

Linnaea borealis in bloom, under my Oregon cedar.[50]

ॐ

Martinez, October 22, 1887

Dear Mrs. Carr

I told Mr. Dewing that I thought you could write Southern
California better than anybody else that I knew, and that he better let
you try your hand on an article or two. As to compensation I know
very little about it. Go ahead and write an article and send in your bill
is my advice. I may say, however, that not more than magazine rates

will be paid as far as I can make out. Little has been written as yet. I have finished some four numbers now mostly in print with fine illustrations by the best artists: Hill, Keith, Moran, Rix, etc., on the passes, forests, Yosemite, etc. Have to write Alaska, Sierra Lakes, Shasta, San Rafael Redwoods, etc., (*and run the ranch*) and edit the whole compound business. The first three numbers are about to be published. Monterey was written by a Mr. Fiske. Bartlett has written Oakland and probably will write Santa Cruz and Clear Lake. I think you can have San Diego and Santa Barbara; at least I have not heard of anyone in these fields as yet.

Picturesque America is about the style and kind of stuff required. Nothing that savors in the least of advertising booming, etc. can be allowed, but latitude wide as you please in picturesque description and choice of objects. Should have abundance of flowery brush, birds, bears, priests of the olden time, adobes gray, old oaks. Old Spanish life but still more fully should the life, Yankee life, of today, in its picturesque aspects be portrayed. Olive orchards, orange, nut trees, vineyards, groups of gatherers of the sunny harvests, views of the main towns, etc., etc., etc. I guess you know what I mean. No scent, flavor, savor of commercial advertisement or any sort of favoritism as to places written or pictured. What a bright appreciative traveler would like to see and hear is what is wanted as near as I can make out.

Write an article anyhow of say from 4000 to 5000 words and send in your bill and see what you can get; then you will know what to do afterward. The money part of the affair I have nothing whatever to do with and do not know what anybody has received for work already done.

With cordial regards to the Doctor and all of you, I am,

Ever yours truly,
John Muir

In choosing subjects for photographs be careful to avoid commonplace prettiness in walks, gardens, cottages, conservatories, etc. such as may be seen in almost any country. Let them be telling of the locality and strictly special, as well as picturesque. Now then, I guess you've got about enough—getting even on you for early lectures, Hamlet's advice to the players, etc.[51]

∾

Martinez, January 12, 1888

Dear Mrs. Carr

I can appreciate your difficulty in getting under way with that article—so many diverse winds of doctrine. I saw from your first manuscript that you had difficulty in getting launched. You were evidently trying to do too much. No matter about the jogs and lifts of the Cordilleras and the resulting influence on human whims and purses, etc. Just pitch in and paint your pictures—whatever you see that interests you, and the changes if any that may be desired may easily be made. If you look for and listen for more instructions you will write nothing freely. Just pitch in and finish in whatever way now seems best in the light you have, remembering always that it is Picturesque California you are sketching and not philosophy of oranges and town lots south of the new Mason and Dixon Line. Look at the landscapes as the sun looks at them.

Fine preaching, isn't it? Your article will be first-rate, I have no doubt, though the introduction will have to be cut off mostly. It reads too much like the preface of some Professor's big book. Strike right out into the midst of your pictures and let the boundaries take care of themselves. Remember me to the doctor.

Ever yours cordially,

J. Muir

[*John Muir*]

Have not yet seen your last manuscript.[52]

∾

Martinez, January 30, 1888

Dear Mrs. Carr

My knowledge of Southern California is not sufficiently close to enable me to follow you well in your descriptions and the manuscript is so mixed and disjointed that I cannot in some places find out where or in what direction you are driving. The pages not being numbered is I suppose the chief cause of the apparent confusion.

I think that you had better put the article together yourself writing freely without sense of haste—taking all the time you require to make the work satisfactory to yourself. This you will now be able to do since the company have or will indicate—definitely what to omit and what to include and the relative importance of the sections, etc., etc.

I first thought after confuring [*sic*] with the publishers that I could put the material in shape and thus save you further trouble. But my ignorance I find is too thick for the purpose and too comprehensive.

In talking over the country yesterday with Messrs. Dewing and Oge it seemed best that you should not attempt to cover so much territory with so thin a layer of words but rather that you should give a good solid instructive, lively and shining picture of Pasadena, the Blest and the Old Mexican and Young American Angels with all their flowers, gravel beds and groves, etc., etc., and padres. Mr. Oge, however, promised to write you particulars and I need say nothing more than good luck and don't forget the arithmetical signs for the top of pages.

Weather funereal and fungoid. With best wishes to yourself and the Doctor and Al and Ned, I am ever truly

J. M.

[*John Muir*][53]

∾

Martinez, February 17, 1889

Dear Mrs. Carr

I will do the best I can about the return of the photographs, but fear some of them may be lost. I have been trying to get back many of my pencil sketches without success so far.

That was a grand booming train of "Carrs" you had lately. I didn't know there were so many brothers. The Doctor must have enjoyed their visit very much and lived the early morning days over again.

Wanda has just recovered from scarlet fever and I have had anxious weeks of nursing. Little Helen was taken to Grandpa's by her mother and has escaped the contagion so far. I am now in the old house alone waiting for weather and sulphur to sweeten things when the family may venture back. Had a good time on Rainier.

Cordially yours,

John Muir[54]

∿

July 16, [1889]

Dear John

Around the evening lamp I was skimming the London Times of
June 28, reading aloud to the family; came across this,

"Dr. Nansen's journey across the Greenland ice."

"At the Royal Geog. Society on Monday night, Dr. Fridtoff
Nansen, the Greenland explorer, gave a description of his journey
across the inland ice of Greenland from east to west."

(Many Lords of high title, Sir Samuel Baker, and others present.)
"Dr. Nansen was received with warm cheers. A great many fine
colored sketches of Greenland scenes, and the sledge upon which he
made the journey was shown, with a fine map of the country."

Dr. Nansen remarked that since the discovery of Greenland 900
years ago its interior had remained a mystery, and successively
sketched the explorations after 1869, when Edward Whymper and
Dr. Robert Brown tried it from the shores of Disco Bay, and failed.
Then came the more fortunate Nordenskiold (1870), Jensen and
others (1878), Nordenskiold again in 1883; etc.

All these explorations were made from the west coast; Dr.
Nansen's plan was to start from the east coast and work through to
the west, where the Danish Esquimaux settlements would afford relief
after the exhausting journey.

A generous Dane, Mr. Augustin Gamel, provided the means.
Norwegian seaman and Lapp servants completed the expedition. They
sailed for Iceland which they reached in June 1888, changed to a Norwegian sealing ship July 17th, leaving this in their boats, after 12 days'
coasting reached the land at Anoritok (61 degrees 30 minutes N. L.)
on the 29 July.

Then forced their way northwards along the coast until August 15,
when they disembarked and commenced their inland journey, intending to reach the settlement on Disco Bay. For twelve days found hard
travelling, pulling their sledges; they altered their course to a more
westerly direction, making for the settlement of Godthaab. September 1
found them 9000 feet above the sea level, on an extensive ice plateau,
like a frozen sea. Cold severe, thermometer falling below the scale
nights. September 19, a favorable wind sprang up, when the travellers

lashed their sledges together, hoisted sails, and holding on to the sledges standing in their Norwegian "skis" or snowshoes, rattled down the western slope until they reached the zone of iceless land on the west coast, on the 26 reaching the fjord called Ameralik. There they made a boat of their canvas tent, in which two of the party reached the Danish settlement Godthaab, arriving on October 3, and immediately sending a relief party in boats, for those left behind.…

The expedition Dr. N[ansen] believes has proved the whole interior of Greenland to be covered by an immense shield-shaped cap of ice and snow which in places must be 5000–6000 feet in thickness. A great point of interest was the comparatively low temperature of the interior. Dr. N[ansen] thought the best way of solving the problems of the great ice age was to examine the places where similar conditions now exist as the expedition had done in Greenland, which had many characteristics of Scotland and Scandinavia.

Love to all in Strentzel-Muir families, and to the Swett family— congratulate J. S. for us.

J. C. C.

[Jeanne C. Carr][55]

 co

The California Illustrated Magazine
The California Publishing Company
San Francisco,
December 5, 1891

Dearest of Friends

Can you not write for us a biographical sketch of John Muir such as you outlined when I was visiting you; one taken from his letters largely! I would like to publish it before the Century publishes the one by my father if possible.

I have written to the Cosmopolitan and they promise an early appearance of your article, but that may mean some months yet. If we could afford the fifty dollars I would withdraw it from there and publish it in ours: but we cannot just yet. We can pay you about twenty-five dollars for the Muir article. Will you do it?

I am so grieved to learn that you have been ill, but trust that you are better again. Did you ever mail me the Doctor's book? I never received it: but as you wrote saying it would be sent by the same mail, I felt afraid of its possible miscarriage. I will have a copy of the Holiday magazine to send you in a few days.

Have the winter excursionists begun to pour in yet?

Take good care of yourself and God bless you.

> Lovingly your friend
> Emelie T. Y. Parkhurst
> Mrs. E. T. Y. Parkhurst
> Assistant Editor[56]

&

Martinez, November 5, 1894

My dear Mrs. Carr

I take pleasure in sending you with this a copy of my first book. You will say that I should have written it long ago, but I begrudged the time of my young mountain-climbing days.

We received your note and newspaper clippings and the Muir peak. I left Mrs. Muir to answer it, but suppose she has not.

I am at work on another book. And in many ways am very busy.

We are all well. Wanda is a woman and considerably taller than her mother. Helen is very smart and may write some day. I told a Mr. Drake of the *Century Magazine* to call on you a week ago. He is to be in Pasadena two months.

With kindest regards to the Doctor and the boys, I am,

> Cordially yours,
> John Muir[57]

&

[*November/December, 1894?*]

[*John Muir*]

[Fragment of letter]

... for I had a pleasure early in this month worthy to have been shared with you. I put out my hand for you once or twice when a

magnificenter view than the rest of the Upper Himalayas was unfolded. Trees, trees, trees, our pines over again, straight columns,
infinite in numbers, and the great imperial photographs give the
appearance of *immensity* in heights and distances. *It must be so.* God
has done His best with men and mountains in Asia.

A Mr. Smith who has travelled everywhere, offered my friends the
use of his *Albums* for a few days. One great Imperial Album has
hundreds of beautifully colored photographs of the people of Japan,
Soochow, and India—in all their various avocations; another of
scenery in Japan. The other two immense folios were the largest-sized
photos of Himalayan scenery and Indian buildings and cities. John,
the *vale of Cashmere* has not yet been seen or sung. The "Taj Mahal,"
the tomb of a beautiful beloved woman, caused me to put my hand
upon my mouth. Inspired marble? Yes, light, fleecy as clouds upon
Tessiak, spiritual as water in its most spiritual mood, *"frozen music,"*
perhaps, but melting into a smile of love. Dear dervish, let's go and
see 'em our two selves!

The old year wanes—I give you its last breath, the saddest of years
to me. I shall love it for the sacred sorrow it has brought. Thank God
for it—for its pure associations and aspirations. For you, beloved
friend, I am always grateful, and my heart always builds precious
hopes upon you.

Jeanne Carr[58]

ॐ

[*Pasadena, California*],
December 18, 1894

Dear John

The mother said in her letter that you had not heard of Flora
Congar's death until through me; and as I am driving myself into
every kind of occupation which diverts my attention from the great
emptiness of our home, I will give you the singular experience it
brought to memory and under my observation.

You may or may not remember that Congar was a trained and
really excellent practitioner of medicine; in the early months of our
residence here, he was called to the sick bed of a lovely little girl, the

prize pupil in our public school. As he did not return, Mrs. Congar
sent over to my cottage and requested me to stay with her, as she
feared he would be gone all night. I complied, and she, not feeling
well, retired, leaving me enjoying a book by the fire.

After midnight, I heard his step and presently he came into the
sitting room and dropped into a rocking chair as if utterly exhausted.

I stepped to the kitchen and brought him a cup of tea or coffee
from the still warm stove, which he took very gratefully; and soon
after broke out in a suppressed tone—"My God! my eyes, *these very
eyes* Mrs. Carr, have seen the curtains lifted; I have watched the most
beautiful thing my eyes will ever see, *the whole process of
reimbodiment.* I want to tell you *now,* before I forget one feature of
it." And so he did very impressively, but without waking Mrs.
Congar; and whatever the hard, cold facts might be, I always believed
in the honesty and sincerity of the narrator. When he had finished he
said, "If it is possible, and I die first, I will try to make you understand
how *natural* it is, no *super* about it!!"

I went at his request to his death bed; and he assured me that he
had just seen the spirit of a little daughter buried at Salt Lake; and
that his mother came and went all through the previous night. He was
as clear in mind as I ever saw him. And, now, of Flora, whose death
occurred more than a year ago, let me tell you, with a bit of preface.

There was a festival gotten up for a benefit to the Unitarian-
Universalist Church to which all liberal souls were invited; with a
dancing floor for the young under an enormous oak tree gay with
lanterns; a favorite band hidden on the Bank of the Arroyo Seco
discoursing and other attractions. I took with me Ruth Finner, a little
woman who as Ruth Burnett was in the University of Wisconsin in
your day; and a lovely lady with (well concealed) mediumistic powers.
I, with no more intention or expectation of any occult proceedings
than I have at this moment. It was a very gay and festive scene; the
band playing and dancing in full swing when Ruth came to me with a
strange look on her face and said, "I have just seen Dr. Congar under
those trees; never saw him more distinctly in my life." She knew him
well in Wisconsin and here. Not long after Mrs. Hoff reported a
similar experience. This was long after his decease. The morning
brought the whole story of the accident which occurred on the

Carmelita property through which the party drove on their ride homeward.

Flora was the only one seriously injured, and her dislocated ankle was set in plastered dressings within half an hour. She was in splendid health when the accident occurred, and on the eve of a very promising entrance into happy marriage with the only child of J. F. Crank, a wealthy and prominent citizen. But it seemed that no skill could save her; Mrs. Congar has apparently lost interest in life, for Flora was her idol. The house is rented as a boarding house; Mrs. Congar and LuLu live in rooms on the east side and take their meals outside. Howard stays at the mine and has no fondness for work or study, but has only the bad habit of continued cigarette smoking.

Out of my own experience I cannot understand how one can so completely lose interest in the life that now is or the infinite vanity of performers. I have not lost my affection for one that life has brought to my shanty of a soul, when it grows into a temple each will have his statue and inscription.

I enjoy the book more and more, taking it in sips and dips. You ought to bring Louie and the girls, and we will take you to Echo Mountain and make a Lion of you for the growing menagerie.

G. Wharton James inquired if I had ever met Mr. Muir; would like to make his acquaintance. "So would I; G. Wharton, it should be made every seven years." Measured thus we shall soon need to be introduced.

Jeanne Carr

Embrace each for me, beginning with grandma.[59]

∾

Martinez, January 7, 1895

My dear Mrs. Carr

We are all glad that you so wisely work and bear up under your bereavement. All this passing from life to life, however gloriously hopeful is ever sad, and they are truly blest who have the strength and faith to work on and enjoy on without halting or hasting like a star, as Goethe says or like a glacier, as I say.

All those cases of spirit-sight seem strange and most of us have to go without it as best we can.

[*John Muir*][60]

∾

Pasadena, Sunday, [*1895?*]

Dear John

I have felt like writing you a long old time letter, in remembrance of August days in 1873, but it is impossible to reach personal enjoyments in the midst of so pressing family cares. But two photos last night received from Lillian Scidmore, a Madison girl who now hails from Washington City and who has been travelling in Alaskan waters this summer—photos of the *Muir* glacier—impel me to ask you to do yourself and her the pleasure of calling upon her at the Occident Hotel, San Francisco. She will be in Frisco all through the Conclave. She is bright, responsive, and an excellent raconteur.

You know that both for your sake and the darlings of your heart, I rejoice in all that gives you honor and happiness, and am always,

Yours faithfully,

Jeanne Carr[61]

∾

Martinez, November 12, 1895

My dear Mrs. Carr

Your kind note just received. I hope to get to Pasadena some time after the rush of grape troubles are over for the season and of course will see you all with great pleasure. But you will probably be in San Francisco before my southern flight is made and we will look for a visit from you. We are all pretty well. Mrs. Strentzel the invalid is much better than she was a few months ago and will be very glad to see you. It was on my last summer's ramble in the Sierra that I fell in with Mr. Lukens and he was very kind to me when I was hungry and weary. With kind regards to the boys, I am,

Ever yours,

John Muir[62]

∾

Pasadena, Cal., June 12, 1897

Dear Mr. Muir

I am sorry to hear you are not well, and hope you will soon recover. I have been very poorly and at times am very much discouraged about my health. I wish I could live near Crockers—then I believe I would get well.

Your article in *Harper's*, like everything you have written, is grand and will do more good than all other efforts put together. While on my last trip this summer I found timber in the San Gabriel Reservation that far excel any I had found before in these mountains. I had used up most of my plates before reaching the fine timber, so I have only a few views, but will return if I am well enough and can then send you some photos of conifers that will astonish you. It was the last of May [*when*] I was there and [*we*] were compelled to return the way we went on account of deep snow, where there would have been no snow if there had not been such dense timber to shield it from the sunshine. We found snow at 6000 feet and at 8000 feet the ground was still one-third covered.

I thought I had written to you about Mrs. Carr, but from your letter I must have neglected to do so. Mrs. Carr is at the Crocker home for old ladies in San Francisco, where she was taken about three months ago. A guardian was appointed by the Court for her, as her mind is nearly gone. She could not dress herself, and would get lost on her own place. Her memory of long past events is perfectly clear. She can talk for hours of past events, but things of today or last hours she knows nothing of the next time you meet her. We all feel very badly [*because*] of her condition. I hope when you are in San Francisco you will call on her.

I will watch for your other articles, I assure you. With kindest regards from us all to you and family, I am,

Respectfully,

T. P. Lukens

[*Theodore Parker Lukens*]

Little Lottie says, "I have only got two men I love—Mr. Muir and Grandpa."[63]

∾

Martinez, November 13, 1901

My dear Lukens

I heartily thank you for the generous lot of fine photographs, they are beautiful and also interesting as tree and forest studies. I have not yet heard a word about Mrs. Carr since she went to live with Dr. Carr's brother near Santa Paula. Please let me know how she is. The letters and papers I want are those I wrote her during a long correspondence begun about 1865 after leaving the State University of Wisconsin. She repeatedly promised to collect and send them to me, but I suppose on account of failing memory this had not been done. Many thanks for your offer to secure them.

My new book is just out, I'll send copies to you and Mrs. [Helen Lukens] Jones as soon as they arrive. I'm at work on another but hope to see you before it is finished. With love to all your family.

I am cordially yours,
John Muir

Your forest work is admirable and must soon gain wider and better recognition.[64]

∾

Martinez, December 18, 1901

Dear Mr. Lukens

I was shocked by the news in your last letter as to the treatment of poor Mrs. Carr by her keeper. I thought of going at once to see her legal guardian, but since I knew no one in Templeton I felt I could not be useful in finding a proper keeper. Surely the guardian can have no difficulty in doing this duty.

I hope the news is not true or at least it will prove greatly exaggerated. Anyhow she must be faithfully cared for and supplied with every comfort she requires. Let me know as soon as possible the facts of the case and what is needed that I can supply and greatly oblige

Your friend
John Muir[65]

ↄ

Templeton, December 18, 1903

John Muir, Esq.

Martinez

Dear Sir

Sister Jeanne C. Carr passed away December 14th and my wife has gone to Oakland with her remains to bury them in the family lot in the Oakland Cemetery. Her last days were peaceful, she gradually sank to her rest and did not seem to suffer much pain. She was 78 years old last May.

Yours very truly

E. M. Carr

[*Elijah Melanthon Carr*][66]

Epilogue

Whereas history takes facts and bends them to fit a particular model of interpretation, letters, though difficult to interpret without facts, express common truth. The letters of John Muir and Jeanne C. Carr refresh our interpretation of history, covering old ground with new insights and providing the foundation for new vantage points. Letters have an honesty that cannot be hidden. To a close friend we bare our soul. In and through the details of life that characteristically make us who we are and in and through the secrets we divulge only to those closest to us, we share our story, and in the telling and the hearing of our story we find ourselves on common ground—we no longer feel alone.

The letters of John Muir and Jeanne C. Carr break the barrier of loneliness—each reaching out to the other beyond family ties to draw upon the fellowship rooted in their faith and in their love of nature. Through their letters we are drawn into the friendship they shared and are richer for the experience.

The writings of John Muir call us home to mountain temples and sugar pines, to water ouzels and larks, to *Calypso borealis* and *Cassiope*. His books and articles provide opportunities for us to be forever changed, forever refreshed. To Jeanne C. Carr we owe a debt of gratitude for what she saw in Muir that resulted in his articulate and insightful descriptions of nature and wilderness.

There are not many people or books or things that transform us. For me Muir's thousand-mile journey from Kentucky to Florida was transforming experience. Muir's ideas and observations resonated against my own thoughts and beliefs, and his convictions strengthened my own resolve. For those who are Muir devotees and for Muir scholars, may *Kindred and Related Spirits: The Letters of John Muir and Jeanne C. Carr* add something to your knowledge of John Muir and Jeanne Carr. To those for whom these letters are an introduction, a bibliography of selected readings is included in this volume. May this be the beginning of an adventure in the study of America's wilderness.[1]

"When we try to pick out anything by itself,
we find it hitched to everything else in the universe."
John Muir[2]

NOTES

ABBREVIATIONS

JCCP   Jeanne C. Carr Papers. Huntington Library.
JMP   John Muir Papers. Holt-Atherton Department of Special Collections, University of the Pacific Libraries. Copyright 1984 Muir-Hanna Trust.
Letters   John Muir. *Letters to A Friend: Written to Mrs. Ezra Carr, 1866–1879.* Boston: Houghton Mifflin, 1915; reprint, Dunwoody, Georgia: Norman Berg, 1973.
SFDEB   *San Francisco Daily Evening Bulletin.*
UJJM   John Muir. *John of the Mountains: The Unpublished Journals of John Muir,* ed. Linnie Marsh Wolfe. Boston: Houghton Mifflin Co., 1938; reprint, Madison: University of Wisconsin Press, 1979.

FOREWORD

1. Carol Gilligan, *In A Different Voice: Psychological Theory and Women's Development* (Cambridge: Harvard University Press, 1982).

2. Barbara Welter, "The Cult of True Womanhood: 1820–1860," *American Quarterly* 18 (Summer 1966): 151–74.

INTRODUCTION

1. Ezra S. Carr, his family, and his friends attributed his resignation from the University of Wisconsin to conflict that arose from academic scrutiny for his views contrary to the academic paradigm. Paul A. Chadbourne, the Chancellor of the University of Wisconsin at the time Carr resigned, suggested Ezra Carr was not fit for his professorship. According to Chadbourne, Carr was aware of his academic limitations. See Paul A. Chadbourne, President, Williams College, to W. D. Whitney, February 26, 1874, The Gilman Papers, II, 17, 308hG48P, University Archives, The Bancroft Library, University of California, Berkeley.

2. Ezra Smith Carr was born August 8, 1847.

3. According to Daniel C. Gilman, President of the University of California, Ezra Carr's knowledge of agriculture was "behind hand." He was unable to make proper chemical analysis, had never made any experiments in any department of agriculture, was frequently absent from faculty meetings and lectures, made the agricultural college too easy for the students, marshalled public opinion against the university and its board, and proposed expendi-

tures in the department of agriculture that included an item for personal use (a model farm house in which he expected to reside). The fact that Jeanne Carr wrote letters for her husband though his name appeared as signator apparently led to concerns over his competency. Futhermore, Ezra Carr was well known for disputing with colleagues, the Board of Regents, and the president of the University of California. See Verne A. Stadtman, *The University of California 1868–1968* (New York: McGraw-Hill Book Co., 1970), 76–78. See also Ezra S. Carr, *The University of California and its relation to industrial education: as shown by Prof. Carr's reply to the grangers and mechanics* (San Francisco: B. Dore and Co., 1874).

4. John Henry Carr was born February 27, 1852.

5. Edward Carver Carr was born December 5, 1848, and died in November 1929; Albert (Allie) Lee Carr was born July 14, 1857, and died January 14, 1937.

6. Annie Wanda Muir was born March 25, 1881; Helen Lillian Muir was born January 23, 1886.

7. UJJM, 439.

8. George Wharton James, "John Muir: Geologist, Explorer, Naturalist," *The Craftsman* 7 (March 1905): 637–67. John Muir, Martinez, to George Wharton James, May 17, 1905, JMP, A15:08532.

9. John Muir, Martinez, to Robert Underwood Johnson, December 15, 1906, JMP, A16:08986.

10. George Wharton James, Buena Vista Sanitorium, San Francisco, to John Muir, July 16, 1908, JMP, A17:09826. John Muir, Martinez, to Theodore P. Lukens, November 13, 1901, Lukens Collection, Box 2, Huntington Library.

11. "Muir Heirs Open Startling Court War Over Rights to Noted Naturalist's Letters," *Los Angeles Examiner,* February 4, 1915, p. 1, col. 6, p. 2, cols. 4–5. William F. and Maymie B. Kimes, *John Muir: A Reading Bibliography* (Fresno: Panorama West Books, 1986), 95. John Muir, *Letters to a Friend: Written to Mrs. Ezra S. Carr, 1866–1879* (Boston: Houghton Mifflin, 1915; reprint, Dunwoody, Georgia: Norman Berg, 1973).

12. John Muir, "For the Boston Recorder. THE CALYPSO BOREALIS. Botanical Enthusiasm. From Prof. J. D. Butler," *Boston Recorder,* December 21, 1866, 1; reprint, William Frederic Badè, *The Life and Letters of John Muir,* vol. 1 (Boston: Houghton Mifflin, 1924), 120–21; reprint, *John Muir: His Life and Letters and Other Writings,* ed. Terry Gifford (Seattle: The Mountaineers, 1996), 70–71. See Jeanne C. Carr, Madison, to John Muir, March 15, 1867, JMP, A1:00946. John Muir, "Yosemite Glaciers. The Ice Streams of the Great Valley. Their Progress and Present Condition. Scenes Among the Glacier Beds. (From an Occasional Correspondent of the Tribune.) Yosemite Valley, Cal., September 28, 1871," *New York Daily Tribune,* December 5, 1871, p. 8, cols. 5–6. Muir referred to Samuel Kneeland's paper "On the Glaciers of the Yosemite Valley," read before the Boston Society of Natural History, February 21, 1872. See *Proceedings of the Boston Society of Natural History* 15 (Boston: Boston Society of Natural History, 1872), 36–47. John Muir, Yosemite Valley, to Jeanne C. Carr, October 8, 1872, JMP, A2:01176.

John Muir, Yosemite Valley, to Jeanne C. Carr, March 30, 1873, JMP, A2: 01254. Muir referred to Joseph Le Conte's glacial studies "On Some of the Ancient Glaciers of the Sierra," read before the California Academy of Science, September 16, 1872. See *The American Journal of Science and Arts* 5, 3rd series (May 1873): 21ff.

13. Muir's letter to Carr dated August 7, 1870, was destroyed according to his request. Vroman's transcribed copy was cut, and William Frederic Badè's transcribed copy was also partially cut. Muir's letter to Carr dated Spring 1872 was destroyed according to his request, and Vroman's transcribed copy was cut. Muir's letter to Carr dated August 5, 1872, was destroyed, and Vroman's transcribed copy was cut. Muir's letter to Carr dated September 13, 1872, was destroyed according to his request, and Vroman's transcribed copy was cut.

14. Frank E. Buske introduced the extant letters Elvira Hutchings wrote to Jeanne Carr and the May 27, 1873, letter Carr wrote to Muir in "An Episode In The Yosemite: To Love Is Painful," *The John Muir Newsletter* 7 (Spring 1997): 1, 3–6. James Hutchings sent a letter to Carr enclosing a note from Elvira Hutchings. Elvira requested that Hutchings read it, have Dr. Albert Kellogg (who was still in the Valley) read it, and then send it to Carr. Unwilling, perhaps patiently waiting, Hutchings chose to leave the matter to God's loving kindness and his "own hearts devoted and unwavering love," rather than comment on Elvira's note. Unable to comprehend Elvira's "utterances," Hutchings wondered if she meant there was an undercurrent of resolve to make their home happy or whether she meant that there was to be "a private and individual Juggernaut of self-sacrifice for a self-chosen victim." Hutchings suggested that before the "sad trouble" came there were few homes more happy than theirs. He believed he and Elvira shared sympathies and tastes. Recognizing that hotel-keeping made him too often a little peevish, he felt Elvira should have understood the cause and "charmed it away." Hutchings believed that the best of us need God's constant presence to lift us into the light and love and usefulness of a true life. If Carr saw Elvira he asked that she give Elvira the note to her he had enclosed. Hoping to do all that he could to make his home happy, Hutchings did not believe Elvira if true to herself as well as to others should expect more. In faith Elvira would have to meet him with an equal desire. See James Hutchings, Yosemite, to Jeanne C. Carr, September 15, 1873, JCCP, CA 110.

15. Muir's letter to Carr dated April 15, 1871, was cut. Vroman's transcribed copy is complete. Muir's letter to Carr dated April 1872 was destroyed. Vroman's transcribed copy was cut. See also *Letters*, 159–61. Muir's letter to Carr dated October 8, 1872, is complete. Vroman's transcribed copy is also complete. (Muir's list of sixteen letters included a seventeenth letter. Attached to Vroman's transcribed copy of Muir's letter of October 8, 1872, was his letter to Carr dated October 1872. (Carr may have placed both letters in the same envelope.) This was the letter Muir wanted expurgated in part and is the reason the October 8, 1872, letter is complete. Muir requested that the postscript of the letter of October 1872 be cut in part. John Muir, Yosemite, to Jeanne C. Carr, September–October 1871, JMP, A2:00981.

16. John Muir, Tahoe City, to Jeanne C. Carr, November 3, 1873, JMP, A2:01315. For Carr's return to Berkeley and her recollections of traveling with Muir, Kellogg, and Keith, see Jeanne C. Carr, University of California, Oakland, California, to Louie Strentzel, October 29, 1873, JMP, B2:01312.

17. JMP, A2:00906; JMP, A22:13203.

18. Jeanne C. Carr, to John Muir, December 18, 1894, JMP, A8:04719. John Muir, 1419 Taylor Street, San Francisco, to Jeanne C. Carr, January 12, 1876, JMP, A3:01524.

19. John Muir, "As it Appears to John Muir," *Oakland Daily Evening Tribune*, September 6, 1890, p. 4, col. 1; John P. Irish, "Muir and Yosemite. John P. Irish has something to say in reply," *Oakland Daily Evening Tribune*, September 8, 1890; John Muir, "John Muir in Yosemite. He Never Cut Down a Single Tree in the Valley. Twenty Years Ago He Was Employed by Mr. Hutchings to Saw Lumber From Fallen Timber," *Oakland Daily Evening Tribune*, September 16, 1890, p. 5, col. 5. Mrs. J. B. McChesney was resolute in reminiscences collected by William Frederic Badè that the relation Muir and Carr shared was misunderstood and distorted. See Mrs. J. B. McChesney's remarks in JMP, A51:00004–00006.

20. While every attempt has been made to secure all of Jeanne C. Carr's extant letters, one letter remains elusive. For Carr's letter to Muir regarding Muir's friendship with Elvira Hutchings see Jeanne C. Carr, University of California, Oakland, California, to John Muir, May 27, 1873, in Buske, "An Episode In The Yosemite: To Love Is Painful," *The John Muir Newsletter* (Spring 1997): 5. A portion of one sentence of a letter Carr wrote to Muir in October 1871 was published in Linnie Marsh Wolfe, *Son of the Wilderness: The Life of John Muir* (New York: Alfred A. Knopf, 1945; reprint, Madison: The University of Wisconsin Press, 1978), 154.

PART ONE: 1865–1868

1. Jeanne C. Carr, "Biographical Notes on John Muir," c. 1892, JCCP, CA 40.

2. Jeanne C. Carr, "My Own Story," c. 1886, JCCP, CA 28; Helen Hunt Jackson, "One Woman and Sunshine," c. 1880, JCCP, HM 11908.

3. For a discussion of Daniel Muir's relation to the Disciples of Christ see Mark Stoll, "God and John Muir: A Psychological Interpretation of John Muir's Journey from the Campbellites to the 'Range of Light,'" in *John Muir: Life and Work,* ed. Sally Miller (Albuquerque: University of New Mexico Press, 1993), 64–81. See also Carl Wayne Hensley, "Rhetorical Vision and the Persuasion of a Historical Movement: The Disciples of Christ in Nineteenth Century American Culture," *The Quarterly Journal of Speech* 61 (February 1975): 250–64.

4. William Frederic Badè, *The Life and Letters of John Muir,* vol. 1 (Boston: Houghton Mifflin, 1924), 121; reprint, *John Muir: His Life and Letters and Other Writings,* ed. Terry Gifford (Seattle: The Mountaineers, 1996), 71.

5. Alphonse de Lamartine, *The Stonemason of Saint Point. A Village Tale* (London: G. Routledge and Co., 1851).

6. Walter R. Brooks, *God in Nature and Life* (New York: Anson D. F. Randolph and Co., 1889), 18–22, 135, 211.

7. Jeanne C. Carr, "John Muir," *The Californian* 2 (June 1892): 92.

8. Lamartine, *The Stonemason of Saint Point,* 37–51; John Muir, *A Thousand-Mile Walk to the Gulf,* ed. William Frederic Badè (Boston: Houghton Mifflin Co., 1916), 98; reprint, *A Thousand-Mile Walk to the Gulf,* in *John Muir: The Eight Wilderness Discovery Books,* with an introduction by Terry Gifford (London: Diadem Books, 1992), 148.

9. Muir, *A Thousand-Mile Walk to the Gulf,* 139; reprint, *A Thousand-Mile Walk to the Gulf, The Eight Wilderness Discovery Books,* Gifford, 161.

10. *Letters,* 8–15.

11. JMP A1:00382.

12. *Letters,* 1–6.

13. JMP, A1:00461. Carr selected Lamartine's stonemason as an example to Muir of a life lived in Christian service in relation to nature. The stonemason expounded a nature catechism emblematic of the life Carr hoped for Muir. See Lamartine, *The Stonemason of Saint Point.*

14. *Letters,* 6–8.

15. JMP, A1:00473. Thomas Buchanan Read (1822–1872), poet and painter of allegorical subjects. Perhaps his best known paintings are "The Spirit of the Waterfall," "The Star of Bethlehem," and "Cleopatra and Her Barge."

16. "For the Boston Recorder. THE CALYPSO BOREALIS. Botanical Enthusiasm. From Prof. J. D. Butler," *Boston Recorder,* December 21, 1866, 1; reprint, Badè, *The Life and Letters of John Muir,* vol. 1, 120–21; *John Muir: His Life and Letters and Other Writings,* Gifford, 70–71.

17. JMP, A1:00496.

18. *Letters,* 15–16.

19. *Letters,* 16–19.

20. JMP, A1:00519. Carr's reference to her best beloved friend was to the Reverend Walter R. Brooks. She met Brooks in 1856 in Madison, Wisconsin, where he was the minister at the First Baptist Church of Madison. Brooks left Wisconsin to become the pastor of the Baptist Church in Hamilton, New York. He also lectured in natural history at Colgate University. Carr valued his friendship and thought of him as the second Thoreau.

21. JMP, A1:00535. Carr referred to Louis Figuier, *The World Before the Deluge* (New York: D. Appleton and Co., 1869), and *The Vegetable World: Being A History of Plants, With Their Botanical Descriptions and Peculiar Properties* (New York: D. Appleton and Co., 1867).

22. *Letters,* 19–21.

23. JMP, A1:00546.

24. *Letters,* 21–23.

25. *Letters,* 23–25.

26. *Letters,* 25–31. JMP, A1:00571.

27. JMP, A1:00582.

28. *Letters,* 31–32. JMP, A1:00587. Leo Lesquereux's theory of the formation of prairies is put forth in *The Flora of the Dakota Group: A Posthumous Work,* F. H. Knowlton, ed. (Washington: Government Printing Office, 1891), and also in Lesquereux, "Cretaceous Fossil Plants: From Minnesota," in *The Geological and Natural History Survey of Minnesota. 1885–1892. The Geology of Minnesota, Vol. III, Part I, of The Final Report. Paleontology* (Minneapolis: Harrison and Smith, 1895), 1–22.

29. *Letters,* 33–35.

30. JMP, B1:00594.

31. Carr, "John Muir," *The Californian* 2 (June 1892): 92.

32. *Letters,* 35–36.

33. JMP, B1:00624.

34. JMP, A1:00626.

PART TWO: 1868–1869

1. Jeanne C. Carr, "Our California Correspondence," *Western Farmer,* December 10, 1868, and December 15, 1868.

2. Jeanne C. Carr, "John Muir," *The Californian* 2 (June 1892): 93.

3. Elvira's third child, William Mason Hutchings, was born in August 1869.

4. John Muir, Yosemite, to J. B. McChesney, September 19, 1871, JMP, A2:00967. In "A Sabbath in the Yo Semite" written by Carr in the 1890s, she suggested that humanity should go to the fields, consider the lilies, and ask of the birds and of the mountains rather than inquire into metaphysics. To know something about God required retiring into the silent places of the Earth, where, ungrieved by the discord of human life, each person may watch the working of miracles and read the lessons of truth and wisdom. Jeanne C. Carr, "A Sabbath in the Yo Semite," c. 1890, JCCP, CA 37. Sandra Sizer Frankiel, author of *California's Spiritual Frontiers,* has commented that many Californians of Anglo-Protestant background developed an image of themselves as expansive, open, social beings, unique in their potential for development. They were searching for "the best and truest" as they moved into the future, and their natural environment reflected their traits. Awed by the natural wonders, the land became an allegory for their spiritual understanding. See Sandra Sizer Frankiel, *California's Spiritual Frontiers: Religious Alternatives in Anglo-Protestantism, 1850–1910* (Berkeley: University of California Press, 1988), 15–16.

5. John Muir wrote to Mrs. James D. Butler regarding his intuition that her husband, Dr. James D. Butler, was in the Valley; see John Muir, Headwaters of the Tuolumne near Castle Peak, to Mrs. James D. Butler, August 1869, JMP, A2:745.

6. *Letters,* 36–43. JMP, A22:13237. In length, content, and tone, Muir's July 19, 1868, letter to Catharine Merrill is inordinately similar to his letter of July 26 sent to Carr. Muir wrote to Merrill that he had not heard from her for a long time. He was lonesome and had not received a single letter from

anyone since he departed from Florida. "Flowers and fate" had carried him to California, where he reveled and luxuriated in its mountains and plants and bright sky for more than a hundred days. See John Muir, Hopeton County, California, At a farm-house near Snelling on Merced river, California, to Catharine Merrill, July 19, 1868, JMP, A1:00635.

7. JMP, A1:00647. Frederic Edwin Church (1826–1900), American landscape painter, member of the Hudson River School, and student of Thomas Cole. Church painted grand landscapes inclusive of the full range of western hemispheric geography as well as exotic foreign landscapes. Perhaps his best known painting is "Heart of the Andes," completed in 1859. See Ralph Waldo Emerson, "Woodnotes. I.," "Woodnotes. II.," in *Poems,* 5th ed. (Boston: Phillips, Sampson and Co., 1856), 67–74, 75–93.

8. *Letters,* 43–48.

9. *Letters,* 48–52.

10. JMP, A2:00711.

11. *Letters,* 54–59.

12. *Letters,* 59–61. See "The Song of Nature," Ralph Waldo Emerson, *May-Day and Other Pieces* (Boston: Ticknor and Fields, 1867), 128–33.

13. *Letters,* 62–65.

14. JMP, A2:00739. On July 1, 1869, Carr wrote that it was evening time. She had been riding alone in the Valley in the transept of the Cathedral among the mighty pines. "The sighing of the wind in the pine leaves, the music of the distant cascades, mingled in one sublime vesper service, the most soul satisfying I have ever known." There in the Valley the invisible things of God from the foundation of the world were clearly seen. There Carr met Jehovah face to face. Jeanne C. Carr, "Letters From The Yo Semite Valley," Yosemite, California, July 1, 1869, JCCP, Scrapbook I, 11, 13. For a further description of Carr's first excursion in Yosemite Valley see Jeanne C. Carr, "Miscellaneous Notes," (c. 1892), JCCP, CA 25.

15. JMP, A2:00754.

16. *Letters,* 66–70.

17. JMP, A2:00761.

18. *Letters,* 70–71.

19. *Letters,* 71–73.

PART THREE: 1870

1. Jeanne C. Carr, "Notes on David Douglas," c. 1890, JCCP, CA32.

2. Patrick Barry, Pocket Diary 1870, vol. 6, #12, Ellwanger and Barry Co. Papers, Box 48, BB.E47, Rare Book Collection, University Archives, Rush Rhees Library, University of Rochester.

3. It is not possible to determine the content of the Walter R. Brooks material Carr sent to Muir. For the collection of Brooks's sermons, lectures, and prayers, see Walter R. Brooks, *God in Nature and Life* (New York: Anson D. F. Randolph and Co., 1889).

4. See Joseph Le Conte, *A Journal of Ramblings Through the High Sierras of California by the "University Excursion Party,"* (San Francisco: Fran-

cis & Valentine, 1875; reprint, Yosemite National Park: Yosemite Association Series, 1994).

5. JMP A2:00783. Rumphius's "Flora Javonensis" was a reference to Karl Ludwig Blume's *Flora Javae*, published with Joanne Baptista Fischer (Bruxelles: J. Frank, 1828).

6. *Letters*, 73–77.

7. *Letters*, 77–80. JMP, A2:00823.

8. JMP, A2:00825. Carr referred to George B. Emerson, *A Report on the Trees and Shrubs Growing Naturally in the Forests of Massachusetts: Published Agreeably to an Order of the Legislature, by the Commissioners on the Zoological and Botanical Survey of the State* (Boston: Dutton and Wentworth, 1846); and Jacob Bigelow, *American Medical Botany, Being A Collection of the Native Medicinal Plants of the United States, Containing Their Botanical History and Chemical Analysis, and Properties and Uses in Medicine, Diet and the Arts, With Coloured Engravings* (Boston: Cummings and Hilliard, 1817–1820).

9. *Letters*, 80–85. JMP, A2:00826. See Henry David Thoreau, *The Maine Woods* (Boston: Ticknor and Fields, 1864).

10. JMP, A2:00856. In the Walter R. Brooks letters that Carr forwarded to Muir, Brooks emphasized a connection between Christian faith and nature. Carr was hopeful that Brooks's ideas would influence Muir toward a life as an interpreter of nature and wilderness, and as a facilitator of the message of the "Divine" manifest in wilderness. See Walter R. Brooks, *God in Nature and Life*.

11. JMP, B2:00587.

12. *Letters*, 85–90. JMP, A2:00858. See Theresa Yelverton, *Zanita: A Tale of the Yo-semite* (New York: Hurd and Houghton, 1872; reprint, Berkeley, Ten Speed Press, 1991).

13. *Letters*, 117–18. JMP, A2:00862.

14. *Letters*, 90–93. Joseph Le Conte's account of his ramblings was published as *A Journal of Ramblings Through the High Sierra of California by the "University Excursion Party"* (San Francisco: Francis & Valentine, 1875; reprint, Yosemite National Park: Yosemite Association Series, 1994).

15. JMP, A2:00876.

16. JMP, A2:00883.

17. *Letters*, 93–96.

18. JMP, A2:00881. Theresa Yelverton became lost in a snowstorm while riding out of Yosemite Valley. For an account of her ordeal see Mary Viola Lawrence, "Summer With A Countess," *The Overland Monthly* 7 (November 1871): 477–79.

PART FOUR: 1871–1872

1. James Bradley Thayer, *A Western Journey with Mr. Emerson* (Boston: Little, Brown and Co., 1884).

2. Jeanne C. Carr, "Female Education In The United States," *California Teacher*, c. 1870, Huntington Library, JCCP, Scrapbook I, 74.

3. Henry Edwards, to John Muir, August 25, 1871, JMP, A2:00956. William Frederic Badè, *The Life and Letters of John Muir*, vol. 1 (Houghton Mifflin Co., 1924), 264; reprint, *John Muir: His Life and Letters and Other Writings*, ed. Terry Gifford (Seattle: The Mountaineers, 1996), 137.

4. *Letters*, 96–101.

5. *Letters*, 119–23. JMP, A2:00906. Muir briefly described his upper Yosemite Falls experience in a letter to his sister Sarah Muir Galloway two days after he wrote to Carr. In a rudimentary telling of the story, he noted that he climbed the mountain to the foot of the upper Yosemite Falls carrying bread and two blankets to spend the night on the rocks and enjoy the water. Drenched by the falls in a way he could scarcely tell, perhaps for fear of worrying her (though he didn't seem to think it would bother Carr), he said the adventure nearly cut all (meaning his life?). John Muir, In the Sawmill, Yosemite Valley, April 5, 1871, to Sarah Muir Galloway, JMP, A2:00916.

6. JMP, A2:00917. The editor of this work was unable to determine to whom Muir referred in directing his condolences to Carr in this letter.

7. JMP, A2:00923. Ezra S. Carr was a colleague of Louis Agassiz, who was a member of Ralph Waldo Emerson's inner circle of literary and scientific friends. Jeanne Carr may have been introduced to Emerson before January 1867. Emerson, however, did not mention Carr in his notebook prior to January 1867, when he stopped in Madison, Wisconsin, on his lecture tour during which Carr participated in social events held in his honor. As a result of Carr's acquaintance with Emerson, she introduced Emerson to Muir. For Emerson's visit with Carr following his excursion in the Valley and his meeting with Muir see Badè, *The Life and Letters of John Muir*, vol. 1, 258; reprint, *John Muir: His Life and Letters and Other Writings*, Gifford 134. For Emerson's lecture on "Society" to the Madison Institute on January 26, 1867, see "Emerson," *Wisconsin State Journal*, Monday, January 28, 1867. James Bradley Thayer, who traveled with Emerson, documented Emerson's trip to California and his meeting with Muir in Yosemite Valley. See Thayer, *A Western Journey with Mr. Emerson*.

8. JMP, A2:00924.

9. JMP, A2:00926.

10. JMP, A2:00927.

11. JMP, A2:00936.

12. JMP, A2:00939.

13. JMP, B2:01128.

14. *Letters*, 102–4.

15. *Letters*, 104–11. JMP, A2:00958. Muir referred to John Tyndall's *Hours of Exercise in the Alps* (London: Longmans, Green, and Co., 1871).

16. *Letters*, 155–59. JMP, A2:00981.

17. JMP, A2:01008.

18. JMP, A2:01017. Carr referred to Theresa Yelverton's articles "With The Soeurs At The Golden Horn," *The Overland Monthly* 7 (July 1871): 9–21, and "The Maison-Mere Of The Soeurs," *The Overland Monthly* 7 (September 1871): 249–58. See Theresa Yelverton, *Zanita: A Tale of the Yo-semite* (New York: Hurd and Houghton, 1872; reprint, Berkeley, Ten Speed Press,

1991). The Marsh to whom Carr referred may have been George Perkins Marsh (1801–1882), diplomat and author. Marsh was born in Woodstock, Vermont, not far from Castleton, Vermont, where Carr was born. The Carrs and Marsh were probably acquainted. Marsh published his seminal book *Man and Nature, or Physical Geography as Modified by Human Action* in 1864.

PART FIVE: 1872

1. Theresa Yelverton, *Zanita: A Tale of the Yo-semite* (New York: Hurd and Houghton, 1872; reprint, Berkeley, Ten Speed Press, 1991); Theresa Yelverton, "With the Soeurs At The Golden Horn," *The Overland Monthly* 7 (July 1871): 9–21; and "The Maison-Mere of the Soeurs," *The Overland Monthly* 7 (September 1871): 249–58. Theresa Yelverton wrote to Muir (Kenmuir) from Hong Kong complaining that the publisher had changed the title of her book from *The Daughters of Ahwahnee* to *Zanita*. Sailing to Hong Kong, she stopped at the Sandwich Islands (Hawaiian Islands), where she saw vegetation she knew would delight Jeanne Carr. See Theresa Yelverton, Hong Kong, to Kenmuir, January 22, 1872, JMP: A2:01033.

2. See John Muir's letter on earthquakes, "Extracts from a letter from John Muir, on the effects of the earthquake of March 26, 1872, in the Yosemite Valley," read by Dr. Samuel Kneeland at the meeting of the Boston Society of Natural History, May 15, 1872, *Proceedings of the Boston Society of Natural History* 15 (Boston: Boston Society of Natural History, 1872), 185–86.

3. Samuel Kneeland, "On the Glaciers of the Yosemite Valley," Boston Society of Natural History, February 21, 1872, *Proceedings of the Boston Society of Natural History* 15 (Boston: Boston Society of Natural History, 1872), 36–47. For Samuel Kneeland's influence on Muir's studies see William Frederic Badè, *The Life and Letters of John Muir*, vol. 1 (Boston: Houghton Mifflin, 1924), 309; reprint, *John Muir: His Life and Letters and Other Writings*, ed. Terry Gifford (Seattle: The Mountaineers, 1996), 157. Joseph Le Conte's paper on glacial formation, "On Some of the Ancient Glaciers of the Sierra," was read before the California Academy of Science on September 16, 1872. See *The American Journal of Science and Arts*, 3d series, 5 (May 1873): 21ff.

4. Muir wrote to his sister Sarah Muir Galloway that his friends had compelled him to sit for his portrait in town. Terribly dazed and confused with the dust and din and heavy sticky air of San Francisco, Muir did not believe his picture was worth having, but he would have a copy sent to her—he had none. John Muir to Sarah Muir Galloway, December 19, 1872, JMP, A2:01211.

5. Jeanne C. Carr, Oakland, to the Editor, *The Overland Monthly*, January 17, 1872, *Overland Monthly* files, C. H. 97, The Bancroft Library, University of California, Berkeley. Carr sent Muir's letter to *The Overland Monthly*, where it was published in April 1872. See John Muir, "Yosemite Valley in Flood," *The Overland Monthly* 8 (April 1872): 347–50; reprint, Muir, *The Yosemite* (New York: The Century Co., 1912), 53–60.

6. JMP, A2:01040. Ezra S. Carr took Muir's letter to Jeanne C. Carr, "Jubilee of the Waters," to *The Overland Monthly,* where it was published as "Living Glaciers of California," *The Overland Monthly* 9 (December 1872): 547–49. See John Muir, "Bears," unpublished essay, JMP, B34:02018.

7. *Letters,* 111–13. JMP, A2:01048; JMP, A22:13195. Muir referred to his article "Yosemite Glaciers. The Ice Streams of the Great Valley. Their Progress and Present Condition. Scenes Among the Glacier Beds. (From an Occasional Correspondent of the Tribune.) Yosemite Valley, Cal., September 28, 1871," *New York Daily Tribune,* December 5, 1871, p. 8, cols. 5–6.

8. John Muir, Yosemite Valley, to Charles Stoddard, February 20, [*1872*], Keeler Collection, Box 4, Huntington Library.

9. JMP, A2:01198. Albert Bierstadt (1830–1902), landscape painter of heroic and grandiose romantic paintings of America's natural beauty. Bierstadt made his first trip to California in 1859; his second in 1863, spending six months in Yosemite and San Francisco; his third in 1871, staying three years. From his San Francisco studio he made trips to remote areas of the Sierra. Perhaps his best-known paintings of California are "Sunset Among the Sierra Mountains" and "Great Trees of California."

10. JMP, A2:01062.

11. JMP, A2:01065. Muir referred to his article "Twenty Hill Hollow," *The Overland Monthly* 9 (July 1872): 80–86; reprint, John Muir, *A Thousand-Mile Walk to the Gulf* (Houghton Mifflin, 1916), 192–212. John Ruskin's observations on repose and moderation may be found in "Of Repose, Or The Type Of Divine Permanence," "Of Moderation, Or The Type Of Government By Law," and "Of Vital Beauty. First, As Relative," in *Modern Painters,* Part III, vol. 2 (New York: John Wiley, 1855), 64–70, 80–84, 88–99.

12. *Letters,* 159–61. JMP, A22:13140.

13. JMP, A2:01091.

14. *Letters,* 113–16. Muir referred to his "letters" sent to the *New York Daily Tribune* and published through April 23, 1872. These included "Yosemite Glaciers. The Ice Streams of the Great Valley. Their Progress and Present Condition. Scenes Among the Glacier Beds. (From an Occasional Correspondent of the Tribune.) Yosemite Valley, Cal., September 28, 1871," *New York Daily Tribune,* December 5, 1871, p. 8, cols. 5–6, and "Yosemite in Winter," *New York Daily Tribune,* [January 1, 1872?]. William F. and Maymie B. Kimes were unable to locate "Yosemite in Winter" while researching *John Muir: A Reading Bibliography* (Palo Alto: William P. Wreden, 1977), 4–5. See John Muir, "IN THE YO-SEMITE. Holidays Among the Rocks. Wild Weather—A Picturesque Christmas Dinner—Idyllic Amusements—Poetic Storms—A Paradise of Clouds. Yo-Semite Valley, Jan. 1," *New York Weekly Tribune,* March 13, 1872, p. 3, cols. 4–5.

15. JMP, A2:01115.

16. *Letters,* 118–19. JMP, A2:01120.

17. JMP, A2:01122.

18. *Letters,* 123–25. Muir received the first volume of Sir Charles Lyell's *Principles of Geology; or The Modern Changes of the Earth and Its Inhabi-*

tants Considered as Illustrative of Geology, vol. 1, 11th ed. (New York: D. Appleton & Co., 1872). The lamp to which Muir referred is probably the St. Germain lamp given to him by Mrs. Kate N. Daggett, to whom he wrote a thank you letter in December 1872. See JMP, A2:01228.

19. *Letters*, 125–27.

20. JMP, A2:01138.

21. *Letters*, 128–30. JMP, A2:01132.

22. JMP, A2:01140.

23. *Letters*, 116–17; 130–32.

24. *Letters*, 153–54. JMP, A2:01148.

25. *Letters*, 132.

26. JMP, A2:01171.

27. JMP, A2:01163. Between April 1872 and September 1872 one essay written by Muir appeared in the *New York Daily Tribune*, "Yosemite in Spring. The Reign of the Earthquake—The Beauties of The Falls—The Time for Tourists. Yosemite Valley, May 7," *New York Daily Tribune*, July 11, 1872, p. 2. See John Muir, "Yosemite in Spring. The Reign of the Earthquake—The Beauties of the Falls—The Time for Tourists. Yosemite Valley, May 7," *New York Weekly Tribune*, August 14, 1872, p. 2, col 5.

28. *Letters*, 143–45. JMP, A22:13251.

29. JMP, A2:01172. The Agassizes departed from Oakland, California, with Muir's article "Yosemite Glaciers. The Ice Streams of the Great Valley. Their Progress and Present Condition. Scenes Among the Glacier Beds. (From an Occasional Correspondent of the Tribune.) Yosemite Valley, Cal., September 28, 1871," *New York Daily Tribune*, December 5, 1871, p. 8. Carr offered to send Muir the second volume of Sir Charles Lyell's *Principles of Geology; or, The Modern Changes of the Earth and Its Inhabitants Considered as Illustrative of Geology*, 11th ed. (New York: D. Appleton & Co., 1872).

30. *Letters*, 133–38, 140–42. JMP, A2:01176. Muir referred to Samuel Kneeland's paper "On the Glaciers of the Yosemite Valley," read before the Boston Society of Natural History, February 21, 1872. See *Proceedings of the Boston Society of Natural History* 15, 36–47. Muir's letter to Carr that described his experiments on glaciers was the basis for "Living Glaciers of California," *The Overland Monthly* 9 (December 1872): 547–49. See Muir, "Living Glaciers of California," *Harper's New Monthly Magazine* 51 (November 1875): 769–76; reprint, Muir, *The Mountains of California* (New York: The Century Co., 1894), 28–35.

31. *Letters*, 138. JMP, A2:01192. Ralph Waldo Emerson sent Muir Sampson Reed's *Observations on the Growth of the Mind* (Chicago: E. B. Myers and Chandler, 1867).

32. *Letters*, 139–40. Muir referred to the "Preface" to John Tyndall, *Hours of Exercise in the Alps* (London: Longmans, Green, and Co., 1871), vii–viii. Tyndall suggested that his interest in fine scenery could not be wholly the result of his own early associations with nature and his love for nature. He accounted for his close relation with nature by concluding that ancestral relations with the appreciation of natural scenery resulted in a genera-

tional development. Tyndall attributed the emotion that a fine landscape produced in him to earlier excitations, "some of them actual, but most of them nascent."

33. JMP, A2:01221.

PART SIX: 1873

1. John Muir, Yosemite Valley, to Mrs. Kate N. Daggett, December 30, 1872, JMP, A2:01228.

2. Jeanne C. Carr, University of California, Oakland, California, to Mr. Hallidie, March 4, 1873, CU-1, Box 1, Folder 4, University Archives, The Bancroft Library, University of California, Berkeley. Ezra S. Carr, Oakland, to Gentlemen of the Board of Regents, February 26, 1874, University Archives, College of Agriculture, 1:5, The Bancroft Library, University of California, Berkeley.

3. John Ruskin, *Modern Painters. By A Graduate of Oxford*, 5 vols. (New York: J. Wiley, 1857–1860). See *The Works of John Ruskin*, vols. 1–12 (New York: John Wiley and Sons, 1886); *The Works of John Ruskin*, eds. E. T. Cook and Alexander Wedderburn, vols. 3–7 (New York: Longmans, 1903–1912); Terry Gifford, "Muir's Ruskin: John Muir's Reservations About Ruskin Reviewed," in *John Muir in Historical Perspective*, ed. Sally Miller (New York: Peter Lang, 1999), 137–50. For the historical background on Ruskin's understanding of mountains see Marjorie Hope Nicolson, *Mountain Gloom and Mountain Glory: The Development of the Aesthetics of the Infinite* (Ithaca: Cornell University Press, 1959; reprinted, Seattle: University of Washington Press, 1997).

4. John Muir, Yosemite Valley, to J. B. McChesney, January 10, 1873, JMP, A2:01234.

5. See Jeanne C. Carr's articles "The Rural Homes of California," *California Horticulturist* 3 (February 1873): 39–41; "Flower Studies," *Illustrated Press* 1 (February 1873); "The Rural Homes of California," *California Horticulturist* 3 (March 1873): 69–72; "Flower Studies.—No. 2.," *Illustrated Press* 1 (March 1873); "Flower Studies.—No. 3," *Illustrated Press* 1 (April 1873); "California Flower Studies.—No. 4," *Illustrated Press* 1 (May 1873); "Nursery and Residence of W. F. Kelsey, Oakland, Cal.," *California Horticulturalist* 3 (May 1873): 147–48; "California Flower Studies.—No. 5," *Illustrated Press* 1 (July 1873).

6. For the letters of Elvira Hutchings to Jeanne C. Carr and the Jeanne C. Carr May 27, 1873, letter to John Muir regarding the relation between Muir and Elvira Hutchings see Frank C. Buske, "An Episode In The Yosemite: To Love Is Painful," *The John Muir Newsletter* 7 (Spring 1997); 1, 3–6.

7. Jeanne C. Carr, "Mrs. Carr's Lecture on the Big Tuolumne Canyon, Before the Oakland Farming Club. October 10th," c. 1873, JCCP, CA 20.

8. "Mrs. Carr's Remarks On The Big Tuolumne Canyon, Etc.," *Illustrated Press* 1 (October 1873).

9. Jeanne C. Carr, "In the Sierras. The Lovers of Science Penetrating

Untrodden Heights in the Mountain Wilderness," *Home Journal,* September 10, 1873, JCCP, Scrapbook I, 17; "Yosemite and the Great New Canyon," *Oakland Daily News,* August 11, 1873; Jeanne C. Carr, "Glaciers of California," c. 1874, JCCP, CA 21, 3; Jeanne C. Carr, "The Flowers of California," *California Farmer,* c. 1875, JCCP, Scrapbook I, 16.

10. Jeanne C. Carr, "Shadow Lake—headwaters of Merced River, 15 miles above Yo Semite," sketch, reverse side entry, 1873, Pasadena Historical Museum, Jeanne C. Carr Papers.

11. For Muir's remarks on human love see John Muir, journal entry, March 15, [1873?] in *John of the Mountains: The Unpublished Journals of John Muir,* ed. Linnie Marsh Wolfe (Boston: Houghton Mifflin, 1938; reprint, Madison: University of Wisconsin Press, 1979), 138.

12. JMP, A2:01237. See Jeanne C. Carr, to Mr. Hallidie, March 4, 1873; E. S. Carr, to the Gentlemen of the Board of Regents, February 26, 1874. Carr referred to Muir's article "On Actual Glaciers in California," *Silliman's Journal of Science and Arts* 5 (January 1873): 69–71; reprint of "Living Glaciers of California," *The Overland Monthly* 9 (December 1872): 547–49. See Jeanne C. Carr, "The Rural Homes of California" *California Horticulturist* (February 1873): 39–41, and "The Rural Homes of California" (March 1873): 69–72.

13. *Letters,* 145–47. The two essays Muir referred to in his letter to Carr later appeared as articles: "A Geologist's Winter Walk," *The Overland Monthly* 10 (April 1873): 355–58, and "Hetch-Hetchy Valley," *The Overland Monthly* 11 (July 1873): 42–50. Carr took the letter Muir wrote to her about his Tenaya Canyon jaunt to *The Overland Monthly,* where it was published as "A Geologist's Winter Walk." Muir referred to Joseph Le Conte's glacial research "On Some of the Ancient Glaciers of the Sierras," a paper read before the California Academy of Science, September 16, 1872; reprint, *The American Journal of Science and Arts,* 3d series, 5 (May 1873): 21ff.

14. *Letters,* 147–48. Muir's reference to articles Carr sent to the *Overland Monthly* between April 1873 and 1875 included the following published essays: "Exploration of the Great Tuolumne Cañon," 11 (August 1873): 139–47; "Wild Sheep of California," 12 (April 1874): 358–63; "Studies in the Sierra. No. I—Mountain Sculpture," 12 (May 1874): 393–403; "Studies in the Sierra. No. II.—Mountain Sculpture.—Origin of Yosemite Valleys," 12 (June 1874): 489–500; "Studies in the Sierra. No. III.—Ancient Glaciers and Their Pathways," 13 (July 1874): 67–79; "Studies in the Sierra, No. IV.— Glacial Denudation," 13 (August 1874): 174–84; "By-Ways of Yosemite Travel. Bloody Cañon," 13 (September 1874): 267–73; "Studies in the Sierra. No. V.—Post-Glacial Denudation," 13 (November 1874): 393–402; "Studies in the Sierra. No. VI.—Formation of Soils," 13 (December 1874): 530–40; "Studies in the Sierra. No. VII.—Mountain Building," 14 (January 1875), 64–73; "Wild Wool," 14 (April 1875): 361–66; "Flood-Storm in the Sierra," 14 (June 1875): 489–96.

15. *Letters,* 148–49. Muir referred to his article "Hetch Hetchy Valley," *Boston Weekly Transcript,* 25 March 1873, p. 2.

16. *Letters,* 149–50.

17. *Letters*, 151–52. JMP, A2:01272. Muir referred to his articles "Exploration of the Great Tuolumne Cañon," *The Overland Monthly*: 139–47; "Wild Sheep of California," *The Overland Monthly*: 358–63, reprint, Muir, *The Mountains of California* (New York: The Century Co., 1894), 300–324; and "Studies in the Sierra. No. 1—Mountain Sculpture," *The Overland Monthly*: 393–403.

18. *Letters*, 154.

19. JMP, B2:01284.

20. JMP, A2:01298. From Elvira Hutchings's perspective, by the summer of 1873, her marriage to James Hutchings had become hopelessly irreconcilable. She had married Hutchings in 1860, when she was seventeen and he was thirty-nine. The twenty-two-year age difference lent itself to marital misgivings that Elvira shared with Muir at some point prior to May 1870. In 1873 Muir would not have been surprised that Elvira intended to leave her husband. She wrote to Muir shortly before September 13, 1873, regarding her plan. She was well and looking forward to a new life. Muir had known her when she was "weak in body and mind, when deeply hurt and most anxious." Now strong, she believed she had approached him (Muir) in her loneliness, like a bird to a cedar in a storm, as she would have gone to Christ had He been there in human form. Elvira's letter to Muir may be found in Stephen Fox, *John Muir and His Legacy: The American Conservation Movement* (Boston: Little, Brown and Co., 1981), 25. It appears that Muir did not read the letter. He sent it to Jeanne Carr. If she wanted him to read it she could bring it to Lake Tahoe where Carr and Muir planned to meet in November. (Muir did not flee the Valley to put distance between himself and Elvira. The reunion with Carr in Lake Tahoe had been planned during the summer because Carr had to leave the Valley to return to Oakland to prepare for a move to Berkeley. Muir spent the winter writing in Oakland. He returned to the Valley the following August.) Elvira did leave her husband briefly in September 1873, but she returned to the Valley. James Hutchings sought compensation under the preemption laws that resulted from the state control of Yosemite Valley. (Yosemite became a state park in 1864 under federal legislation.) Following the receipt of $24,000, Hutchings closed his hotel. James and Elvira departed from the Valley together in 1874 and moved to San Francisco. There Elvira left her husband. Muir kept the undated and unidentified letter in an envelope marked "Mrs. Hutchings." William Frederic Badè wrote to Gertrude (Cosie) Hutchings Mills on April 11, 1923, regarding this letter. "An intimate document, [*it*] is noble in its spirit, and does great credit both to her [*Elvira*] and to John Muir." William Frederic Badè, to Gertrude Hutchings Mills, April 11, 1923, JMP, Series 5A, Correspondence.

21. JMP, A2:01300.

22. JMP, A2:01302.

23. *Letters*, 164–66.

24. *Letters*, 162–64.

25. JMP, B2:01312.

26. *Letters*, 167–68. JMP, A2:01315. The bereavement to which Muir referred in his letter to Carr was the death of Carr's son, Ezra Smith Carr, on

October 23, 1873. A railroad brakeman, he was crushed and killed between two railroad cars in Alameda, California. For the obituary of Ezra S. Carr see the *Daily Alta California,* October 25, 1873. For the Strentzels' concerns for the Carrs and their condolences, see Louisiana Erwin Strentzel, "Diary," October 26, 1873, Louisiana Erwin Strentzel Papers, C-F16:5, The Bancroft Library, University of California, Berkeley. See Anna E. Dickinson's condolences in Anne E. Dickinson, Pittsburgh, to Jeanne C. Carr, November 24, 1873, JCCP, CA 82.

PART SEVEN: *1874–1875*

1. Verne A. Stadtman, *The University of California 1868–1968* (New York: McGraw-Hill Book Co., 1970), 71–74. See "The University Squabble," *San Francisco Alta,* August 6, 1874, p. 2, col. 1; "More Resolutions Concerning the Removal of Professor Carr," *San Francisco Alta,* August 18, 1874, p. 1, col. 1. The Carrs were advocates of William E. Channing's ideas on the elevation of the laboring classes. Channing stated that faith in labor celebrated labor but not as the sole work of life. Labor was to be joined with higher means of improvement—study, meditation, society, and relaxation. See William E. Channing, "On the Elevation of the Laboring Classes," in *The Works of William E. Channing* (Boston: American Unitarian Association, 1877), 36–66.

2. Ezra S. Carr's account of the history of the Pacific Coast Grange was published as *The Patrons of Husbandry On The Pacific Coast* (San Francisco: A. L. Bancroft and Co., 1875). Charles Warren Stoddard, to Jeanne C. Carr, July 8, 1874, JCCP, CA 168.

3. Sarah J. McChesney Reminiscence of John Muir, 1916, Badè Papers, 1915–1923, JMP, A51:00004. John Muir, "Studies in the Sierra. No. 1—Mountain Sculpture," *The Overland Monthly* 12 (May 1874): 393–403; "Studies in the Sierra. No. II.—Mountain Sculpture.—Origin of Yosemite Valleys," *The Overland Monthly* 12 (June 1874): 489–500; "Studies in the Sierra. No. III.—Ancient Glaciers and Their Pathways," *The Overland Monthly* 13 (July 1874): 67–79; "Studies in the Sierra, No. IV.—Glacial Denudation," *The Overland Monthly* 13 (August 1874): 174–84; "By-Ways of Yosemite Travel. Bloody Cañon," *The Overland Monthly* 13 (September 1874): 267–73; "Studies in the Sierra. No. V.—Post-Glacial Denudation," *The Overland Monthly* 13 (November 1874): 393–402; "Studies in the Sierra. No. VI.—Formation of Soils," *The Overland Monthly* 13 (December 1874): 530–40; "Studies in the Sierra. No. VII.—Mountain Building," *The Overland Monthly* 14 (January 1875): 64–73.

4. John Muir, "Salmon Breeding. The Establishment on McCloud River. John Muir, the Naturalist Gives a Graphic Description of What is Being Done. (Special Correspondent of the Bulletin.) U.S. Salmon Breeding Establishment on the McCloud River, Shasta Co., October 24, 1874," SFDEB, October 29, 1874, p. 1, col. 1; "Shasta in Winter. John Muir, the Geologist and Explorer, Ascends It. A Hard Perilous Undertaking—Among the Glaciers, Lava-beds, and Storm-clouds. (Special Correspondence of the Bulletin.) Sisson's Station,

November 24, 1874," SFDEB, December 2, 1874, p. 1, col. 3; "Shasta Game. Hunting the Wild Sheep and Mule Deer—Exciting Sport Among the Lava Cliffs—John Muir Tells What He Saw and Did. (Special Correspondent of the Bulletin.) Sisson's Station, Near Mount Shasta, Nov. 29, 1874," SFDEB, December 12, 1874, p. 8, col. 1; "Modoc Memories. A Visit to the Lava Beds by Muir the Geologist and Explorer—The Spot where Gen. Canby Fell—Sad Relics of the War. (From Our Special Correspondent.)," SFDEB, December 28, 1874, p. 1, col. 4; "Shasta Bees. A Honeyful Region—The Bee Lands—A Summer Paradise. (From Our Special Correspondent.) Sisson's Station near Mt. Shasta, December 17, 1874," SFDEB, January 5, 1875, p. 2, col. 5.

5. John Muir, "Wild Wool," *The Overland Monthly* 14 (April 1875): 361–66.

6. Jeanne C. Carr, University of California, Oakland, Cal., to Louie Wanda Strentzel, October 29, 1873, JMP, 2:01312.

7. Louie Wanda Strentzel, Alhambra, to Jeanne C. Carr, March 21, 1875, JMP, B3:01482. See Jeanne C. Carr, Oakland, to Louie Wanda Strentzel, April 19, 1875, JMP, B3:01492; Jeanne C. Carr, to Louie Wanda Strentzel, February 16, 1876, JMP, B3:01535.

8. Jeanne C. Carr, "Birds and Caterpillars—A Hardshell Sermon," *Pacific Rural Press*, May 22, 1875. See Jeanne C. Carr, "The Flowers of California," *California Farmer*, c. 1875, JCCP, Scrapbook I, 16. "The Granger Picnic," *Oakland Daily Transcript*, May 31, 1875.

9. "Summering in the Sierra. John Muir Discourses of Sierra Forests, Etc.—The Glorious Solitudes of Nature—Pine Nuts as Food—Tuolumne Meadows—Mono Pass—A Lovely Lake. (Special Correspondence of the Bulletin.) Mono Lake, July, 1875," SFDEB, August 3, 1875, p. 1, cols. 2–3; "Summering in the Sierra. A New Yosemite—The King's River Valley. It is Geographically Described by John Muir. Glorious Scenery, Magnificent Forests, Lovely Waterfalls—El Capitan and Three Brothers Reproduced—The Valley at Night. (From Our Own Correspondent.) Yosemite Valley, August 5, 1875," SFDEB, August 13, 1875, p.1, cols. 1–2; "Mount Whitney. Its Ascent by John Muir, the Explorer and Geologist. Different Routes—The Ascent from the East—A Minor Yosemite—Glacier Meadows and Glacier Lakes—Glorious Views—Successive Ascents. (Special Correspondence of the Bulletin.) Independence, Inyo County, August 17, 1875," SFDEB, August 24, 1875, p. 1, cols. 2–3; "Summering in the Sierra. John Muir's Description of a Wonderful Region. Owens Valley and Its Lava Floods—The Conflict Between Frost and Fire—Mono Valley—Dead Lakes—A Mountain Character. (Special Correspondence of the Bulletin.) Yosemite Valley, September, 1875," SFDEB, September 15, 1875, p. 1, cols. 3–4; "Summering in the Sierra. A Bit of Forest-Study by John Muir. The Royal Sequoia—Its Beauty and Impressiveness—Its Cones and Timber—Doom of the Coniferae—A Forest Hermit. (From Our Own Correspondent.) Fresno Grove of Big Trees, Sept., 1875," SFDEB, September 21, 1875, p. 1, col. 1; "Summering in the Sierra. The Giant Forests of the Kaweah. Something about the Sequoia Gigantea of the South Fork of King's River—Measurements of Largest Trees by John Muir. (Special Correspondence of the Bulletin.) Pluno [Plano], Cal., October 19, 1875," SFDEB,

October 22, 1875, p. 1, col. 5; "Summering in the Sierra. Tulare Levels. John Muir Comes Down From the Mountains—Exuberant Farmers—The Story of an Irrigation Ditch—Blessed Ministry of Water. (Special Correspondence of the Bulletin.) Grangerville, Tulare Co., October 25th," SFDEB, November 17, 1875, p. 1, col. 4; "South Dome, Its Ascent by George Anderson and John Muir—Hard Climbing but a Glorious View—Botany of the Dome—Yosemite in Late Autumn. (From Our Special Correspondent.) Yosemite Valley, November 10, 1875," SFDEB, November 18, 1875, p. 1, col. 1; "Summer in the Sierra. John Muir Shakes the Dust of the Town from his Feet and Flees to the Mountains. The Calaveras Grove—Some Facts About the Sequoia System. (Special Correspondence of the Bulletin.) Big Tree Grove, July 13, 1876," SFDEB, July 20, 1876, p. 1, col. 1; "Summering in the Sierra. John Muir Discourses of the Ancient River Channels. Their Importance as Gold Fountains—Eccentric Characters. (Special Correspondence of the Bulletin.) Murphy's Camp, Calaveras County, July 17th," SFDEB, July 26, 1876, p. 1, col. 4; "Summer in the Sierra. 'The Season' at the Yosemite Valley—A Disquisition on Tourists—In Memoriam—Lamon's Grave. (From Our Own Correspondent.) Yosemite Valley, August 20, 1876," SFDEB, August 24, 1876, p. 1, col. 5; "Summering in the Sierra. The Summit of South Dome—Yosemite Tourists—An Irrepressible Mountain Climber. (From Our Own Correspondent.) Yosemite Valley, August 28, 1876," SFDEB, September 6, 1876, p. 1, col. 4. For the obituary Jeanne Carr prepared on James Lamon, see Jeanne C. Carr, "The Farmer of the Yosemite Valley," Oakland, May 26, 1875, JCCP, Scrapbook I, 70.

10. UJJM, 220, 229.

11. UJJM, 230, 234.

12. UJJM, 235. Jeanne C. Carr, "Idustrial [sic] University for Women," n.d., JCCP, Scrapbook I, 152. See Jeanne C. Carr, "Professional Training Schools for Girls," *Pacific Rural Press,* n.d., JCCP, Scrapbook I, 44; "Mrs. E. S. Carr's Address. (Delivered on the occasion of the graduation of the Normal School of the San Francisco Girl's High School, May 24th, and published by request of the audience.)," n.d., JCCP, Scrapbook I, 55–56. See Jeanne C. Carr, "Woman and Land," *Pasadena & Valley Union,* February 23, 1884.

13. George Wharton James, "A Letter From The Yosemite Valley," *The Craftsman* 7 (March 1905): 654–65. JMP, A3:01431.

14. John Muir, Yosemite Valley, to Jeanne C. Carr, September 27, 1874, Huntington Library, HM 17357. See Katharine Hooker's letter to John Muir, August 3, 1907, in which she noted the receipt of his letter illustrated with "charming and quaint" grasshopper tracks. Katharine Hooker, West Adams Street, Los Angeles, to John Muir, August 3, 1907, JMP, A16:09194.

15. *Letters,* 168–69. JMP, A3:01445.

16. *Letters,* 170–72. Muir's "short letter" was published as "Salmon Breeding. The Establishment of McCloud River. John Muir, The Naturalist Gives a Graphic Description of What is Being Done. (Special Correspondent of the Bulletin.) U. S. Salmon Breeding Establishment on the McCloud River, Shasta Co., October 24, 1874," SFDEB, October 29, 1874, 1.

17. JMP, A3:01452. Carr referred to Muir's article "Studies in the Sierra.

No. V.—Post-Glacial Denudation," *The Overland Monthly* 13 (November 1874): 393–402; reprint, *John Muir's Studies in the Sierra* (San Francisco: The Sierra Club, 1950), 62–74.

18. *Letters,* 172–74.

19. *Letters,* 174–76.

20. *Letters,* 176–78. The account of Muir's experience in Yuba County was his final contribution to the *Overland Monthly.* See John Muir, "Flood-Storm in the Sierra," *The Overland Monthly* 14 (June 1875): 489–96; incorporated, in part, in the chapter "The Rivers Floods," in Muir, *The Mountains of California* (New York: The Century Co., 1894), 258–70. For a discussion of Muir on his return to the "Knox House" following his experience in the storm in Yuba County, see William Frederic Badè, *The Life and Letters of John Muir,* vol. 2 (Boston: Houghton Mifflin, 1924), 44–46; reprint, *John Muir: His Life and Letters and Other Writings,* ed. Terry Gifford (Seattle: The Mountaineers, 1996), 214.

21. JMP, A3:01489.

22. *Letters,* 178–79.

23. JMP, A3:01498. Carr met James Lamon in Yosemite Valley in 1869 and visited him again in 1873. She noted that he was not only the earliest real inhabitant and cultivator of the Valley, but that he was the only one whose improvements did nothing to mar its natural beauty. Lamon's summer log house where he lived alone was nestled under towering pines. His orchard and strawberry patch revealed only a touch of a human hand, "like a caress upon the mellow earth." Fences were hidden with ferns. The wilderness was near and abundant. Carr recalled sitting in the log house doorway eating raspberries from broad rubus leaves. Inside the cabin was a generous fireplace, a couch, shelves for books and magazines, and hiding places for winter stores of apples and potatoes. Squirrels and birds were frequent visitors. For her complete reminiscence of Lamon in the Valley, see Carr, "The Farmer of the Yosemite Valley," JCCP, Scrapbook I, 70.

24. JMP, A3:01502.

25. *Letters,* 180.

PART EIGHT: 1876–1903

1. John Muir, "God's First Temples: How Shall We Preserve Our Forests? The Question Considered by John Muir, the Californian Geologist—The Views of a Practical Man and a Scientific Observer—A Profoundly Interesting Article. (Communicated To The Record-Union)," *Sacramento Daily Union,* February 5, 1876, p. 8, cols. 6–7.

2. Jeanne C. Carr, "Department of Education, Teachers' Institute in Siskiyou—Notes of Travel Northward—Honor to Del Norte. Shasta-Ward," *Sacramento Record-Union,* May 17, 1876.

3. Jeanne C. Carr, Chicago, to Louie Wanda Strentzel, May 20, 1876, JMP, B3:01557. "Woman's True Sphere: Mrs. Jennie C. Carr's Efforts in the Cause of Labor Education," *Daily Alta California and San Francisco Times,* September 4, 1876. Louisiana Erwin Strentzel, "Diary," October 4–6, 1876,

Louisiana Erwin Strentzel Papers, C-F16:5, The Bancroft Library, University of California, Berkeley.

4. The notice of John Henry Carr's suicide, "A Sad Affair," appeared in the *Daily Alta California* on April 10, 1877, p. 1, col. 5. Jeanne C. Carr, Marysville, to Mr. and Mrs. J. B. McChesney, April 25, 1877, JMP, B3: 01610; Louisiana Erwin Strentzel "Diary," April 11, 1877, Louisiana Erwin Strentzel Papers, C-F16.5, The Bancroft Library, University of California, Berkeley. Mary A. Livermore wrote a touching letter to Jeanne Carr in July in which she empathized with Carr and described her own personal feelings of loss when her child died. See Mary A. Livermore, Melrose, Massachusetts, to Jeanne C. Carr, July 22, 1877, JCCP, CA 133.

5. John Muir, "City of Saints. The Grand Wasatch Mountains—A Graphic Description of Salt Lake City—Mormon Men and Women—Latter-Day Boys and Girls. (From Our Own Correspondent.) Salt Lake City, May 15, 1877," SFDEB, May 22, 1877, p. 1, col. 3; "A Great Storm. Fierce War of the Elements in the Salt Lake Basin—The Wasatch Mountains Capped with Snow—A Magnificent Sight. (From Our Own Correspondent.) Salt Lake City, May 19, 1877," SFDEB, May 25, 1877, p. 1: col. 3; "Notes from Utah. John Muir the Naturalist, on Bathing in Salt Lake—A Glorious Swim—Erroneous Impressions Corrected. (Special Correspondent of the Bulletin.) Lake Point, Utah, May 20, 1877," SFDEB, June 14, 1877, p. 1: col. 1; "Mormon Lilies. Liliaceous Wonders—A Mountain Covered with Flowers—Gorgeous Lily Gardens—A Sublime Scene—The Queen of All. (Special Correspondence of the Bulletin.) Salt Lake, July 1877," SFDEB, July 19, 1877, p. 4, cols. 1–2.

6. Jeanne C. Carr, Sacramento, to Dr. and Mrs. John Strentzel, September 16, 1877, JMP, B3:01630. Asa Gray, Palace Hotel, San Francisco, to Jeanne C. Carr, September 2, 1877, JCCP, CA 98. UJJM, 236–41. See Mrs. Annie Kennedy Bidwell's Reminiscences of John Muir, JMP A51:00009.

7. A. L. Carr, "Genesis and Development of Carmelita," n.d., Pasadena Historical Museum, Jeanne C. Carr Papers, 2–5; Helen Hunt Jackson, "One Woman and Sunshine," c. 1880, Helen Hunt Jackson Papers, HM 11908, Huntington Library.

8. Carr, "Genesis and Development of Carmelita," 1–3; Jackson, "One Woman and Sunshine," 2–7. W. A. T. Stratton, Petaluma, to Jeanne C. Carr, October 21, 1879, JCCP, CA 172; Marshall P. Wilder, Dorchester, to Jeanne C. Carr, April 17, 1882, JCCP, CA 179.

9. John Muir, "The Humming-Bird of the California Water-Falls," *Scribner's Monthly* 15 (February 1878): 545–54. John Muir, "Pyramid Lake. The Largest Body of Water West of Lake Superior—Charming Description of Little Known Country—A Rival of Lake Tahoe. (Correspondence of the Bulletin.) Reno, Nev., July 28, 1878," SFDEB, July 31, 1878, p. 4, col. 1; "Nevada Farms. John Muir on the Agricultural Resources of Our Sister State—Mountain and Valley Ranches—Virgin Wilds—Irrigation and Artesian Wells. (Special Correspondence of the Bulletin.) Ward, Nevada, September 29, 1878," SFDEB, October 5, 1878, p. 1, col. 5–6; "Nevada Forests. Coniferous Trees in the Great Basin—The Timber Line. Pine Nut Forest—Pine Nuts as Food—Pine Nut Harvests. (Special Correspondence of the Bulletin.) Eureka, Nev.,

October 22, 1878," SFDEB, October 31, 1878, p. 1, cols. 4–5; "Nevada's Timber Belt. Early Winter in the Pine Woods—More About Nevada Conifers, Fox-tail Pine and Rocky Mountain Spruce—The Home of Happy Birds—A Mountain Excursion—A Splendid View. (Special Correspondence of the Bulletin.) Pioche, Nevada, October 20, 1878," SFDEB, November 19, 1878, p. 4, cols. 1–2; "Glacial Phenomena in Nevada. Interesting Discoveries by John Muir. Glacial Traces—Lateral Moraines—How the Valleys Were Formed. (Special Correspondence of the Bulletin.) Eureka, Nev., November 28, 1878," SFDEB, December 5, 1878, p. 4, cols. 1–2; "Nevada's Dead Towns. A New Country Thickly Strewn with Ruins of Mining Towns—How Capital has been Squandered. Roving Tendencies of Miners—Wonderful Energy of Mining Men. (Special Correspondence of the Bulletin.)," SFDEB, January 15, 1879, p. 1, col. 1. Muir's bee-pasture articles were published by the *Century Magazine* in 1882. See John Muir, "Bee-Pastures of California: In Two Parts:—I," *The Century Magazine* 24 (n.s., v. 2) (June 1882): 222–29; "Bee-Pastures of California: In Two Parts:—II," *The Century Magazine* 24 (n.s., v. 2) (July 1882): 388–96.

  10. Jeanne C. Carr, "Our Teachers," *San Francisco Patron*, April 29, 1882, JCCP, Scrapbook I, 79. Jeanne C. Carr, "Pasadena Hedges," *Pasadena Star-News*, May 3, 1923.

  11. John Muir, Victoria, British Columbia, to Louie Wanda Strentzel, July 10, 1879, JMP, A3:01899; Louie Wanda Strentzel, Alhambra, to John Muir, October 9, 1897, JMP, A3:01928; Louie Wanda Strentzel, Alhambra, to John Muir, December 1, 1879, JMP, A3:01934. John Muir, "Notes of a Naturalist. A Rough Passage—Sea-Sickness. Sea and Coast Scenery. British Columbia—Glacial Phenomena. (Correspondence of the Bulletin.) Victoria, V. I., June 25, 1879," SFDEB, August 27, 1879, p. 4, col. 1; "Notes of a Naturalist. John Muir on Puget Sound and Its Lovely Scenery. Forest Belts—Mount Rainier—Thriving Towns—Coal Fields. (Special Correspondence of the Bulletin.) Seattle, Washington Territory, June 28, 1879," SFDEB, August 29, 1879, p. 1, col. 3; "Notes of a Naturalist. John Muir in Alaska—Wrangel Island and its Picturesque Attractions. Summer Days that Have No End—Pictures of Sound Life. Life Among the Indians—Boat Life—Wild Berries. (Special Correspondence of the Bulletin.) Fort Wrangel, Alaska, August 8, 1879," SFDEB, September 6, 1879, p. 1, col. 4; "Alaska Glaciers. An Ounalaska Yosemite. Glacial Theology and Sermons in Ice. The Rocks, Plants, and Trees of Alaska. (Correspondence of the Bulletin.) Fort Wrangel, Alaska, September 5, 1879," SFDEB, September 23, 1879, p. 4, col. 1; "Alaska Glaciers. Graphic Description Of the Yosemite Of The Far Northwest—A Living, Moving Glacier In All Its Sublimity And Grandeur. (Correspondence of the Bulletin.) Fort Wrangel, Alaska, Ter., September 7, 1879," SFDEB, September 27, 1879, p. 1, col. 1; "Alaska Coast Scenery. Sailing Among the Islands—Delightful Views. Wonderful Variety of Lovely Pictures. Effects of Glaciation—An Archipelago of Evergreen Isles. (Special Correspondence of the Bulletin.) Fort Wrangel, Alaska, Sept. 25, 1879," SFDEB, October 29, 1879, p. 4, col. 1; "Alaska Forests. Evergreens—The Yellow Cedar and its Various Uses. The White Spruce—Pines and Cottonwoods—Firs and Hardwoods.

Extent and Commercial Value of Alaska Forests—The 'Devil's Club.' (Special Correspondence of the Bulletin.) Fort Wrangel, October 8, 1879," SFDEB, October 30, 1879, p. 4, cols. 1–2; "Wanderings in Alaska. A Lovely Sail—Majestic Mountain Views—More Glaciers. Visit to a Deserted Indian Village. Habitations of the Natives—Carved Images and Other Relics—Indian Rites—A Doomed Race. Fort Wrangel, October 12, 1879," SFDEB, November 1, 1879, p. 1, col. 4; "Alaska Climate. Some Popular Errors Corrected—A Good Country to Live In. An Alaska Summer Day—Glorious Sunsets. Bright and Cloudy Weather—Rainfall—Temperature—Alaska Winters. (Special Correspondence of the Bulletin.) Fort Wrangel, October 16, 1879," SFDEB, November 8, 1879, p. 1, cols. 4–5; "Alaska Gold Fields. A Country Moderately Rich in the Precious Metals. The Cassiar and Other Mines—Mining Prospects—Geological Changes. (Special Correspondence of the Bulletin.) Sitka, December 23, 1879," SFDEB, January 10, 1880, p. 4, col. 1; "Alaska Rivers. Their Number and Characteristics—The Stickine. Sublime Alpine Scenery—An Alaska Canyon. Glacier Mud—Stupendous Glacial Phenomena. (Special Correspondence of the Bulletin.) Sitka, December 27, 1879," SFDEB, January 20, 1880, p. 4, cols. 3–4.

12. Jeanne C. Carr, Pasadena, to Louisiana E. Strentzel, May 1880, JMP, B4:02054.

13. John Muir, "Some Alaska Notes. Dull Times at Sitka and Fort Wrangel—Indians Turned Smugglers. (From Our Special Correspondent.) Fort Wrangel, August 14, 1880," SFDEB, August 25, 1880, p. 3, col. 9; "Alaska Land. John Muir Revisits the Scene of Last Year's Exploration. A Land of Abundance—A Canoe Voyage Among the Islands and Icebergs. Magnificent Scenery—The Hoona Indians—Among the Salmon. (Special Correspondence of the Bulletin.) In Camp, Near Camp Fanshaw, August 18, 1880," SFDEB, September 25, 1880, p. 4, cols. 6–8; "Alaska Land. A Canoe Voyage Among the Islands and Icebergs. Sum Dum Bay—Enormous Glaciers—Gold Mines—Products and Future Development of Alaska. (Special Correspondence of the Bulletin.) Sum Dum Bay, Alaska, August 22, 1880," SFDEB, October 7, 1880, p. 1, col.1; "Alaska Land. An Eventful Day—Revelling Among the Glacial Monarchs. Fountain Source of Ice-Rivers—Wild Goats—Music of the Cascades. (Special Correspondence of the Bulletin.) Cascade Camp, Sum Dum Bay, August 19, 1880," SFDEB, October 9, 1880, p. 4, col. 1; "Alaska Land. Perilous Adventure—Shooting the Rapids. A Typical Young Yosemite—Royal Glaciers—Alaska Flora. (Special Correspondence of the Bulletin.) Gold Camp, Sum Dum Bay, Alaska, August 20, 1880," SFDEB, October 16, 1880, p. 4, col. 3; "Alaska Land. Among the Glaciers, Cascades and Yosemite Rocks. How Nature Works in Icy Solitudes—Rock Sculpture. Searching for the King of Glaciers. An Alaska Sunday. (Special Correspondence of the Bulletin.) Sum Dum Bay, August 29, 1880," SFDEB, October 23, 1880, p. 4, col. 1; "Alaska Land. A Perfect Day—Nature's Ceaseless Work—Pushing Northward. Indian Superstitions—The Tahkou River Indians—Magnificent Glacial Scenery—Gorgeous Sunset. (Special Correspondence of the Bulletin.) Mouth of Tahkou River, Alaska, August 24, 1880," SFDEB, November 13, 1880, p. 4, cols. 1–2. See John Muir, *Stickeen: The Story of A*

Dog (Boston: Houghton Mifflin Co., 1915). John Muir, to Mary L. Swett, March 29, 1881, JMP A4:02199.

14. John Muir, "The Corwin's Cruise. At Ounalaska—An Aleutian Storm and Landscape, Snow Barriers and Glacier Footprints on the Aleutian Group. (Special Correspondence of the Bulletin.) Ounalaska, May 18, 1881," SFDEB, June 20, 1881, p. 1, col. 1; "At St. Paul. The Fur Seals of the Pribilof Group—Habits of the Natives—The Annual Catch of Fur Seals—Physical Appearance of the Islands. St. Paul, Alaska, May 23, 1881," SFDEB, July 13, 1881, p. 1, col. 1; "On the Siberian Coast. The Corwin Enters the Arctic— First News of the Missing Whalers—A Story of Death and Disaster—In the Ice Pack—Over the Ice in an Esquimo Sleigh—Reluctance of Esquimos to Leave Their Homes. Steamer Corwin, Kapkan, Siberia, May 31, 1881," SFDEB, July 13, 1881, p.1, cols. 2–3; "Pushing Northwestward. The Corwin Meets With A Disaster—The Rudder Smashed by Ice Floes—Getting Up a Sleigh Party—Landing on Kolintchin Island, 6 P.M., June 2, 1881," SFDEB, July 13, 1881, p. 1, cols. 3–4; "An Anchor. Weathering a Gale in St. Laurence Bay—Social Intercourse with the Natives—An Esquimo Orator—A Great Reindeer Owner—Native Appetite for Strong Drink—Glacier Markings. Steamer Corwin, St. Laurence Bay, Siberia, June 6, 1881," SFDEB, July 13, 1881, p. 1, cols. 4–5; "Dodging The Ice. The Corwin Hard Pressed—Crowded by the Drifted Pack on a Lee Shore—An Esquimo Baby—Repairing the Damages to the Ship—The Wreck of the Schooner—Loleta—Plover Bay. Steamer Corwin, Plover Bay, June 15, 1881," SFDEB, July 13, 1881, p. 1, col. 5; "The Aleutian Islands. Geological Notes of the Group—Glaciers and Volcanoes. Fauna and Flora of the Group—Agricultural Notes—The Inhabitants. (Special Correspondence of the Bulletin.)...(By the Alaska Commercial Company's steamer Dora...the following delayed letter...came to hand:) Ounalaska, May 21, 1881," SFDEB, July 25, 1881, p. 1, col. 3; "Near Cape Serdze. Rejoined by the Land Party—Confirmation of the Discovery of Wreck of the Vigilant—List of Relics Recovered. Steamer Corwin (Off the Tchuchi Village of Tapikan, near Cape Serdze, Siberia), June 29, 1881," SFDEB, August 15, 1881, p. 3, col. 7; "St. Laurence Island. Arctic Volcanoes—A Land of Lava and Craters—A Ghastly Scene in an Arctic Golgotha—The Work of a Famine. Steamer Corwin, St. Laurence Island, Alaska, July 3, 1881," SFDEB, August 15, 1881, p. 3, cols. 7–8; "Return to St. Michael's. Preparing for Another Cruise—The Busy Season at St. Michael's—San Francisco Prospectors Heard From—Fauna and Flora—Volcanic Cones. St. Michael's, Alaska, July 8, 1881," SFDEB, August 15, 1881, p. 3, col. 8; "At St. Michael's. An Arctic Summer Scene—Description of the Trading Post—Yukon River Indian Trappers—Outfitting the Corwin. St. Michael's Alaska, June 20, 1881," SFDEB, August 16, 1881, p. 1, col. 1; "At Metchigme Bay. Glacier Work at Plover Bay—A Crazy Native—His Idiosyncracies and Attempted Suicide. Steamer Corwin. Near the Mouth of Metchigme Bay, On the west side of Behring Strait, June 27, 1881," SFDEB, August 16, 1881, p. 1, cols. 1–2; "At East Cape. Ashore—A Siberian Village—The Arctic Hunter's Luxurious Home— Arctic Cemeteries—Botanizing on the Siberian Shore—Tracing the Ice Floods. Steamer Corwin, East Cape, Siberia, July 1, 1881," SFDEB, August 16, 1881,

p. 1, col. 2; "The Jeanette Search. Exploration of Herald Island—No Signs of the Missing Ship. Dangers of Arctic Exploration—Fauna and Flora of the North. (Special Correspondence of the Bulletin.) Steamer Corwin (Off Herald Island), Arctic Ocean, July 31, 1881," SFDEB, September 28, 1881, p. 4, col. 3; "Wrangel Island, Conflict with the Ice—A Struggle to Reach Shore. The Corwin in an Arctic River—Acquisition to the National Domain. Steamer Corwin, Off Point Barrow, August 16, 1881," SFDEB, September 29, 1881, p. 1, col. 3; "On Wrangel Island. Wreckage Found on the Beach—Condition of the Soil. Improbability of Any Landing Having Been Made by Captain De Long. Difficulties Which Beset the Corwin—Narrow Escape from the Ice. (Special Correspondent of the Bulletin.) . . . Steamer Corwin, Off Point Barrow, Alaska, August 17, 1881," SFDEB, October 22, 1881, p. 4. col. 3; "Perils of Whaling. The Corwin Among the Whaling Fleet Off Point Barrow. Destruction of Whaling Ships by Ice—Esquimaux Wreckers. (Special Correspondence of the Bulletin.) Steamer Corwin, off Point Barrow, August 18, 1881," SFDEB, October 24, 1881, p. 3, cols. 7–8; "Out Of The Arctic. The Most Northerly Coal Mine in the World. The Corwin in a Gale—Effects of the Northern Current. The Diomedes—Dangers to Navigation in Behring [sic] Strait. The Point Barrow Signal Service Expedition—What It Expects to Do. (Special Correspondence of the Bulletin). Steamer Corwin (Plover Bay, Siberia), August 25, 1881," SFDEB, October 25, 1881, p. 1, cols. 1–2; "In Plover Bay. Reindeer Farming on the Arctic Shores of Siberia. Graphic Description of Reindeer Farmers and their Flocks. Glacier Groovings—Desolate Appearance of the Land. (Special Correspondence of the Bulletin.) Steamer Corwin, Plover Bay, Siberia, August 26, 1881," SFDEB, October 26, 1881, p. 1, cols. 1–2; "An Ice-Bound Shore. Cruising along the Edge of 'the Pack'—Off Wrangel Land. 'Hove to' in an Arctic Gale—The Corwin's Misadventures. Aboriginal Merchant Middlemen of Two Continents. (Special Correspondence of the Bulletin.) Steamer Corwin, Arctic Ocean, Between Herald Shoals and Point Hope, September 3, 1881," SFDEB, October 27, 1881, p. 3, col. 6; "Homeward Bound. End of the Corwin's Cruise in the Arctic Ocean. Elephant Point—A Fossil Glacier and its Exuberant Vegetation. Shipwrecked Prospectors—An Alaskan Silver Mine and Oonalaska Scenery. (Special Correspondent of the Bulletin.) Steamer Corwin, Oonalaska, October 4, 1881," SFDEB, October 31, 1881, p. 1, col. 1.

15. Jeanne C. Carr, "Partial List of Ornamental Trees and Shrubs at Carmelita," 1883, JCCP, CA 189; Charles Francis Saunders, *The Story of Carmelita: Its Associations and Its Trees* (Pasadena: A. C. Vroman, 1918), 21–54. Jeanne C. Carr to Dr. and Mrs. Louisiana E. Strentzel, February 1, 1883, JMP, B4:02472. William A. Spalding, *The Orange: Its Culture in California with a Brief Discussion of the Lemon, Lime, and Other Citrus Fruits* (Riverside: Press and Horticulturist Steam Print, 1885), 3.

16. Jeanne C. Carr, "Woman and Land," *Pasadena & Valley Union*, February 23, 1884. Jackson, "One Woman and Sunshine," 15. Jeanne C. Carr, "Throop University, Pasadena," *The Californian* 2 (September 1892): 565–78.

17. The Carrs sold the three-acre lot to Isaac Banta, who built the Los Angeles House Hotel on the corner of Fair Oaks Avenue and Colorado Street.

See J. W. Wood, *Pasadena, California Historical and Personal: A Complete History of the Organization of the Indiana Colony* (J. W. Wood, 1917), 141, 258. A. L. Carr, "The Trail of Yesterday," n.d., 105–15, Jeanne C. Carr Papers, Pasadena Historical Society. Jeanne C. Carr, "Pasadena. The Crown of the Valley del Rio de San Gabriel," *Los Angeles Daily Times*, September 16, 1885.

18. An undated letter from Daniel Muir to his son John Muir tells of the Christian orthodoxy of Daniel Muir's faith and of the relationship he shared with John. Writing while recovering from a seven-week bout with diarrhea and gnawing abdominal pain, Daniel Muir wrote that he had cast all his burden upon God forever. He believed the Lord, three in One, to whom all glory was given forever, was doing great things for him. God's grace was sufficient for him and he found perfect happiness in God, whose love was shed abroad in his heart, God who was unto him wisdom, righteousness, sanctification, and redemption. Daniel told John that he loved him with a love above parental or human, prayed for him in the Holy Spirit, and sent God's blessings upon him. Daniel Muir, to John Muir, n.d., JMP, Series 5A.

19. John Muir, ed., *Picturesque California and the Region West of the Rocky Moutains, from Alaska to Mexico* (San Francisco: The J. Dewing Co., 1888); Jeanne C. Carr, "The Heart of Southern California," in *Picturesque California*, 161–92.

20. Muir and Keith climbed Mount Rainier with E. S. Ingraham, superintendent of schools in Seattle; David Waldo Bass, an attorney; Charles V. Piper, a botanist; A. C. Warner, a photographer; N. O. Booth, a young nature enthusiast; and Henry Loomis, unidentified. They were guided by the local postmaster, Philemon Beecher Van Trump. Linnie Marsh Wolfe, *Son of the Wilderness: The Life of John Muir* (New York: Alfred A. Knopf, 1945; reprint, Madison: University of Wisconsin Press, 1978), 239. UJJM, 295.

21. Louie Strentzel Muir, to John Muir, August 9, 1888, JMP, A5:03138.

22. Carr's understanding of irrigation and forest planning may be attributed to Theodore Parker Lukens, a friend and resident of Pasadena. Though the following articles postdate Carr, see Theodore P. Lukens's articles on forests, irrigation, and agriculture, "Why Forests Are Needed: They Would Hold Back Half the Rain and Prevent Disastrous Floods," *Water and Forest* 1 (1902): 13; "The Relation of Forestry to Agriculture," *Pacific Rural Press,* October 4, 1902; "Effects of Forests on Water Supply," *Forestry and Irrigation* 10 (1904): 465–69. See Shirley Sargent, *Theodore Parker Lukens: Father of Forestry* (Los Angeles: Dawson Book Shop, 1969), 54–87.

23. See Robert Underwood Johnson, *Remembered Yesterdays* (Boston: Little, Brown, & Co., 1923), 287–88.

24. John Muir, "Yosemite Valley. Beauties of the Landscape in Early Summer. Late Changes in the Valley—Lack of Plan a Serious Impediment to Improvement—John Muir's Views. Yosemite Valley, June 21, 1889," SFDEB, June 27, 1889, p. 1, cols. 5–6; "Forests of the Sierra. The Destruction that is Being Wrought in the Mountains. John Muir's Protest against the Wantonness of the Sheep-Herder and Lumberman—Value of the Forests," SFDEB, June 29, 1889, p. 1, col. 6; John Muir, "The Treasures of the Yosemite," *The Century Magazine* 40 (August 1890): 483–500; "Features of the Proposed

Yosemite National Park," *The Century Magazine* 40 (September 1890): 656–67. UJJM, 299–300.

25. John Muir, "As it Appears to John Muir," *Oakland Daily Evening Tribune,* September 6, 1890, p. 4, col. 1; John P. Irish, "Muir and Yosemite. John P. Irish has something to say in reply," *Oakland Daily Evening Tribune,* September 8, 1890; John Muir, "John Muir in Yosemite. He Never Cut Down a Single Tree in the Valley. Twenty Years Ago He Was Employed by Mr. Hutchings to Saw Lumber From Fallen Timber," *Oakland Daily Evening Tribune,* September 16, 1890, p. 5, col. 5. See Jeanne C. Carr, to Mrs. Mary L. Swett, c. 1893, The Irving Stone Papers, BANC MSS 95/205 cz, The Bancroft Library, University of California, Berkeley.

26. Jeanne C. Carr, "Pasadena Homes: A Summary of the Year's Progress," *Daily Commercial,* September 7, 1881.

27. UJJM, 322–23. Jeanne C. Carr, "John Muir," *The Californian* 2 (September 1892): 565–78.

28. "New Buildings. A List of Those Erected Here during 1892," *Pasadena Daily Evening Star,* January 28, 1883.

29. John Muir, *The Mountains of California* (New York: The Century Co., 1894). John Muir, *Letters to a Friend: Written to Mrs. Ezra Carr, 1866–1879* (Boston: Houghton Mifflin, 1915; reprint, Dunwoody, Georgia: Norman Berg, 1973).

30. UJJM, 334–37. John Muir, "The Discovery of Glacier Bay," *The Century Magazine* 50 (June 1895): 234–47.

31. UJJM, 354–55.

32. Jeanne C. Carr, to Elizabeth Mills, September 8, 1896, JCCP, CA63; John Muir, Martinez, to Joseph C. Pickard, after February 15, 1901, JMP, A11:06848.

33. John Muir, "National Parks and Forest Reservations," *Harper's Weekly* 41 (June 5, 1897): 563–67; John Muir, "The American Forests," *The Atlantic Monthly* 80 (August 1897): 145–57.

34. "Wild Parks and Forest Reservations of the West," *The Atlantic Monthly* 81 (January 1898): 15–28.

35. UJJM, 384–85, 421. For a discussion of John Muir and John Burroughs see Wolfe, *Son of the Wilderness,* 280–87. See Muir's tribute to Burroughs's experience on the Bering Sea, John Muir, "The True Story of J. B. and Behring [sic] Sea," UJJM, 422–26. See John Muir, *Travels in Alaska* (Boston: Houghton Mifflin Co., 1915).

36. John Muir, "Hunting Big Redwoods," *The Atlantic Monthly* 88 (September 1901): 304–20. John Muir, *Our National Parks* (Boston: Houghton Mifflin and Co., 1901).

37. See John Muir, "The Tuolumne Yosemite In Danger," *The Outlook* 87 (November 2, 1907): 486–89; John Muir, "The Hetch-Hetchy Valley," *Sierra Club Bulletin* 6 (January 1908): 211–20; Stephen Fox, *John Muir and His Legacy: The American Conservation Movement* (Boston: Little, Brown and Co., 1981), 139–47.

38. Jeanne C. Carr's obituary appeared in the *San Luis Obispo Semi-Weekly Breeze,* December 22, 1903, p. 8, col. 4. Saunders, *The Story of*

Carmelita, 15. For Carr's reminiscence of James Hope's portrait of her, see Jeanne C. Carr, Oakland, to John Muir, February 3, 1872, JMP, A2:01237.

39. *Letters,* 182–83.

40. *Letters,* 180–82.

41. *Letters,* 183–85.

42. *Letters,* 185–87. See Orville H. Congar and Jeanne C. Carr correspondence, November 27, 1876–February 17, 1877, Jeanne C. Carr Papers, Pasadena Historical Museum. See Harold D. Carew, *History of Pasadena and the San Gabriel Valley, California,* vol. 1 (Chicago: S. J. Clarke Publishing Co., 1930), 428. Descriptions of Carmelita may be found in Jackson, "One Woman and Sunshine," Helen Hunt Jackson Papers, Huntington Library; "Beautiful Carmelita," *Pasadena Star,* July 1, 1886, JCCP, Scrapbook I, 84; "Carmelita (Little Garden)," n.d., Jeanne C. Carr Papers, Pasadena Historical Museum; A. L. Carr, "Genesis and Development of Carmelita," Jeanne C. Carr Papers, Pasadena Historical Museum; A. L. Carr, "The Trail of Yesterday," Jeanne C. Carr Papers, Pasadena Historical Museum; Saunders, *The Story of Carmelita. Its Associations and Its Trees.*

43. *Letters,* 187–89. Muir sent several letters to the SFDEB where they were published as "Semi-Tropical California. John Muir Describes the Sun Valley of San Gabriel. Some Facts about Orange Culture—A Fruit Land—A California Colony—Hints to Invalids. (Special Correspondence of the Bulletin.) San Gabriel Valley, September 1, 1877," SFDEB, September 7, 1877, p. 1; reprint, Muir, *Steep Trails. California, Utah, Nevada, Washington, Oregon, The Grand Cañon* (Boston: Houghton Mifflin, 1918), 136–44; and "In the San Gabriel. An Excursion by John Muir—Hot Weather and Plenty of Chaparral—A Glorious View—Rattlesnakes and Bear Tracks. (Special Correspondence of the Bulletin.)," SFDEB, September 11, 1877, p. 1; reprint, *Steep Trails,* 145–53.

44. *Letters,* 189–90.

45. JMP, A3:01849.

46. *Letters,* 190–93. Muir referred to George Gordon, *The Pinetum: Being A Synopsis Of All The Coniferous Plants At Present Known, With Descriptions, History and Synonyms, And A Comprehensive Systematic Index,* 2d ed. (London: Henry G. Bohn, 1875). The Rexford "citrus book" to which Muir referred could not be located. Muir's reference to the "orange book" may be to a book on citrus or may be to a book on trees published by the Orange Judd Company of New York who began publication in the early 1850s. Eben Eugene Rexford (1848–1916) may be the Rexford to whom Muir referred. Rexford published books on home floriculture, ornamental plants, and vegetable and small fruit growing for amateur gardeners from the 1890s until 1909. Though these dates postdate 1879, he may have published a book on citrus culture prior to 1879. In 1890 the Orange Judd Company published Eben Eugene Rexford's *Home Floriculture: A Practical Guide to the Treatment of Flowering and Other Ornamental Plants in the House and Garden.* None of the chapters include a discussion of oranges. The articles written by Muir that appeared in *Scribner's* between April 1879 and October 1881 included "In The Heart of the California Alps," *Scribner's Monthly* 20

(July 1880): 345–52; reprint, Muir, *The Mountains of California* (New York: The Century Co., 1894), 48–73; "Coniferous Forests of the Sierra Nevada. I," *Scribner's Monthly* 2 (September 1881): 710–23; reprint, *The Mountains of California*, 139–72; and "Coniferous Forests of the Sierra Nevada. II," *Scribner's Monthly* 22 (October 1881): 921–31; reprint, *The Mountains of California*, 172–79, 200–25. The essays written by Muir prior to April 9, 1879, were published as follows: "Great Evils from Destruction of Forests," *San Francisco Real Estate Circular*, vol. 14, No. 6, April 1879, 2; "Bee-Pastures of California: In Two Parts:—I.," *The Century Magazine* (June 1882): 222–29; and "Bee-Pastures of California In Two Parts:—II.," *The Century Magazine* (July 1882): 388–96.

47. *Letters*, 53.

48. *Letters*, 193–94.

49. JMP, B4:02054.

50. JMP, A4:02057.

51. JMP, A5:03010. See William Cullen Bryant, *Picturesque America; or, The Land We Live In. A delineation by pen and pencil of the mountains, rivers, lakes, forests, waterfalls, shores, canyons, valleys, cities, and other picturesque features of our country. With illustrations on steel and wood, by eminent American artists*, 2 vols., 2d ed. (New York: D. Appleton, 1872). See Jeanne C. Carr, "The Heart of Southern California," in *Picturesque California and the Region West of the Rocky Mountains, from Alaska to Mexico*, ed. John Muir (San Francisco: J. Dewing Co. in 1888).

52. JMP, A5:03035.

53. John Muir, Martinez, to Jeanne C. Carr, January 30, 1888, JCCP, CA146.

54. JMP, A6:03229.

55. JMP, A6:03304.

56. JMP, B7:03847. Jeanne C. Carr's article "John Muir" provides the only evidence Muir sent Carr a description of his experience in Bonaventure Cemetery during or immediately following his stay there. See John Muir to Jeanne C. Carr, September-October, 1867, in Jeanne C. Carr, "John Muir," *The Californian* (June 1892): 92. Parkhurst referred to Ezra Slocum Carr's book *The University of California and its relation to industrial education as shown by Prof. Carr's reply to the grangers and mechanics* (San Francisco: B. Dore and Co., 1874) or to *The Patrons of Husbandry On The Pacific Coast* (San Francisco: A. L. Bancroft and Co., 1875).

57. JMP, A8:04647. Muir sent Carr a copy of his first book, *The Mountains of California* (New York: The Century Co., 1894).

58. JMP, A6:03621. Ezra Slocum Carr died on November 27, 1894. Jeanne Carr's comment about "the saddest of years" referred to Ezra's death that year. See Galen Clark's December 3, 1894, letter to Jeanne C. Carr in which he consoled Carr and noted Muir should have dedicated "his book" [*The Mountains of California*] to her, "as no one person has given to to [*sic*] him the great encouragement and assistance which you have." Galen Clark, Yosemite Valley, to Jeanne C. Carr, December 3, 1894, JMP B8:04683.

59. JMP, A8:04719.

60. JMP, A8:04759.

61. JMP, A8:05072.

62. JMP, A8:05047.

63. JMP A9:05548. Lukens referred to Muir's article "The National Parks and Forest Reservations," *Harper's Weekly* 41 (June 5, 1897): 563–67.

64. John Muir, Martinez, to Theodore P. Lukens, November 13, 1901, Huntington Library, Lukens Collection, Box 2. Muir referred to his "new book," *Our National Parks* (Boston and New York: Houghton Mifflin and Co., 1901).

65. John Muir, Martinez, to Theodore P. Lukens, December 18, 1901, Huntington Library, Lukens Collection, Box 2.

66. JMP, A13:07830.

EPILOGUE

1. John Muir, *A Thousand-Mile Walk to the Gulf* (Boston: Houghton Mifflin Co., 1916); reprint, *"A Thousand-Mile Walk to the Gulf,"* in *John Muir: The Eight Wilderness Discovery Books,* with an introduction by Terry Gifford (London: Diadem Books, 1992).

2. John Muir, *My First Summer in the Sierra* (Boston and New York: Houghton Mifflin Co., 1911), 110.

LIST OF MISSING LETTERS

1. Jeanne C. Carr, Scrapbook, n.d., JMP, Series 7B; John Muir, List, 1909, JMP, A22:13084; William Frederic Badè, c. 1920s, List, JMP, A22: 13086.

GLOSSARY OF
BOTANICALS IN LETTERS

Abies amabilis (*Picea amabilis*) (Pacific Silver Fir) (Pinaceae: Pine Family), evergreen tree, ashy gray bark, seed cones 6 inches in length, subalpine forests, Siskiyou County to British Columbia.

Abies concolor (Silver Fir, White Fir, Balsam Fir) (Pinaceae: Pine Family), evergreen tree, 140–60 feet tall, covered to ground with branches arranged loosely in tiers, ashy bark, scraggly needles, green with bluish cast, flat and bluntly pointed, seed cones 3¼–4½ inches in length, barrel-shaped, yellow-green to olive green and brown, stand upright on branches, on topmost part of crown, cool climate, tolerant to shade, north-facing slopes, pure stands, mixed forests, southern Cascades and Siskiyous.

Abies grandis (*Picea grandis*) (Grand Fir) (Pinaceae: Pine Family), evergreen tree, 75–200 feet tall, thick and furrowed brownish bark, needles dark green above, whitish beneath, redwood, Douglas-fir, mixed-evergreen forests, coastal mountains, northern California to British Columbia.

Abies williamsonii = *Tsuga mertensiana* (Western Hemlock, Mountain Hemlock) (Pinaceae: Pine Family), evergreen tree, 70–100 feet tall, slightly tapered trunk, pendant slender branches with drooping frond-like branches, dark, cinnamon-scaled bark, shaded with blue or purple, blunt light bluish-green or pale blue needles, thin delicate scaled cones, bright bluish purple, occasionally pale yellow-green, ⅜–3 inches long, to 10,000 feet elevation, exposed ridges and slopes at high altitudes, along the High Sierra to the canyon of the south fork of King's River.

Adiantum (Maidenhair fern) (Adiantaceae: Maidenhair Family), fern, 10–18 inches high, black stalks, moist woods, shaded hillsides along rivers and streams. Var. (*A. pedatum; A. capillus-veneris; A. tenerum; A. emarginatum*).

Agave americana (American Aloe, Century Plant) (Agavaceae: Agave Family), plant, stalk 20–40 feet tall.

Agrostis scabra (Hairgrass) (Gramineae: Grass Family), grass, purplish, 1–3 feet tall, moist mountain meadows, fields, open woods, 3,500–10,000 feet elevation.

Alder (Mountain Alder) (*Alnus tenuifolia*) (Betulaceae: Birch Family), tree, height to 30 feet, wet areas, to 10,000 feet elevation. Var. (*A. rhombifolia,* White Alder), egg-shaped 2–5 inch long leaves, light gray trunk, broad whitish markings, height to 80 feet, stream banks, to 8,000 feet elevation; (*A. rubra,* Red Alder), coarsely toothed leaves, gray-white patchy bark, blooms January–March, along streams, coastal range, Santa Cruz County to Alaska.

Alpine Aster (*Asteralpigenus*) (Compositae: Sunflower Family), wildflower, pink-to-purple ray flowers and contrasting yellow disk flowers, blossoms atop 2–16 inch stem, prostrate, inflorescence rises as plant matures, leaves grass-like, mountain meadows, 6,000–10,000 feet elevation, June–September.

Amaranth (*Amaranthus*) (Amaranthaceae: Amaranth Family), wildflower, green flowers in bristly spikes, egg- or lance-shaped leaves, 1–6 feet high, garden and waste place weed, late summer and fall.

Anemone nemorosa (Windflower) (Ranunculaceae: Buttercup Family), wildflower, summer- and autumn-flowering perennial, white, blue, red, greenish flowers.

Anemone nuttalliana (*A. patens*) (Pasqueflower) (Ranunculaceae: Buttercup Family), wildflower, blue, purple, white flowers, silky-hairy stem, 3–6 inches high, dry prairie, April–June.

Apple (*Pyrus*) (Rosaceae: Rose Family), small to medium tree, shrub, some thorny, simple evenly serrated leaves, flowers in clusters, blooms in spring. Var. (*Pyrus malus,* Domestic Apple), small tree, 20–30 feet tall, brownish scaly bark, white or pinkish flowers, April–June, fruit appears in September–November, hedgerows, along fences, and old farms.

Aquilegia (Columbine: "dovelike") (Ranunculaceae: Buttercup Family), wildflower, large nodding red, yellow, blue, or white flowers, deeply lobed leaflets, spring and early summer. Var. (*Aquilegia formosa:* "beautiful eagle," Crimson Columbine), red flowers, exclusively pollinated by Hawk Moth, pendulous blossoms from 24–48 inch stem, moist ground, coniferous forests up to 10,500 feet elevation, along seeps and mountain streams, Nevada Fall trail, under seeping rock walls near end of trail, April–June; (*A. pubescens,* Coville's Columbine), white flowers, contrasting yellow stamens protrude as in *A. formosa,* blossoms 1½ inches across, creamy-white, pink, yellow, or lavender, rock crevices above timberline, June–August.

Arborvitae (*Thuja*) (Cupressaceae: Cypress Family), evergreen tree or shrub, stout erect or horizontal branches, moist or wet soil, swamps.

Arethusa (*A. bulbosa*) (Dragon's Mouth, Swamp Pink) (Orchidaceae: Orchid Family), orchid, magenta-pink solitary flower (June–July), 1–2 inches long, single slender grass-like leaf (appears after flower has withered), *Sphagnum* bogs.

Ash (*Fraxinus*) (Oleaceae: Olive Family), deciduous tree. Var. (*Fraxinus dipetala,* Flowering Ash, Two-Petal Ash), small tree, shrub, 6–20 feet tall, dry foothills, chaparral, below 3,500 feet elevation, Sierra Nevada foothills, Shasta County south; (*F. latifolia,* Oregon Ash), 80 feet tall, 4 feet diameter, flood plains, canyons, near streams, below 5,500 feet elevation, western Sierra Nevada, north Kern County to Modoc County.

Aspen (*Populus*) (Salicaceae: Willow Family), slender deciduous tree, 20–40 feet tall, soft pale furrowed bark, whitish wood, stream borders, damp slopes, 6,000–10,000 feet elevation. Var. (*P. tremuloides,* Quaking Aspen), 75 feet tall, invader of open spaces, 6,000–10,000 feet elevation, golden in autumn.

Aspidium aculeatum = Polystichum braunii (Braun's Holly Fern, Prickly Shield Fern) (Dryopteridaceae: Fern Family), fern, chaffy stalks, 1–2 feet high, deep rocky woods, Green Mountains and Smuggler's Notch, Mount Mansfield, Vermont (1807).

Aspidium fragrans = Dryopteris fragrans (Shield Fern, Wood Fern) (Dryopteridaceae: Fern Family), fern, fronds 4–12 inches, cold climate, cliff crevices, mossy rocks.

Aspidium lonchitis = Polystichum (Mountain Holly Fern) (Dryopteridaceae: Fern Family), fern, ½–1 foot high, cool shaded rocks and hillsides, mostly on limestone.

Aspidium marginale = Dryopteris marginalis (Evergreen Wood Fern) (Dryopteridaceae: Fern Family), fern, several inches to 3 feet high, chaffy stalks, shiny scales, blue-green fronds, bare rocks, moist clammy swamps, under trees and grapevines, flourishes throughout winter; likeness to Crested Shield Fern.

Aspidium spinulosum = Dryopteris carthusiana (Spinulose Wood Fern) (Aspleniaceae: Spleenwort Family), fern, common European type, rare in North America, 1–2½ feet high, few pale-brown scales on stalks, tops of mountains. Var. (*Dryopteris intermedia*), wood fern, large, chaffy stalks, brown dark-centered scales, rich green outward curving fronds, fallen trees, decaying stumps.

Asplenium acrostichoides = Polystichum acrostichoides (Christmas Fern) (Aspleniaceae: Spleenwort Family), evergreen fern, 1–3 feet high, dull green, large patches, rich woods, near water, boggy ground or edge of clear brook, not common.

Beech (*Fagus*) (Fagaceae: Oak Family), early deciduous forest tree, 60–80 feet tall, smooth light bark, strongly veined, taper-pointed toothed leaves, triangular nut, rich bottomland, upland soils. Var. (*Fagus ferruginea, American Beech*).

Birch (*Betula*) (Betulaceae: Birch Family), tree, spicy-aromatic twigs, brown or yellow-gray bark, sessile scaly buds, flowers in early spring along with leaves.

Boraginaceae (Borage Family), herb, shrub, tree, usually rough-hairy (Heliotrope, Comfrey, Blueweed, Forget-Me-Not, Bugloss, Stickseed, Lungwort).

Botrychium lunarioides (Assume: *B. lunaria*) (Moonwort) (Ophioglossaceae: Adder's Tongue Family), fern, 3–12 inches high, dry pastures, open fields and meadows, June–August.

Bracken Fern (*Pteridium aquilinum*) (Dennstaedtiaceae: Bracken Family), fern, 1–4 feet high, occasionally higher, most widely distributed fern, dry, open woods, sunny hillsides, moist sheltered valleys.

Briar Rose (*Rosa Eglanteria, R. rubiginosa*) (Sweet Briar) (Rosaceae: Rose Family), shrub, pink to whitish flowers, pastures, waste places, May–July.

Bryanthus (Mountain Heather) (Ericaceae: Heath Family), much-branched, low evergreen shrub, heathlike, rose-purple to pinkish flowers, rocky, moist ground, 6,000–12,000 feet elevation, Sierra Nevada from Tulare County to Mount Lassen, July–August. (See Sierra Heather.)

Buckeye (*Aesculus*) (Hippocastanaceae: Horse-chestnut Family), deciduous tree, 30 feet tall, leaves 4–8 inches long, 5–7 fine toothed leaflets, white to rose-colored flowers in large clusters 4–8 inches long, blooms in May–June, fruit in thick pear-shaped three-parted husk without prickles, 1–3 large shiny brown poisonous nuts, ripening and falling in October, canyons and foothills to 4,000 feet elevation, coastal ranges and Sierra. Var. (*Aesculus californica*, Californica Buckeye), borders of streams, 2,000–3,000 feet elevation, valley of the south fork of the Salmon River, Siskiyou County, coastal range to San Luis Obispo County, western slope of Sierra.

Calami (Assume: *Calamintha*) (Labiatae: Mint Family). Var. (*Calamintha grandiflora*), small to medium plant, large pink flowers in cluster, rocky places, open woodland, embankments, shaded habitats, Spain eastward to Turkey; (*C. nepeta*, Lesser Calamint), medium to tall, white, pale lilac flowers, dry, hedgerows, fallow fields, waste places, Spain-Turkey; (*C. incana*), smaller pink flowers, Greece; (*C. clinopodium*, Wild Basil), pinkish-purple flowers, dry grassy stony habitats, roadsides, embankments, northern Africa.

California Hazel (*Corylus cornuta, C. californica*) (Betulaceae: Birch Family), common California shrub, small tree, 3–10 feet high, egg-shaped leaves, 2–4 inches across, flowers in early spring, edible nuts appear in autumn, shaded areas, wooded slopes, near streams and creeks, coastal ranges. Var. (*Corylus maxima*, Giant Filbert).

Calla (*Richardia*) (Araceae: Arum Family). Var. (*Richardia africana*, Calla Lily), plant, common house culture, native of Cape of Good Hope, glossy-green leaves, large white singular flowers; (*R. albo-maculata*, Spotted Calla), leaves with oblong white blotches, greenish-white flowers; (*R. hastata*, Yellow Calla), greenish-yellow flowers.

Calopogon (*C. pulchellus*: "beautiful beard") (Swamp Pink) (Orchidaceae: Orchid Family), orchid, 3–15 magenta-pink flowers at summit of stalk, 8–12 inches high, white beard, yellow and crimson tips (flowers late spring through summer), bulb-like tuber produces single elongated grass-like leaf, *Sphagnum* bogs, peaty meadows, eastern United States, Canada, common.

Calypso borealis (Fairy Slipper) (Orchidaceae: Orchid Family), orchid, single flower, one inch long, scoop-shaped lip crested with yellow hairs, marked with purple (variegated purple, pink, and yellow), resembles Lady's Slipper, single egg-shaped leaf, cold bogs, wet woods, bulbs resting in moss, northern New England to Michigan and northward, spring. Var. (*Calypso bulbosa*), mid-spring pink flower atop slender 4–6 inch long stem, northern west coast, common in Humboldt and Del Norte counties.

Camptosorus rhizophyllus = Asplenium rhizophyllum (Walking Fern, Walking Leaf) (Aspleniaceae: Spleenwort Family), fern, 4–18 inches high, light-green stalks, long simple fronds tapering toward the apex often rooting and forming a new plant, prefers limestone rocks, found on sandstone, shale, conglomerate, decaying trees, uncommon.

Carex novae-angliae (New England Sedge) (Cyperaceae: Sedge Family), grass, greenish-purple, husk-like flowers, moist open woods.

Carex panicea (Cyperaceae: Sedge Family), grass, rush-like, loosely husked flowers, moist ground, open woods.

Carpetweed (*Mollugo verticillata*) (Molluginaceae: Carpetweed Family), wildflower, prostrate plant, long-stalked white flowers, leaves ½–1 inch long, garden, waste-place weed, June–September.

Cassiope (*Cassiope mertensiana*) = *Harrimanella* (Sierra Heather, White Heather) (Ericaceae: Heath Family), wildflower, small Alpine moss-like creeping heather, matted evergreen shrub, fir-like needle foliage, small bell-shaped nodding white flowers, red sepals attached to base, singly on ends of 4–14 inch long branches, clings to moist rocky outcroppings at or above timberline, Sierra Nevada, Fresno County north, coastal ranges, Trinity County to Siskiyou County, above Vogelsang High Sierra Camp, July–August.

Cherry Rose (Assume: Bitter Cherry) (*Prunus emarginata*) (Rosaceae: Rose Family), shrub, small tree, deciduous, 3–10 feet tall, spreading crooked branches, dark green oblong leaves, white flowers in round-topped clusters (April–May), bright red cherries (late summer), below 9,000 feet elevation, rocky slopes, ravines, dry woods, coniferous forests, along roadsides entering Sierra national forests and parks.

Chiogenes hispidula = *Gaultheria hispidula* (Creeping Snowberry) (Ericaceae: Heath Family), evergreen creeping plant, leaves 3–4 inches long, bright white berries, aromatic flavor of Birch, peat-bogs, mossy mountain woods, evergreen shade, common northward.

Citrus sinensis (Sweet Orange) (Rutaceae: Rue Family), round-topped tree, oblong-ovate leaves, 2–4½ inches long, light green to olive green or dark green, white flowers, fruit, oval to flattened or subglobose, thin and tight peel, sweet pulp, 10–13 segments, cultivated in Texas, California, and Florida, considered to be native of southeastern Asia.

Climacium americanum (Tree Moss) (Bryaceae: Bryum Family), moss, erect scaly stem, tree-like, trunk and spreading leafy branches, common in shady woods, damp places, decayed logs, roots of trees, east of Rocky Mountains; closely allied to C. *dendroides*.

Coast Hemlock (*Tsuga heterophylla*) (Pinaceae: Pine Family), evergreen tree, 100–200 feet tall, deeply furrowed brown bark, "Octopus Tree," long roots entwine over fallen logs, needle-like leaves on drooping branches, dark green above, whitish beneath, solitary cylindrical cones, ½ to 1 inch long, hang from ends of branchlets, northwestern California to Alaska.

Compositae = Asteraceae, largest family of flowering plants, 20,000 species, many blossoms, individual flowers very small and clustered (cluster mistaken for single flower in the daisy, aster, or sunflower), green, yellowish, or yellow flowers.

Cypripedium arietinum (Ram's-head Lady's Slipper) (Orchidaceae: Orchid Family), orchid, single flower, ½–¾ inch long, drooping inflated hollow purplish pouch, veined with crimson on outside, tapers to point, broad veined leaves, 6–15 inches high, cold woods, bogs, late spring, Maine to Minnesota, rare.

Cystopteris bulbifera (Bulblet Bladder Fern) (Aspleniaceae: Spleenwort Family), fern, 1–3 feet high, light-colored, brittle stalks, vine-like, slender, feathery fronds, wet rocks, prefers limestone, falling water, clinging to rocks wet with spray.

Dicranum (Feather Mosses) (Dicranaceae: Feather Moss Family).

Dielytra = *Dicentra eximia* (Bleeding Heart) (Fumariaceae: Fumitory Family), woodland wildflower, 1–2 feet high, dangling white or pink heart-shaped flowers, ½–¾ inch long, rich woods, shaded ledges, spring–fall.

Dodecatheon meadia (American Cowslip, Shooting Star) (Primulaceae: Primrose Family), wildflower, stalk 6–12 inches high, pink, lilac, or white flowers in an umbel, flower lobes bent backwards, open rich woods, meadows, river banks, April–June.

Dogwood (Cornaceae, Dogwood Family). Var. (*Cornus stolonifera,* Creek Dogwood, Red Osier), shrub, 9–15 feet tall, red branches, small white four-petaled bracts in cluster on branch tip, red leaves (fall), lakeshores, stream banks, northern Sierra, June–July; (*C. nuttallii,* Pacific Dogwood), 100 feet tall, creamy-white bracts, 2–3 inches long, button-like center cluster of tiny green flowers, red-orange fruit/crimson leaves (fall), under 6,000 feet elevation; (*C. glabrata,* Smooth Dogwood, Brown Dogwood), small tree, 20 feet tall, white bracts, thickets below 5,000 feet elevation, more frequent in coastal ranges; (*C. sessilis,* Blackfruit Dogwood), northern Sierra.

Douglas Fir (*Pseudotsuga menziesii*) (Pinaceae: Pine Family), pine tree, dark gray bark, light green needles, drooping stems, 3–4 inch long cones, common in redwood forest, second in size only to coastal redwoods.

Dwarf Oak (*Quercus humilis*) (Fagaceae: Oak Family), shrub, 2–4 feet high, small acorns, poor soil, sandy barrens.

Elm (*Ulmus*) (Ulmaceae: Elm Family), tree, 16–45 feet tall, moist, fertile soil, upland woods. Var. (*U. americana,* White or American Elm; *U. rubra,* Slippery or Red Elm; *U. thomasii,* Rock Elm; *U. alata,* Winged Elm; *U. serotina,* September Elm).

Erigenia (*E. bulbosa*) (Pepper and Salt) (Umbelliferae: Parsley Family), wildflower, 6 inches high, small white flowers, purple stamens, rich woods, harbinger of spring, March–April.

Eriogonum (Polygonaceae: Buckwheat Family), herb, shrub, native to western United States, several to many flowers in umbrella-like clusters. Var. (*Eriogonum nudum,* Nude Buckwheat), 12–36 inches high, ¾-inch white or pink flowers at stem tips, leaves whorled at base, lying flat on ground, foothills to timberline, roadsides, open forests, May–December; (*E. ovalifolium,* Alpine Buckwheat, Oval-leafed Buckwheat), dense mat, wind-swept alpine country, umbrella-like clusters of flowers, creamy yellow to burgundy as season progresses, silver gray leaves, July–August; (*E. roseum,* Rosy Buckwheat), erect, branchless stem, 12–24 inches high, clusters of tiny pompon-like flowers bundled tightly together clasping stem at regular intervals, dry sandy flats, meadow fringes, below 5,000 feet elevation, June–October; (*E. wrightii,* Wright's Buckwheat), late bloomer, dry sage-like, stems rise out of thick woody tuft of lance-like leaves, white and pink flowers tightly clustered along stem prostrate from weight, dry rocky places, along Tioga Road, July–September.

Evening Primrose (*Oenothera hookeri*) (Onagraceae: Evening Primrose Family), wildflower, lance-like leaves, creamy yellow flowers, open late evening, pollinated by Hawk Moth, meadow fringes, roadsides, June–October.

Fumaria (Fumaria officinalis) (Fumariaceae: Fumitory Family), weed, 6–36 inches high, light green leaves, dense cluster of small pinkish crimson-tipped flowers, old gardens, waste places, dung-heaps, April–July. Var. (*F. parviflora*).

Gentian (*Gentiana*) (Gentianaceae: Gentian Family), herb, solitary or clustered flowers, woods, damp ground, late summer–autumn.

Geoglossum glutinosum (Slimy Earthtongue) (Geoglossaceae: Earthtongue Family), cup fungi, small, variously shaped, often brightly colored, scattered or in small groups in soil, decaying roots and logs.

Geraniaceae (Geranium Family), 800 species; may have been *(Geranium richardsonii*, Wild Geranium, Cranesbill), pale pink flowers at end of 12–24 inch branched stem, palm-shaped leaves, moist mountain meadows, July–August; cultivated: *Pelargonium.*

Goldenrod (Compositae: Sunflower Family). Var. (*Solidago canadensis*, Meadow Goldenrod), wildflower, vibrant yellow florets, 3–7 inches long, bottle brush appearance, multiple lance-like, sharply toothed leaves, smooth stem, 1–5 feet high, 3,000–8,000 feet elevation, Yosemite meadows, moist roadsides, July–September; (*Solidago occidentalis*, Narrow Goldenrod), small yellow flower heads, smooth stem, lance-like 6 inch long leaves, 32 inches high, 8,000 feet elevation, July–September.

Gramineae (Grass Family), herb, usually hollow stemmed, 4,500 species.

Heliotrope (*Heliotropium*) (Boraginaceae: Borage Family), herb, low shrubby plant, small white or bluish flowers, roadsides and meadows, summer.

Hemizonia virgata = Holocarpha virgata (Compositae: Sunflower Family), wildflower, 8–48 inches high, yellow flowers, bloom May–September, abundant in sun-baked soils, to 2,500 feet elevation, Sierra foothills, inner coastal ranges, California (31 species), June–November.

Hemlock (*Tsuga Canadensis*) (Pinaceae: Pine Family), common forest tree, 60–100 feet tall, tannin-rich bark, short-flat needles, green above and whitish beneath, oval cones, ½ inch long, two eastern and two Northwestern species, hills, swamps.

Hepatica (Liverleaf) (Ranunculaceae: Buttercup Family), wildflower, related to *Anemone,* named for liver-shaped thickish leaf, hairy stem, solitary blue, pale lilac, or pinkish-white flowers, ½ to 1 inch wide, dry rocky woods, amid brown leaves and debris, early spring. Var. (*H. americana; H. acutiloba; H. triloba*).

Honeysuckle (*Lonicera*) (Caprifoliaceae: Honeysuckle Family), shrub, vine, herb, tubular white, yellowish, pink flowers, blue or red berries. Var. (*Lonicera villosa*, Mountain Fly; *L. oblongifolia*, Swamp Fly; *L. canadensis*, American Fly; *L. tatarica*, Tartarian; *L. morrowi*, Morrow's).

Hoya (Wax Plant) (Asclepiadaceae: Milkweed Family). Var. (*Hoya carnosa*), house plant, thick fleshy oval leaves, white flowers, India.

Hypnea (Bryaceae: True Moss Family), moss, pale olive green.

Hypnum splendens (Bryaceae: True Moss Family), moss, thin closely entangled mat, deep pine woods, mountains, common.

Isopyrum (False Rue Anemone) (Ranunculaceae: Buttercup Family), wildflower, 4–10 inches high, white flowers, ½–¾ inch wide, in small clusters, rich woods, spring.

Juniperus occidentalis (Western Juniper) (Cupressaceae: Cypress Family), tree, shrub on dry rocky slopes and toward northern limits of range, 20 feet tall, bright cinnamon-red bark, gray-green denticulately fringed leaves, blue-black fruit, 6,000–10,000 feet elevation, summits and upper slopes of Sierra.

Koeleria cristata (Junegrass) (Gramineae: Grass Family), cattail grass, 1–3 feet high, 2–4 barely acute flowers, dry hills, open woods, sandy soil; allied to *Dactylis* (Orchard Grass).

Laurel (*Kalmia polifolia*). Var. (*Kalmia microplylla*) (Alpine Laurel, Sheepkill) (Ericaceae: Heath Family), evergreen, smooth small shrub, cup-shaped clustered rose-colored flowers, ½ inch wide, subalpine and alpine meadows, poisonous.

Leguminosae (Pea Family), one of three largest families of flowering plants, 13,000 species, irregular flowers of sweet-pea type (Lupines, Clovers, Indigos, Psoraleas).

Libocedrus decurrens = *Calocedrus decurrens* (Incense Cedar) (Cupressaceae: Cedar Family), large evergreen, aromatic, cones ripen August–September, seeds shed mid-winter, dry, well drained soil, rock outcroppings, alluvial flood plains, occasionally in redwood forests, canyons, slopes, northern California to southern Oregon, southern Nevada to Baja, California.

Lichen (Ascomycetes: Fungi Family), plant, alga, or microscopic green or blue-green algae and fungus in symbiotic association, forms thallus (single independent plant), not differentiated into stem and leaves, pale yellowish green or mineral gray, includes organisms important in weathering and breaking down rocks or tree bark.

Lilium pardalinum (*L. californicum*) (Tiger Lily) (Liliaceae: Lily Family), wildflower, large colonies, stems 2–3 feet high, long narrow leaves, orange flowers, purple spots, moist shady redwood and mixed evergreen forests, along streams, up to 6,000 feet elevation, once common, uprooted for cultivation, coastal ranges, Sierra Nevada south to Kern County, June–September.

Linnaea borealis (Twinflower) (Caprifoliaceae: Honeysuckle Family), trailing plant, slender creeping stems, pair of fragrant, nodding, pink, funnel-shaped flowers on each flower stalk, ½ inch long, small round evergreen leaves, moist mossy woods, cold northern forest bogs, rare, June–August.

Madotheca (*Porella*) (Liverwort) (Porellaceae: Liverwort Family), green to brown, robust, 8 inches high, usually dull when dry.

Maple (*Acer*) (Aceraceae: Maple Family), tree, 60–70 species, widely distributed throughout northern hemisphere, palmately lobed leaves, flowers appears with or after leaves, limpid sweet sap of some American species manufactured into sugar.

Mimulus (Monkey Flower) (Scrophulariaceae: Figwort Family), wildflower, tubular shaped five-petaled blossoms, two lips turned up, three down. Var. (*Mimulus tilingii,* Alpine Monkey Flower), wet places, 8,000–11,000 feet elevation, June–September; (*M. guttatus,* Common Monkey Flower), flowers ½–2 inches, dotted with color or plain yellow, multiple blossoms, smooth oval leaves, 4–36 inch stems, June–September; (*M. cardinales,* Scarlet Monkey Flower), red flowers, yellow stamens, 4,000–7,000 feet elevation, rare, April–September; (*M. layneae,* Layne's Monkey Flower), dark rose blossoms, white throat (red spots), ½–1 inch, oval leaves on 4–12 inch stem, below 7,500 feet elevation, May–August; (*Diplacus aurantiacus,* Sticky Monkey Flower), branched stalks, dark green narrow sticky leaves, bright orange funnel-shaped flowers, March–July.

Mint (*Mentha*) (Labiatae: Mint Family), herb, common. Var. (*Mentha arvensis,* Field Mint), 6–24 inch square stem, sharply toothed leaves, 1½–3 inches long, lilac flowers, moist meadows, occasionally dry soil, June–September.

Moose Maple (*Acer pensylvanicum*) (Aceraceae: Maple Family), small tree, 15–20 feet tall, smooth greenish bark, large broad leaves, eastern mountains.

Mountain Maple (*Acer glabrum*) (Aceraceae: Maple Family), small tree, shrub, 6–20 feet tall, moist to fairly dry slopes, canyons, 5,000–9,000 feet elevation, coniferous forests, Sierra Nevada and northern coastal ranges. Var. (*A. diffusum*).

Myosotis (*M. scorpioides*) (Scorpion Grass, Mouse-Ear, Forget-Me-Not) (Boraginaceae: Borage Family), wildflower, 12–20 inches high, small clustered blue flowers with yellow eye, wet ground, muddy shores, late spring–fall.

Myrtle (*Myrica californica*) (Wax Myrtle) (Myricaceae: Bayberry Family), shrub, evergreen, glossy dark green fragrant leaves.

Nevada Pine (Assume: Nevada Nut Pine) (*Pinus monophylla*) (Single-Leaf Pinon) (Pinaceae: Pine Family), tree, 15–20 feet tall, short trunk, divided near ground into several spreading stems, short thick branches, edible seeds, dry gravelly slopes and mesas, 2,500–9,000 feet elevation, Utah to California, eastern foothills Sierra Nevada (some western slope).

Oregon Cedar (*Chamaecyparis lawsoniana*) (Port Orford Cedar) (Cupressaceae: Cypress Family), tree, 100–175 feet tall, long loose narrow-ridged bark with reddish tinge beneath, dark russet-brown berry-like cones clustered on upper branchlets, 0–5,000 feet elevation, Pacific Coast.

Oreodoxa regia (Royal Palm) (Arecaceae: Palm Family), palm tree, 80–100 feet tall, trunk rising from abruptly enlarged base, gradually tapering, deep green pinnate leaves, 10–12 feet long, Cuba, Everglades, western Caribbean; largely cultivated as ornamental tree.

Osmunda cinnamomea (Cinnamon Fern) (Osmundaceae: Cinnamon Fern Family), fern, cinnamon-colored spore-cases, crown shaped, 1–5 feet high, swamps, wet woods, muck, May.

Osmunda claytoniana (Interrupted Fern) (Osmundaceae: Cinnamon Fern Family), fern, 2–4 feet high, margins of swamps, open moist woods, May.

Osmunda regalis (Royal Fern) (Osmundaceae: Cinnamon Fern Family), fern, smooth pale-green fronds, 1–6 feet high, rich soil, wet woods, swampy fields shielded from sun, May.

Panicum clandestinum (Gramineae: Grass Family), grass, 1–3 feet high, leafy top, taper-pointed, common, June–September.

Panicum depauperatum (Gramineae: Grass Family), grass, 6–12 inches, few-flowered, dry woods and hills, common, June.

Picea sitchensis (Sitka Spruce) (Pinaceae: Pine Family), tree, 125–200 feet tall, reddish-brown bark, rough textured branches, needles whitish on upper surface, bright green beneath, cones, 2–4 inches long, coastal mountains, northern California to Alaska, cool, moist areas, clinging mosses and ferns cover trunk.

Pinus albicaulus (Whitebark Pine) (Pinaceae: Pine Family), timberline tree or shrub, 15–30 feet tall, 1–3 inch dark purple cones, 7,000–12,000 feet elevation, Sierra Nevada and northward.

Pinus flexilis (Limber Pine) (Pinaceae: Pine Family), pine tree, needles, and twigs similar to Whitebark Pine, 3–6 inch elongated light brown cones, eastern slopes of Sierra Nevada, 5,000–12,000 feet elevation.

Pinus ponderosa (Western Yellow Pine) (Pinaceae: Pine Family), pine tree, 200 feet tall, massive trunk, short thick many-forked often pendulous branches, generally turned upward at the ends, dark brown, nearly black bark, irregularly divided into plates, needles in clusters of 3, 5–10 inches long, dark yellow-green, mountain slopes, dry valleys, high mesas, western North America from British Columbia to Mexico.

Poa alsodes (Meadow Grass) (Gramineae: Grass Family), grass, 2¼–4 feet high, rich, moist woods, hillsides, May–June.

Poa pratensis (Green, Common Meadow Grass, Kentucky Bluegrass, June Grass) (Gramineae: Grass Family), grass, 1–3 feet high, early flowering, open woods, meadows, altitudes below alpine regions, May–July.

Polemoniaceae (Phlox Family), 260 species in western United States; may have been (*Phlox diffusa:* "spreading flame") (Spreading Phlox), small shrub, 4–12 inch branches, short needle-like leaves, white or lilac flowers, rocky or sandy plots, mid-to-upper elevations, early bloomer, June–August.

Poplar (Lombardy Poplar) (*Populus nigra*) (Black Poplar) (Salicaceae: Willow Family), tall thin tree, dull gray branches, dark furrowed bark. Var. (*P. dilatata; P. fastigiata*).

Portulaca (Portulacaceae: Purslane Family), trailing weed, succulent fleshy leaves, yellow, white, red flowers, solitary or in clusters, open in morning sun, cultivated and waste ground, common, summer.

Primula (*P. suffrutescens*) (Sierra Primrose, First Blooming) (Primulaceae: Primrose Family), wildflower, spatula-shaped fringed leaves, magenta flowers, stem 3–4 inches high, rocky ledges, crevices below slow-melting snowbanks, July–August.

Proteaceae (Protea Family), shrub, tree, alternate, simple or divided leaves, racemes, spikes, or heads of irregular brightly colored flowers, southern hemisphere to tropical regions, rare in northern hemisphere, some known for medical properties and for edible seeds. Macadamia nuts are the best known in the United States, grown as ornamentals.

Pulsatilla (*Anemone occidentalis*) (Windflower) (Ranunculaceae: Buttercup Family), wildflower, white or purplish flowers, dry rocky slopes, July–August.

Purslane (*Portulaca oleracea*) (Portulacaceae: Purslane Family), wildflower, prostrate, small yellow, whitish, green or reddish flowers, fleshy garden and waste-place weed, grows out of cracks in concrete sidewalks, summer.

Red Maple (*Acer rubrum*) (Aceraceae: Maple Family), small tree, reddish twigs, swamps, scarlet, crimson, yellowish flowers, leaves bright crimson in early autumn, alluvial soils, wet woods.

Redwood (*Sequoia sempervirens*) (Taxodiaceae: Taxodium Family), evergreen tree, 300–350 feet tall, 12–16 feet diameter, thick rich reddish-brown bark, deep furrows running length of tree, dark green flat needle-like leaves, small cones, 1 inch long, capable of sprouting from roots of parent tree, flats, slopes, below 2,000 feet elevation, coastal fog belt, may attain age of 1,500 years.

Rubiaceae (Madder Family), related to Honeysuckle family; may have been (*Galium,* Bedstraw), wildflower, creeper, appears as vine, hairy four-sided stem, 1–5 feet high, whorled leaves, tiny whitish-green clustered flowers, 2–5 on stalk, Yosemite's moist shaded areas, redwood and mixed evergreen forests, blooms March–April.

Salix discolor (Pussy Willow) (Salicaceae: Willow Family), shrub, small tree, 25 feet tall, light brown bark tinged with red, divided by shallow fissures, elliptic leaves, bright green above, silvery white below, broad yellow midrib, 3–5 inches long, furry flower catkins, silvery white, 1 inch long, late winter, very early spring, moist meadows, banks of streams and lakes, common.

Salvia (Sage) (Labiatae: Mint Family), herb, blue (violet) flowers, 1 inch long, spring–early summer.

Sanguinaria (*S. canadensis*) (Bloodroot) (Papaveraceae: Poppy Family), wildflower, 3–6 inches high, single white flowers, 1–1½ inch wide, orange-red sap (toxic alkaloid), rich woods, early spring, first flower to appear with *Hepatica.*

Sarcoscypha occidentalis (Western Scarlet Cup) (Sarcoscyphaceae: Elf Cup Family), fungi, slender stalk, shallow cup, ¼–½ inch long, interior bright red, fading to pink, exterior lighter, smooth or wrinkled at base, solitary or clustered on buried sticks in deciduous forests, fallen hardwood branches in wet places, early spring.

Scarlet Oak (*Quercus coccinea*) (Fagaceae: Oak Family), deciduous tree, 70–80 feet tall, smooth shiny leaves, 3–6 inches long, medium-sized acorns, dry, sandy soil, forests, roadsides.

Scolopendrium officinarum = *Phyllitis scolopendrium* (Hart's Tongue Fern) (Aspleniaceae: Spleenwort Family), fern, fronds 12–18 inches high, 1–3 inches wide, limestone rocks, sink-holes.

Scrophulariaceae (Figwort Family), ornamental, 3,000 species, wildflowers, (foxgloves, snapdragons, speedwells, beardtongues); may have been (*Scrophularia californica,* California Bee Plant), common in open places, 3–5 feet high, toothed-spear shaped leaves, square stem, small reddish clustered flowers, spring.

Sedum (*S. obtusatum*) (Stonecrop) (Crassulaceae: Orpine Family), wildflower, delicate small succulent, thick fleshy leaves, bright red 2–6 inch stem, early blossoms (yellow), fade pink as season progresses, 4,000 feet to timberline, grow from cracks and crevices, May–August.

Sedum rosea (Roseroot) (Crassulaceae: Orpine Family), succulent, thick fleshy oval leaves, red cluster flowers, ¼ inch wide, stout 2–6 inch stems, sprouts early spring, moist areas at and above timberline, Sierra Nevada, May–July.

Selaginella (*S. densa*) (Spike-Moss) (Selaginellaceae: Club Moss Family), moss, dense opaque spreading moss, gray-green, erect cones, prairie soil, dry calcareous rock outcrops.

Sequoia (*Sequoiadendron giganteum*) (Taxodiaceae: Taxodium Family), Big Tree, 100–200 feet tall, 10–20 feet diameter, red-brown bark, up to 24 inches thick, needles ⅛–¼ inch long, cones ½–2½ inches long, isolated groves, western slopes, Sierra Nevada, 5,000–8,200 feet elevation, may attain age of 1,000–3,5000 years.

Sierra Heather (*Phyllodoce breweri*) (Mountain Heather) (Ericaceae: Heath Family), wildflower, evergreen, fir needle-like leaves along woody stem, pink-red bell-shaped blossoms, ½ inch wide, clustered at end of 6–12 inch stem, subalpine forest and rocky outcroppings above timberline, June–July.

Snow Flower (Snow Plant) (*Sarcodes sanguinea*) (Pyrolaceae: Wintergreen Family), wildflower, lacks chlorophyll, incapable of photosynthesis, fleshy red crowded leaves, 4–12 inches high, thick humus of forest floor, nourished by decaying material in soil, 4,000–8,000 feet elevation, Santa Rosa and San Jacinto Mountains, Sierra Nevada, northern coastal range to Oregon, May–July.

Sphagnum (*Sphagnobrya*) (Sphagnaceae: Peat-moss Family), moss, whitish green, large spongy patches cover acres of bog, crowd and support one another, up to 12 inches tall, associated with Cranberries, Sundews, and Orchids.

Spiraea (*S. densiflora*) (Meadowsweet) (Rosaceae: Rose Family), deciduous shrub, 36 inches high, white or pale-pink flowers in branching clusters, ⅛–¼ inch wide, moist rocky areas below melting snow or seeps, middle to upper elevations, rock crevices, July–August.

Stipa spartea (Porcupine Grass) (Gramineae: Grass Family), grass, 1½–3 feet high, plains and prairies, May–July.

Struthiopteris germanica = *Matteuccia struthiopteris* (Ostrich-Fern) (Onocleaceae: Sensitive Fern Family), fern, rich green plume-like fronds, 2–5 feet high, along streams, moist woods.

Sugar Pine (*Pinus lambertiana*) (Pinaceae: Pine Family), largest pine, 180–220 feet tall, largest cones, 10–24 inches long, common forest, deep soils, mountain slopes, sides of ravines and canyons, along western slopes of Sierra Nevada, 2,500–9,000 feet elevation, may live for 600 years.

Tamarack (Larch) (*Larix*) (Pinaceae: Pine Family), northern conifer, slender, 50–120 feet tall, dark needles, 1 inch long, shed in fall, small scaly cones, flowers in earliest spring before leaves. Var. (*Larix americana,* American Larch).

Tea Rose (*Rosa indica*) (Rosaceae: Rose Family), miniature rose.

Thalictrum anemonoides (*Rue Anemone*) (Ranunculaceae: Buttercup Family), wildflower, white (rarely pinkish) flowers, early spring, woods, common; resembles *Anemone nemorosa.*

Thyme (*Thymus*) (*Thymus serpyllum,* Wild Thyme) (Lamiaceae: Mint Family), herb, upland woods and fields, June–September, commonly cultivated.

Umbelliferae (Carrot Family), aromatic herbs (Marsh Pennywort, Snakeroot, Hedge Parsley, Sweet Cicely, Coriander, Bishop's Weed, Poison Hemlock, Water Parsnip, Lovage, Water Hemlock, Parsnip, Angelica, Cow Parsnip, Ranger Buttons).

Victoria regia (*Victoria amazonica*) (Nymphaeaceae: Water-Lily Family), giant water-lily, aquatic perennial herb, 3–6 foot floating round flattened leaves with upturned edges, stalk attached at middle of lower surface, numerous large floating cream petaled flowers with intoxicating fragrance, tropical South America, cultivated in northern hemisphere. *V. amazonica* was popular in England in the mid-nineteenth century, where immense glasshouses were built to grow and display them.

Violet (*Viola*) (Violaceae: Violet Family), wildflower, 300 species, white, dark violet, lavender, yellow flowers, moist slopes, meadows, open woods, uncommon in Sierra Nevada.

Western Azalea (*Rhododendron occidentale*) (Ericaceae: Heath Family), deep-green shrub, to 10 feet tall, cluster blossoms, white or pinkish-white funnel-star-shaped flowers, 1–2 inches long, along streams, moist meadows, redwood and mixed evergreen forests, Yosemite Valley, Merced River, June–July.

Willow (*Salix*) (Saliaceae: Willow Family), trees, shrubs, 160–170 species, 70 found in North America, of these 24 attain the size and habit of trees, scaly bark, soft wood, slender terete tough branchlets often easily separated at the joints, slender leaves, stalked or sessile flowers in early spring, banks of streams, low moist ground, alpine summits of mountains.

Woodwardia (Chain Fern) (Blechnaceae: Fern Family), fern. Var. (*Woodwardia virginica:* Virginia Chain Fern), widely creeping and branching, 2 to more than 3 feet tall, glossy fronds, rusty-backed with regular double row of sori (fruit-dots), bogs, swamps, marshes, shallow ponds, rooted in mud, wet meadows among *Calopogon,* fruits more freely in sun than in shade.

Yarrow (*Achillea lanulosa*) (Compositae: Sunflower Family), fern-like leaves with pungent odor, 1–3 feet high, flat-topped clustered tiny white flowers, open flats to timberline, April–September. Var. (*A. millefolium,* Common Yarrow; *A. ptarmica,* Sneezewort).

BIBLIOGRAPHIES

BIBLIOGRAPHY OF BOTANICAL SOURCES

Bailey, L. H. *Manual of Cultivated Plants: Most Commonly Grown in the Continental United States and Canada.* Revised ed. New York: Macmillan Co., 1949.

Blamey, Marjorie, and Christopher Grey-Wilson. *Mediterranean Wild Flowers.* St. Helier, Jersey: HarperCollins, 1993.

Conrad, Henry S. *How to Know the Mosses and Liverworts: Pictured-Keys for Determining Many of the North American Mosses and Liverworts, with Suggestions and Aids for Their Study.* Revised ed. Dubuque: William C. Brown Co., 1956.

Gleason, Henry A., and Arthur Cronquist. *Manual of Vascular Plants of Northeastern United States and Adjacent Canada.* Princeton: D. Van Nostrund and Co., 1963; 2d ed. Bronx: The New York Botanical Garden, 1991.

Gray, Asa. *Field, Forest, and Garden Botany: A Simple Introduction to the Common Plants of the United States East of the 100th Meridian, Both Wild and Cultivated.* Revised. New York: American Book Co., 1895.

———. *Manual of Botany of the Northern United States: Including the District East of the Mississippi and North of North Carolina and Tennessee, Arranged According to the Natural System.* 5th ed. New York: Ivison, Blakeman, Taylor & Co., 1879.

Hickman, James C. *The Jepson Manual: Higher Plants of California.* Berkeley: University of California Press, 1993.

Hitchcock, A. S. *Manual of the Grasses of the United States.* Vol. 1 and 2. 2d ed. New York: Dover Publications, 1971.

Horn, Elizabeth L. *Sierra Nevada Wildflowers.* Missoula, Montana: Mountain Press Publishing Co., 1998.

Hylander, Clarence J. *The Macmillan Wild Flower Book.* New York: Macmillan Co., 1854.

Lesquereux, Leo, and Thomas P. James. *Manual of the Mosses of North America.* Boston: S. E. Cassino and Co., 1884.

Lyons, Kathleen, and Mary Beth Cooney-Lazaneo. *Plants of the Coast Redwood Region.* Boulder Creek, California: Looking Press, 1988.

Mabberley, D. J. *The Plant-Book: A Portable Dictionary of the Higher Plants.* New York: Cambridge University Press, 1987.

McKnight, Kent H., and Vera B. McKnight. *A Field Guide to Mushrooms: North America.* Boston: Houghton Mifflin, 1987.

Munz, Philip A. *California Mountain Wildflowers*. Berkeley: University of California Press, 1963.

Munz, Philip A., and David D. Keck. *A California Flora*. Berkeley: University of California Press, 1959.

Newcomb, Lawrence. *Newcomb's Wildflower Guide*. Boston: Little, Brown and Co., 1977.

Orr, Robert T., and Margaret C. Orr. *Wildflowers of Western America*. New York: Alfred A. Knopf, 1974.

Parsons, Frances Theodora. *How to Know the Ferns: A Guide to the Names, Haunts, and Habits of Our Common Ferns*. New York: Charles Scribner's Sons, 1899.

Petrides, George A. *A Field Guide to Trees and Shrubs*, 2d ed. Boston: Houghton Mifflin, 1972.

———. *Trees of the California Sierra Nevada*. Williamston, Michigan: Backpacker Field Guide Series, 1996.

Pusateri, Samuel J. *Flora of Our Sierran National Parks: Yosemite—Sequoia and Kings Canyon (Including Many Valley and Foothill Plants)*. Tulare, California: Carl and Irving Printers, 1963.

Sargent, Charles Sprague. *Manual of the Trees of North America*. 2 vols. 2d ed. New York: Dover Publications, 1961.

Vines, Robert A. *Trees, Shrubs and Woody Vines of the Southwest*. Austin: University of Texas Press, 1960.

Vitt, Dale H., Janet E. Marsh, and Robin B. Bovey. *Mosses, Lichens & Ferns of Northwest North America*. Seattle: University of Washington Press, 1988.

Wilson, Lynn, Jim Wilson, and Jeff Nicholas. *Wildflowers of Yosemite*. El Portal, California: Sierra Press, 1992.

ARTICLES AND MANUSCRIPTS BY JEANNE C. CARR: 1846–1893

"A Tale of Truth." *Temperance Herald*. Transcribed February 14, 1846. JCCP, Scrapbook I, n.p.

"A Day Among the Hubbardton Lakes." October 1850. JCCP, CA 17.

"The Working Mans [*sic*] Home." (c. 1850?). JCCP, CA 18.

"Journal." May 12–June 23, 1851. JCCP, CA 19.

"Letters to Young Mothers. No. 1." *The Esculapian*, n.d. JCCP, Scrapbook I, Annexed following p. 152.

"Letters to Young Mothers. No. 2. Dress." *The Esculapian*, (c. 1853). JCCP, Scrapbook I, Annexed following p. 152.

"Cultivation of Annuals." *Wisconsin Farmer* 9 (April 1857): 147–48.

"My Rose-Garden." *Wisconsin Farmer* 9 (May 1857): 183–84.

"Amos Dean." *Wisconsin State Journal*. Transcribed February 5, 1868. JCCP, Scrapbook I, 36.

"Our California Correspondence." *Western Farmer*, December 10, 1868.

"Our California Correspondence." *Western Farmer*, December 15, 1868.

"Letters From the Yo Semite Valley." Transcribed July 1, 1869. JCCP, Scrapbook I, 11, 13.

"An Hour In the Hebrew Synagogue." May 7, 1870. San Francisco. JCCP, Scrapbook I, n.p.

"Female Education in the United States." *California Teacher,* (c. 1870). JCCP, Scrapbook I, 74.

"The Rural Homes of California." *California Horticulturist* 3 (February 1873): 39–41.

"Flower Studies." *Illustrated Press* 1 (February 1873).

"Flower Studies.—No. 2." *Illustrated Press* 1 (March 1873).

"The Rural Homes of California." *California Horticulturist* 3 (March 1873): 69–72.

"Flower Studies.—No. 3." *Illustrated Press* 1 (April 1873).

"California Flower Studies.—No. 4." *Illustrated Press* 1 (May 1873).

"Nursery and Residence of W. F. Kelsey, Oakland, Cal." *California Horticulturist* 3 (May 1873): 147–48.

"California Flower Studies.—No. 5." *Illustrated Press* 1 (July 1873).

"In the Sierras. The Lovers of Science Penetrating Untrodden Heights in the Mountain Wilderness." *Home Journal,* September 10, 1873. JCCP, Scrapbook 1, 17.

"Mrs. Carr's Remarks On The Big Tuolumne Canon, Etc." *Illustrated Press* 1 (October 1873).

"Mrs. Carr's Lecture on the Big Tuolumne Canon, Before the Oakland Farming Club. October 10th." (c. 1873). JCCP, CA 20.

"Narrative Fragment." (c. 1873?). JMP, E51:00234.

Glaciers of California." (c. 1874). JCCP, CA 21.

"A Beautiful Art." *Pacific Rural Press,* February 20, 1875. JCCP, Scrapbook I, 67.

"Birds and Caterpillars—A Hardshell Sermon." *Pacific Rural Press,* May 22, 1875. JCCP, Scrapbook I, n.p.

"The Farmer of the Yosemite Valley." May 26, 1875. JCCP, Scrapbook I, 70.

"The Holy Child." December 1875. JCCP, CA 23.

"Christmas." (c. 1875). JCCP, CA 22.

"The Flowers of California." *California Farmer,* (c. 1875). JCCP, Scrapbook I, 16.

"Miscellaneous Notes." (c. 1875–1890). JCCP, CA 25.

"Housekeeping A Fine Art; or The Ideal Home." *Record Union,* January 1, 1876. JCCP, Scrapbook I, 57–58.

"Department of Education: Teachers' Institute in Siskiyou—Notes of Travel Northward—Honor to Del Norte. Shasta-Ward." *Sacramento Record Union,* May 17, 1876.

"How To See California." *Daily Record-Union,* September 30, 1878.

"Thanksgiving and Giving Thanks." *Pacific Rural Press,* November 27, 1880. JCCP, Scrapbook I, 78.

"Pasadena Homes: A Summary of the Year's Progress." *Daily Commercial,* September 7, 1881.

"Our Teachers." *San Francisco Patron,* April 29, 1882. JCCP, Scrapbook I, 79.

"Fruit and Vine." August 24, 1882. JCCP, Scrapbook I, 71.

"Partial List of Ornamental Trees and Shrubs at Carmelita." 1883. JCCP, CA 189.

"The San Gabriel Valley." In *A Southern California Paradise, (In the suburbs of Los Angeles.) Being a historic and descriptive account of Pasadena, San Gabriel, Sierra Madre, and La Canada; with important reference to Los Angeles and all Southern California, and containing map and illustrations, 61–66.* Edited by R. W. C. Farnsworth. Pasadena: R. W. C. Farnsworth, 1883.

"Woman and Land." *Pasadena & Valley Union,* February 23, 1884.

"What Shall We Do With Our Fruit!" *Pasadena & Valley Union,* March 15, 1884.

"The Festival of the Rose. Santa Barbara, April 15–19, 1884." April 22, 1884. JCCP, Scrapbook II, 78.

"Pasadena, The Crown of the Valley del Rio de San Gabriel." *Los Angeles Daily Times,* September 16, 1885.

"Helen Hunt Jackson." (c. 1885). JCCP, Scrapbook 1, Annexed after p. 80.

"My Own Story." (c. 1886). JCCP, CA 28.

"The Heart of Southern California," 161–92. In *Picturesque California.* Edited by John Muir. New York: J. Dewing Co., 1888; reprint, Philadelphia: Running Press, 1976.

"Hotel San Gabriel." Chicago: Donohue & Henneberry, (c. 1880s). Rare Book Collection, The Huntington Library.

"'South California.' State Division from the Southern Standpoint." May 30, 1890. JCCP, Scrapbook II, 59.

"Pasadena," 316. In *Illustrated History of Los Angeles County, California.* Chicago: Lewis Publishing Co., 1889.

"The Late Frederick Billings." *San Francisco Bulletin,* October 8, 1890. JCCP, Scrapbook II, 57.

"Bomoseen: A New England Tale." (c. 1890?). JCCP, CA 30.

"Description and Early History of Southern California." (c. 1890). JCCP, CA 31.

"Manuscript on Wild Flowers of California." (c. 1890?). JCCP, CA 36.

"Manuscript Relating to Landscape Gardening." (c. 1890). JCCP, CA 35.

"Notes on David Douglas." (c. 1890). JCCP, CA 32.

"Notes on Selecting and Planting Trees." (c. 1890). JCCP, CA 33.

"A Sabbath in the Yo Semite." (c. 1890). JCCP, CA 37.

"The Blessed Cora of San Luis Rey." *The Californian* 1 (October 1891): 61–71.

"John Muir." *The Californian* 2 (June 1892): 88–94.

"Throop University, Pasadena." *The Californian* 2 (September 1892): 565–78.

"Among the Basket Makers." *The Californian* 2 (October 1892): 597–610.

"Biographical Notes on John Muir." (c. 1892). JCCP, CA 40.

"Pasadena—The Crown of the Valley," 80–87. In *Annual Publication of the Historical Society of Southern California, Los Angeles, 1893.* Los Angeles: Historical Society of Southern California, 1893.

"Steamer Journey from New York to San Francisco in October 1869." (c. 1893). JCCP, CA 41.

"Recollections of Helen Hunt; and the Genesis of the Novel, Ramona." (c. 1895). JCCP, CA 44.

"Pasadena Hedges." *Pasadena Star-News,* May 3, 1923.

"A Compromise." n.d. JCCP, Scrapbook I, 48–49.

"Deacon Gorum's Temptation." n.d. JCCP, Scrapbook I, 23.

"Deacon Gorum's Temptation." n.d. JCCP, Scrapbook I, 27.

"The Deacon's Temptation." n.d. JCCP, Scrapbook I, 21–22.

"The Deacon's Temptation. A Story of Yesterday." n.d. JCCP, Scrapbook I, 19–23, 25–28.

"Hard Times Here—Why and How Cured." n.d. JCCP, Scrapbook II, Annexed after p. 43.

"Idustrial [*sic*] University for Women." n.d. JCCP, Scrapbook I, 152.

"My Schoolmates. No. 2. Jessie Lewis." *Temperance Herald,* n.d. JCCP, Scrapbook I, n.p.

"Professional Training Schools for Girls." *Pacific Rural Press,* n.d. JCCP, Scrapbook I, 44.

SELECTED READINGS FOR FURTHER STUDY

Books by John Muir

The Mountains of California. New York: The Century Co., 1894.

Our National Parks. Boston and New York: Houghton Mifflin and Co., 1901.

Stickeen. Boston and New York: Houghton Mifflin Co., 1909.

My First Summer in the Sierra. Boston and New York: Houghton Mifflin Co., 1911.

The Yosemite. New York: The Century Co., 1912.

The Story of My Boyhood and Youth. Boston and New York: Houghton Mifflin Co., 1913.

Travels in Alaska. Boston and New York: Houghton Mifflin Co., 1915.

A Thousand-Mile Walk to the Gulf. Boston and New York: Houghton Mifflin Co., 1916.

The Cruise of the Corwin. Boston and New York: Houghton Mifflin Co., 1917.

Steep Trails. Boston and New York: Houghton Mifflin Co., 1918.

Collections of the Writings of John Muir

Muir, John. *To Yosemite and Beyond. Writings from the Years 1863 to 1875.* Edited by Robert Engberg and Donald Wesling. Madison: The University of Wisconsin Press, 1980; reprint, Salt Lake City: The University of Utah Press, 1999.

———. *John Muir: His Life and Letters and Other Writings.* With an Introduction by Terry Gifford. London: Baton Wicks, 1996.

———. *John Muir's "Stickeen" and The Lessons of Nature.* Edited by Ronald H. Limbaugh. Fairbanks: The University of Alaska Press, 1996.

———. *Letters from Alaska.* Edited by Robert Engberg and Bruce Merrell. Madison: The University of Wisconsin Press, 1993.

————. *The Eight Wilderness Discovery Books.* With an Introduction by Terry Gifford. London: Diadem Books, 1992.

————. *Muir Among the Animals: The Wildlife Writings of John Muir.* Edited by Lisa Mighetto. Sierra Club: Sierra Club Books, 1986.

————. *Dear Papa: Letters Between John Muir and His Daughter Wanda.* Edited by Jean Hanna Clark and Shirley Sargent. Fresno: Panorama West Books, 1985.

————. *John of the Mountains: The Unpublished Journals of John Muir.* Edited by Linnie Marsh Wolfe. Boston: Houghton Mifflin Co., 1938; reprint, Madison: The University of Wisconsin Press, 1979.

————. *The Life and Letters of John Muir.* 2 vols. Edited by William Frederic Badè. Boston: Houghton Mifflin Co., 1924.

Other Books and Articles

Albanese, Catherine L. *Nature Religion in America: From the Algonkian Indians to the New Age.* Chicago: The University of Chicago Press, 1990.

Austin, Richard Cartwright. *Baptized Into Wilderness: A Christian Perspective on John Muir.* 2d ed. Abington: Virginia Press, 1991.

Cohen, Michael. *The Pathless Way: John Muir and the American Wilderness.* Madison: The University of Wisconsin Press, 1984.

Ehrlich, Gretel. *John Muir: Nature's Visionary.* Washington, D.C.: National Geographic Society, 2000.

Fleck, Richard F. "John Muir's Homage to Henry David Thoreau." *Pacific Historian* 29 (Summer-Fall 1985): 54–64.

Fox, Stephen. *John Muir and His Legacy: The American Conservation Movement.* Boston: Little, Brown and Co., 1981.

Holmes, Stephen. *The Young John Muir, An Environmental Biography.* Madison: The University of Wisconsin Press, 1999.

Limbaugh, Ronald H. "The Nature of Muir's Religion." *Pacific Historian* 29 (Summer-Fall 1985): 16–29.

Miller, Sally M., ed. *John Muir in Historical Perspective.* New York: Peter Lang, 1999.

————. *John Muir: Life and Work.* Albuquerque: The University of New Mexico Press, 1990.

Nash, Roderick. *Wilderness and the American Mind.* 3d ed. New Haven: Yale University Press, 1990.

Schofield, Edmund A. "John Muir's Yankee Friends and Mentors: The New England Connection." *Pacific Historian* 29 (Summer-Fall 1985): 65–89.

Sheats, Paul D. "John Muir's Glacial Gospel." *Pacific Historian* 29 (Summer–Fall 1985): 42–52.

Stoll, Mark. *Protestantism, Capitalism, and Nature in America.* Albuquerque: The University of New Mexico Press, 1997.

Turner, Richard. *Rediscovering America: John Muir in His Times and Ours.* New York: Viking Press, 1985.

Wadden, Kathleen Anne. "John Muir and the Community of Nature." *Pacific Historian* 29 (Summer-Fall 1985): 94–102.

Williams, Dennis C. "A World of Light: John Muir, Christianity and Nature in the Post-Darwinian World." Ph.D. diss., Texas Tech University, 1992.

Wolfe, Linnie Marsh, ed. *Son of the Wilderness: The Life of John Muir.* New York: Alfred A. Knopf, 1945; reprint, Madison: The University of Wisconsin Press, 1978.

Worster, Donald. *The Wealth of Nature: Environmental History and the Ecological Imagination.* New York: Oxford University Press, 1993.

Yelverton, Theresa. *Zanita: A Tale of the Yo-semite.* New York: Hurd and Houghton, 1872; reprint, Berkeley: Ten Speed Press, 1991.

CHRONOLOGY OF EVENTS

1825   Jane (Jeanne) Caroline Smith born Castleton, Vermont, May 12.

1834   J. C. Smith entered Castleton Seminary.

1838   John Muir born Dunbar, Scotland, April 21.

1842   Ezra Slocum Carr, professor of chemistry, joined faculty, Castleton Medical College.

1844   Jeanne Caroline Smith married Ezra Slocum Carr, February 15.

1846   J. C. Carr published "A Tale of Truth," *Temperance Herald.*

1847   Ezra Smith Carr born August 8.

1848   Edward Carver Carr born December 5.

1849   Muir family emigrated to Wisconsin, settled at Fountain Lake farm.

1852   John Henry Carr born February 27.

1853   J. Muir became interested in literature; began to invent mechanical devices. J. C. Carr published "Letters to Young Mothers. No. 1" and "Letters to Young Mothers. No. 2. Dress," *The Esculapian.*

1856   Ezra S. Carr joined faculty as professor of natural history and chemistry at University of Wisconsin. Carr family moved to 114 Gilman Street, Madison, Wisconsin.

1857   Muir family moved to Hickory Hill farm, Wisconsin. J. C. Carr published "Cultivation of Annuals" and "My Rose-Garden" in *Wisconsin Farmer.* Albert (Allie) Lee Carr born July 14.

1859   James Mason Hutchings bought the Upper Hotel in Yosemite Valley and took up a claim of 160 adjacent acres.

1860   J. Muir left for Madison, Wisconsin, to exhibit inventions at Wisconsin State Agricultural Society Fair; worked in Prairie du Chien with Norman Wiard. J. Muir and J. C. Carr met at fair. Josiah D. Whitney, head of California Geological Survey, explored and mapped Coastal Range and the Sierra.

1861   J. Muir entered the University of Wisconsin, Madison.

1862   J. Muir introduced to the study of botany by fellow-student Milton S. Griswold.

1863   J. Muir left University of Wisconsin for "University of the Wilderness" at end of spring term.

1864   Yosemite Valley and Mariposa Big Tree Grove granted to California by President Abraham Lincoln, first wilderness park in United States.

1864–1866 J. Muir traveled to Canada, botanized, and worked for William H. Trout and Charles Jay, rake and broom-handle factory near Meaford, Canada.

1865   J. C. Carr and J. Muir began correspondence.

1866   J. Muir found *Calypso borealis*; returned to United States from Canada; went to Indianapolis, worked for Osgood & Smith, carriage manufacturing company.

1867   J. Muir nearly blinded by eye injury in accident at Osgood & Smith, vowed to study nature; walked from Kentucky to Florida on thousand-mile walk to Gulf of Mexico; wrote first journal.

1868   J. Muir arrived San Francisco, March 28; first visit to Yosemite Valley; spent winter in Sierra foothills; wrote first California journal. Ezra S. Carr dismissed by University of Wisconsin over academic controversy. Carr family sailed to California. J.C. Carr published "Our California Correspondence," *Western Farmer*.

1868–1869 J. Muir sheepherder for "Smokey Jack"; studied Sierra geology and botany.

1869   J. Muir spent first summer in Sierra with Pat Delaney's sheep; employed by James M. Hutchings, operated sawmill and guide. J. C. Carr visited Yosemite, June-July. Ezra S. Carr appointed professor of agriculture, agricultural chemistry, and horticulture, University of California. Carr family resided in Oakland.

1869–1873 J. Muir headquarters in Yosemite Valley; explored Sierra for evidence of glacial action.

1870 J. Muir rambled with Joseph Le Conte and his students in Yosemite high country. J. C. Carr published "Female Education In The United States," *California Teacher.* Therese Yelverton in Yosemite.

1871 J. Muir published first article on glaciers, "Yosemite Glaciers," *New York Daily Tribune,* December 5; resumed work as sawyer for Hutchings (January), quit in July. Ralph Waldo Emerson visited Yosemite, where he met J. Muir; named Sequoia "Samoset."

1872 Jeanne C. Carr submitted Muir's letter to *Overland Monthly,* "Yosemite Valley in Flood," published in April. J. Muir first ascent of Mount Ritter; visited Oakland for two weeks.

1873 J. Muir, J. C. Carr, Albert Kellogg, and William Keith explored Tuolumne Canyon and Sierra Range. Emily Pelton visited Yosemite. J. Muir in Oakland with J. B. McChesneys until September 1874; wrote Sierra series for *Overland Monthly;* first excursion south of Yosemite to Kings Canyon; first ascent of Mount Whitney, September-October. J. C. Carr planted thirty species of pine trees, University of California, Berkeley; published "The Rural Homes of California," *California Horticulturist,* "Flower Studies," *Illustrated Press,* and "In the Sierras. The Lovers of Science Penetrating Untrodden Heights in the Mountain Wilderness," *Home Journal.* Ezra S. and J. C. Carr helped organize California grange. Ezra Smith Carr, a railroad brakeman, crushed between two railroad cars, died October 23.

1874–1876 J. Muir began intensive study of trees.

1874 Ezra S. Carr and grangers locked in dispute with President David C. Gilman and Board of Regents, University of California, over future of university; Ezra S. Carr dismissed. Carrs served on grange committees. J. Muir met Dr. John T. Strentzel, Mrs. Louisiana Erwin, and daughter Louie Wanda; returned to Sierra; climbed Shasta.

1875 J. C. Carr published "A Beautiful Art" and "Birds and Caterpillars—A Hardshell Sermon," *Pacific Rural Press.* Ezra

S. Carr elected California State Superintendent of Public Instruction; J. C. Carr appointed Deputy Superintendent of Public Instruction. J. Muir resided with Swett family in San Francisco; three-month trip with mule "Brownie" through Southern Sierra.

1876   J. Muir returned to San Francisco, lived with Swett family; published "God's First Temples," *Sacramento Semi-Weekly Record Union,* urged federal control of forests; first public lecture.

1877   J. Muir explored Great Basin; traveled through San Gabriel Mountains; conducted Shasta excursion with Asa Gray, Sir Joseph Hooker, Bidwell Party. J. C. Carr purchased forty-two acres in Pasadena, began to cultivate Carmelita; served on California state board of grange with Louie Wanda Strentzel. John Henry Carr committed suicide with a Smith & Wesson revolver, April 9.

1877–1878 J. Muir returned to San Francisco; lived with Swett family; wrote and lectured.

1878   J. Muir to Martinez; joined Coast and Geodetic Survey reconnaissance of 39th parallel in Utah and Nevada.

1879   J. Muir engaged to Louie Wanda Strentzel of Martinez, California; first Alaskan expedition. J. C. Carr began to transform Carmelita from wilderness into garden.

1880   J. Muir and Louie Wanda Strentzel married, April 14. J. Muir, second trip to Alaska, July-September; Taylor Glacier with the dog Stickeen. J. C. and Ezra S. Carr retired to Carmelita.

1881   Annie Wanda Muir born March 25. J. Muir worked Strentzel ranch to learn fruit business; cruised in Alaskan and Arctic waters aboard *Corwin,* May-October.

1882–1887 J. Muir managed fruit farm, Martinez.

1883   J. C. Carr published "The San Gabriel Valley," in *A Southern California Paradise,* ed. R. W. C. Farnsworth. Carmelita became boarding house.

1884   J. C. Carr published "Woman and Land," *Pasadena & Valley Union.* J. Muir first and only trip to Yosemite Valley with wife, Louie.

1885   Death of Muir's father, Daniel Muir.

1886   Helen Lillian Muir born January 23.

1887   J. Muir edited and contributed and J. C. Carr contributed to
            Picturesque California.

1888   J. Muir ascended Mount Rainier.

1889   J. Muir collaborated with Robert Underwood Johnson on the
            creation of Yosemite National Park through articles and lobby
            effort.

1890   J. Muir published "The Treasures of the Yosemite" (August)
            and "Features of the Proposed Yosemite National Park"
            (September), *Century*; fourth trip to Alaska. J. C. Carr refuted
            John P. Irish's accusation that Muir sawed lumber for J. M.
            Hutchings in Yosemite Valley. Yosemite National Park bill
            passed in October.

1891   J. C. Carr published "The Blessed Cora of San Luis Rey,"
            Californian; trustee Throop Polytechnic Institute (forerunner
            of Caltech). Dr. John Strentzel died.

1891–1892   J. Muir relieved of Martinez ranch responsibilities. J. Muir
            helped organize Sierra Club, served as first president; promoted
            recession of Yosemite Valley to federal government.

1892   J. C. Carr sold Carmelita, moved to cottage on Kensington
            Street; published "John Muir," "Throop University, Pasadena,"
            and "Among the Basket Makers," *Californian*.

1893   J. Muir visited Chicago World's Fair, Boston, New York, and
            Europe, including Dunbar, Scotland.

1894   J. Muir published first book, *Mountains of California*. Ezra
            Slocum Carr died, November 27.

1895   J. Muir trip from Tahoe to Tuolumne Canyon and Yosemite
            Valley; met Theodore P. Lukens in Hetch Hetchy; trip to
            Southern California; visited Lukens; lectured at Throop
            Polytechnic Institute and Pasadena High School.

1896   Death of Muir's mother, Anne Gilrye Muir. J. Muir traveled
            with Forestry Commission; fifth trip to Alaska.

1897   J. C. Carr sold Kensington Street cottage; experienced mental
            and physical exhaustion; entered Crocker Home for Old
            Ladies, San Francisco; experienced loss of memory, dementia.
            J. Muir sixth trip to Alaska.

1899   J. Muir seventh trip to Alaska; joined the Harriman-Alaska
            Expedition.

1900–1901   J. C. Carr resided with Elijah Melancthon Carr, Ezra S. Carr's
            brother, on ranch, Santa Paula, Ventura County, California.

1901   Theodore Roosevelt became president. J. Muir wrote
            Roosevelt about America's natural resources; published second
            book, *Our National Parks*; requested Theodore P. Lukens
            retrieve letters written to J. C. Carr.

1902   J. Muir began fight to save Hetch Hetchy Valley.

1903   J. Muir guided and camped with President Roosevelt in
            Yosemite; world tour with Charles S. Sargent to study trees.
            Jeanne C. Carr died in Templeton, San Luis Obispo County,
            California, December 14; buried in Carr plot, Mountain View
            Cemetery, Oakland, California.

1905   Louie Wanda Strentzel Muir died, August 6. Recession of
            Yosemite Valley to federal government.

1906   J. Muir explored Arizona and Petrified Forest; opposed the
            damming of Hetch Hetchy Valley.

1909   J. Muir published *Stickeen*.

1911   J. Muir published *My First Summer in the Sierra*. Death of
            William Keith.

1911–1912   J. Muir traveled to South America and Africa.

1912   J. Muir published *The Yosemite*.

1913   J. Muir published *The Story of My Boyhood and Youth*. Death
            of John Swett. Fight to save Hetch Hetchy lost, December 19.

1914   J. Muir died in California Hospital, Los Angeles, December 24;
            buried in Strentzel Cemetery, Alhambra Valley, Martinez.

LIST OF LETTERS

DATE	AUTHOR	ADDRESSEE	WRITTEN FROM	PAGE
May 2, 1867	John Muir	Jeanne C. Carr	Indianapolis	51
June 9, 1867	John Muir	Jeanne C. Carr	Indianapolis	52
[August, 1867]	John Muir	Jeanne C. Carr	[Portage City]	53
August 14, 1867	Jeanne C. Carr	John Muir	Madison	56
August 30, 1867	John Muir	Jeanne C. Carr	Indianapolis	57
September 9, [1867]	John Muir	Jeanne C. Carr	Among the Hills of Bear Creek, seven miles southeast of Burkesville, Kentucky	57
September 14, 1867	Jeanne C. Carr	Ada [Brooks]	Madison, Wisconsin	59
September–October, 1867	John Muir	Jeanne C. Carr	[unknown]	59
November 8, [1867]	John Muir	Jeanne C. Carr	Cedar Keys, [Florida]	60
1868				
May 10, 1868	Jeanne C. Carr	Merrill Moores	Madison, Wisconsin	60
May 25, [1868]	Jeanne C. Carr	John Muir	Madison	61
July 26, 1868	John Muir	Jeanne C. Carr	Near Snelling, Merced Co., California	71
August 31, 1868	E. S. [Ezra S.] and Jeanne C. Carr	John Muir	Castleton, Vermont	74
November 1, [1868]	John Muir	Jeanne C. Carr	At a sheep ranch between the Tuolumne and Stanislaus rivers	78

DATE	AUTHOR	ADDRESSEE	WRITTEN FROM	PAGE
1869				
February 24, 1869	John Muir	Jeanne C. Carr	Near Snellings, Merced Co., [California]	80
March 28, 1869	Jeanne C. Carr	John Muir	San Mateo	82
May 16, 1869	John Muir	Jeanne C. Carr	Seven miles north from Snellings	84
May 20, 1869	John Muir	Jeanne C. Carr	Hopeton	86
July 11, 1869	John Muir	Jeanne C. Carr	Five miles west of Yosemite	87
July 13			A few miles north of Yosemite	88
July 30, [1869]	Jeanne C. Carr	John Muir	Yosemite	89
September 28, 1869	Jeanne C. Carr	John Muir	Oakland, California	91
October 3, 1869	John Muir	Jeanne C. Carr	Two miles below La Grange	91
October, [1869]	E. S. [Ezra S.] and Jeanne C. Carr	John Muir	Oakland, Alameda County, Corner 11th and Webster Streets	93
November 15, 1869	John Muir	Jeanne C. and E. S. Carr [Ezra S.]	La Grange	94
December 6, 1869	John Muir	Jeanne C. Carr	Yosemite	94
1870				
January 22, 1870	Jeanne C. Carr	John Muir	Oakland	104
April 5, 1870 April 13	John Muir	Jeanne C. Carr	Yosemite	105
May 17, [1870]	John Muir	Jeanne C. Carr	Yosemite	106
May 28, [1870]	Jeanne C. Carr	John Muir	Oakland	108

DATE	AUTHOR	ADDRESSEE	WRITTEN FROM	PAGE
May 29, [1870]	John Muir	Jeanne C. Carr	Yosemite	110
[July 10, 1870]	Jeanne C. Carr	John Muir	Oakland	112
July 10, 1870	Jeanne C. Carr	Mrs. Robert C. Waterston [C. L. Waterston]	Oakland, California, Corner 11th and Webster Streets	113
July 29, [1870]	John Muir	Jeanne C. Carr	Yosemite	114
[August 7, 1870]	John Muir	Jeanne C. Carr	[Yosemite]	116
August 20, [1870]	John Muir	Jeanne C. Carr	Yosemite	117
October 2, [1870]	Jeanne C. Carr	John Muir	Oakland	118
Nut-Time, [Autumn, 1870]	John Muir	Jeanne C. Carr	Squirrelville, Sequoia Co.	119
November 4, [1870]	John Muir	Jeanne C. Carr	Tuolumne River, two miles below La Grange	121
December 22, [1870]	John Muir	Jeanne C. Carr	Near La Grange, California	123
1871				
[Spring, 1871]	John Muir	Jeanne C. Carr	Yosemite	133
Midnight [April 3, 1871]	John Muir	Jeanne C. Carr	[Yosemite]	135
April 15, [1871]	John Muir	Jeanne C. Carr	Yosemite	137
May 1, [1871]	Jeanne C. Carr	John Muir	[Oakland]	138
[May 8, 1871]	John Muir	Ralph Waldo Emerson	Yosemite Valley	139
May 16, [1871]	Jeanne C. Carr	John Muir	[San Mateo]	140
May 24, [1871]	Jeanne C. Carr	John Muir	San Mateo	140
June 22, [1871]	John Muir	Jeanne C. Carr	[Yosemite]	142

DATE	AUTHOR	ADDRESSEE	WRITTEN FROM	PAGE
June 30, [1871]	Jeanne C. Carr	John Muir	Oakland	143
July 10, 1871	C. L. W[aterston] Mrs. Robert C. Waterston	Jeanne C. Carr	71 Chester Square, Boston	144
August 13, [1871]	John Muir	Jeanne C. Carr	Yosemite	146
September 8, [1871]	John Muir	Jeanne C. Carr	Yosemite	147
September or October, 1871	John Muir	Jeanne C. Carr	Yosemite	150
December 11, 1871 January 8, 1872	John Muir	Jeanne C. Carr	Yosemite	152
December 31, [1871]	Jeanne C. Carr	John Muir	Oakland	154
1872				
January 17, 1872	Jeanne C. Carr	Editor, Overland	Oakland	166
February 4, 1872	Jeanne C. Carr	John Muir	Oakland	166
February 13, 1872	John Muir	Jeanne C. Carr	Yosemite Valley	168
February 20 [1872]	John Muir	[Charles Warren] Stoddard	Yosemite Valley	169
[Late February, 1872?]	Jeanne C. Carr	John Muir	[Oakland]	170
[February 26, 1872] March 3, 1872	Jeanne C. Carr	John Muir	[San Mateo]	171
March 16, [1872]	John Muir	Jeanne C. Carr	Yosemite Valley	172
[April, 1872]	John Muir	Jeanne C. Carr	New Sentinel Hotel	174
April 9, 1872	Jeanne C. Carr	John Muir	San Mateo	175
April 23, 1872	John Muir	Jeanne C. Carr	New Sentinel Hotel	176
May 12, 1872	John Muir	Jeanne C. Carr	Yosemite Valley	177

DATE	AUTHOR	ADDRESSEE	WRITTEN FROM	PAGE
May 31, 1872	John Muir	Jeanne C. Carr	New Sentinel Hotel	178
[Spring, 1872]	John Muir	Jeanne C. Carr	[Yosemite]	179
July 6, 1872	John Muir	Jeanne C. Carr	New Sentinel Hotel, Yosemite Valley	180
July 14, 1872	John Muir	Jeanne C. Carr	New Sentinel Hotel, Yosemite Valley	181
[July, 1872]	Jeanne C. Carr	John Muir	[Oakland]	182
July 27, 1872	John Muir	Jeanne C. Carr	Yosemite Valley	184
August 4, 1872	Mrs. J. P. Moore [M. R. Moore]	John Muir	Oakland, California	185
August 5, 1872	John Muir	Jeanne C. Carr	Yosemite Valley	187
August 28, 1872	John Muir	Jeanne C. Carr	Yosemite Valley	188
September 13, 1872	John Muir	Jeanne C. Carr	Yosemite Valley	189
[September, 1872?]	Jeanne C. Carr	John Muir	[Oakland]	189
September 24, [1872?]	Jeanne C. Carr	John Muir	Oakland	190
[Autumn, 1872]	John Muir	Jeanne C. Carr	[unknown]	191
October 2, [1872]	Jeanne C. Carr	John Muir	Oakland	193
October 8, 1872	John Muir	Jeanne C. Carr	Yosemite Valley	193
[October, 1872]	John Muir	Jeanne C. Carr	[Yosemite]	198
October 14, [1872]	John Muir	Jeanne C. Carr	Yosemite	199
December 25, 1872	John Muir	Jeanne C. Carr	Yosemite Valley	199

1873

February 3, [1873]	Jeanne C. Carr	John Muir	Oakland	213
March 30, 1873	John Muir	Jeanne C. Carr	Yosemite Valley	214

DATE	AUTHOR	ADDRESSEE	WRITTEN FROM	PAGE
April 1, 1873	John Muir	Jeanne C. Carr	[Yosemite]	215
April 13, 1873	John Muir	Jeanne C. Carr	Yosemite Valley	216
April 19, 1873	John Muir	Jeanne C. Carr	Yosemite Valley	216
May 15, 1873	John Muir	Jeanne C. Carr	Yosemite Valley	217
June 7, 1873	John Muir	Jeanne C. Carr	Yosemite Valley	218
July 11, 1873	Jeanne C. Carr	Ezra S. Carr	Yosemite Valley	218
September 13, [1873]	John Muir	Jeanne C. Carr	Clark's Station	221
September 15, [1873]	John Muir	Jeanne C. Carr	Clark's	222
September [27, 1873]	John Muir	Jeanne C. Carr	Camp on South Fork, San Joaquin, near divide of San Joaquin and Kings River	222
October 2, [1873]	John Muir	Jeanne C. Carr	Camp in dear bonnie grove where the pines meet the foothill oaks. About 8 or 10 miles SE from the confluence of the N fork of Kings River with the trunk	224
October 16, 1873	John Muir	Jeanne C. Carr	Independence	225
October 29, 1873	E. S. [Ezra S.] and Jeanne C. Carr	Louie [Strentzel]	University of California, Oakland, Cal.	227
November 3, [1873]	John Muir	E. S. [Ezra S.] and Jeanne C. Carr	Tahoe City	228
1874				
[September, 1874]	John Muir	Jeanne C. Carr	Yosemite Valley	241
September 27, 1874	John Muir	Jeanne C. Carr	Yosemite Valley	250

DATE	AUTHOR	ADDRESSEE	WRITTEN FROM	PAGE
1894				
November 5, 1894	John Muir	Jeanne C. Carr	Martinez	303
[November/December, 1894?]	Jeanne C. Carr	John Muir	[unknown]	303
December 18, 1894	Jeanne C. Carr	John Muir	[Pasadena, California]	304
1895				
January 7, 1895	John Muir	Jeanne C. Carr	Martinez	306
[1895?]	Jeanne C. Carr	John Muir	Pasadena	307
November 12, 1895	John Muir	Jeanne C. Carr	Martinez	307
1897				
June 12, 1897	T. P. Lukens [Theodore Parker]	John Muir	Pasadena, Cal.	308
1901				
November 13, 1901	John Muir	T. P. Lukens [Theodore Parker]	Martinez	309
December 18, 1901	John Muir	T. P. Lukens [Theodore Parker]	Martinez	309
1903				
December 18, 1903	E. M. Carr [Elijah Melanthon]	John Muir	Templeton	310

LIST OF MISSING LETTERS

THIS LIST OF MISSING letters is an attempt to account for correspondence between John Muir and Jeanne C. Carr that is either no longer extant or possibly in private collections and unknown and inaccessible to the editor of this work. That there are missing letters is not an indication of letters having been expurgated, but is rather a reminder that correspondence between Muir and Carr was lost, misplaced over time, or passed on to friends who failed to return the letters. The missing letters are, therefore, a natural occurrence in correspondence that spanned thirty years beginning over 130 years ago.

Three sources have been used to compile this list.[1] First, the letters in this edition are themselves a source of missing letters. Some of the Muir/Carr letters make reference to and are a direct response to a letter or to the receipt of books, plants, and other objects.

Second, Carr created a scrapbook of Muir's letters to her. She glued small white envelopes, usually three to a page, and dated and numbered them 1–100. Into the envelopes she inserted Muir's letters. The date of the compilation of the scrapbook is unknown; however, the last letter in the scrapbook is dated January 12, 1877. The entire corpus of letters that concluded in 1895 is not included. Though neither chronological nor complete, Carr's scrapbook is still a valuable resource. (William Frederic Badè suggested that Carr's dating of the letters in many cases was incorrect. The examination of the scrapbook of envelopes in relation to the chronological list of extant Muir letters to Carr reveals that her accuracy in dating the letters appears less doubtful in most cases and also exposes definite gaps from which some conclusions may be drawn as to missing letters.) Muir had access to Carr's scrapbook in 1909 at the time George Wharton James sought Muir's permission to publish his letters to Carr. He made notations on eight envelopes requesting that the letters in those envelopes be destroyed. For reasons that cannot be determined Muir's request was not complied with in the case of four of the letters written to Carr on August 7, 1870, Spring 1872, August 5, 1872, and September 13, 1872. These letters are extant. The other four letters were excised in accordance with Muir's request. Of them three letters were from Muir to Carr (June 2, 1871, May 22, 1872, and December 18, 1872). The fourth letter was from Carr to Muir (June 1, 1873). (Muir created a list of letters he wanted expurgated in part or in whole at the same time he had access to Carr's scrapbook. He requested that eight letters be destroyed in full and that eight have sections cut. The eight he requested to be destroyed are the same letters he marked in Carr's scrapbook.)

Third, in the 1920s Badè created a list of thirty-one missing Muir letters.

Drawn from Carr's scrapbook, the list indicated that fragmentary parts of five letters were located and that other letters were recovered. Badè's list is a source for further analysis.

DATE	AUTHOR	ADDRESSEE	WRITTEN FROM
Before September 13, 1865	Jeanne C. Carr	John Muir	Madison, Wisconsin
?	John Muir	Jeanne C. Carr	Near Meaford, Canada
After January 21, 1866	Jeanne C. Carr	John Muir	
Before October 12, 1866	John Muir	Jeanne C. Carr	
After October 12, 1866 Before December 16, 1866 (*Calypso borealis* letter taken by James D. Butler)	John Muir	Jeanne C. Carr	
On or after December 16, 1866 but before December 25, 1866 (Book: *The Stonemason of Saint Point*)	Jeanne C. Carr	John Muir	
After June 9, 1867 Before August?	Jeanne C. Carr	John Muir	
Fall 1867 (Probably after September 9, 1867, but before November 8, 1867)	John Muir	Jeanne C. Carr	
Before November 8, 1867	Jeanne C. Carr	John Muir	
After November 8, 1867	Jeanne C. Carr	John Muir	
July 1868	John Muir	Jeanne C. Carr	Hopeton
Before February 24, 1869 (Two Letters)	Jeanne C. Carr	John Muir	
After March 28, 1869 Before May 16, 1869	Jeanne C. Carr	John Muir	

DATE	AUTHOR	ADDRESSEE	WRITTEN FROM
After March 28, 1869 Before May 20, 1869	Jeanne C. Carr	John Muir	
May 31, 1869	John Muir	Jeanne C. Carr	
June 22, 1869	Jeanne C. Carr	John Muir	
June?–July 1869 (eight letters)	Jeanne C. Carr	John Muir	
February 4, 1870?	John Muir	Jeanne C. Carr	
May 7, 1870	Jeanne C. Carr	John Muir	
After July 10, 1870 Before August 7, 1870	Jeanne C. Carr	John Muir	
November 19, 1870	Jeanne C. Carr	John Muir	
After November 19, 1870	Jeanne C. Carr	John Muir	
Before February 14, 1871	Jeanne C. Carr	John Muir	
February 14, 1871	Jeanne C. Carr	John Muir	
Before May 24, 1871 (two letters?)	John Muir	Jeanne C. Carr	
June 2, 1871	John Muir	Jeanne C. Carr	Yosemite Valley
After June 30, 1871	Jeanne C. Carr	John Muir	
Before September 8, 1871	Jeanne C. Carr	John Muir	
After September 8, 1871 (October 7, 1871?)	Jeanne C. Carr	John Muir	
October 1871 (letter, box of berries, and Liebig's extract)	Jeanne C. Carr	John Muir	
October–Early December 1871?	Jeanne C. Carr	John Muir	

DATE	AUTHOR	ADDRESSEE	WRITTEN FROM
Before September/ October 1871	John Muir	Jeanne C. Carr	
November 1, 1871	Jeanne C. Carr	John Muir	
February 4, 1872	Jeanne C. Carr	John Muir	
February 8, 1872	Jeanne C. Carr	John Muir	
After April 9, 1872 Before May 31, 1872	Jeanne C. Carr	John Muir	
April 15, 1872	Jeanne C. Carr	John Muir	
After April 15 Before July 6, 1872	Jeanne C. Carr	John Muir	
April 23, 1872?	John Muir	Jeanne C. Carr	
Before May 12, 1872 (box of plants)	Jeanne C. Carr	John Muir	
May 22, 1872	John Muir	Jeanne C. Carr	
Before July 14, 1872	Jeanne C. Carr	John Muir	
August 23, 1872	Jeanne C. Carr	John Muir	
(Month?), 18th, Before September 24, 1872	John Muir	Jeanne C. Carr	
September 17, 1872	John Muir	Jeanne C. Carr	Yosemite
December 18, 1872	John Muir	Jeanne C. Carr	
After December 25, 1872 Before February 3, 1873	John Muir	Jeanne C. Carr	
Before February 3, 1873 (two letters)	Jeanne C. Carr	John Muir	
May 27, 1873	Jeanne C. Carr	John Muir	University of California, Oakland

DATE	AUTHOR	ADDRESSEE	WRITTEN FROM
June 1, 1873	Jeanne C. Carr	John Muir	Oakland
Before September 13, 1873	Jeanne C. Carr	John Muir	
Before December 9, 1874? (card and letter)	Jeanne C. Carr	John Muir	
(Month?), 17th Before December 21, 1874	Jeanne C. Carr	John Muir	
Before April 15, 1875	Jeanne C. Carr	John Muir	
Before July 31, 1875?	Jeanne C. Carr	John Muir	
Before November 3, 1875?	Jeanne C. Carr	John Muir	
Before April 3, 1876? (letter?)	Jeanne C. Carr	John Muir	
January 12, 1877?	John Muir	Jeanne C. Carr	
Before August 12, 1877	Jeanne C. Carr	John Muir	
Before February 18, 1879?	Jeanne C. Carr	John Muir	
Before April 9, 1879?	Jeanne C. Carr	John Muir	
Before October 22, 1887?	Jeanne C. Carr	John Muir	
Before January 12, 1888?	Jeanne C. Carr	John Muir	
Before January 30, 1888	Jeanne C. Carr	John Muir	
Before February 17, 1889	Jeanne C. Carr	John Muir	
Before November 5, 1894	Jeanne C. Carr	John Muir	
Before November 12, 1895	Jeanne C. Carr	John Muir	

INDEX

Abies spp. (Fir), 213, *343*
Agave americana (American Aloe, Century Plant), 109, 111, *343*
Agassiz, Louis, 116, 131, 163, 190, 193, 321n7, 324n29
agricultural reform, 7, 129, 233, 240. *See also* grange; social reform
Agrostis scabra (Hairgrass), 55, *343*
Alaska, Muir's trips to, 271, 272, 282, 283–84
Aquilegia sp. (Columbine), 138
Armes, William D., 278
art and artists, in Yosemite Valley, 164. *See also* Bierstadt, Albert; Keith, William; Simms, Billy
Aspidium spp. (ferns), 26, 35, 345
Atlantic Monthly, 159, 171, 282, 283, 284
Avery, Benjamin P., 165, 207

Badé, William Frederic, 315n13, 327n20, 381–82
Banta, Isaac, 336n17
Barry, Patrick, 101
Bass, David Waldo, 337n20
Bidwell, John & Annie Kennedy, 268
Bierstadt, Albert, 160, 170, 323n9
Bigelow, Jacob, 109
Bolivian Commercial and Colonization Company, 102–103, 118–19
Boston Historical Society, 194
Boston Recorder, 12, 23, 24, 40–42, 43
Boston Transcript, 216

botany: and Carr on fungi, 37; and Carr on gardens of California, 109; and Carr's description of Vermont, 75–76; Carr on teaching of, 83; and friendship between Carr and Muir, 3; and influence of Douglas on Carr, 100; Muir on flowers and ferns of Wisconsin, 53–54; Muir on flowers of San Joaquin Valley, 72–74; Muir on Illinois prairies, 54–55; Muir's descriptions of Yosemite Valley, 81, 95, 105, 111, 120, 201, 202, 293; Muir's observations in Canada, 35, 40–42, 53; and studies of Carr and Muir, 17–18, 22. *See also* horticulture
Botrychium lunarioides (Moonwort), 35, 345
Brooks, Ada, 26, 28
Brooks, Walter R., 5, 24–25, 101, 129, 140, 317n20, 319n3, 320n10
Bryanthus sp. (Mountain Heather), 259
Bugbee, Sumner W., 274
Burroughs, John, 280, 283
Buske, Frank E., 315n14
Butler, Henry, 1, 2
Butler, James D., 2, 12, 23, 24, 43, 69, 91, 93–94

Cable, George Washington, 280
California: and Ezra Carr as State Superintendent of Public Instruction, 233, 239, 265; and Jeanne C. Carr as Deputy Superintendent of Public Instruction, 7, 239, 265;

ABOUT THE EDITOR

BONNIE JOHANNA GISEL has a Ph.D. in nineteenth-century American cultural history from Drew University and an M.Div. from Harvard Divinity School. An environmentalist and naturalist, she is the interim director for the John Muir Center for Regional Studies, a visiting professor of environmental studies at the University of the Pacific, and an adjunct assistant professor of cultural history and humanities at Drew University. She lives in Stockton, California.